P9-ECZ-207

THE REFLOWERING OF MALAYSIAN ISLAM

MODERN RELIGIOUS RADICALS AND THEIR ROOTS

Judith Nagata

UNIVERSITY OF BRITISH COLUMBIA PRESS
VANCOUVER
1984

THE REFLOWERING OF MALAYSIAN ISLAM

Modern Religious Radicals and Their Roots

This book has been published with the help of a grant
from the Social Science Federation of Canada,
using funds provided by the Social Sciences
and Humanities Research Council.

Canadian Cataloguing in Publication Data

Nagata, Judith A., 1940-
    The reflowering of Malaysian Islam

Includes index.
Bibliography: p.
ISBN 0-7748-0195-6

1. Islam – Malaysia. 2. Da'wah (Islam)
I. Title.
BP63.M27N33 1984   297'.09595   C84-091001-0

This book is printed on acid-free paper.

International Standard Book Number 0-7748-0195-6

Printed in Canada

To Shuichi
who suffered through it all

Contents

Preface

The surface layer of books often conceals a deeper stratum of much human co-operation and joint activity, some of which forms the very bedrock on which the book is built. Were it not for the solid support, both direct and indirect, contributed by my many colleagues, friends, assistants, and "informants" in Malaysia, each in their own distinctive way, this particular book would have had no foundation at all. In this respect, like most anthropological endeavours based on field research, it is a product of a more collective conscience and effort, distilled from a variety of local sources and drawing from the reflections of some very reflective people. This is not to evade or defuse the responsibility for the views expressed in the following pages, for their selection, presentation, and organization are entirely mine.

The peripatetic nature of the research whose results are recorded below took me to many parts of the Malay Peninsula (West Malaysia), to universities, colleges and schools, to government offices and departments, to religious meetings, lectures, conferences and other events, and most important of all, into the generously opened homes and inner sancta of numerous Malays and other Malaysians, rural and urban, from all walks of life. It is these latter to whom I probably owe the greatest debt for their willingness to stretch the limits of their religious and cultural traditions of tolerance in order to accommodate the questions and interests of a white female infidel who was so unexpectedly launched into their life and whose purposes and goals must often have appeared somewhat remote and incongruent with their own. This, of course, is the mark of the anthropologist in many places. Yet whatever their private thoughts, ulama, religious teachers, and kampung residents of all ages were unfailingly courteous in the Malay way and generous in sharing their religious and other personal views and in allowing me to attend their group events. I deliberately refrain from acknowledging them all by name—not from bias, nor even from the pressure of sheer numbers—but out of respect for their confidence and personal integrity on topics sometimes contentious or sensitive.

Among my university and other more "public" academic colleagues are some names I wish to go on record for their constant support, co-operation, and sharing of ideas on the contemporary social and religious scene of Malaysia, as well as lubricating the wheels of travel, access, and movement in the country. At Penang's Universiti Sains Malaysia are: Dr. Chandra Muzaffar, Dr. Loke Lok Ee, Encik Mohd, Razha Haji Abdul Rashid, Dr. Kamal Salleh, then dean of the School of Comparative Social Sciences, and Dr. Wan Halim, its present dean. Warm friendships and support also came from Encik Eza-nee Ahmad, agricultural research officer of MARDI in Kajang; Dr. Halim Ali of Universiti Kebangsaan; and to Encik Sharudin Ma'aruf of Kuala Lumpur. As well, the wives of many of the above provided their own support and hospitality, not to mention close and nurturant friendships which I still cherish.

I owe a special debt of gratitude to the efforts of six stalwart undergraduates from Universiti Sains Malaysia whose service as male Malay Muslim assistants were indispensible in certain delicate social and religious events and situations where my own status and qualifications obviously could not take me. Their grasp of my interests was quick to develop, and the energy with which they covered the Kedah countryside on their motorcycles was matched by their attention to detail and sense of problem, as they observed, not just participated in local religious events, and saw their own culture with new eyes. My six faithful assistants were: Ismail b. Yumus, Wan Bukhari B. Wan Daud, Ahmad Nasir Khosri, Narudin Awang Itam, Mohd. Sahar B. Mohd. Noor, and Muhammad Yusoff Osman. At this point too, it would be ungrateful of me not to acknowledge, with the deepest respect and appreciation, the unquestioning and ever open hospitality regularly extended to me and to my band of student assistants at the home of religious teacher and alim, Haji Abdul Rashid and family in Alor Setar, Kedah, and whose own deep knowledge and resources I tapped on many occasions. To my gratitude is now added deep regret at his recent passing.

Outside Malaysia, I had the good fortune to be offered a part-time position as a Foreign Research Fellow at the Institute for Southeast Asian Studies in Singapore (ISEAS), which I visited periodically to use the fine library and thoughtfully provided office and support services. Most important of all, however, was the opportunity to enjoy the varied and stimulating company and conversation of the other denizens of the ISEAS, and to cross paths with all manner of scholars from several continents. The seminars at ISEAS were one of the most rewarding aspects of my research. I particularly wish the names of the Institute's Director, Professor K. S. Sandhu, and its Research Officer, Dr. Sharon Siddique, to go on record here. To these must be added my contacts with members of the National University of Singapore, especially Dr. Anthony Walker and Dr. Tan Chee Beng and wives.

I trust that those of my other friends and colleagues whose names have not been singled out in this brief acknowledgement will understand that their friendship and support do not go unappreciated, but will long be remembered in ways that go beyond their immediate contribution to this volume.

I leave to the end, not for lack of recognition, but that it might stand out and remain in the memory, my financial benefactors, equally as indispensable as my other type of support. From the Social Science Research Council (U.S.) I was fortunate enough to receive a Post-Doctoral Southeast Asia Research Fellowship for 1979-80, and from the Social Sciences and Humanities Research Council of Canada I benefited from a Leave Fellowship to complement my sabbatical in the same year. I wish both of these agencies to know that their generosity is appreciated (and has even borne some fruit!).

Introduction

The point of take-off for the present volume was the *dakwah* movement in Malaysia, which is a parochial form of a more widespread, and by now familiar, revitalization process in the broader Islamic world.

As a force in contemporary Malay and Muslim society, the rise and flowering of dakwah is one of the principal and most visible developments of the 1970's. Its impact extends far beyond the bounds of religion in a theological sense and inevitably touches the interests and sensitivities of non-Muslims too. The established equation of certain kinds of identities, religious, ethnic or "racial," and cultural, and their implied oppositions have long determined the heartbeat of Malaysian social and political life, such that a change or reinforcement of any one of these elements is bound to make waves throughout the entire, somewhat precariously balanced system.

One of the ongoing issues in the Malay world, which has gathered intensity and urgency from the colonial early twentieth century to the present, has been the definition of the various "races" as a basis for rights and obligations, and hence their relationships with one another.

In the definition of Malay status, Islam has historically played a pivotal role, sometimes relaxing, sometimes tightening the ethnic boundary. The most recent "dakwah period" has seen a general trend in the latter direction, an intensification of Malay-Muslim sentiments with all its attendant political repercussions, and it has generated some very self-conscious and searching debates over the position of non-Malay Muslims, especially new converts. For the latter, dakwah has created many additional problems, in addition to those of personal identity.

In keeping with the traditions of Malaysian pluralism, religious and ethnic identities have long gone hand in hand. These are among the apparent responses to, or possibly symptoms of, the forces fueling dakwah in the Malay community and of other religious revivals erupting in the major communities in Malaysia. Among the Chinese, a variety of forms of revitalization are taking place, including an assortment of millenarian-type, syncretic movements, several versions of charismatic Christianity, and renewed cultivation of a "purer," more canonical brand of Theravada Buddhism, all of which are clearly manifestations of Chinese identity as much as of any more "universalistic'' preoccupations with theological issues per se. Likewise, some Hindu Indians are showing a resurgence of interest in a more intellectualized form of their faith, not to mention the enormous popularity of the cult of Sai Baba, a guru resident in South India. Any major religious movement bears organizational burdens of defining its perimeters, its membership, and, even more crucially, its leadership, whose legitimacy must be established. Leaders as much as ideologies are usually on trial, and as I shall try to show, the latter are often evaluated in the light of the former, as the purveyors of the new ideas and mediators of the message. Part of the interest of the recent revival in Malaysia lies in its internal diversity and in the competing claims of the leaders of an assortment of movements which collectively come under the locally popular rubric of dakwah. Some of these movements are nationally known and organized, and their leaders representatives of specific interests, platforms and constituencies, while others are merely heads of local cults, rooted in a single rural community.

It is easy to describe such leaders as ''charismatic,'' a glib and much over-worked term, which often obscures rather than sheds light on its subject. Its use begs rather than answers questions, such as the ''bargaining'' aspects of leader-follower relations, and its applicability in Malaysian dakwah will be raised in subsequent chapters.

Pursuing the theme that religious ideologies and symbols frequently become the handmaiden of both incumbent and of would-be leaders, whether in the Buddhist *sangha*, the Christian church, or the Muslim *ummat*, it is but a short step from religious revitalization to political intrigue. In practice, religion and politics have more in common than might at first be imagined. In the final analysis, after all, both are concerned with power, and also with meaning. They both provide templates for a social order, for unity and integration. Even the principles and symbols of authority may overlap: divine kings and politically active religious movements are familiar across the ages and the world. Both appeal to principles that claim to transcend the trivia of the mundane world. Both can be frighteningly dogmatic, demanding, and imperious in compelling conformity.

Unlike Christianity, Islam has never even pretended to uphold a separation of church and state. To the contrary, it has unabashedly affirmed, in many different times and places, the rightness of the involvement of both its leaders and followers in social, community, and hence political affairs, always blurring the western distinction between the secular and the sacred. The political dimension can be as blatant as in the Muslim Brotherhoods (*Al-Ikhwan al-Muslimin*) of contemporary Egypt and Syria, or at the other end of the spectrum, they may take the form of the subtle, yet deeply pervasive socializing influence of the Sufi mystic or religious guru in their small, exclusive, and personal congregations, as in much of pre-twentieth-century, rural

Southeast Asia. True to form, Islamic symbols have been widely used in Malaysia as a source of authority and legitimacy for the launching and defence of the various policies and programmes of those in, or aspiring to, power. In response to the relatively new dakwah revival movements, whose leaders must first acquire their legitimacy de novo, the incumbent government and other political élites have likewise begun to invoke Islamic modes and metaphors to their own advantage. These are calculated to deflect challenges to the existing status quo from other dakwah quarters, in a bid to join where beating, or even changing, the rules of the game is clearly out of the question. For Malay opposition leaders also, notably those in the forefront of the largely rural-based, religiously oriented party PAS (*Partai Al-Islamin Se-Malaysia*), invocation of Islam as the basis of their appeal to a heavily peasant constituency is as old as the party. But even before the formation of PAS in the 1950's, rural leadership and mobilization was long under the influence of religious teachers and scholars (*ulama*), who often rivalled secular headmen and who provide much of the motive force of PAS today. It is in the leadership of these men that the delicate balance between the strength of personal character, "charismatic" or other appeal in the local community, and "pure" ideology is most clearly displayed, both historically and in the recent dakwah revival. The brands of dakwah purveyed by the representatives of other interests and constituencies, such as those of urbanites, youth, or government, are potential threats to the established authority of the ulama, in some ways independent of the content of the teaching itself. As I try to show in Chapters 2 and 5, the close dependence of ideological acceptability on the reputation and credibility of the leader raises some crucial questions about the nature of orthodoxy. As often as not, the message is judged according to the medium, or the man who delivers it, and this in turn is based on the relationship he has established with a specific constituency. In this traditional feature of Islamic authority lies one of its principal weaknesses and strengths: a lack of sustained or institutionalized central control or single ultimate "court of appeal." Taken together, these factors make the competing claims and accusations of the various organizations and cults of the contemporary revival particularly difficult to assess and evaluate.

Finally, the present Islamic resurgence in Malaysia has proven a useful vehicle for the flexing of the political muscles of an otherwise almost politically emasculated royalty. As a result of colonial arrangements continued after Independence (1957), the traditional powers of the reigning ruler of each Malay state[1] were restricted to the assumedly innocuous and ineffectual realm of "Malay Religion and Custom" (to be discussed more fully in Chapters 1 and 2). These powers are now being groomed to new effect. Under the general public mood and consciousness of matters religious, some sultans are converting their originally rather nominal and vestigial religious authority into real power, through control of state religious councils and projects and through more direct and calculated involvement in state religious affairs. These newly discovered powers have been used on the one hand as a counterfoil to the prevailing political dominance of federal government and bureaucratic élites (Chapter 3) and, on the other, to rally the masses, their subjects, in the name of Islam. These loyalties must usually be tapped discreetly. The alleged support of the Sultan of Kedah for the outlawed religious crusading people's army (*Sabilullah*) and its implications for peasant and rural politics propels him perilously close to the forbidden brink of personal power politics (see Chapter 3). In such matters, the sultan trades on the alleged historical "blind loyalty" (cf. Chandra Muzaffar 1979) of his subjects to their feudal ruler, even though objective peasant interests as a class could be said to diverge radically from his own.

Islam in Malaysia therefore is many things to many people, and this is nowhere more striking than in the heady religious atmosphere of dakwah. To return for a moment to its role as an ethnic boundary-marker, as a symbol of Malayness, it is apparent that Islam simultaneously unites and divides. On one level it strives to exclude non-Muslims from access to Malay status even by conversion, while on another level, even within the Malay-Muslim community, the diverse interpretations of Islam by different dakwah and other elements have a divisive effect. In this respect, the so-called "dakwah movement" is by no means a monolithic or unitary phenomenon, but seems to follow the cracks and seams already present in Malay society. In subsequent chapters I shall explore in more detail this seeming paradox: Islam is the membrane which keeps the Malays and non-Malays apart and is also a source of internal fragmentation among the Malays.

Reflections on the forms and meanings of dakwah in the Malaysian context inevitably lead to a reconsideration of just what is "universalistic" about a universalistic religion such as Islam. To what extent can a body of broadly accepted, transcendent norms prevail in the face of such particularistic ties and pulls as those of peoplehood, of ethnicity, and of nationalism? In Malaysia, the de facto appropriation of Islam to Malayness, as noted, has rendered the position of non-Malay Muslims somewhat problematic (see Chapter 7). This kind of appropriation of a so-called universalistic religion to particularistic ends is by no means confined to Malaysia or to Islam, and it has been reported, for example, for Buddhism as used by the Sinhalese in Sri Lanka (Obeyesekere 1975) and for Christianity among some of the hill peoples of Burma (von der Mehden 1963). When confronted with the problem in terms of formal theology, most knowledgeable Malay Muslims would recognize the spiritual equality and unity of all members of the unmat, regardless of "race" or origin. Certainly some of the contemporary dakwah leaders, such as ABIM's past president, Anwar Ibrahim (see Chapter 4), publicly condemn *assabiyah* or "racism" as un-Islamic. But in practice, many dakwah participants do not necessarily follow such universalistic principles in their daily life and behave "as if" Islam were largely the preserve of Malays alone. The history of the volatile and shifting relationships between religious and other social boundaries is the basis of much of Chapter 7.

The many local forms and variations of Islamic practice in Malaysia, as elsewhere, whether of the revivalist variety or not, has implications for studies of religious sectarianism. Most Malay Muslims vigorously deny the existence of "sects" in a western/Christian sense, and the more informed of them attribute such misuse of the term to the misunderstanding of "western Orientalists."[2] While there may be grounds for this accusation in a number of cases, it cannot be allowed to close entirely the debate over the status of ideological and organizational cleavages within the broader religious community. We should attempt to pluck out and disentangle the two principal strands by which Christian sectarianism has been studied in the past, derived from the very separate traditions of theology and sociology, and apply these to reveal the generic problems of religious differentiation.[3] The theological approach usually attempts to apply traditionally Christian notions of orthodoxy and degrees of deviance from some canonical norm, although even here the standards are hardly absolute, and the tendency to pursue a mythical orthodoxy has had something of the quality of a quest for the holy grail (cf. Troeltsch 1931; Wilson 1975). Social scientists, on the other hand, have tended to pay more attention to micro-political issues such as the problems of leadership and its legitimacy, to techniques of mobilizing a following, and to competition with other would-be leaders. It also pays more attention to organizational problems and to the nature of the social and experiential bonds by which the "sect" is held together. One possible marriage of these two lines, which could transcend the specifics of Islam or Christianity, is attempted in Chapter 2. In this, the ideological correctness or "orthodoxy" can largely be judged by reference to the local acceptability of the bearer and interpreter of the ideas within a particular community or congregation. This position gives a slight edge to the primacy of the political over the purely ideological. In all fairness, the test of each case ideally should rest on an attempt, after the fashion of social anthropology, to analyse the nature and basis of the attachments of the follower to the sect or movement and, by implication, to its leader, whether predicated on shared ideas, shared experience, or shared identity. Finally, and also in keeping with the social anthropological approach, religious sects and movements need to be placed in a broader context of other political, economic, and social developments to which they are often a response. In the Islamic revival, it is clear that the various branches of the dakwah movement each serve a special constituency and its needs, whether rural, urban, young, old, more or less educated, politically active, or passive, and so on.

To come full circle, what the recent Islamic revitalization in Malaysia consists of remains to be determined precisely. It has popularly and loosely been labelled the "dakwah movement" with a meaning peculiar to the local Malaysian scene. The generic term dakwah is as old as the faith itself and, after the five pillars, integral to the observances of all Muslims. Its literal meaning of a "call" or "invitation" to the faith is grounded in its purpose to convert the unbeliever. More commonly nowadays, its goal is to revive the spirit and reinspire lapsed members ("born Muslims") to a greater zeal and devotion. It enjoins greater commitment to a study of the scriptures, to incorporation of them into daily life, and to the obligation of reminding fellow Muslims of their religious duties, both by example and by formal exegesis. While most active dakwah propagators explicitly reject force (*paksa*) as a means of achieving their objectives, the existing, powerful, informal social pressures in many segments of Malay-Muslim society exert forces of their own. Chapter 5 explores the topography of the principal networks of influence and dissemination of dakwah ideas.

Manifestations of dakwah, as currently perceived in Malaysia, range from private, almost invisible exercises in personal piety and devotion, involving a meticulous observance of the obligatory prayers, fasting, and personal morality, to a series of highly visible, and sometimes dramatic, public behaviours and rituals, which have contributed to a heightening of religious consciousness in general in Malaysia. Probably the most immediate and highest visual impact lies in changes in style of dress. The sarung-clad girls and women of the 1960's and early 1970's have been transformed by renewed ideals of Islamic feminine modesty into virtual facsimiles of their Arab sisters in the Middle East. Now they are shrouded in many-layered and loose garments (*baju kurung*), which obscure all hint of body form. Malay women have also adopted a modified short head veil (*mini-telekung*) somewhat resembling the nun's wimple, although usually they still reveal the face. A small minority do veil the entire face and even cover their hands and feet with gloves and socks. Men are also affecting Arab style costume in the form of long, green or white robes (*jubah*), turbans (*serban*), and leather sandals. Other attempts to follow Arabic customs among some dakwah participants include styles of eating and a conscious cultivation of Arabic language and art, all of which illustrates again how the ideals of a "universalistic" religion can easily slip into an identification with a particular people and its non-religious culture. For some dakwah followers, Islam and Arabness, like Islam and Malayness, are inseparable.

In the light of such perceptions it may well be asked how contemporary forms of dakwah revitalization may be characterized in religious terms. The epithets "fundamentalist," "reformist," and "revivalist" are variously heard on different fronts, but these may sometimes reflect the standards of the observer as much as of the participant. Malays are probably most offended by the term reformist, for it implies that there are wrongs in the faith to be rectified, a reflection, it is alleged, of the biases of critical western orientalist judges, falsely applying the canons and history of Christianity and of the Protestant Reformation in particular. The arrogance of such observers is compounded when they try to evaluate the "motives," as opposed to the actions, of those involved in the religious movements. Irritation with the reformist interpretation has been fueled by the writings of Muslim scholars of various national backgrounds, for example, the academic Talal Asad of Kuwait and the Pakistani preacher and guru Maulana Al-Maudoodi. The works of Maudoodi are virtually required reading across the international community of young Muslim scholars and students, and from his work many young dakwah Malays draw their inspiration and guidance. All these protestations, however, cannot be allowed to obscure the reality, recognized by some "non-orientalist" and highly respected Muslim scholars, of explicit reform programmes. They are to be found in the nineteenth-century-Egyptian writings and actions of such as Mohammed Abduh and Al Afghani who espoused a form of modernization acceptable to Islam, in the works of such modern socialist Muslims as Algeria's Fazhur Rahman, and in Dahlan's Muhammadiyah movement in Indonesia. For the reformers of this category, Islam must cultivate two elements not found in the current revival in Malaysia. In Malaysia there is little preoccupation with *ijtihad*, by which is meant the constant review and reinterpretation of Koranic and Prophetic injunctions in the light of the changing needs of society. By and large, Malaysian dakwah eschews this approach to the faith, advocating in its place a return to a more literal rendering of the scriptures and the traditions of the Prophet (*Hadith*), which partly explains the renewed emulation of Arab dress and custom. In this sense it is undeniably fundamentalistic. But ultimately, even reform Islam, with its accompanying emphasis on purification of the faith, as in the zealous purging of syncretic, non-Islamic religious intrusions (such as Hindu-origin Malay customs), and its attempts to penetrate to the elemental morality and intent of the original teachings when swept free of the crust of custom, also has fundamentalist tendencies. The *Kaum Muda* (literally "Young Faction") episode among the Malays of the 1920's and 1930's came closest in that country to a reformist movement (see Roff 1967). The movement was an attempt, inspired largely by non-Malay Muslims (Middle Eastern, Arab, and Indonesian) to purge Malay Islam of its Indic accretions and politically to challenge the feudal authority of the sultans and of the multi-layered bureaucracy who combined to administer Islam in the peninsula. Little emphasis was placed on ijtihad per se. Certainly the term ijtihad is rarely heard in contemporary dakwah circles, but then neither are the equivalents for the terms fundamentalist or reformist. Dakwah has become the all-embracing and all-meaning term, intuitively understood and experienced, but less often deeply analysed, to cover the spectrum of deepened religious consciousness and culture now prevailing. Its *Verstehen* to participants clusters along the lines of "returning to the holy faith" (*kembalikan ke agama suci*) or "for the sake of God" (*kerana Allah*). Other strands of the religious culture subsumed by the rise of dakwah will be unravelled in subsequent chapters.

It will now be apparent that "dakwah" has acquired a culturally specific meaning in Malaysia as opposed to its generic significance for most of the rest of the Islamic world. Malaysian dakwah refers principally to a set of more highly organized urban-based movements, largely supported by highly educated youth, who often received their schooling overseas. The three best-known movements are the Malaysian Islamic Youth League, whose Malay acronym is ABIM, Darul Arqam, and Jemaat Tabligh, whose activities are examined in Chapter 4. Partly in response to these movements, and underscoring their not-so-covert political aspects, is a parallel series of government-sponsored dakwah institutions, deliberately named so as to create an ideological antidote as well as a political counterforce. There is simultaneously a continuing ferment of religious activity in many rural areas under the auspices of more traditional religious scholars and teachers whose roles as local leaders have considerable historical depth. This activity is not a direct offshoot of the recent urban dakwah activity, but more representative of a continuing, older religious tradition rooted in conservative village society. Rural leaders have not been impervious to changing winds and currents from outside, whether from other parts of the Muslim world or from their own urban neighbours. Often, however, jealousy of their own established authority and social pre-eminence in their rural domains has diluted the enthusiasm to make common cause with urban revivalists and other outsiders, even when there may be a general ideological and theological consensus. A few rural religious leaders have gone their own ways, and responded to the revival spirit by instigating highly localized idiosyncratic cult-like movements of their own, some with ancient Sufi elements (see Chapter 2).

Everywhere among Malays, there is evidence of a generally enhanced religious consciousness, whether emanating from direct personal commitment and experience or from a sensibility to the tenor of the times. It is evident in mosques overflowing at Friday prayer, in the orientation of the arts and the content of radio and television programming, and in the growing numbers actively involved in one of the formal dakwah organizations mentioned.

To the unwary, Christian-centred "orientalist," reference to specific movements or organizations such as ABIM or Darul Arqam may suggest a form of sectarianism which could be misleading. These movements are by no means organizationally discrete, totalitarian, or exclusivist in membership in a manner normally associated with Christian sects. Rather, their appeal is more general, and their membership, if it can be called such, fluid and even eclectic. Many dakwah enthusiasts follow not one, but several of the movements simultaneously, not to mention government dakwah programmes for good measure, by attending lectures, conferences, and other activities. Informal, but often powerful, social pressures are sometimes exerted by colleagues, peers, and other figures important in the life of the individual which may eventually tip the balance in favour of orientation to one movement rather than another, but the more common effect is one of a generally deeper religious commitment regardless of specific affiliation. This fluidity makes the dakwah movement hard to pin down structurally. Its essence consists of a series of religious ideas and symbols that are constantly being reinterpreted and rearranged to accommodate the needs of particular individuals and groups at particular times, rather than of a discrete and rigid ideology with a single or fixed point of reference.

One other characteristic of the current Islamic revival in all parts of the Muslim world is the strength of its anti-western fervour, which has made a deep impression on political attitudes. Insofar as Islam has become a symbol of oil politics, of Arab-Israeli and other ethno/geopolitical conflicts, and as calls for holy wars and crusades (*jihad*) pervade international relations, Islamic revitalization under any name, dakwah or other, is inevitably regarded with some apprehension by non-Muslims. However, the monolithic unity of Islam is often overestimated and exaggerated, for Islamic politics is as much concerned with internal cleavages within specific Muslim countries, such as Malaysia, as with its relations to "infidels." More subtle, however, is the more invidious anti-westernism lurking in recent Muslim attitudes to their own culture and lifestyle, and a renewed sense of a historical tradition and identity. A new confidence and pride, no doubt partly reinforced by politics in the narrow sense, has arisen in Muslim circles over the glories of Islamic civilization in its art, literature, philosophy, as well as theology. With it has burgeoned a new attention to the classical social thinkers of the Muslim world from Ibn Khaldun to Iqbal and now Al Maudoodi. From these scholars an alternate social theory is being fashioned, complete with its own counter lifestyle and solutions to the many social problems facing Muslims in the modern, western-dominated world. The revolution in Iran and the Khomeini solution is, of course, one of the most dramatic examples during the present resurgence and one which has captured the imagination of idealist Muslims everywhere. Another area where this cultural xenophobia towards the west is surfacing among Malaysia's own dakwah followers is in the field of science and education. A growing disenchantment with the grosser products of western technology and with the competitive, aggressive approach to learning, have led to a questioning of the very premises and values on which western science rests. In opposition to the hard, empirical science taught in foreign universities, Muslim students are advocating a return to a more inspirational form of knowledge (*wahyu*), and academic disciplines based on Islamic values in place of the so-called "value-free" sciences, which are, after all, only manifestations of a western bias. In their home countries too, these views are sometimes accompanied by the revivalists' symbolic rejection of the material comforts associated with the west, particularly television and certain styles of furniture. Many forms of western art and entertainment are also against Muslim canons of morality. Commitment to a religious revival therefore can do double duty in satisfying a search for new meanings and identities within traditional civilization and expressing opposition to the west in the form of an Islamic counterculture, whether through the Islamic Brotherhoods in Egypt and Syria or dakwah in Malaysia. Dakwah in the Middle East, as indicated above, has retained its generic meaning without the special connotation it has developed in Malaysia. There are, however, local equivalents to dakwah, which exhibit many striking parallels to their Malaysian counterparts, particularly in the nature of their adherents, who are drawn principally from the young, educated, and urban segments of the population, many of whom are in regular communication with one another across international boundaries.

While certain common elements may be perceived across the Islamic world in the contemporary revitalization period, within each country or area, its specific meanings and directions are partly shaped by local events and issues. In many Muslim countries, Islam is the language in which local politics is played out, whether by dramatic, aggressive confrontation—as in Iran, in the take-over of Mecca's holy of holies, the Masjid Il-Haram by anti-monarchist elements in November 1979, or the activities of the Egyptian and Syrian Brotherhoods—or by the more covert and gentle alliance of Malaysia's ABIM with the religious opposition Malay party PAS.

In Malaysia, the incumbent government élites, increasingly harassed and challenged by the various dakwah elements, attempt to retaliate by a frontal attack on their "orthodoxy," hurling at them accusations of "false teachings" and "deviance," as a means of undermining the authority of their leadership and cause.

What began therefore as an investigation of the easily labelled religious revival, or dakwah, in Malaysia, soon proved to be not so easily defined or confined in practice. As the above comments suggest, dakwah overflows into many domains of Malay and Malaysian life and even beyond, and it redounds on Muslims and non-Muslims alike. If these lateral repercussions in contemporary society may be regarded as the tendrils of the dakwah movement, then we should search for dakwah's roots by delving into Malaysia's Islamic past. Accordingly, the first chapter attempts to reconstruct, through an anthropologist's view of history, the role of Islam in shaping Malay identity and the extent to which it helped to promote early political unity. Also to be reconstructed in the first chapter are the original pathways and networks of communication of the early, itinerant Muslim scholars and teachers from India across Sumatra, Java, South Thailand, and the Malay peninsula.

Anthropologists have long ceased to be confined to the local level alone, to the small village or neighbourhood. Now they must strive to integrate local-level findings with larger and more inclusive organizations and structures and to present some vision of broader patterns and processes. To this exercise, there are no clearly defined limits or guidelines—the system is never really closed—and given the international significance of the Islamic revival, the boundaries are nothing less than the world system. The anthropologist's custom of working from the bottom up, however, does have the advantage of providing some insights that may be overlooked when operating in the reverse direction. From this "parochial" perspective, the observer is less likely to see a religion such as Islam as a monolithic entity, or as a given, an independent variable, but rather as an ever-changing and pulsating series of smaller-scale congregations, groups, and movements, which are themselves dependent on other factors of which Islam is but a composite and varying refraction.

The linkage of dakwah to other places and eras beckons those who would understand its roots on to the territory of the historian and other scholars. In reconstructing the history of Islam in Southeast Asia, I draw upon the works of Drewes and A.H. Johns, while my discussion of its early Sufi components depends heavily upon the studies by Syed Naguib Al-Attas and Trimingham. Roff's penetration into the different ideological strands of Islam, especially the Kaum Muda and *Kaum Tua*, and his analysis of their political and national significance still remains an important yardstick by which contemporary religious events in Malaysia can be judged. Also important is Kessler's bold interpretation of the history of Islamic politics in the east coast state of Kelantan, which has stimulated some timely thoughts on the position of Islam on social inequality and social class. A comparative perspective on dakwah can be gained through attention to events in Indonesia, traditionally home to a series of varied and lively styles and movements in Islam, whose political impact can be seen through the eyes of such writers as Geertz, Peacock, Siegel, Deliar Noer, and Taufik Abdullah. More theoretical quests were set in motion by stimuli from Mendelssohn's thoughtful treatment of ideology and factionalism in sectarianism through his analyses of small-group formations within the Buddhist sangha. This is supplemented by similar material by Kemper on Sri Lankan Buddhism (1980). Further, Jackson's study of the differential appeal of Darul Islam to villagers in Java also suggested more detailed exploration of the relationships between ideology and leadership loyalties, appropriate to the Malaysian scene. Ultimately, however, the most important sources of the materials used in this volume are the original voices and messages of the actors themselves, of the intellectuals, thinkers, scholars, commentators, and critics of the dakwah movement as it continues to unfold in Malaysia. Dakwah is among other things a highly literate movement, and its organizations are prolific sources of books, journals, tracts, reports, inspirational messages, and communiqués in several languages.

The overall approach to dakwah by this anthropologist then is eclectic. It combines a number of strategies and levels of observation, which include an intensive and more "typical" anthropological investigation of a single local area in the "Rice-Bowl" of Kedah, a state in North Malaysia, distinctive for its traditional religious schools, whose teachers, pupils, ideology, and organization were the principal objects of attention. But no comprehensive feeling for the entire range of expression, distribution, and diversity of Islam in Malaysia as a whole could be constructed from one area or community alone, and the whole of West Malaysia really became the effective unit of analysis. This required considerable mobility, and a need to be in many places at different times. The places most intensively covered, however, were the major university campuses where so many of the dakwah followers are concentrated and the urban centres of activity, especially Penang and Kuala Lumpur, supplemented by some comparative incursions across the causeway in Singapore. It entailed interviews with the leaders of the principal religious organizations, including those of the government, and, of course, interaction with countless dakwah followers and attendance at their lectures, conferences, and other activities. In a more typically anthropological style, through personal interaction with members, I tried to understand the basis of the informal groups and networks, the nature of the sanctions and pressures by which dakwah is communicated and reinforced, and how "ideology" is subtly reinterpreted as it passes along these social channels. Such methods helped to reveal the importance attached to particular roles and individuals as models of social behaviour and to valuations of certain types of authority and leadership.

Possibly some Malay or Muslim intellectuals who may eventually come to read this book could see the sinister hand and interpretation of yet another "orientalist" false prophet. Possibly too the Islamic purists are correct in their claims that no non-Muslim can fully grasp the meaning of the faith to the true disciple, particularly at such times of religious ferment as the current one. The anthropologist is accustomed to the doubts and angst encountered when translating one culture into the frames of another and should not ignore this question. However, as a traditional problem in anthropology, it has to be confronted like any other, and Islam is not immune to anthropological methods and attention, even though these—the rejected western forms of science—may not appeal to those personally involved. This does not mean of course that the present anthropologist was not well received by dakwah individuals and organizations. Indeed I have many close friends and colleagues among their number, who have both provided many of my sources and ideas and even read some of mine. I trust that I have not done any injustice in shaping and presenting some of these ideas in my version of an attempt at a value-free social science account which follows.

1

The Religious Route to Nationhood: The Islamic Foundation of Malay Culture and Consciousness

The theme of this chapter is the evolution, over the past three or four centuries, of Malay identity and the importance of Islam in this process. In the light of the central role religion has played in more recent concerns over Malay unity and identity and in shaping the pattern of ethnic relations, a retrospective and longitudinal view may provide some insight into the nature of the bond between Islam and Malayness. In this chapter I deliberately avoid treading the same ground as Roff and other social historians who have covered some of it before. Rather, my purpose here is to rework and to rearrange some of the existing historical material in order to illustrate certain themes and principles which will be drawn upon and elaborated further in subsequent chapters. Of these, one of the most important is the evolution of the concept of the Malay, *Melayu* and its connections with Islam over the past three hundred years.

Ideally, the task should begin at a point before Islam enters the stage, as far as this can be reliably reconstructed without bias from later sources. The existence of some sensitive transcriptions of indigenous historical materials on the early coastal states (*negeri*) of the Malay peninsula and Sumatra helps to make this task easier for the non-historian. Some of these accounts are sufficiently detailed for us to move beyond the background dramas of wars, migrations, major trading expeditions, and royal dynasties towards an understanding of the ethos and authority on which the early states were founded. Two principal types of relationship concern us here. The first revolves around the relationship between the ruler and his people: the nature of political authority and the bond or contract which sustained it. On this, many of the early chronicles wax quite eloquent. The second relationship is somewhat more elusive owing to the aristocratic and courtly bias of the annals: this has to do with the bond which united the common people (*rak'yat*) into some emotional and cultural community independent of more formal ties of political allegiance to the same ruler.

From the commentaries of historians on the best-known Malay chronicles, the consensus emerges that the term "Melayu" was initially associated more closely with ideas of stratification or rank and hierarchy than with ethnicity or social boundaries (Milner 1982:3ff.). This association is particularly explicit in the earliest of the sources analysed, that is, the *Sejarah Melayu*, and to a lesser extent in the *Hikayat Hang Tuah*, both apparently composed in the late seventeenth century[1] (Matheson 1979). Both reflect ideas of the contemporary political organization and state by which people's status and identities were defined.

The term Melayu is first used in connection with a myth of origin, where it refers to a river in Sumatra, near a hill known as Si Guntang. This was the ancestral home of the descendants of Sultan Iskandar Dzu'l-Karnain, mythically identified as the peripatetic Alexander the Great (Matheson 1979:369). It is to members of this dynasty that the epithet Melayu was originally confined, on the principle of lineage or descent, there referred to as *bangsa*. In this period, bangsa was reserved for those of demonstrable royal connection by blood. At this time, even the idea of indigenousness (*asal*) was restricted to those of royal origin (ibid:366-67), in contrast with the more universalistic and parochialized application of these terms in the present day (Nagata 1979). In fact, early perceptions of Malay identity seem to have arisen out of a quest by royal genealogists for some sort of legitimating principle, linking contemporary rulers to forebears of illustrious and even divine origin, the latter very much in the tradition of ancient Indic kingship (Milner 1982). In periods subsequent to that ascribed to the *Sejarah Melayu* and in places ruled by individuals several dynastic steps removed from the first courtly Melayu line, the term continues to perform the same legitimating function for the rulers and is used to validate the authority of the Johor and Pahang royal families (Matheson 1979:359). It is not surprising therefore to find the term *adat*, now used for Malay custom in general, also restricted to courtly ceremony. Vestiges of this meaning still remain today in the concept of *adat-istiadat rajah*, ceremonies in connection with royal rites of passage, such as the installation of the king, where, significantly, the title used for the ruler is Indic rather than Muslim.[2]

It was only through connection with a true "Malay," that is, one of royal descent, that the common people could themselves acquire Malay status. This was achieved by affiliation as *anak Melayu*, or fictive "children" of the rajah, or, as a more explicit status category, as *hamba Melayu* (the rajah's slaves). For the "people" or rak'yat of this period, therefore, Malay identity was defined less on the basis of bangsa than on a political bond, one of loyalty to a ruler or opposition to his enemies. Unlike the notion of descent or birth, as a fixed and inalienable status, the relationship with rulers was transferable, and so, presumably, was one's identity. As far as generalizations can be made, in the traditional Southeast Asian state, the bond between ruler and ruled was essentially a personal one of the classic patron-client variety (cf. Bronson 1977; Andaya 1975; Gullick 1958; Lieberman 1978; Geertz 1980; Milner 1982) whose expressive form was woven into a web of ceremonial glorifying the ruler. More instrumentally, the relationship embodied a dyadic contract, by which loyalty, labour, and services (military, agricultural, corvée, and so forth) were required of the subject in return for certain rewards and protection by the head of state. In this we can perceive the roots of the so-called "feudal" relationship and mentality and of the "protector" ideology as described and deplored by some modern Malay commentators (cf. Alatas 1968, 1979; Chandra Muzaffar 1979), who see this as a system of personal and mental bondage. This will receive more attention later.

The economies of traditional Southeast Asian coastal states, including Malacca in the west of the Malay peninsula, portrayed by the *Sejarah Melayu* as the prototype Malay state, whose rulers traced direct descent from the semi-divine denizens of Si Guntang, were largely mercantile and vulnerable to the weaknesses of dependence on international trade. The advantages of wealth and a certain cosmopolitanism were frequently countered, from the point of view of the ruler, by a highly mobile, shifting population, whose loyalty could sometimes be equally shifting and unreliable. For the ruler, control over riverine trading routes and hinterlands was often tenuous at best, as depicted in Bronson's account of the "dendritic state" (1977). Combined with a situation in which land pressure presented few problems (Gullick 1958; Chandra Muzaffar 1979), which permitted even non-trading peasants to relocate in other areas if it suited their interests, allegiances to rulers could often be fickle, or at best temporary. This rather volatile system was characterized by a constant rearrangement of personal loyalties and social boundaries, especially by units at the bottom of the hierarchy or state, and it resulted in a rather rapid process of creation, dissolution, and reformation of political states in a repetitive pattern which Tambiah has called the "galactic" state (1976). This is also a variant of the classic "segmentary state" known to anthropologists (cf. Fortes and Evans-Pritchard 1940). The modern geopolitical or territorial notion of the state as a grounded entity with relatively (or at least ideally) fixed boundaries thus differs from the latter kind of polity, which may help to explain why the word *tanah* (land or realm) is almost never found in connection with early ideas of Melayu (Matheson 1979:357). Identity was derived from political affiliation and founded on status and rank. Insofar as the bond between residents of the state was regarded as personal, the status of "citizenship" was less a function of territorial or residential position per se than of the tie with a specific overlord. In its broader dimensions, while it lasted, this relationship called for "absolute loyalty" on the part of the subject, together with unqualified obedience, regardless of ethical, moral, or other dimensions of their actions. Thus, even the grossest injustice by the "protector" could be upheld and justified as a form of divine right, the residue of old Indic ideas of kingship. The essence of this concept of royal power is vividly portrayed in the trials and tribulations of Hang Tuah[3] in the service of his ruler (cf. Kassim Ahmad 1964; Alatas 1968:79; Chandra Muzaffar 1979).

Finally, the pomp and circumstance of court ceremonial provided the ritual accolade and context to this unequal relationship (Milner 1982:97ff.), not unlike the exemplary centre of the Balinese "theatre state" as portrayed by Geertz (1980:13). The strategic and ritual importance of intermarriages between the royal sons and daughters of many states in the early Melayu world, including Malacca, Pahang, Johor, Pasir, and Aceh, underscored the hierarchical and rank-tied basis of identity, as opposed to an "ethnic" one, as is true, of course, in dynastic marriages and status "quality control" of modern royalty. Malayness could only be acquired through submission to an unequal and even autocratic relationship, but not, apparently, on the strength of common descent or the sharing of a wider culture by a grass-roots population. It did not connote a "people" nor result in a state based on a "nation." If anything, the position was reversed, whereby a nation has been slowly evolving over the centuries out of prior existing state and political ties, a process which is still continuing today. In seventeenth century Malacca, there were few means by which ordinary "Malays" or subjects could express their unity with each other or their sense of common identity. Presumably local-level loyalties to specific villages or kin existed, and it is assumed that the Malay language was widely used and understood as the trading *lingua franca* of the littoral of the Malay peninsula and much of Sumatra. However, even language (*bahasa*) at this time referred primarily in the literature to courtly language and, by extension, to manners, etiquette, and breeding (Matheson 1979), whose residue is retained in the modern *budi bahasa* with its sense of personal integrity and honouring of status obligations.

The gradual conversion of Melayu from an essentially political to more familiar "ethnic" bond, with greater emphasis on horizontal relationships between commoners of equal status, is first evident from nineteenth-century sources, for example, the *Tuhfat al-Nafis*, subtitled *Sejarah Melayu dan Bugis* ("The History of the Malays and Bugis"), and particularly from the well-known *Hikayat Abdullah*.[4] Now we find references to Malay bangsa in the modern sense of the "Malay people" and to adat as the everyday Malay way of life. Anak or *orang Melayu* were no longer necessarily of royal birth or dependent on a covenant with a ruler, but were the people or rak'yat themselves. Factors accounting for these changes may possibly be sought in two developments on the Malay peninsula. The first, in continuation of the shifting and migration of populations from one state to another, was marked by an intensification of immigration from the more heavily populated Indonesian islands and from India to the relatively open frontier of the Malay peninsula. One consequence of this was a heightened awareness of differences, by origin and interest, tradition and culture, of newly juxtaposed peoples, independent of a vertical referent or connection to a royal patron. Thus, one of the preoccupations of the *Tuhfat al-Nafis* is the relationship between Malays and Bugis and other immigrants such as Arabs, Javanese, Balinese, Chinese, and now the Dutch, as well as with some new categories, including "Muslims" (*orang Islam*) and *Nasrani* (Christians) (Matheson 1979:367). The fact that the author of another of the early chronicles, *Hikayat Abdullah*, was himself an offshoot of an Indian-Arab family and moved in British colonial circles may well have heightened his consciousness of "other" people and of their impact on a more indigenous (*asli*) stratum of the population, now labelled Malay. Under the interests of European colonialism as well, territorial boundaries and ideas about the geopolitical state were becoming more fixed, and status could be acquired through residence in the domain of a particular ruler without the necessity of a personal bond or contract.

The second factor contributing a new dimension to identity was undoubtedly Islam. Where the original concept of Melayu was particularistic and exclusive, Islam is ideally universalistic and transcends political and other status considerations. The horizontal spread and moral equality of the religious community or ummat is in total contrast to the vertical principle of ruler-subject and encourages a different kind of solidarity and identity. In particular, Islam provides its own blueprint for social relationships and community organization. It creates its own ritual-cultural domain within which it enjoins the self-sufficiency of each congregation in matters of religious observance. Ideally, every Muslim community should have the capacity to attend to all the needs of the life cycle and rites of passage of its members, as prescribed by Islam, to calculate all the religious accountables, from taxes to times of prayer and dates for fasting, and to disseminate and transmit the scriptures from generation to generation. On the more practical side, it is also considered desirable for each community to weave its own cloth for winding sheets, make its own paper for religious books, and cultivate sufficient carpentry skills to construct a prayer house or mosque. All of the above are encompassed in the *fardhu khifayah*. Between them, the Koran and Hadith are replete with injunctions for the appropriate conduct of daily life, even to details of controlling bodily emissions and cleansing thereafter, acceptable styles of personal deportment and dress, and diet and modes of food preparation. Islam does, in effect, supply a fairly comprehensive cultural blueprint for life. This may be integrated with, co-exist with, or even conflict with pre-existing customs and with the culture of the secular state. Whichever of the above combinations occurred as Islam was first introduced to the Malay world, one of the effects would undoubtedly have been a rise in the level of cultural consciousness, of choices to be made, substitutes to be weighed in the balance, and with it, a sense of shared interest and commitment that such dialogue, even in conflict, can create. Whether "Malay culture" was eventually to be resolved more in the direction of Islamic—or even Arabic— custom and law, or still wedded to the older strata of pre-Islamic custom became a discussable, debatable issue, from then on rooted in the social life and experience of the peoples affected. Beyond debate and diversity, Islam created a bond of common experience and shared identity.

Islam, like the other "religions of the Book" is also eminently legalistic, and through the application of *fiqh* (jurisprudential and theological interpretations of the Koran) and court of civil law (*hukum Syariah*), it codifies and sanctions the principal domains of personal, family, and social behaviour, including matters of property, inheritance, and commercial activities. The *hukum Islam* further extends to such "criminal" offences and sins as theft, drunkenness, adultery, and murder (*hudud*) which only God can pardon, but for which man can administer specific penalties, also laid down in the scriptures. Finally, the Koran and Hadith are the ultimate sources from which a series of continuous exegeses down the ages by Muslim scholars have attempted to construct theories and models of the ideal polity or state, its leadership, authority, and legitimacy. It is on this point that some of the greatest theological and social conflicts have arisen in Muslim societies in many times and places. Whether condensed into the somewhat unsatisfactory opposition between "secular" and "sacred" authority or refined in more intellectual notions of justice and liberty, a perennial concern in Islam revolves around the quality and foundation of the ties that bind man to man in society, from fellow villager to ruler. The coming of Islam to Malacca and other original "Malay states" was of potential revolutionary significance for the reformulation of the traditional ruler-subject relationship, and within it, the definition of Melayu. While Islam by no means rejects temporal political authority,[5] and indeed extolls a just ruler such as the Caliph Omar II, it does pose a serious practical and ethical dilemma for those faithful faced with a ruler who violates the tenets of the faith, even while himself claiming to be a Muslim. Ethically, the notion of an Indic-style divine king and absolute loyalty conflicts with the authority of religious law, of the Prophet, and of God, the more so if the ruler be unjust. Thus the exploits of some of the early Malacca and other Malay sultans recorded in the *Sejarah Melayu* and *Hikayat Hang Tuah*, as well as the nature of some of the obligations imposed on their subjects, such as corvée (*kerah*), were in opposition to Islamic concepts of justice (cf. Chandra Muzaffar 1979:7; 30ff). The question of authority in a Muslim society is complicated by the fact that, in practice, the emergence of a body of religious scholars and teachers (ulama) may challenge or compete with the established élites both morally and politically. Although historically, some ulama have been pressed into the service of the temporal rulers, as their "Brahmins" or validators, and have often enjoyed high status at court as educators of the royal and aristocratic youth, and even married into their families (Drewes 1958:291), there has always existed a countercurrent of opposition to this authority by ulama who did not necessarily perceive the interests of the moral/religious community as coinciding with those of the state (cf. Gibb 1962:96).

It may be speculated that, just as Islamic ritual culture threw into relief a non-Islamic Malay culture and gave it a name, it introduced a double-edged problem of authority. It set in motion a new political process with an increased potential for tension, uncertainty, ambiguity, and conflict (but also accommodation) between the two principles and their representatives, to which the politics of the modern Federation of Malaysia are not immune. As will be seen in subsequent chapters, issues of the "Islamic state" and of Islamic law versus their western parallels and the limits of the jurisdiction of the sultans constantly resurface in new guises.

It should not be overlooked that the coming of Islam to Southeast Asia was soon to be followed by the arrival of the European Christians. With them emerged a new dichotomy, between believer and infidel, one of whose consequences was the stimulation of a new bond of unity between the sultans, as the erstwhile rajahs were now called, with their subjects against the outsiders, whether Portuguese, Dutch, or British. Undeniably, this helped to solidify another political and cultural dimension and the common identity of the Melayu.

The first ulama of whom there are clear records in the early Islam of the states of Southeast Asia were of Middle Eastern origin and attached to the courts of various North Sumatran sultans, especially those of Aceh and Pasai, where they taught and had substantial followings (Drewes 1958; Johns 1975; Syed Naguib al-Attas 1970; Muhd.Uthman el-Muhammady 1978). Apparently, these early ulama were more in concert with the status quo than in opposition to it and reportedly even competed for royal patronage (Johns 1975:43). While the first Islamic scholars were outsiders, for example, Sayyids from Mecca, Persia, and India, from the sixteenth century on a line of indigenous, Malay or *Jawi* pupils and protégés soon arose (Syed Naguib Al-Attas 1970:8), of whom Hamzah Fansuri, a wandering mystic and poet in the Sufi tradition was the best-known. Hamzah Fansuri wrote fluent Malay, Arabic, and Persian, but he was distinguished by his command of the first and by his literary presentations of Sufism to the Southeast Asian world. Hamzah was later followed by other ulama, some Sufi, some not, of whom one, Shamsuddin (Shams Al-Din), taught at the Acehnese court. Beginning with the reign of Sultan Iskandar Muda of Aceh in the early seventeenth century, there developed a tradition of peripatetic ulama-teachers who fanned out through the islands of the Indonesian archipelago and the Malay peninsula spreading various, and often idiosyncratic, forms of mystical Sufi teachings. Some settled in local communities where they established schools. The importance of Hamzah lies in the fact that he was the first *alim* to write on religious matters entirely in Malay, probably the Pasai variant, and so made available and comprehensible the teachings of the faith to those not conversant with Arabic or Persian. By the pen of Hamzah, the Malay language was moulded into the form of the Arabic mystical quatrain (*sya'ir*) which required considerable ingenuity and innovation and a fluency and power by which the conviction and depth of the religious message could be conveyed. It is also important to recognize that in pre-Islamic days, Malay was not a written language with a script of its own, unlike old Javanese, Balinese, or even Batak. It remained for Islam to provide the Arabic script (Jawi), which was an essential precondition to the development of an effective theological and educational tradition and the foundation of an ulama-guru class. It was at this time too that Malay probably began to replace classical Javanese as the language of some of the Indonesian island courts, high culture, and international etiquette (Al-Attas 1970:73). Nevertheless, it was a Malay readjusted to accommodate a vast new vocabulary of terms and ideas from Arabic and, to a lesser extent, from Persian, particularly in the realms of religion, philosophy, and literature, many of which had no Malay precedent, although others supplied parallels to existing terms of Sanskrit origin.[6] This was the period too, claims al-Attas (1970:78), when Malay was transformed from an "aesthetic" to a "scientific" mode, which subsequently made it capable of handling the vocabulary and concepts of modernization.

Thus began a long and rich tradition of written religious literature in Malay, but in the Arabic (Jawi)[7] script. It encompassed both translations from Arabic originals as well as indigenous Malay commentaries and texts, known as the *Kitab Jawi* (Malay/Jawi books), many of which are still used in prayer houses (*surau*), mosques, and religious schools throughout Muslim Southeast Asia. The importance of the literary tradition established through the spread of Islam and its relationship to the Malay language was probably two-fold and also somewhat circular. First, a widely understood Southeast Asian language was essential as a vehicle for the further propagation of the faith, especially across political boundaries. Second, and in the process of the first, the language acquired a greater cosmopolitan character and international circulation and status, including in the Middle East itself, where it became the second largest "Muslim" language. Certainly it would have had the effect of raising the level of consciousness of linguistic and literary matters to those within the religious community, as the comments of Abdullah Munshi often caustically show.[8] It meant, too, that the Malay language had to adjust itself to the new demands placed upon it in the realm of esoteric new vocabulary and expression of specialized theological Islamic concepts. Some concepts were lifted directly from Arabic, but some "indigenous" Sanskrit terms underwent transformation and acquired new meanings. Thus the Sanskrit *agama* (see n.6 above) became not just "religion," but specifically Islam, with the connotation of the only true religion. All other religions were demoted to the status of *percayaan* (beliefs).

By Abdullah Munshi's time, in the early nineteenth century (1970:53), this literary/religious brand of Malay was the only version of the language formally taught and largely as the medium of religious instruction rather than for its own sake. Indeed, Abdullah Munshi also reports (ibid:280) that some zealous religious teachers favoured the banning of Malay stories as unredeemed by religious content, as though they were the purveyors of false doctrine. Literature and religion thus went hand in hand. It is probably no coincidence that the Malay language, the vessel of Islam, was also the regional trading lingua franca, and many of the first Muslim visitors to the shores of Southeast Asia came on missions of trade first and religion second. A common linguistic medium thus aided both causes.

Extravagant claims are currently fashionable among Malay Muslim revivalists over the debt owed by the Malay language and culture to Islam, and these have been the subject of a number of university seminars and conferences wherein Islam is viewed as the ultimate source of Malay cultural unity, dignity, ethics, morality, civilization, and everything else of value, and the dawn of a "new intellectual age" (*zaman ahkliah*). The greatest heights of spiritual truth (*hakikat*) and depths of self-awareness and knowledge became expressible only through Islam (cf. Muhd.el-Muhammady 1978:17). It is true that Malay culture would now be unimaginable without Islam and also that certain intellectual disciplines such as astronomy, mathematics, and metaphysics owe much to their Middle Eastern origin, travelling on the back of Islam, but the excoriation of the residual, non-Islamic elements of Malay culture as backward (*adat kolot*) or as religiously unorthodox or forbidden (*salah, haram*), may sometimes be overstated by these cultural exegesists. Such negative judgments on the pre-Islamic past tend to be more frequent and vituperative at times of religious revival, as during the Kaum Muda movement earlier in the present century (Roff 1967). As will be seen in subsequent chapters, many eager dakwah advocates see elements of Malay culture not merely as pre- or non-Islamic, but as anti-Islamic (*bertentangan dengan Islam*) and seek to purge them accordingly. Among these customs are an assortment of agricultural and fishing rituals designed to appease malevolent spirits, some magical curing rites, and many practices attached to rites of passage. Yet other religious purists split hairs over such questions as whether the writings of Hamzah Fansuri represent "Islamic literature" or "Malay literature with Islamic elements."

How early and deeply this wealth of Islamic knowledge and spirituality suffused Malay culture, however, is not so clear. For while Islam was officially adopted by the Malacca court early in the fifteenth century, some references to its mode of practice in the *Sejarah Melayu* suggest that the depth of comprehension and subtlety of interpretation was at times superficial and simplistic, whether on the part of the chroniclers or those whom they depicted. Johns (1975:41) relates how religious scholars who solved theological riddles were rewarded by their sultan with gifts of gold and concubines, which suggests more of a Hang Tuah kind of ethic, rooted in a set of acquisitive/courtly, rather than spiritual/intellectual, values. As noted above, the distinction between Islamic and Malay society and culture and its implications for political authority was a concern which consumed Abdullah Munshi in his quest for a Malay identity shorn of its feudal symbols. It became an issue again under the influence of the Kaum Muda, when the legitimacy of the sultans' roles as Heads of Religion was questioned. In the current climate of religious sensitivity, the controversy has surfaced once more, particularly among the dakwah protagonists, albeit in muted form, given that open discussion of royal power is officially prohibited.

Two types of authority are relevant to the political unfolding of the various historical Malay states and of contemporary Malaysia. One line of authority descends through the ulama, validated by God's Word (*firman Tuhan*) through the Koran, and by that of the Prophet in the Hadith, and reinforced by the word of the law (*kata hukama*) of the various exegesists (for example, kata al-Ghazzali) and is of the type known as "inspirational" (wahyu, *nubuwwah*). The other line of authority traces its roots to the Indic idea of kingship and unquestioning "feudal" loyalties described above. This latter type is associated by some commentators not only with the sultans, but also with modern federal government leaders, whose autocratic style and imperiousness and expectations of absolute personal loyalty are claimed to resemble very closely those of traditional royalty (cf. Chandra Muzaffar 1979). Attempts by secular élites to take over the administration of religion and control its doctrine and efforts by some ulama to gild their legitimacy through royal patronage mark the controversial point at which these two paths cross. The debate is fraught with moral and theological, as well as political, problems and casuistry, and it serves to highlight the continuing double strands and double standards in Malay culture which have never been totally integrated.

Extrapolating from the above lengthy digression on early Islam, we are now in a position to venture some conclusions about the nature of Malay culture in a modern sense. Regardless of whether the mesh and individual strands of Islamic and non-Islamic tradition are loosely or tightly woven, in harmony or in tension, the advent of Islam undoubtedly helped to promote the "horizontal" solidarity of the rulers' subjects and, by introducing elements of universalism, encouraged the crossing of such political boundaries as those between Malacca and Aceh through the activities of ulama and travelling Sufi mystics (cf. Mohd Taib Osman 1980). The medium was the common language of Arabic-influenced Malay, or Jawi. Thus even a poet from Makassar could invoke Islam, in the Malay language, and thereby call himself a Malay. It is, of course, always difficult to disentangle history from "myth" in an anthropological sense, particularly when the rendering is by a commentator with a message of his own. Thus modern, dakwah-oriented interpreters tend to see the emergence of a more spiritual basis of identity, which helped to unify the bangsa in much the same way as the early tribes of Arabia were joined by the faith of Muhammad. Such commentators (for example, Baharuddin b.Ahmad 1977:35) note that, beginning in this early colonial period, individuals and groups are identified as much by religion as by bangsa, for example, "Christians" for Europeans, in opposition to the "Muslim national heroes" (*pahlawan Muslim Nasionalis*), such as the Javanese hero, Diponegoro. It could be said that if Islam did not create Malayness, it certainly widened its scope. Yet if Islam succeeded in transcending political boundaries, it did not erase them entirely. The Malays of Malacca, the Acehnese, and the Minangkabau preserved their primary attachment as subjects of their sultans, increasingly defined as "states." Even the lineal offshoots of Malacca, the kingdoms of Johor and Pahang, retained their separate political identity, despite their shared Melayu elements. At the grassroots level, Islamization tended to represent first an emulation of the ruler's choice and second an independent ideological or moral commitment.

The persistence of particularistic identities within political units in the face of a more universalistic ideology has its parallels, and possibly some of its causes, in the character of the ulama themselves. As has been noted (Johns 1975:51), many of them were attached to royal courts and rulers through personal ties similar to those that bound the lesser subjects and depended on their patrons for their status, wealth, marriage alliances, and thus some of their legitimacy. (Of the kind of ulama who opposed royal power, more later.) Ultimately, therefore, the limits of Malay identity, while stretched and partly democratized by Islam, were still constrained by political loyalties and by ties to a certain kind of established authority. By the end of the nineteenth century, most Malay rulers had succeeded in formalizing this association between royal and religious authority by appointing official interpreters of the religious law (*mufti*, or in some states, *Syeikh al-Islam*) who were dependent on princely patronage and upheld the royal power, or, Brahmin-like, even added to its aura. These mufti were empowered to issue doctrinal rulings (*fatwa*) regarded as valid and legally binding on all Muslims resident in the sultan's domain. It follows that, in some cases, their rulings tended to support the political status quo.

The period between the rise of Malacca in the sixteenth century, as chronicled by the *Sejarah Melayu*, and the beginning of the twentieth century saw a progressive trend towards a clearer conception of Malayness in all the sultanates of the Malay peninsula and even beyond. Each state retained its own political autonomy, and this long represented the primary source of identity for the common people, but there was an awareness of a shared language,[9] culture, and faith (Milner 1982). Within each state the degree of integration between religion and other cultural elements, and their identification with the people (rak'yat) had reached the point where the two had become conceptually fused. It is well known that during this period any outsider who converted to Islam was automatically eligible for Malay status, following the adage that to "enter Islam" (*masuk Islam*) was to "become a Malay" (*masuk Melayu*) (Roff 1967; Nagata 1974a; 1979). At this time, most converts would have been of local provenance and usually involved in an intermarriage, so that the equation would rarely have created blatant status incongruities. To the extent that Islam was able to transcend narrow community or parochial identities and interests and generously opened the doors of Malay identity (admittedly then still in a process of flux and consolidation) to all who professed the Muslim faith, the universalism of Islam was honoured. But insofar as the same religious boundary did double duty in delimiting specific peoples and interests, and was in fact becoming appropriated by them, this universalism was reduced to an ethnic particularism. This will be discussed further in Chapter 7.

At this point it is necessary to recognize the intervention of other political events which changed the established patterns of power and authority within the Malay states. Over the course of the nineteenth century, increasing political turmoil resulted from the intrigues of tin-seeking Chinese traders and their secret societies (cf. Khoo 1975) and from unofficial British economic interests, each of which made alliances with various factions of the local ruling families in their respective states. Eventually, the quest for trade and resources led the British to protect their economic interests by political treaties, and so the colonial presence began to creep, state by state, across the Malay peninsula, creating hybrid political offspring in the form of indirect rule.[10] By the time the British had finished clipping the political wings of the traditional rulers in their own states and had engineered a somewhat artificial and doubtful union of all nine states into the Federation of Malaya in 1948, royal power and authority had lost much of its panache and lustre. What remained was an emasculated position, limited largely to the domain of "Malay religion and custom."[11] Formally, this restricted the ruler's scope to the control of religious councils and the appointment of the mufti and mosque officials, which, however, did leave the ruler with some influence in matters of doctrine (fatwa) within his own state. Today the sultans remain as formal Heads of Religion and Custom within their own domains, while the symbolic Head of the Federal State of Malaysia is the King (*Yang di Pertuan Agong*, see Introduction n.1), who also represents religious interests in the two states with no sultans of their own. In non-religious matters, as shown in Chapter 3, the sultans now have to contend with the political encroachment of federal politicians and government bureaucrats, including federally approved chief ministers (*Mentri Besar*), and party influence in the State Assembly.

This period between the first colonial presence and the formation of the Malayan Federation also saw the numerical increase of non-Malay populations, particularly from China and India, but also from Europe. This was probably one of the most important single factors in generating a sense of "Malayness" if only by a principle of opposition and contrast. When the contrast became a symbol of other economic and political interests, however, the scene was set for oppositions of a more serious nature. The immigrants, whether Asian or European, were preoccupied with material gain, largely at the expense of the indigenous population, and neither owed any allegiance to the incumbent political authority of the sultans. This could only widen the gap between the newcomers and sultans' Malay subjects.

The twentieth century, a turbulent era covering the rise and fall of colonialism in a formal sense, has witnessed a continuation of the two contending symbols and bases of authority in Malay society: the Islamic and the more narrowly Malay. During this period, one variant of non-Islamic[12] Malay culture has emerged in the form of a mildly socialistically inclined nationalism, following the Indonesian pattern. In Malaya, the opposition between these two principles of authority was most clearly thrown in to relief over the issue of national independence, which burned intermittently during the 1920's and 1930's, simmered down over the war years, only to flare up once more at the end of the Japanese occupation and the war.

Both elements shared a concern over the status of the Malay population vis-à-vis both the British colonialists and the steadily increasing cohorts of other immigrants, principally Chinese and Indians. Each in its own way wished to chart a course towards greater Malay independence and political autonomy. The Islamic element was largely Arabic-educated and closely identified with the Kaum Muda, many of whom were foreigners from the Middle East, India and Indonesia. Despite their background, they were now permanently settled in Malaya and committed to their adoptive homeland and its political fate. Like the Arab-Tamil-descended Abdullah Munshi before them, they were sufficiently detached from local loyalties to see the Malay situation in a broader context, yet equally anxious themselves to be regarded as Malays, through the common bond of Islam. To this end they found it convenient to invoke the old "masuk Islam/masuk Melayu" equation, but since most of them were resident in the Straits Settlements, [13] outside the jurisdiction of any sultan, they lacked that crucial political tie which was still the hallmark of true Malay status. To the contrary, many of them, in the name of Islamic reformism, went so far as to challenge the validity of royal jurisdiction in religious affairs, which alienated[14] them further from the native-born, who formed the backbone of the so-called Kaum Tua or conservative Malay-Muslims (Roff 1967). The response of the latter was to create a new and contrasting category of "pure Malay" (*Melayu jati*), thereby disengaging the religious and ethnic boundaries once again. At about the same time, a new kind of individual was invented in the form of the "*Bumiputera*"[15] (son of the soil) to separate the true indigenes from the immigrants, even when Muslim. This represented a retreat into an ethnic particularism while implicitly acknowledging the existence of a category of non-Malay Muslims, in a back-handed nod to Islamic universalism. The residue left over after the pure Malays had been filtered out from the other Muslims became known by various epithets, including *Darah Keterunan Kling* (DKK), *Darah Keterunan Arab* (DKA), *Jawi Peranakan*, or *saudara baru* (cf. Roff 1967; Nagata 1974a; 1978; 1979).[16] This explicit blood/origin rationale for their exclusion made Malayness more than ever a matter of descent as much as of political contract.

It was this second group with their narrower interpretation of Malayness which was responsible for a new kind of political loyalty and identity. No longer intractably bound by obligations to royalty, yet often hostile to colonial authority, they espoused a form of nationalism whose focus was the creation of a pan-Malayan solidarity, transcending the old royal states and even the new colonial ones. At its broadest it found its expression in such concepts as *Melayu Raya* (Greater Malaya) and Nusantara.[17] The idea of Malayu Raya was first used by the pre-war, moderately socialist political party, *Kesatuan Melayu Muda* (Union of Young Malays, or KMM), and was reinforced through its association during the 1930's with the Indonesian Masjumi political party.[18] Both the concepts of Nusantara and Melayu Raya are essentially based on the myth of a common culture and people rather than on either existing or proposed political unity. Political divisions which had for so long obscured a common Malay identity by their primary affiliation to such states (negeri) as Aceh, Malacca, Pasai, Minangkabau, Jawa, and so forth, were to be subordinated to a higher level of nationalism which would represent the Malay people as a whole. How far and how soon this far-flung population would find consummation in political union beyond the traditional negeri was never clearly stated, and it was, in any case, relegated to the remote future, making it, as Rustum Sami aptly terms it, a "nation of intent" (1976). This suggests a form of "nationalism without a nation," that is, without full political mobilization, with a rather diffuse notion of culture and lineage, and without a significant role for religion. Whether the nation emerges from the state or the state from a natural outgrowth of self-conscious nationalism seems to depend, in this paradigm, on the point at which the analysis is made and on what level, the negeri or the wider Melayu Raya or Nusantara.

Following the Pacific War, preoccupation with nationalism in a more narrowly political sense intensified and so did the bifurcation between what might crudely be termed the royalist and religious streams. The former represented the group which eventually gave rise to the United Malays National Organization political party (UMNO) and advocates a continued absolute loyalty to an exclusive Malay leadership,[19] whether to the old or new rajahs in the form of the *kerajaan* or government elites. UMNO was preceded in 1945 by an earlier Malay political party, the Malay National Party (MNP), which gave voice to both the religious and left-wing secular elements of Malay nationalism. Although such MNP leaders as Dr. Burhanuddin Al-Helmy (later a founder of the Islamic party PAS) were strongly critical of the Malay aristocracy and royalty, they nonetheless called upon the latter to "lead our race" in the struggle against foreign imperialism and saw the sultans as symbols of the "Malay race" and its derivative, the "nation" (*kebangsaan*) (cf. Funston 1976:61). Insofar as the MNP could envisage a more generous interpretation of Malayness, by extending it to cover anyone willing to identify with the traditional symbols of the Malay world, there was continuity with the more diffuse Malayness of old, but as the influence of the Islamic elements of the party increasingly prevailed, the religious component of individual and political identity once more had to be accommodated. Issues such as these were first raised at the now-celebrated Pan-Malayan Economic Religious Conferences, convened by Dr. Burhanuddin at the equally famous religious school in Gunung Semanggol, Perak. Once again, the competence of the sultans to represent or administer religious affairs was questioned. Interest was also expressed in the creation of a uniform religious affairs department which would unify all the states and the Straits Settlements under a single jurisdiction and standardize Islamic doctrine for Malaya as a whole. It would also have had the effect of pulling from under the feet of the sultans their last vestiges of power and much of their legitimacy.[20] Among the interests of these congresses was the purging of "impure" ritual and other local accretions to Islam (Stockwell 1979:138). The culmination of all this debate and activity was the formation, in 1951, of the *Persatuan Islam Se-Tanah Melayu* (PMIP) (Pan-Malayan Islamic Party), which was renamed the *Partai Islam Se-Malaysia* (PAS) in 1973, under the leadership of Haji Ahmad Fuad bin Hassan.

For the first ten years of its career, the PMIP or PAS was popularly identified with a form of Malay communalism with Islam as an essential component of that identity. In the past it has advocated greater attention to Malay language education, restriction of certain government posts to Malays, and general opposition to the political co-operation with the non-Malays that has been the underpinning of the post-Independence coalitions of the Alliance and National Front. Not surprisingly, PAS has been most successful electorally in the most Malay states of Kelantan and Trengganu, and to a lesser extent in Kedah. Its platform has been consistently for Malay rights and greater prominence of Islam in national institutions. A zone of ambivalence continues to exist, however, over the official PAS attitude to the monarchy. For Kelantan at least, Kessler (1978) has claimed that the entire balance of PAS support is anti-royal and that behind its representation of peasant/class interests can be discerned a continuation of the early radical element from which PAS was born. In Kedah, on the other hand, such anti-royalist sentiments are less apparent. Indeed, the first post-Independence prime minister of Malaysia, Tunku Abdul Rahman, a member of the Kedah royal family, still commands widespread respect, despite his sometimes less-than-meticulous attention to religious obligations and his well-known enjoyment of such entertainments as horse-racing. In other states too, the public causes of PAS have commonly centred on topics close to the heart of the rural Malay who forms the backbone of the party, particularly those pertaining to religious versus secular education, the construction of prayer houses (surau) and mosques, and more particularly over the legitimate authority in these domains. The party regularly and self-righteously challenges UMNO's materialistic and worldly financial and development schemes as false lures designed to woo the rural voter.

The rise of dakwah during the 1970's has undoubtedly fortified PAS's Islamic platform and convictions, but it still leaves a number of other areas to be clarified. With Islam as the new rallying call, PAS is now somewhat more hesitant about identifying Islam too headily with Malayness and on occasion even accuses UMNO politicians of "racism," although the taint of ethnic chauvinism has not been completely eradicated. Today the language of opposition is more often Islam/non-Islam (*Islam/bukan Islam*), and Datuk Asri, long president of PAS, increasingly tended to stress the universalistic-religious dimensions of his party in such declarations as "*semangat keislaman mengatasi semangat nasionalisma*" ("the spirit of Islam will vanquish the spirit of nationalism") (*Utusan Melayu* 14/8/75; *Sarina* 1979:32). It is probably more accurate to say that it is the language of opposition, rather than the opposition itself which has changed. Like most of the dakwah groups, PAS has kept a conspicuous silence over the question of royal authority. Only through subtle and indirect references to such non-Islamic practices and habits as excessive materialism, gambling, and drinking can the latter be assailed and then with caution.

The contemporary cultural, religious, and political situations among the Malays show a community divided, particularly between the two streams which emerged in the pre-war, and even pre-colonial, period. The deepest cleavages still exist over questions of authority and its legitimacy and over the role of Islam. On one side are the supporters of secular authority (principally Party UMNO), the heirs to the "feudal mentality" and the "absolute loyalty" syndrome, described above. Indeed, there are still some Malays who see their primary identity and opposition to non-Malays in terms of an almost atavistic personal allegiance to an individual sultan, as among the Malays of the Riau Islands which, in the modern geopolitical framework, belong to Indonesia (Vivienne Wee, personal communication). In 1979, an association was formed in Malaysia with the aim of restoring the ancient Malacca sultanate in an attempt to recapture the glories of early Malay history. The candidate for sultan was to be drawn from the royal family of Perak, which claims the closest genealogical ties with the last members of the Malacca ruling house (*Watan* 29/2/80). Meanwhile, across the water in North Sumatra, there is talk of similar moves by some coastal Malays to restore the old sultanate of Deli as a symbolic focus of their sense of lost identity (Vivienne Wee, personal communication). On the other side, although the two may not be totally mutually exclusive, stand the advocates of stronger religious leadership, whether in the form of more power to the independent ulama, as in the original PAS formula or of a full-fledged Islamic state,[21] as proposed by some of the more zealous dakwah enthusiasts. For this category, Islam is the most integral part of their identity, although within it there is by no means total consensus over the details of their ideal polity or projected relationships between the Malays and non-Malay Muslims. The popular epithet used to characterize the first kind of Malay is derived from the Bumiputera template, described above. The Bumi Malay is one who is willing to consort and co-operate politically and economically with non-Malays and non-Muslims, but turn these alliances to his own, and to the other Malays', advantage. Through them they gain access to Chinese capital and other material benefits, as well as control of the political balance in such a way as to make their non-Malay "partners" scapegoats where convenient, as a means of vote-getting among their own Malay electorate. Prominent among these are the UMNO "hardliners" who favour western capitalism and technical development, as long as these are directed towards Malay interests. In the broad Bumi category too would be included the royalists and all those who lay their loyalty unconditionally on the line for their secular patrons among the government and bureaucratic élites. This should not be taken to mean that the Bumi Malays are non- or anti-religious. On the contrary, many of them, particularly government and other leaders, make liberal use of Islamic symbols and programmes, both to win votes and to respond to the opposition dakwah or religious Malays in the latters' own idiom. This hybrid form is often referred to as "Islamic Bumiputerism." Each group in its own way invokes Islam to its own ends, yet each places a high priority on Malay rights and privileges, albeit by different routes and in slightly different proportions. Given the intense politicization of these two positions, with religion being pressed into service on both sides, the lines are drawn for inevitable confrontation. The Malays are simultaneously united and divided by their common faith.

The current resurgence of dakwah among certain elements of the Malay-Muslim population must be placed in the context of the lengthy historical sequence from which the present ethnic and political situation has evolved. Far from being a mere fashion or fad imported as if by whim from other parts of the Muslim world, Malay dakwah in the third quarter of the twentieth century resurrects a number of ancient themes about the essential nature of Malayness and the status of the Malay community. Interwoven with its more explicit theological pronouncements are thinly veiled concerns over the relationship between Malays and non-Malays or non-Muslims in a multi-ethnic society and over the legitimacy of the secular power and authority, and even of the state itself. It is not hard to understand why the Islamic revival is perceived as a potential political challenge by the other Bumi Malays. In the cultural domain, the questions raised by the dakwah revivalists are substantially of the same tone as those asked half a century, one and a half centuries, and several centuries ago, namely, the status of Islamic culture in relation to Malay custom (adat), including language. Always an emotive issue, the Malay language has once again assumed symbolic significance through a new twist. Given that by the end of the 1970's, Malay is well on the way to being fully established, at least in the educational system, the latest emphasis is on a reintroduction of the Arabic (Jawi) script and, among the literary set, a promotion of Arabic vocabulary, styles, and spelling both as a means of enhancing the richness of Malay and as a more effective vehicle for Islam (see Chapter 7).

Clearly the dakwah revival reflects issues and interests, cleavages and conflicts long present in Malay society, regardless of the personal religious commitment for the individuals involved. Finally, insofar as questions about Malay identity and the nature of the state are still debatable, Islam will be the key variable in that debate and will be invoked by both streams of Malay as they attempt to chart their own path to full nationhood.

2

The Chain of Religious Knowledge:
Rural Ulama and the Basis of Their Authority

Until only a generation or so ago, Malay society was essentially rural and agricultural, based on a mixed economy of wet rice, fruit and vegetable cultivation, and fishing. The basic social unit was the village or *kampung*, and for most Malays this is still the most meaningful place of reference for personal identity by origin. Regardless of the larger, traditional royal state or negeri to which the individual belonged, day-to-day affairs were administered within the local kampung or cluster of kampungs in a unit known as the *mukim* (parish), and this was also the unit within which most religious affairs were conducted.

For several centuries following the introduction of Islam to Southeast Asia, a distinctive pattern of religious authority and practice was continued, with only minor modifications, until the colonial period in the early twentieth century. Recent changes reflect the pressures of growing urbanization and control of the economy by Malays, intensified educational programmes and policies, modern occupational and lifestyle innovations, and finally, the dakwah revival. In this chapter I describe the traditional rural religious organization and try to assess the extent to which it has succumbed to some of these changes. Much of the contemporary descriptive material and detail is drawn from field research in the northwestern state of Kedah, which is well known for its historically deep tradition of Islamic religious schools and scholarship. Kedah has also long cultivated extensive connections with centres in other parts of the Muslim world and has played a role in other and past religious revivals and movements in Malaya, such as the Kaum Muda of the 1920's and 1930's. Supplementary material is derived from numerous written sources, principally an assortment of Malay annuals and historical documents, religious books, manuscripts and tracts, genealogies (*salasilah*), and other records. I also draw, eclectically, on information and materials pertaining to other parts of the Malay peninsula for a comparative perspective.

The position of the ulama in rural Malay society cannot be assessed without reference to basic Islamic notions of orthodoxy and the possibilities for legitimate ideological variation and/or change. That the Koran, as revealed to the Prophet Mohammed is the ultimate source of all prescriptions and wisdom in Islam is never disputed. The Koran may be supplemented where necessary by the Hadith, which contains the tradition, sayings, and acts of the Prophet (*sunna*) as recorded by his companions. Together, these two form the inspiration from which all else flows. What is disputed, however, is how these "raw" materials should be applied and codified in any systematic blueprint for society and state (cf. Gibb 1962:92). As in other religions, particularly those based on revelation, the burden lies in the interpretation, and the scripture or holy books are merely the beginning of a long chain of exegesis and commentary (*tafsir*) and not a little casuistry, which engage the scholars and philosophers in every age. In cases where both the Koran and the Hadith are regarded as unclear, one theological strategy is that of *qiyās* or the method of analogy, whereby new problems are solved on the basis of old principles, if the parallels seem justifiably close. Qiyās has the option of either doubling back to a literalist and fundamentalist approach to the scriptures or of being used more imaginatively to support innovations in changing societies without forfeiting the spirit of the original. In more recent times, opposition between these two approaches has separated conservative and fundamentalist from more reform-oriented or modernist movements. Islamic history has been marked by shifts in the balance between the two, and the same dichotomy is evident in Malaysia today. Logically too, there is need for a balance. Just as the creative and adaptive use of qiyās could get out of hand to the extent that the end product would bear little resemblance to the original and an uncontrollable heterodoxy develop, so too could an unassailable rigidity set in, with attempts to freeze all Muslim societies of all places and periods into a seventh-century Arabic mould.

Some western "orientalist" scholars of Islam have made much of this first proclivity, particularly in the absence of any centralized religious authority for Islam as a whole, the lack of an ultimate court of appeal or yet of an institutionalized clergy. In practice, however, a substantial degree of self-regulation and consistency developed early in the Islamic era, based on the consensus of a respected and accepted class of scholars and scriptural commentators (ulama), who emerged as arbiters of religious affairs, and started their own "chains" of learning (*isnad*), crossing generations and regions. To some extent, this closure of the ranks with its control over the networks of communication and information flow resulted in a broad agreement over major issues, which is generally accepted by most Muslims as the canon of Islamic orthodoxy or *ijma*. The ijma provides a baseline or standard by which subsequent interpretations can be measured. Both the principle of *ijma* and their own legitimacy in determining it were achieved by the ulama on the strength of one of the Traditions (Hadith) to the effect that they are the heirs of the Prophets (*"bahawa ulama itu warith Nabi-nabi"*), hence qualified to oversee the correct dissemination of religion (*Kamus Sanusi* 1976:81). The transmission of the ijma has never been entirely smooth, nor did it irrevocably close the door to the residual privilege of individual interpretation through the use of qiyās already mentioned or through reason and intellect (*akal*), a process known by the generic term ijtihad.[1] In theory there still remain some points as yet uncovered, for in a world of almost infinite inventions and possibilities, even the ijma cannot be exhaustive. Most Muslim scholars are reluctant to open the door too widely to ijtihad and innovations (*bid'aa*), for fear that, among other things, it could undermine their own authority as well as foment disunity in the Islamic community. Different combinations of the two processes of ijtihad and ijma, under the varying political jurisdiction of different caliphates, resulted eventually in the emergence of four distinct streams (*mazahab*) of Islamic law (Syari'ah), the Maliki, Hanbali, Hanafi, and Syafie. It is to the Syafie that all Malays and most Southeast Asian Muslims belong, while most of Pakistani and Indian origin are Hanafi.

Throughout its history, Islam has nevertheless experienced some abrupt mutational changes, often under charismatic influence of particularly powerful individuals. Messianic leaders (*mahdi*) have arisen in various times and places, bearing messages that transcend and contradict the ijma and established Syari'ah, and attempt to chart new paths (*syar*) to salvation. Among these would be numbered, not only the Shi'ite *mujtahid*, but also many Sufi leaders within the broad Sunni school. From the standpoint of the central core of the four schools, such variants are often considered heretical, even though the leaders themselves can claim a direct line of intellectual descent or connection (isnad; salasilah)[2] with more orthodox ulama or else invoke the right of ijtihad.

Such movements and changes in direction, however, are not just tests of ideological orthodoxy. Clearly they must involve followers and their needs and willingness to accept. They must further accommodate to the interests of power and politics in their area of operation. Islam has never claimed to stand aloof from worldly affairs, nor upheld any distinction between church and state. It is a religion grounded in law, with a strong social underpinning and philosophy. Not surprisingly, therefore, political interests have often influenced the course of religious events and movements and the types of leadership and practice as much as purely doctrinal or ideological concerns. That is, religious divisions may result from political factionalism and loyalty, or opposition, to particular leaders and thus transcend matters of specific belief. Indeed, such commitments may determine the "ideological" content of the movement rather than the reverse (cf. Jackson 1980). To this question I shall return later.

"OFFICIAL" ULAMA AND RELIGIOUS COUNCILS

Given that Islam is self-defined as a *Din*, a total way of life, for which the Syari'ah and other prescriptions for full community living are provided, oppositions between the domain of sacred and secular have never been very meaningful. Indeed, throughout its history, Islam has tended to be highly politicized, and the two types of authority, ulama and royalty, have had to come to some sort of mutual accommodation—or conflict.[3] Islam rarely rejects the principle of secular leadership out of hand and indeed often endorses and respects the just ruler, the defender of the faith, who sets an example to his people, helps the poor, alleviates misery, and is modest and temperate in his personal habits. Religious scholars of the stature of Al-Ghazali and Ibn Khaldun are known to have favoured totalitarian rule rather than weak or no rule at all. This is consistent with the generic idea of authority in Islamic culture, which tends towards the autocratic, based more on command and adherence to the law, than on paternalism or "love" in a Christian sense. In this respect, it mirrors the relationship between man and Allah.

Moral equality of man before God does not necessarily entail social equality. Not only are political hierarchies endorsed, but economic inequalities can be tolerated so long as they are not the fruits of activities religiously forbidden (haram), for example, through undue "exploitation" or use of monetary interest (*riba*) or, to take an instance in modern Malaysia, from the profits of taxes on the sale of pork or liquor by non-Muslim citizens of the state. The idea of the Islamic state is based more on empirical historical precedents than on any specific scriptural canon.[4] No precise details are laid down in the Koran for handling problems of administration or unequal wealth and status, as PAS and dakwah leaders in Malaysia have discovered. The usual model for the Muslim state has been the caliphate, wherein the ruler was acknowledged as both temporal and spiritual leader. As such, he was responsible for the administration of religious law (hukum syari'ah), although his freedom to reinterpret that law (ijtihad) was apparently curtailed by watchful scholastic ulama (Gibb 1962:15). More often than not, however, politics in Muslim states have been characterized by a tension between the two types of authority, with the ulama as a significant counterforce. The current revival forces in Malaysia are no exception to this.

While the village and teaching ulama of the rural Malay areas were relatively independent actors, answerable largely to their own personal followers and pupils, some ulama in the royal courts and capitals were putting down roots as the official spokesmen of their faith and becoming the basis of a more politicized Islam in each state. Eventually this role was institutionalized in the form of State Religious Councils. Partly in order to codify and enforce religious rulings (fatwa), and partly as a result of the colonially sanctioned entrenchment of the sultans as Heads of Malay Religion and Custom in their respective states, the need for a more organized system of religious administration arose. In two states, Kelantan and Pahang, state religious councils were established as early as 1915, but in the rest of the peninsula there were none before 1949. A key figure in most religious councils is the mufti,[5] a royal appointee, charged with interpretation of disputed points of doctrine and issuing fatwa which are then legally binding for Muslims in that state alone. Even in the 1980's, this represents the limits of centralization and control over Islamic doctrine in Malaysia, despite federal government attempts to override state autonomy by all manner of national programmes and institutions (see Chapters 3 and 6).

Most state religious councils are divided into two sections, one dealing mainly with matters of doctrine, the other with day-to-day administration of religious projects. Religion has not escaped bureaucratization, and special departments, along the lines of the civil service, now exist for collection of religious taxes (*fitrah* and *zakat*), for control of religious schools, operation of the Syari'ah court, registration of births, marriages, deaths, and new converts, and the trusteeship of religious endowments and properties. Religious councils in the modern age now also sponsor information offices and special investment and development schemes to finance charities and other operations. Most religious councils today have their own dakwah departments or programmes, in order to keep abreast of the "rising religious tide," and to "integrate the Muslim community," by drawing the population away from the exclusive sway of local village ulama. Some idea of the expanded sphere of financial operations of modern religious councils is provided by the case of Kedah, where income generated from a variety of agricultural schemes is being applied to such projects as the construction of a new hostel in Cairo for Kedah students studying at Al-Azhar University in conjunction with the Past Scholars of the Middle East Association of Kedah (*Persatuan Bekas Mahasiswa Timur Tengah Kedah*).

Over the past few years, a noticeable trend in the direction of centralization has been observable in many religious councils. In Kedah this has been marked by a complete takeover of the tithe/tax collection, from the traditional local (mukim) level, to a bureaucratic organization centred on the state capital. Significantly, the taxes are now known as zakat rajah (royal zakat), as opposed to the original zakat *peribadi*, which connotes a "gift from the heart," truly voluntary and given out of compassion rather than under coercion. The growing centralization of religious control by the council has occurred partly at the expense of the independence of the old kampung religion and the local ulama. Imams and other mosque officials in each area are now usually appointed by the council and paid salaries from zakat. Now too, the entire independent rural religious school system is under review and under the threat of council "aid" and intervention in the form of "approved" teachers and curricula to assist the traditional ulama and teachers in their educational enterprises. In its invasion of new areas and activities, the religious councils are creating something of a state within a state, whereby a wide assortment of enterprises are gradually drawn into the sphere of Islam, and religious activities are increasingly bureaucratized and politicized.

Given that each sultan is Head of Religion in his own state, with powers of appointing religious council officials, both directly and through the Executive Council of the state ruling political party (EXCO), he is in a strategic position which can be turned to his advantage. On occasion, he is able to use religious issues to flex his otherwise rather atrophied political muscles against other authorities. The Sultans of Pahang and of Kedah both used their positions to assert a measure of independence from the federal government when they refused to participate in the National Dakwah Month in 1978. The ruler of Kedah also annually directs his religious council to determine the dates and working hours of the fasting month of Ramadhan independently of those decreed by the civil service in Kuala Lumpur. In 1978, the religious council of the state of Johor, under the influence of its sultan, who has a number of differences of opinion with the federal centre, also announced its decision to tighten controls over "lapsed" Muslims and even to extend the jurisdiction of the Syari'ah court to cover the moral behaviour of non-Muslims (*Berita Minggu* 4/11/79). In these limited but symbolic ways, some sultans attempt to restore a few grains of the old authority. Another, more traditional means of encroaching farther on religious pastures has been by strategic marriages of some royalty into prestigious Arab-descended ulama families. The royal houses of Kedah and Perlis in particular and, to a lesser degree, Johor have pursued the marriage alliance route to religious prestige, through families claiming descent from the Prophet, and thus the titles of *Syed* and *Syarifah*. In Kedah it is said by those who are intimately connected with the grass-roots religious scene that the sultan is a powerful symbolic focus in the underground religious army

Jihad fil Sabilullah (fight for the cause of God), which has for several decades led the Islamic crusade on behalf of the certain elements of the Malay-Muslim population against the unbelievers (*jahiliyah*), including those Malays who co-operate with other religious and ethnic groups. Currently, this army appears to be most active in connection with the Malay/Muslim irredentist movements in South Thailand.[6] It is rumoured, for example (though it is understandably difficult to verify), that at a nod from the sultan, Sabilullah activities can be started or stopped, and certainly this is the popular perception of his powers. This is probably as close as it is currently possible for latter-day rulers in Malaysia to regain their traditional "protector" status.

It is not only through the involvement of the ruler that religion is drawn into power politics. Even within the Malay-Muslim community, religious divisions increasingly follow party lines, between PAS and UMNO.[7] Theoretically, the sultan is "above party politics" and so may fraternize with UMNO and government élites, who tend to share the similar lifestyles and educational backgrounds of the colonial tradition, and may support federal programmes. Sometimes, however, as noted in the cases of Kedah and Pahang, they maintain their distance and independence from these constraints, and this is reflected in their religious appointments. In the case of Kedah, a number of key positions in the religious court are held by nominees of the UMNO-dominated state EXCO, while several other religious council officials, some of whom were appointed at the time that PAS was in the Front, (see note 7 above) have remained. There is, therefore, even within the religious council itself, a cast and a set ready made for subtle plots and politicking along party lines, which the ruler can at times turn to his own advantage. It must not be automatically assumed that all ulama who hold positions in religious councils, or even those who become mufti, necessarily support the political status quo at all times. Some mufti have been notoriously outspoken, regardless of royal interest. For example, Haji Wan Musa, mufti of Kelantan in the early years of the twentieth century, publicly objected to the religious council's use of tithes for the construction of a lavish new mosque in the state capital of Kota Bahru at the expense of the poor and indigent, for which he was eventually forced to step down by his ruler (Mohd. Salleh b. Wan Musa 1974:157). Syed Yusof Ali Abdullah, recently deceased (1980) mufti of Trengganu, also made some unpopular fatwa by opposing family planning programmes to which the state government was committed. In other matters, however, he supported official policies and predilections in setting the fasting dates by the sighting of the moon instead of the calendar and allowing women to become air-hostesses. For this, he was permitted to remain in office.

THE "INDEPENDENT" ULAMA

Within the ranks of religious authorities, one segment in particular has long drawn the attention and opposition of the "established" ulama. These are the Sufi[8] mystics, who tend to cultivate a separate chain of intellectual / theological authority (isnad) and to be peripatetic. Sufi leaders depend for their influence more on an intensely personal bond with their followers, within the context of brotherhoods (*tarikat, taifa*), organizations based on *Gemeinschaft* and other particularistic relationships (cf. Trimingham 1971:233; 239). Despite their apparent other-worldly orientation, their political potential cannot be ignored, for many mediaeval Middle Eastern Sufi heads of *zawiyah* and *hanaqah* (variants of religious brotherhoods) posed challenges to the scholastic and "official" ulama. Usually their personal and factional oppositions were couched in ideological form, for the Sufi stress on the development of inner spiritual illumination in the quest for a mystical path to the Oneness of God encouraged greater individual autonomy and the dangers of ijtihad, or worse, rank heresy. Consequently, the Sufi were often seen as subversive by legalistic ulama and other political authorities. The existence of a personal "love" rather than a law-based bond, reinforced by the intensity of shared spiritual experiences, chanting, and trances within Sufi groups, created the kind of powerful sodality characteristic of some Christian sects. Some Sufi movements even had millenarian tendencies. When these elements were transported to isolated communities in outlying rural areas by itinerant Sufi proselytizers, fear of their potential powers by the political centre can well be imagined. Sufi practices first began in the sixteenth century, but reached their apogee in the eighteenth and nineteenth centuries, by which time several distinct traditions had crystallized. Among the principal ones are the *Naqsyabandiyah*, *Qadiriyyah*, *Samariyyah*, and *Ahmadiyyah*, and a number of lesser ones, all with offshoots in India and Southeast Asia (Al-Attas 1963). Opponents among the scholarly ulama often used the brand of heresy as their principal weapon against Sufi leaders, although in practice, most Sufi teachings could be demonstrated to be firmly grounded in the Koran (Gibb 1962:135). This reflects the perennial problem of ultimate authority in Islam, although Sufi followers are wont to quote the Prophet's statement from the Hadith that there are "three hundred and sixty pathways to the eternal truth."

In Southeast Asia, partly because of its geographical marginality and the strength of the Sufi influence in isolated rural settlements, Sufism was by and large at the core of the Islamic folk or "little tradition" in the area. As such, and like folk Catholicism in Latin America, or folk Buddhism in parts of the Southeast Asian highlands, the local version of the faith has often been varied and embellished by customs of other origin. In the case of Malay

Islam, the Indic religious substratum from which Malay custom (adat) is largely derived, still surfaces in many important areas of life, including most rites of passage and reverence for the graves of holy men (*keramat*). These provide plenty of grist for the theological mill of more militant scholastic ulama, or dakwah revivalists and other fundamentalists, as they did for Kaum Muda reformists. Finally, they excite political apprehensions, because of their local power bases, in most political authorities at all levels.

Such was the reception accorded to Hamzah Fansuri, who, as noted in Chapter 1, was the first Southeast Asian Muslim to write extensively in Malay and who was known as an itinerant mystic and Sufi in sixteenth century Aceh. Branded as a heretic by his successors at the Acehnese royal court, for example, by Nur'l-Din Al-Raniri, many of his works were burned for bearing a "Vedantic" imprint (al-Attas 1970:20). One might suspect, however, that this had something to do with the fact that Hamzah was not the supporter or religious legitimator of any major political leader or interest or 'protector." He was not an Islamic Hang Tuah. In Hamzah's time, and until about the end of the nineteenth century, most of the rural areas of the Malay peninsula, South Thailand (Patani), and Sumatra were still largely terra nova to Islam, but they were progressively opened up to the new faith by missionaries, both Sufi and non-Sufi, some from India and the Middle East. The language used by the messengers was usually the indigenous Malay, given the growing currency of Jawi, with Arabic reserved for study and prayers.

Prior to their forays into the villages, these ulama as well as the official Muslim court judges and registrars (*kathis*), were often attached to the capital and court, where they officiated at the principal mosque and at royal ceremonies. Most rulers also retained mufti or specially appointed religious advisers, some of whom were of Arab provenance, as in the case of Trengganu. These men also gave religious instruction to the children and other members of royal and aristocratic families.

Of the nineteenth-century Malay states, it was the most northerly ones, Perlis, Kedah, Kelantan, Trengganu, and Patani, in what is now southern Thailand, which had the most vigorous traditional of rural religious learning. Kelantan, like Aceh, was sometimes known as the "verandah of Mecca" (*serambi Mekah*), and even in the early nineteenth century, several Kelanta- nese ulama had received much of their education in the Holy City. As these men returned to their homeland, steeped in Arabic and religious scholar- ship, elevated in social as well as ritual status in their parochial communities of respectful fellow-villagers, demand for their services grew. Many were petitioned to return to their natal kampung to teach or establish a school. Other returning ulama, aware of the deficiencies of the religious instruction locally available, invited colleagues met in Mecca to join them in new areas.

Such was the case, for example, in the community of Sabak Bernam, Selangor. On his return, the first local village boy who had managed to achieve the difficult and expensive feat of completing a course of studies in Mecca was able to motivate the kampung people to contribute funds for the building of two new schools on the "Arabic" model, and additional Middle-East-trained teachers were invited down from Kedah to staff them (Mohd. Jani Naim 1979:54). Likewise, when another "local boy made good," simple Mohd. Yusuf from the small Kampung Kenali, Kelantan, returned in glory, after many trials and tribulations in his quest for a Middle Eastern education, he was named for his home kampung "Tok Kenali." Eventually, he became one of the most renowned and sought-after teachers in the Malay tradition, with a reputation throughout Malaya and Thailand (Abdullah al-Qarib b. Haji Salleh 1974). Today, a generation after his death, Tok Kenali is still one of the most illustrious links in the isnad chain for most Malay teachers, a surprisingly large number of whom claim to have studied with him, however briefly. As a further accolade of success and distinction, many returning scholars appended to their names, as a sort of mnemonic device, epithets or suffixes of the place where they studied and acquired their legitimacy or scholarship "licence." Thus one Kelantan guru became known as Tok Khurasani, in reference to Afghanistan, where he reputedly studied. Similarly, humble, Negri Sembilan-born Mohd. Saleh b. Baki, later to achieve permanent fame and respect as the founder of the Al-Masriyyah religious school in Bukit Mertajam, Province Wellesley, was professionally known as Haji Saleh Masri, after the Malay term for Egypt (*Mesir*), where he received his religious education.

Other influential rural ulama and teachers (guru) were outsiders by origin, who came like the proverbial "stranger," as a messenger from the unknown, to deliver the locals from affliction or apathy. The personal names and histories of a number of early teachers of high reputation are evidence of this marginal/stranger status. There were in the Malay states several "al-Patanis" suggesting an origin from that region in Thailand with its highly respected religious tradition, for example, Syaikh Daud b. Abdullah al-Patani, a title which proved to be useful currency in Kelantan and Kedah. Many Kedah ulama were of Sumatran or even Indian origin. Others used Arab patronymics to the same effect, even though a traceable genealogical connection to any actual Arab family was tortuous at best (but equally tortuous to disprove). These men "free-lanced" their way into new areas, partly on the strength of such myths of illustrious religious backgrounds, reinforced by personal persuasion and acceptability. The status of outsider or stranger may be associated with a certain detachment and aloofness from local society which is at times conducive to courageous and abrupt deviations from tradition, as happened on the arrival of the non-Malay immigrant bearers of the

Kaum Muda teachings on to Malay soil. Some of the more dramatic or "deviant" religious cults and movements, including the more spectacular displays of Sufism, which erupt from time to time in different parts of the Malay peninsula, are led by men of this sort. As will be seen, this is a process which has not ceased in the 1970's and 1980's. One particularly dramatic event in Johor, in October 1980, involved an attack on a local police station by a cohort of frenzied Muslim "extremists," believing themselves to be mystically invulnerable to the inevitable hail of police bullets. This was apparently the culmination of the activities of a particular cult, which had been created and cultivated in opposition to the "worldly" representatives of despised officialdom by a pair of Muslim refugees from Kampuchea. They emerged on the Malay scene "out of the blue" as it were, as messengers from God. Outsiders, of course, unlike the returning local-born, have a built-in liminality, and part of their status and reputation lies in the mystery of their origins. They are whatever they choose to make themselves, supported by diffuse and often unverifiable myths and titles, whose acceptance is a de facto acknowledgment of their legitimacy. Claim to any Arab connection almost always opened the doors of religious acceptability in the Malay world, and sometimes elaborate biographies and genealogies were carefully cultivated and circulated. As an example, the past mufti of Trengganu, who carried an Arabic family name (Al-Zawawi), was known to have "originated" (*berasal*) from the region of Saudi Arabia and to have studied in Egypt. His more traceable history in Southeast Asia, however, starts in Singapore. Through contacts made with the Sultan of Trengganu in that city, he was invited to become state mufti, whence he despatched a number of his offspring for education in the Middle East to continue the connection. This mufti's predecessor in Trengganu was also an Arab, Syeikh Hassan al-Yamani, from Mecca, who married into the family of well-known religious teachers in Bukit Mertajam who were descended from Mohd. Saleh al-Masri (see Appendix: Genealogy No. 1), thereby adding further kudos to that line. As noted above, others claiming Arab origin often married into the royal houses, thus conferring on the latter an additional religious "halo effect" as one half of a mutual legitimation process.

For the "independent" ulama, that is, those whose position is not dependent on connections with royalty or religious councils, legitimacy is still largely a matter of demonstration of personal skills and scholarship, of careful management of personal relations, and the creation of an individual reputation. This, in turn, is heavily influenced by the nature of the particular "congregation" he aims to lead. All religious leaders must have followers, and the needs of the latter are a crucial ingredient in the establishment of a successful leadership. The relationship can be likened to the striking of a tacit "bargain," whose conditions and operation follow principles similar to those of the "big-man" recruiting his men (cf. Sahlins 1963; Bailey 1971), whereby some social manoeuvering ensures satisfaction and benefits to both sides. Of course, some ulama are more autocratic than others in the imposition of their will and may exploit the origin myths and stranger value which awe many villagers. Ultimately, most become integrated into the social life of a particular village constituency, albeit in an élite role. This pattern of recipro-cal benefit between religious leader and follower seems to be widespread throughout the Muslim world (cf. Gilsenan 1976; Green 1978; Jackson 1980). For his part, the individual alim must demonstrate, to the satisfaction of his village constituency, an ability to read and expound knowledgeably upon the Koran and Hadith, and a command of Arabic, sometimes with an Arabic accent even when pronouncing Malay. The alim is also expected to be familiar with Islamic history, law and jurisprudence (*usuluddin*; fiqh), and even with astronomy—for the calculation of times of prayer and fasting dates. All ulama were able to lead the prayer, although, as we shall see, this duty has recently become a matter of bureaucratic control, largely confined to religious council-appointed imams. In addition, duties of the ulama including officiating at the appropriate prayers and rituals (*baca doa*) of all social activities and rites of passage requiring such services, for example, funerals, births, and weddings, and ceremonies for opening new houses, farewells, the Prophet's Birthday, and so on. On the strength of these abili-ties, as well as his personal character, the alim is often sought for his counsel, words of wisdom, and judgment on local disputes and problems, in some cases even displacing the local village headman in this area. Until the advent of the state religious council, he was also accustomed to issue rulings (fatwa) in local controversies, and even now, unofficial fatwa by village ulama are often quietly accepted in their own domains. Generally speaking, however, rural ulama are rarely called upon to issue fatwa or statements on major theological questions of the kind that ijtihad are made of, and are more in demand to pronounce upon the *remeh temeh*, or details of everyday life, as they affect the experience of the peasant, for example, involuntary touching of dogs or other unclean things or the fine calculations of the alcoholic content of a traditional rice wine.[9] These skills and services are all further legitimated by the charter of the all-important intellectual genealogy (isnad, salasilah) described above. The question of who studied with whom provides not only the accolade and approval of an established teacher or scholar, but also a critical link between the local community and the wider Islamic world. It creates a chain of intermediaries across time and space, in one dimension endowing it with a historical depth and association with an ancient and venerable tradition of scholarship, and in the other, relating each alim to "famous names" elsewhere, whether in Malaysia, Sumatra, Thailand, India, or the Middle East, in increasing order of status. In the case of Malaysia, two of the most renowned teachers were Tok Kenali and Tok Khurasani, already mentioned, and out of twelve ulama/guru whose schools and life-histories were the object of my research in Kedah, fully ten claimed to have studied with one of these two men at some point in their career. Reputation breeds reputation.

In the chain of scholarship, connections with the Middle East take precedence over all others, and the aura of the Holy Land is a powerful one. In the absence of a personal guru/disciple or kinship/marriage relationship, the isnad can be established by a university degree such as one from Cairo's Al-Azhar, although even here studies frequently involve more personal ties than in many western universities. Finally, it was the rare alim who was not also a returned pilgrim (*haji*), having passed at least one season in the Holy Land. On occasion, however, conflicts between ties with the Middle East and Malay status have emerged, where Islam and Malayness have been seen not to coincide. The most dramatic expression of such conflict was at the time of the Kaum Muda/Kaum Tua controversy, when locally entrenched and respected conservative Malays (Kaum Tua), loyal to their sultans, opposed the immigrant, often Middle Eastern, representatives of the Kaum Muda, who seemed to be attempting to dictate the terms of Malay society. Here, ethnicity clearly cut deeply into religious and ideological solidarity.

The rural ulama further cultivated a distinctive style of life and somewhat élitist religious exclusiveness through strategies of kinship and marriage alliance. Although by no means a totally endogamous stratum, there was a strong tendency for ulama to take wives from the families of other ulama, both local and from more distant places. From the genealogies of a sample of twelve ulama in one region of Kedah, out of a total of twenty-seven wives (as a result of some polygynous marriages), seventeen wives were daughters of other religious leaders, while eighteen out of thirty-seven sons-in-law were either sons of ulama or carefully selected pupils in their own religious schools. The net was spread even wider by strategic multiple marriages, and religious leaders generally had a higher rate of polygyny than the average villager. There were practical advantages to marrying women from other religious families. First, some of the wives were able to assist in the instruction of girl pupils and in such tasks as attending to the ablutions of female corpses. The value of second and subsequent, wives in the tasks of cooking and hospitality which engaged the households of ulama more than the average villager must also not be overlooked.

It may be instructive to look at the family connections of one Kedah alim in more detail, for a sample portrait of others in the same calling. The son of an official at the court of the Rajah of Perlis, his mother's brother, father's brother, and several cousins were all mosque officials or kathis (religious court registrars) and religious instructors to the children of the Rajah of Perlis. His sister married an imam, and his sister's son, brother's son, and brother's daughter all became religious teachers (*ustaz*) at local secular schools. On his mother's side, this alim was descended from an Arab line of Syeikhs and also related to the Mufti of Perlis, to the Head of the Perlis State Religious Council, and to the Head of one locally famous Adabi Religious School. This same family on his mother's side also provided several spouses for lesser members of the Perlis royal family and one of Malaysia's ambassadors to India.

Marriage alliances with families of Arab and other Middle Eastern origin are even more desirable, and such unions have often been made sometimes with the daughters of their teachers, during the sojourns of ulama overseas. Other alliances have been made more indirectly, by fictive kinship, as when Malay ulama are adopted into the families of visiting Arab scholars. Such was the case of the already-mentioned Mufti of Trengganu, Syeikh Hassan Al-Yamani, who relinquished that post to return to Mecca in 1953, but not before he had adopted (*angkat*) several promising young Malay pupils who had studied with him at various times and also taken as one of his wives the daughter of the founder of a well-known religious school (Al Masriyah) in Bukit Mertajam, Province Wellesley. One of the adopted Malay sons also married another daughter of the same school's family. In this manner, the Malay family were incorporated into the kinship network of the highly respected and prestigious Saudi Arabian Yamani lineage (which has also produced the well-known oil minister and ambassador to London). Since the time of the first alliances, the two families have maintained a very close relationship, marked by regular intervisiting between Malaysia and Saudi Arabia, and there is no doubt that the "Arab connection" has elevated the religious and social status of the Malay branch of the family and of its school. (See Appendix: Genealogy No. 1).

Kinship and marriage ties were also used by ulama to open up other networks of influence and advantage, principally through alliances with wealthy farmers and even with scions of aristocratic and royal families. Royal unions were often initiated when illustrious ulama were invited to teach members of distinguished families. These arrangements simultaneously conferred blessings (*berkat*) on the families of the students, as well as considerable material returns to the family of the religious teacher. Rewards for service, in addition to the gift of a spouse, often included land endowments (*wakaf*) from the patron/father-in-law, and sometimes also provision of a building for a school, a trip to Mecca, or other funds to make the teacher independent of the day-to-day and hand-to-mouth existence of the average peasant. Thus they were freed for the relative leisure of the life of the literati. The independence of these ulama was sometimes bought at a price, and there is record of at least one alim who refused the daughter of his patron—a member of a

Perlis royal family—in marriage, for fear that the property being offered as a dowry was "ill-gotten" (haram) by the strict standards of Islam or obtained through some form of illegal "collaboration" (*makan harta syubhat*). Invariably, in such marriages, the client alim was excused most of the normal expenses of a Malay marriage,[10] save for the "marriage gold" (*mas kahwin*), obligatory in Islam as the personal payment of a groom to his wife, a nominal sum of approximately M$20.

For all the problems of transport and communications in nineteenth- and early twentieth-century rural Malaya and its feeder regions of Sumatra and Patani, the extent and effectiveness of the networks between widespread ulama families and far-flung patrons is remarkable. Reputations travelled rapidly, often faster than their possessors. Returnees from the Middle East were eagerly anticipated with offers of schools and pupils, and the assurance of loyal village followings. Thus in 1905, a star pupil like Fakih Mohd. Saleh, from Seremban, Negri Sembilan, had made so deep an impression on his teachers in Bukit Mertajam both before and during his studies in Egypt, that he was greeted upon his return to Malaya by a wealthy businessman, Tuan Haji Abbas, together with the offer of an endowment of land for a school, the gift to be consummated by the hand of his daughter in marriage. In virtually one stroke, Fakih Mohd. Became *Tuan Saleh al-Masri* (Master Saleh the Egyptian), the founder of a new "Arabic" school and a man of independent means, while his father-in-law/patron acquired blessings (berkat) and a stamp of respectability on his money and name.

While marriage ties provided the path to wealth for some guru, others generated their own. Some ulama were quite canny businessmen on their own account (Saman b. Sariff n.d.:93-94), active in the printing and trade of religious books (the tools of their trade) and other religious objects, including *songkok* (religious hats for males), and assorted local crafts, across wide areas of North Malaya, South Thailand, and Sumatra, often following their genealogical and professional networks. Many of them too, on their trips to Mecca, helped to support themselves through the sale of batik cloth and items from their homeland. The operation of small eating shops was another popular enterprise among ulama, and even the well-endowed Tuan Saleh al-Masri supplemented his income with the proceeds of a substantial eating establishment attached to his school. Proceeds from the endowments of rice and land also fulfilled the same needs, and in this case, the field labour was frequently one of the tasks required of pupils between their hours of study and prayer.

It is probably no accident that many ulama originated from families who were wealthier than average. For not only were the expenses of education and travel appropriate to the aspiring scholar considerable by Malay peasant standards, but the family also needed to be sufficiently stable financially to sacrifice free labour to higher pursuits. There is evidence that many ulama in the Muda "Rice Bowl" area of Kedah today are in the upper quarter of the rural population in terms of wealth and are equally as well endowed as many of the secular leaders at the village level, for example, village headmen, *penghulu*, and local UMNO party leaders (cf. Mansur Othman 1978). For the area close to the Kedah-Perlis border, Othman Ismail (1974) reports that over 50 per cent of the ulama and other religious leaders have more than 10 *relong* (7.5 acres) of land, and 8 per cent possess over 20 relong (15 acres), as compared with the average of 5 relong (3.75 acres) held by almost 70 per cent (69.7) of ordinary villagers in the area (Lim, Gibbons & Shukor 1980). It does not escape even the casual observer that in their respective kampungs it is the ulama who generally have the finest houses and cars, whatever their expressed disdain for worldly goods. In many a school compound, the Volvo — a prestige model in Malaysia — standing discreetly in the shade is more than likely to belong to the guru. The wealth factor also helps to explain the concentration of ulama and religious school traditions in certain areas, namely, the richest rice lands of the norther plains, in Perlis, Kedah, Kelantan, and Trengganu and geographically stretching into South Thailand.[11] These areas were able to generate a sufficient surplus for the voluntary contributions of rice and other commodities, usually labelled zakat peribadi or *sedekah* (charity) by the loyal and respectful villagers and followers. Some parents made a further, more personal commitment of their children to a particular alim or guru through an institution known as *ikat tangan* or "tying the hands." This could be compared to a form of godparental relationship, involving the alim in the moral and spiritual tutelage of the child, and reciprocally binding the parents to an annual gift, (in money or kind), for each child so tied. This relationship between the seniors may persist long after the children in question have grown up and moved to a town or university, but as in the case of godparents in other faiths, the moral tie is not supposed to lapse.

The criteria for acceptance of ulama and teachers in local village society generally extended far beyond the purely ritual or religious in a narrow sense. Given the pre-Islamic (Indic) sources of a goodly portion of Malay adat, and many of the customary practices accompanying even Muslim rites, the two strands have often become so intertwined that they cannot be unravelled without seriously damaging the fibre of the social institutions and activities into which they are woven.[12] In the case of weddings, for example, the simple Islamic contract (*akad nikah*) strictly requires only the signatures of a Muslim registrar (kathi), of the groom, the bride's male representative (*wali*), and two witnesses. But for the Malay, this is merely the prelude. Socially, the most important events are the Hindu-style sitting in state (*bersanding*) of the bridal pair on an embellished dais (*pelamin*), the public display of the gifts exchanged between the two families, a substantial feast (*kenduri*), and often entertainment. Many village Malays do not consider a couple as legally married until they have undergone these additional social rituals, regardless of their religious status. Likewise, traditional Malay custom has an extensive repertoire of rites in addition to those required by Islam, marking various stages in the individual life, and even pre-life, cycle, from pregnancy, to birth, the first public presentation of the baby (*berendul*), the first hair-shaving (*akika*), ear-piercing (*cucuk telinga*), and feasts for all manner of special occasions, including illness and other crises. All are basically Indic in origin, but they have come to require the services of Islamic officiants and Koranic verses for their full consummation. On all these occasions an alim is asked to read prayers (baca doa) and a fragment from the Koran, and to lend his presence and blessing. Whatever their level of theological awareness—Islamic or non-Islamic—or personal conviction as to the validity of these practices, the ulama normally take on these duties without demur as part of the bargain and process of mutual accommodation between villager and religious leaders. Other commonly mixed obligations which blend Islamic and pre-Islamic roles, involve some ulama as curers (*bomoh*; *pawang*). The syncretism may be illustrated by the kinds of cure offered, for example, an infusion of traditional herbs, to which has been added some shredded pages printed with Arabic verses. Even the invocation of spirits for curing is acceptable, as long as no attempt is made to by-pass the power of God and the spirits used are recognized in the Koran (for example, *jinn* or *roh*). Some ulama have also established reputations in the Malay martial arts (*silat*), which have a large and devoted following among both rural and urban Malays, male and female, of all ages. Fundamentally, there is nothing in the physical training of the body or in of some of the aesthetic dance and musical accompaniments of basic silat to contravene Islam, but in its more evolved or specialized forms, silat has incorporated into its rituals Islamic prayers, performances in mosques, and the invocation of God in certain invulnerability cults.

The combination of silat and the grace of God is believed by some to render immunity to bullets and other forms of attack, thus conferring superhuman powers on the practitioner and an ability even to vanquish the devil (*syaitan*). Such cults tend to be surprisingly compatible with certain Sufi practices involving chanting and trances. Sufism cultivates the surrender of self to a variety of spiritual powers, of whom God is sometimes more like an awesome Primus inter pares. This kind of combination of cult and magical elements is akin to the generic type of mysticism known as *suluk* or *kebatinan*, strong in Java and other parts of Indonesia, which has become one of the targets of attack by some of the dakwah revivalists. More contentious still is the question of the religious merits of certain practices which have intermittently been singled out for criticism from the time of the Kaum Muda to the present and which have to do with the placation of the spirits of land and sea. Some religious leaders in Kedah and Penang are still known to perform the "*puja pantai*," or sea spirit ritual, on behalf of local fishermen, and condone the *Mandi Safar*, an annual water-rite which has been rationalized as a form of purification during the mournful month of Safar[13] in the Islamic calendar. Nowadays, under growing dakwah pressure, few ulama admit publicly to performing these rites. Either they are conducted in secrecy or at night (cf. Mohd. Razha Hj. Abdul Rashid, personal communication) or handed over to another, non-alim practitioner or pawang, so dividing the labour between the more orthodox Islamic and the non-Islamic Malay tradition.

The deep roots of Sufism in rural Islam, already noted, still bear fruit in the form of sporadic mini-cults and other idiosyncratic practices which recur with great regularity throughout Malaysia. Sufi-like activities range from orderly, weekly Thursday-night (before the Sabbath) meditation and chanting sessions (*zikir*), to nocturnal processions to the graves and shrines of holy men and guru, often ending in trances and "speaking in tongues" (*syatu/syathiyyat*). In some cases, behaviour resembling "drunkenness" (*mabuk*) and other ecstatic forms of devotion are the means by which the devotees seek their personal path to God. A celebrated case came to public attention in Kedah in 1979 when the leader of a particular cult known as the *Tarikat Auratismailiyyah* was brought before the Syari'ah religious court accused of "false teachings" against the "true religion" (*ajaran sesat, bertentang dengan Islam*). At the hearing, one elderly couple called as witnesses complained, to the amusement of the court, and with genuine regret, that when they had participated in these activities, they had not been nimble enough to keep up with the "jumping around" required in some dance dramas (*melompak macam Mak Yong*) and flagellation with rattan whips which had apparently seized those in trance (*Bintang Timur* 6/3/80; *Utusan Malaysia* 24/10/79). They also complained that the young girls were flocking to the leader and that women were leaving their husbands for this "Mahdi" (messiah). So highly regarded is the cult leader, it appears, that his followers, who comprise about 60 per cent of the adult members of his home kampung, collectively contributed to a fund to send him on two trips to Mecca despite their own poverty, according to interviews with local inhabitants. It is said that on the first occasion a few hints were dropped by the then aspiring leader, when he was allegedly found in tears by some of his devotees after a dream in which "Allah commanded him to perform the pilgrimage (*haj*)." As he did not have the means to go, the villagers promptly pooled their resources on his behalf.

When such emotions, commitment, and loyalties are found in association with kebatinan and silat elements, or invulnerability cults, then a formidable, and potentially combustible mix can result. Such was probably the case in the dramatic 1980 attack on the Johor police station by the group led by the two Kampucheans. So strong was their belief in their invincibility, that they were prepared to confront the inevitable bullets armed only with a *kris* (Malay knife). Stockwell (1979:151-61) documents a series of such movements, marking several major periods of crisis in Malay history from the Perak Wars at the end of the nineteenth century to the Malayan Union proposition in 1946-48.

One fairly widespread variant of these tarikat cults is known as the *Ajaran Taslim*. The basic thrust of its teaching is one of simplication of the formal requirements (five pillars) of Islam as far as possible, by substituting personal vows and spiritual dedication for the five regular daily prayers and fasting and by transmuting the pilgrimage obligation into a visit to some local shrine. Emphasis is on the individual's relationship with God, dispensing with religious intermediaries and institutions. In Kedah and Penang, the Taslim beliefs are particularly strong in the *Tarikat Mufaridiyah*, popularly known as the *Matahari* (Sun) cult,[14] of which at least three communities date back as far as the time of the Kaum Muda movement. Members of the Taslim communities known to the writer in Penang and Kedah are normally ostracized and even taunted by their more orthodox Muslim neighbours. Stories are popularly circulated to the effect that Taslim leaders exercise first-night rights to all new brides, after the fashion of droit du seigneur, and seduce other women and that when they climb the hill which is said to be in lieu of the haj, they are in reality only going to "relieve themselves."

Their uncontrollable and unpredictable character, and their potential political strength, makes all such cults objects of suspicion by more institutionalized Islam, particularly those in alliance with religious courts and secular governments (cf. Mohd Taib Osman 1980). When, on occasion, they are persecuted by the Syari'ah, it is invariably justified on theological grounds, but fear of the power of the leader is usually the real principal concern. To this I shall return.

At this point it might be appropriate to comment on the "charismatic" content of cult and religious leadership. Evidence for the kind of innovative and creative "surprise" element (cf. Andelson 1980), extraordinary supernatural gifts, and extreme personal magnetism of such men as the leader of the prosecuted Auratismailiyyah group described above and of some of the rebellious mahdi of colonial days is strongly suggestive of a classic (Weberian) charisma. But the concept has probably been overworked in practice, for as I have tried to show, the position of most of the ulama in the Malay rural tradition is better likened to that of the party to a contract, whereby the leader needs the follower as much as the reverse. In order to articulate and represent, dramatically or otherwise, the needs and interests of his people or constituents, a leader must also discharge certain obligations and sometimes even rely upon props to support his position. Thus for the average alim, his power and appeal may lie as much in the attractiveness of his family and scholarly connections, wealth, and personal and ritual services, as in any magnetically transcendent personality, and it is negotiated as much as unilaterally imposed (cf. Spencer 1973). In dispensing benefits both tangible and intangible, sacred and secular, some ulama may be said to assume a patronal rather than a truly charismatic role. The nature of this bargain between leader and follower, as the essence of the "charisma," can probably be seen as the root of the attraction between the members of the Johor group and their Kampuchean leaders. Most of the followers were apparently dissatisfied residents of government (FELDA)[15] land schemes and ready for an alternative. When this seemingly presented itself in the form of a new (mahdi) leadership miraculously appearing, the timing and the rapprochement were perfectly co-ordinated. The Kampucheans' mystique and acceptability was no doubt enhanced by the "stranger" effect, by the drama of those emerging from the unknown, as though God's response to a call or need. Even these men, however, had to legitimate themselves initially through a local authority, in this case, the resident imam of one of the FELDA communities, who was himself converted and thus drew to the newcomers' fold much of his own original constituency. This is but one example of myriads of messianic-like, mystical cults which have recurred in rural Malay Islam and other parts of the Muslim world for centuries. The important part, however, is that of the negotiated nature of the leader-follower relationship, in its broadest, unselfconscious sense, and of legitimacy itself, which leads to the conclusion that even charisma is open to bargains based on a solid foundation of mutual needs and benefits.

ULAMA AS TEACHERS: THE RELIGIOUS SCHOOL

Finally, we come to the role of the alim as religious teacher or guru *agama* (a Sanskrit term). The "chain" of knowledge has always been sustained by the long and didactic tradition of teacher-disciple relationships, and the institution of the school is a venerable one in Islam (cf. Eickelman 1979; Green 1978; Peacock 1978). In both the ancient and modern Middle East and India the *madrasah* taught not only the Scriptures and Islamic law, but also such subjects as astronomy, mathematics, languages, and other secular subjects cultivated in Arabic civilization.[16]

One of the first references to religious schools, or rather to Koranic instruction, in Malaya is found in Abdullah Munshi's Malacca in the early nineteenth century. As described by Abdullah, the schools at this period consisted of little more than a few pupils clustered around a scholar to whom they were entrusted, in body and soul, by their parents to study the Koran. "Studying the Koran" meant learning to recite the scriptures from start to finish (*mentelaah*), sometimes including even the punctuation marks, in an Arabic they often did not fully comprehend and usually without benefit of explanation or exegesis. Those who actually memorized the entire holy book (*menghafal*) were entitled to call themselves *hafiz*. There were, however, some teachers who also gave instruction in Islamic law (fiqh) and expounded on the doctrine of the Unity of God (*Tauhid*). In the cause of completing the formidable task of reading and memorizing the Koran, the commitment of children to guru by parents was total and permitted the use of sometimes intimidating instruments and punishments of lazy or wayward pupils (cf. Hill 1970:41). This kind of education, at the very least, conferred the benefits of literacy, in the Jawi script, on the young males who were exposed to it. On completion of the first full reading of the Koran to the teacher's satisfaction, it was customary for the pupil's family to sponsor a large feast (*Khatam Koran*), at which the boy demonstrated his reading skills. This was accompanied by a ceremonial presentation of such gifts as cloth, money, chickens, and cooked food to the guru by the grateful parents. In such rituals both the intellectual and social standing of the guru was publicly acknowledged and enhanced, and it increased with every "graduation." As a result, more pupils would be sent to him, and his reputation would grow.

Formal religious schools came relatively late to the Malay peninsula, and until the end of the nineteenth century most religious instruction took place in the homes of the guru themselves. Some guru, particularly if they were simultaneously an imam, *bilal*, *khatib*,[17] or other official, taught in the surau or mosque and included the rudiments of the obligatory prayers, fasting, and other requirements of the practising Muslim. These were often the nucleus of the first schools, especially in larger centres, and in Kelantan's capital of Kota Bharu, the grand mosque of Muhammed (Masjid Besar Muhammed) was the focus of learning. Another old and venerable tradition of religious learning in nineteenth-century Malaya was in Trengganu, around the area of modern Kampung Besut. Apparently this was already acknowledged as an important centre in Abdullah's time, and as we shall see in Chapter 5, the area still retains its reputation for its lively, and sometimes anti-establishment, religious activity. The mosque school in Malaya was merely the replication of a much older tradition in Mecca, Medina, and Cairo, where pupils actively sought out ulama in the famous mosques of Masjid il-Haram, Masjid an-Nawawiy, and Masjid Al-Azhar respectively.

Religious instruction in Malaya followed two basic styles and was reflected in two distinct types of school (cf. Mokhtar Mohamad 1974-75). The first was called *umumi* (general), the second *nizami*, after the style of school pioneered by Nizam Al-Muluk in eleventh-century Baghdad. The umumi type was originally the most common, and like the home-based groups from which they grew, they offered little more than the rote learning and recitation, or mentelaah, techniques described. Students were not generally encouraged to ask questions, giving rise to a style of passive learning, often called *menadah*, in which the image is of the pupil as an empty vessel, or receptacle, to be filled. The degree of refinement and accomplishment varied considerably from guru to guru, however, and some were able to offer far more. Only rarely did they offer the more specialized subjects of history or jurisprudence. When taught at all, the latter was presented anecdotally and consisted mainly of earthly homilies and examples placed solidly in a Malay peasant context. Topics most often covered were, and are, the mutual obligation of parents and children, husband and wife, how to choose a good wife, and counsel on proper male and female deportment. Also stressed was the importance of Muslim solidarity in the local community, particularly as expressed in attendance at mosque and funerals. Material values are generally belittled and even denounced while the virtues of agriculture—here drawing from the lore of the Hadith—are extolled. In umumi schools the sultan was, and is, invariably portrayed as the "Shadow of Allah on earth," so long as he does not obviously or blatantly violate the principles of the Koran. Accordingly, in umumi philosophy, rebels against the ruler should be severely punished, just as the holy war or jihad is enjoined upon those who oppose Islam.

Most umumi teachers used at least one or two supplementary adjuncts to learning in the form of the Kitab Jawi (religious books in literary Malay, but written in the Arabic script) and popularly known as the *kitab kuning* (yellow books) after their rather antique physical condition and appearance. Most of these kitab were composed by Malay-speaking scholars from various parts of Southeast Asia (cf. Mohd Nor b. Ngah 1980). The names of the authors provide the clue as to their provenance, for example, al-Fatani from Patani, al-Palembang from the Sumatran town of that name, and most used printing presses operated by themselves or fellow ulama, although later, in the twentieth century, some of the larger centres such as Kota Bharu, Penang, and Singapore developed more commercial printing facilities. Some of the kitab recounted the age-old theme of the creation of heaven and earth, others provided commentary on the Koran (tafsir), while yet others dealt with selected aspects of Islamic law or of the various Sufi tarikat. The more detailed exegeses were used more often in the nizami schools.

Pupils in the traditional umumi schools normally sat on the floor, had no blackboard, and repeated everything in chorus after their teacher, who was, as in Abdullah Munshi's day, usually swift and unerring in the use of his stick on dissident pupils. Since the guru was alone, pupils at different levels or at different stages of the Koran, regardless of age, sat in separate clusters in corners of the same room, and practised reciting to each other in the style of the proverbial village school. Generally, the teacher would employ one or more of his more advanced, promising, or favoured pupils as a helper (*ketua mutalaah*), and these young men sometimes became candidates for the hand of their guru's daughter and even his potential successors to the school (see Appendix: Genealogies). These were also the youth most likely to be sponsored by the school or local community to continue their studies elsewhere, either in Malaya or overseas, as were Mohd. Saleh al-Masri, Tok Kenali, and several of the Kedah ulama in my own research.

Both the mode of instruction and the style of life in the religious schools were highly authoritarian. As Geertz has chronicled for the *pesantren* schools in Java, not only were pupils subjected to physical chastisement by their guru where deemed necessary, but they were also pressed into service on their master's land, in his house and compound, and for any other business project for which he required assistance. Many adult Malay males, who went through this early experience in common, now joke with one another about the "long stick of the guru," and it is even featured in Malay cartoons, as part of the essence of Malay childhood, shared and remembered. In the early days, and until the Pacific war, pupils were kept apart from mainstream kampung society by boundaries both physical—fences and prohibitions on visiting outside—and symbolic—strictly enforced regulations about correct Malay dress, religious caps (songkok), prohibitions on sports, music and other worldly or childish activities, and, later, also on radios. They were housed in simple, even makeshift, huts or *pondok*, which eventually gave rise to the generic term for most rural religious schools in the Malay peninsula—the "pondok school." In the pondok the students slept, cooked for themselves, ate, and studied, sometimes singly, but more often in groups of two or three. These structures filled the compound surrounding the guru's house and the prayerhouse, and sometimes, for want of space, became so closely packed that the boys could crawl from the window of one to another without touching the ground. Girl pupils were often lodged in the guru's house under the vigilant eye of his wife or wives. Days began with the dawn prayer (*subur*), followed by long mornings of Koran reading, the midday prayer (*zohor*), with more study and physical work filling the afternoons until the evening prayers and meal.

Alongside the youthful students in the school compounds there was often a parallel contingent of older disciples who assembled to sit at the feet of a popular guru for voluntary religious studies and self-improvement. While some of the older followers merely attended Thursday night lectures, others actually retired permanently to the peaceful and ascetic life of the pondok, which they treated as a kind of "old folk's" or retirement home, filling that final and uncertain span between making the pilgrimage, where possible, and the afterlife (*akhirat*). Many are widowed, most too old to continue farming, and not a few reluctant to remain as full-time dependents on younger members of their family. Socially, they also find companionship within their own age and generation set, itself an important line of cleavage in Malay society, and in this new setting recreate a more venerable form of the mosque men's groups and women's co-operative groups of an earlier stage of life. Now freed from the major material preoccupations of this life, they can prepare for the next. The pondok of the older people are usually more desirably located, closer to the house of guru (*pondok dalam*), or "interior" pondok, while those of the youth are on the fringes of the compound, "external" or *pondok luar*. The number of pupils, both old and young, varies from a handful to several hundred, in which case a veritable, and quite self-sufficient community can be created, parallel to that of the surrounding kampung, by which it is regarded with considerable respect, and sometimes even referred to as "*mulia*" or noble. The younger students are expected to show respect for their elders within the pondok community. In pondok conditions, where pupils share almost all their daily activities and experiences, as well as prayer, study, Sufi sessions, and even silat training, an intense form of solidarity was usually engendered, as in boarding schools elsewhere. Despite the authoritarian and even harsh régime of the system, strong bonds of physical, moral, and spiritual dependence also developed between guru and pupil such that "whatever the guru says is right" ("*apa yang dikatakan Tok Guru adalah benar bagi murid*"). Young boys would earnestly repeat such phrases to me, captured by this powerful force in their life. Those who shared such common experiences early in life developed strong attachments, not only to the teacher, but also to each other, from which grew an "old boy" network enduring for many years afterwards. Often they form the foundation of adult roles in such secular situations as participating on village committees and in political party activities.

As noted, the umumi type of pondok school was limited in academic scope and unable to prepare its students directly for advanced religious institutions, whether universities in the Middle East or, more recently, local Malaysian institutions of higher religious learning, without some upgrading. Among the latter are the Islamic College (*Kolej Islam*) in Petaling Jaya, Kota Bharu's Nilam Puri Centre for Higher Religious Studies, and the Faculty of Islamic Studies at the National University (*Universiti Kebangsaan*). By contrast, the nizami school or madrasah style is able to provide such qualifications. The madrasah or Arabic school — until recently all its instruction was in Arabic — offers, in addition to the basic Koranic training available in umumi schools, a full academic curriculum of Islamic law, jurisprudence, astronomy, mathematics, ethics, history, geography, and Malay and other languages up to a standard equivalent to the Arabic grades of *Thanawi* and *Syahadah*. These qualify the graduate for entrance to a Middle Eastern university, and over the years many Malay students have graduated directly from Malay madrasah to Al-Azhar, for example, although the problem of funding has always been a pressing one. It is partly for this reason that the Kedah Ex-Middle Eastern Students' Association launched a project to build a hostel in Cairo for its present and future students at Al-Azhar, and more recently, the Kedah religious council has offered a limited number of scholarships for advanced religious study overseas. In one or two exceptional instances too, graduates of established Kedah madrasah whose guru are well-connected with the Middle East, and the quality of whose education is unquestioned, are encouraged to enter certain institutions there, sometimes with the addition of some financial aid.

Even in madrasah, a "submerged" umumi element was often to be found, with traditional Koranic instruction filling half the day and academic subjects occupying the balance. In some madrasah the pupils continued to live in pondok, with all the associated restrictions on their social life, although madrasah did not normally cater to the needs of older people. Those with adequate financial foundation and organization had, however, substituted for the pondok a dormitory style of residence, in which meals were either catered on a contractual basis by an eating shop, by the guru's womenfolk, or by some semi-autonomous enterprise of the guru himself, as in the case of the "restaurant" run by Tuan Mohd. Saleh al-Masri in his school (Al Masriyyah). Dormitory students are normally subject to some fee (*yuran*), which favours those from families with slightly more means. Thus even in such fully fledged boarding school types of madrasah as Maktab Mahmud in the capital of Kedah, a small minority of poor, rural students, whose only hope of remaining in the school required severe personal deprivation, had created an isolated cluster of pondok on the perimeter of the school's property, where they still courteously brewed tea for the visiting anthropologist.

The "golden age" for both types of religious school in Malaya was probably the period between the turn of the century and the late 1950's, a period when pupils with the means would not hesitate to travel from one region to another in order to study with a specific guru. During this era, the schools reached their maximum size, and the ulama interviewed in Kedah proudly cited records from the 1930's and 1940's of schools with over eight hundred pupils, which of course required the master guru to employ assistant teachers in what were sometimes highly organized educational enterprises. At this time too, the religious schools performed several important functions in Malay society other than the most immediate and obvious, which partly accounts for their popularity. First, they were frequently the only source of education available to rural kampung children, where the newly instituted colonial schools were still a rarity. Even when the latter became more numerous and accessible, the religious schools were usually preferred, for fear of religious "contamination" at the British Christian schools. Since Independence (1957), however, and the steadily increasing availability in rural areas of Malay National schools and the blossoming of opportunities for secondary and tertiary education for the Malays of the younger generation, the occupational sights of kampung youth and their parents have been set ambitiously on civil service and other professional secular jobs. As a result, the purely religious school has begun to lose some of its old appeal. Now, rather than catering to the brighter youth, and to those from the better endowed families, able to make the necessary gifts and contributions to the guru and his school, the contemporary religious school is more likely to receive the drop-out from the government school, for reasons either of failure or of poverty.[18] Somewhat ironically, among the first students to forsake the cloisters of the religious schools were the sons of the guru themselves,[19] who had both the means and the inclination to seek newly emerging opportunities in secular life (see Appendices 1 and 2). Offspring of religious teachers who are now in their twenties or early thirties are quite numerous in the universities, in the civil service, and in the still relatively prestigious occupations of bus drivers, bank tellers, telephone operators, and secular school teachers. All of the six offspring of the above-mentioned Syeikh Abdullah Yusuf, Mufti of Trengganu, entered such secular occupations as law and medicine, and one became an airline stewardess. Some offspring of the guru of that generation took the plunge for themselves and ran away as boys from their fathers' houses, to avoid co-optation into the religious life, thus breaking some of the hereditary ulama tradition. There are histories, too, of some sons of religious houses, sent in great anticipation to study in the holy places of Cairo or Mecca, who switched from religious to secular subjects, for example, to aerodynamics or engineering, and returned home to take up other vocations. In adjusting to the situation, the ideal of most guru is now to have sons and daughters strategically scattered across a broad spectrum of occupations, secular and religious, for maximum network and status advantage. As often as not, this has resulted in the handing over of the school in the next generation to someone other than the son. The most favoured alternative, as mentioned, has been to cultivate a promising pupil as successor and even son-in-law. From my own sample of twenty-six transitions or take-overs in ten pondok schools over three generations in Kedah, only nine went to sons. Nine others went to sons-in-law who were also pupils, four to pupils who were not sons-in-law, three to assorted other kin, namely, wife's brother, sister's son, and brother's son, and one to an adopted son (see Appendix 1: Genealogies).

The decline in enrolment in religious schools has set in motion a vicious cycle. As fewer graduates of a purely pondok education have been able to find secular jobs when in competition with candidates from government schools and as religious opportunities are on the decline owing to the popularity of secular education, fewer young people are willing to commit themselves to an exclusively religious education, and this reduces still further the openings for new religious teachers. Observers of the religious scene in Malaysia are even worried that the once respected title of ustaz, a religious teacher of lesser standing than a guru with his own establishment, is losing its lustre and is less sought after than the glamorous professional and civil service roles. To most modern youth, the job of ustaz suggests failure to pass the promotional examinations of the government school system (Lupti Ibrahim 1980:45ff). In the face of these trends, however, the ulama and guru have not been totally immobile. As far back as 1948, in anticipation of some of these changes, an early decision by the newly formed Kedah Ulama Association resulted in the implementation of a programme of more "progressive" schools, in which both traditional religious and elements of the newly popular, secular, examination-based system were combined. The association even instituted special training for their own teachers (*Latehan Normal*) for this new dual role. One of the fruits of this decision was the now well-established Maktab Mahmud secondary school in Kedah's capital, Alor Setar. This school actually sits squarely in the (nizami) Arabic/madrasah school tradition and was able to provide its students with both options on graduation, religious and secular.

Two other factors have also contributed to the decline of the more traditional religious school. One is the increasing centralization of the state religious council. In most states, and especially in Kedah, monopoly of the zakat tax by the religious council has reduced the resources available for voluntary financial support of the old schools, which have consequently become more dependent on funds from distribution of the zakat rajah by the religious council. The council has further assumed the responsibility for issuing licences (*surat tauliah*) to all teaching ulama, thus reducing their academic freedom and independence and changing the basis of their authority. It is not yet clear in Kedah whether licences already held will have to be renewed or re-examined, although in Johor, it has been explicitly stated that all ulama are to be reassessed for new surat. In tightening their control, the religious councils in most states have proposed some form of centralization of all religious education in a co-ordinated network of "people's religious schools" (*sekolah agama rak'yat*) of the madrasah type, but also offering the full series of secular, national promotional examinations of the lower, middle, and higher school certificates.[20] This relates to the second change. Recently, the federal Ministry of Education has also planted its foot in the door of the religious schools by increasing the pressure for accommodation to the national curriculum and examination system, particularly at the secondary level. In addition, the ministry would like to impose controls of its own, including the screening of teachers. Compliance with ministry conditions brings with it certain financial advantages in the form of funds[21] for new buildings, laboratories, equipment, and higher salaries for teachers (*Bintang Timur* 26/2/80; *Berita Minggu* 9/3/80). Salaries for teachers for the religious council or in private traditional schools have never been able to compete with government scales, and this, too, has contributed to the slow demise of the religious school. Finally, the Education Ministry contributes to the construction of hostels and dormitories to replace the old pondok. Most religious guru, however, having seen the writing on the wall, are preparing themselves in a variety of ways. Some, as noted, are remarkably skilful entrepreneurs and have been able to put to good use endowments of rice land attached to their schools (in some cases as much as 40 relong or 30 acres), while others have developed printing services, book stores, and even a bus company. One cultivates a very successful market gardening enterprise, using his pupils' labour on the school vegetable patch and for sales. Those less well endowed are becoming resigned to at least a modicum of co-operation with either the ministry or other religious councils as the only alternative to permanent closure. These schools are often the first candidates for conversion to the sekolah agama rak'yat (people's religious schools), with its compromise between traditional religious and modern secular learning. In many such schools, a symbolic division is maintained by partitioning the day into "secular" morning and "religious" afternoons or the reverse, with different teachers, subjects, and didactic styles in each programme.[22] These new-style people's schools, as a form of modern madrasah, are currently growing in popularity among rural parents in the states where they have been instituted, namely, Kedah, Kelantan, Perak, Trengganu and Pahang. They satisfy the parents who wish to ensure that their children receive a sound religious education, but who do not wish to cut them off from other options and opportunities. Furthermore, the students themselves will have a choice of employment on graduation.

In some of the original pondok schools, where the two types of programmes are maintained almost intact and relatively unintegrated, the old people can still be accommodated in the religious section, and indeed they are increasingly the only sustaining force for what would otherwise be but a shell of the past. As the old total system and way of life of the residential pondok for youngsters loses its attraction in favour of the less intensive two- or three-hour maximum now possible with the "two-tier" day, the pondok face dereliction. Only those whose guru have a substantial elderly following are able to redeploy their resources. In a few, probably about a half a dozen in total in all of Kedah, the guru's personal popularity is so great that there is actually a waiting list for access to a pondok hut by individuals or couples preparing for retirement. In one village, old people are willing to pay as much as M$1,000 a year for the rental of a pondok in the school compound, which is a substantial commitment in Malay peasant society. These old people often continue the custom of "ikat tangan," or "tying" their grandchildren to their revered guru, thus guaranteeing small but regular financial contributions for a number of years to come. This does not, of course, necessarily commit the children themselves to a full-time religious education or personal bond with the guru. Like the godparent of the *compadrazgo* relationship elsewhere, the critical bond is that between those on the senior generation level.

Where traditional pondok schools have failed to adapt to the changes now taking place, they have "died," leaving the alim or guru with residual functions as part-time lecturer, Sufi, or silat leader only. One or two cases exist of a vestigial old people's community remaining intact and in residence in the original pondok even after the death of the old guru and, in the absence of a successor, the closure of the school. Such communities are mere shells of their past, and slowly lose their elevated status and moral superiority in relation to the rest of the villagers.

THE ULAMA AS A STATUS GROUP

Whatever the nature of the "bargain" between ulama and their congregations, there can be little doubt as to the asymmetrical nature the relationship between the two parties or over the degree of respect commanded by most ulama. They tend to maintain what they consider an appropriate social distance and a certain aloofness without incurring the accusation of arrogance (*sombong*). Generally, they refrain from participation in the more mundane, trivial, or profane daily rounds of sports, entertainment, and other social activities, reserving their presence for religious and ritual services. This does not mean that the homes of the ulama are closed to visits from villagers, although the latter are normally suitably deferential, and sometimes hesitant in manner in the presence of *Tok Guru*. Of course, some ulama are more accessible (*mesra*) than others, and this is reflected in their popular appellation: the most loved are addressed by "*Pak*" the term for "father," for example, Pak Ya, Pak Ngah Haji Omar, while the more remote are referred to by the "grandfather" term Tok, for example, Tok Haji Yusuf. The most distant and revered of all became *Tuan* ("sir"), for example, Tuan Haji Abbas, Tuan Mohd. Saleh. In the original system, the strict segregation of students and school from kampung life reinforced this distance which lent it, if not enchantment, at least an aura of reverence and awe. Subtle reminders of their contacts with the Middle East or Arabs also added to the effect. Often the ulama were referred to as mulia (noble in character) and were further set apart by their tendency to endogamy. Reciprocally, the villagers were not only deferential, but often willing to gain berkat (blessing) by volunteering labour on the alim's land. Whether or not a villager had ever been a full-time denizen of a pondok or merely a part-time pupil of a particular alim, the imprint of the latter's views was often powerful and could have political implications, as will be seen. Finally, the ulama were, and still are, acknowledged to be among the wealthier elements of the rural population in land and business, which helped to sustain congruence in style between them and the aristocratic and royal families into which they sometimes married. In the early days too, many of the pupils came from families of above-average means, although there were always a minority of very poor boys who struggled and made tremendous sacrifices for religious study, and their life in the pondok was one of severe physical deprivation. In all of these respects, the ulama could be said to represent a distinct and élite status group in the Weberian sense, based on a code of honour, a certain ethic, and style of life, often reinforced by the "prestige of descent." As an élite status group, they were parallel to the secular élites, particularly the village headmen (*ketua kampung*), penghulu, and lower-level government bureaucrats (cf. Syed Husin Ali 1975). In this sense too, they could be likened to a "class fraction" within the Malay rural leadership (cf. Poulantzas 1973).

THE ULAMA AS A POLITICAL FORCE

A sense should be emerging, from several points already made, of the potential and actual political influence and capacities of the ulama. It takes little imagination to understand the impact, in their own small home domain, of those ulama who are incorporated as supporters of the status quo, whether religious councils, sultans, or other political élites. Aside from this, ulama have wielded tremendous power in their own schools and kampungs, through their control over key stages of socialization of the youth when subliminal — or not so subliminal — political messages are most effective. Some ulama, indeed, are known for sending political messages home to the pupils' parents via the medium of the school, as they did most successfully at the time of the 1946 Malayan Union scheme, which they virulently opposed (Ahmad Kamar 1979). Several Kedah ulama today still instruct their older pupils how to vote and make this an explicit condition of the latter's residence in their pondok, of attendance at their lectures and Sufi sessions, and eligibility for his ritual services. Despite their apparent individualism and independence within their own constituencies, the organizational and co-operative capacities of the ulama must not be underestimated as the formation of the ulama associations in various states, as well as across their boundaries, testifies.

Beyond this diffuse capacity for political influence, many ulama are more blatantly involved in party politics. The party of choice for many ulama is PAS, the Islamic party, which contributes financially to many religious schools to encourage the training of future leaders, and so the connection comes full circle. At the national level, the founders of PAS were largely of educational background (cf. Funston 1976:69ff). Among their ranks are the great names of PAS history such as Ustaz Abu Bakar, Dr. Burhanuddin, Haji Ahmad Fuad bin Hassan (PAS's first president), Ustaz Othman Hamzah, and Syed Abdullah Hamid Al-Edrus. PAS's most recent president, Datuk Asri is entirely typical of this pattern. He originated from a traditional Kelantanese family who provided him with a strong religious education, and he subsequently married the daughter (Datin Sakinah) of a well-known Sumatran alim and guru of the celebrated religious school Maahad Il-Ilya Assyariff in Gunung Semanggol, Perak, where the embryonic organization (PAS) held its formative meetings. Since the end of 1982, the PAS leadership has passed into the orbit of a new and younger cohort of religious leaders in Trengganu.

The Kedah branch of PAS is notable for its high ulama membership, particularly in positions of party leadership. These include some of the most famous names in the Kedah guru tradition: Haji Abbas Nasution of the now defunct Sekolah Arab Al-Sakhiniyah in Pulau Pisang; Haji Othman Yunus of the Madrasah Al-Nadah, Bukit Besar; Haji Abu Bakar Palestain, Pondok Ayer Itam; Tok Haji Hussein, Sekolah Menegah Ugama Raudzatul Ulum, Langgar; Haji Wan Leh, Sekolah Arab Mukarrimul Akhlak, Kampung Chagar; Lebai Isa, Al-Madrasah Ahmadiya, to name the most prominent. Most of these men were in at the founding of the party and are still active in its affairs, as are also many of their past pupils once they pass through the doors of the school into the wider political world.

Of the PAS leaders who are not also ulama or guru, most appear to have, by way of education, an all-Malay, religious, and often a pondok background, with only a minority coming out of the English-medium, government, or secular schools.[23] Mansur's survey (1978) comparing the origins of PAS and UMNO élites in the Muda area of Kedah finds that the principal differentiation between the two lies in education, marked by the predominantly religious school background of the former, rather than by significant differences in landholding or wealth. This is supported by material from yet another Kedah district, Tanjung Pauh, where 57 per cent of the local PAS leaders have some kind of religious status (alim, guru, ustaz, imam, *lebai*, [teacher of lesser status] bilal and so forth), and 61 per cent are from a pondok background (Othman Ismail 1974:83). What is also striking is the degree to which kinship and marriage ties provide a framework for the organization of PAS party branches at the village cluster level, so that the head is likely to be the father of the secretary, uncle to the treasurer, cousin of many committee members, married to the daughter of another member, and all are finally "old boys" of the same pondok.

In the state religious council the situation is somewhat more complex. Some ulama here are undeniably political appointees of the UMNO State EXCO, hence "co-opted" to that party's interests. However, dating from the years of the brief alliance between PAS and other parties of the National Front (1972-78), there remain a number of ulama from that party too, so that the religious council cannot be characterized as unequivocally supportive of the status quo. PAS council members can thus play the opposition role from inside and lobby against certain proposed UMNO appointments or projects, as well as lend a moderating voice in favour of their PAS ulama colleagues "outside," when they are threatened, for example, with withdrawal of their licences to teach and preach (*Utusan Malaysia* 22/10/79). Council appointees who are to be sent out to distant rural areas as mosque officials or as headmasters of the new people's schools, tend to be of the UMNO persuasion, which, at the local level, carries with it the potential for considerable animosity with the established local ulama and guru and their loyal PAS constituents. Where the imam and his assistants are seen as "government men" (*orang kerajaan*), extreme PAS suppoters have been known to refuse to pray at the mosque, preferring instead to follow the prayer with "their own" Tok Guru, whom they regard as of higher ritual status, hence more legitimate. There is no doubt that some ulama do not discourage such sentiments. The "government/independent" division within the ranks of the religious also creates a weakness in the kinship and marriage-cemented status group unity of the religious élites, for few PAS ulama would seek the hand of the daughter of an UMNO imam.[24] Indeed, a few religious families have been known to have irrevocably split along party lines, so that all social interaction and commensality has ceased entirely; such a break occurred in the ranks of the offspring generation of Haji Abbas Nasution, one of the most illustrious charter members of PAS Kedah.

The political component of personal/religious relations in many rural kampungs has reached critical proportions. In a bid to retain their religious authority in the face of the erosion of the traditional pondok school system, threats of revision of surat tauliah, and so on, some ulama have tried to compensate by a more aggressive "promotion" of their own services. They encourage villagers to make greater use of ritual and ceremonial accompaniments to their social activities, on pain of being accused of religious laxity.

Threatened by the loss of their élite status, and seeking alternate areas of authority, some ulama are playing purely for power, and bids for legitimacy are increasingly taking the form of *"kafir-mengafir"* between PAS ulama and followers and those with UMNO connections. In this process political opposition is phrased in religious language, and one side accuses the other of being less than Islamic or purveyors of false teachings, hence like au unbeliever (kafir). The mass media are often invoked to press even more widely and publicly accusations of deviance and heresy (*menyeleweng, songsang*), especially by the UMNO faction. Furthermore, not only do the two factions refuse to pray at the same mosque, but PAS ulama will convince villagers that meat slaughtered by UMNO members is unclean (haram) and that marriages solemnized by UMNO religious officials are invalid (*tidak sah*). In some cases, ulama have even stubbornly issued fatwa to that effect, advising the unfortunate couple to remarry. The ultimate symbol of non-recognition in Malay society and any Muslim community is when one group refuses to eat with, attend the funerals of, or pray in the mosque of the other, and in these events, too, PAS and UMNO members do not co-operate. Thus political opposition is expressed in religious idiom, and religious issues are politicized. While PAS accuses the opposition of being infidels (kafir), the latter retaliate with their own religious campaigns and programmes, advising the villagers "not to use Islam to gain power, but rather to use power for the sake of religion" (*"jangan mempergunakan agama Islam untuk mendapatkan kuasa, sebaliknya menggunakan kuasa untuk agama"*).

One or two celebrated cases involve the screening of the content of the lectures and sermons of the ulama by UMNO officials for any hint of political subversion and policing the speakers along their customary lecture circuits and meetings. Ulama have been accused of suggesting that UMNO supporters "will never get to heaven," and a few have even been taken before the Syari'ah court on such grounds. In a recent case in Kampung Besut, Trengganu, the defendant alim was alleged to have referred to the prime minister of Malaysia as a hypocrite and heretic (*murtad*), traitor to Islam (*Watan* 11/4/80). During the trial, even the validity of the court hearing itself was challenged for the alim claimed that all the court officials were UMNO representatives, and one even a senator of the federal government as well as a member of the state religious council (ibid). These ties, the defendant asserted, contaminated their oaths and testimony and made them invalid. For their part, UMNO and government factions mobilize ulama support wherever possible to curb the "excesses" of their more independent-minded brethren through the institutions of the religious councils and state ulama associations. At such conventions they usually manage to pass symbolic resolutions to the effect that the Islamic community, that is, the Malays, must not be split (*berpecah*), that Muslims should concentrate on being more devout and pay less attention to *tasawuuf* (Sufism), and above all, that they not mix religion and politics. This is a clear attack on the strategy and persons of the rural leadership.

This last injunction has invariably proved to be in vain, for local political campaigns, especially in such states as Kedah, Kelantan, and Trengganu have been fought in just such terms, many very abrasively. The two political parties make liberal use of Islamic symbols and exhortations, for when one flings the religious gauntlet down, the other cannot fail to take it up. When PAS campaigners accuse their UMNO opponents of a preoccupation with the material and cosmetic aspects of religion through the construction of bigger and more elaborate mosques, staging expensive Koran-reading competitions, and funding religious projects with lottery proceeds, UMNO counters with criticism that PAS leaders are denying their constituents the fruits of legitimate technical progress, modernization, and general welfare, none of which conflicts with Islam.[25] Successful candidates in elections on both sides claim the intervention of the "hand of God," and they make vows (*nazar*) to shave their heads by way of gratitude to Allah, as did the winner of one by-election at Bukit Raya in 1980. For their part, UMNO ulama are increasingly able to play patrons controlling disbursement of government favours influencing the direction of rural programmes and so on. Beneath the surface drama runs, as in shadow play, the sub-theme, or possibly the real theme, of a contest for a more basic kind of power and legitimacy, deeper than that of ephemeral party politics. This reverts back to the age-old, never-resolved ambivalence and tension between religious and non-religious élites, or even over what is religious and what is not. The contest also reflects the two strands of Malay identity. UMNO represents the Bumi Malay, champion of the absolute loyalty mentality, and above all of Malay ethnic unity (despite differences of opinion with specific individual sultans). The ulama, for the most part, insist on the primacy of "religious" values in determining leadership, but in elections they carefully skirt the delicate issue of the role of the sultan, if only because it is an officially sensitive topic, not to be debated publicly.

Probably the most ambitious attempt by UMNO to discredit PAS via religion was on the occasion of the peasant demonstration in the Kedah capital in 1980 (see Chapter 7), for which a scapegoat had to be found. From a show of force over prices and payments for rice, UMNO quickly constructed a conspiracy theory in which the villain was the underground Holy Army (*Pertubuhan Angkatan Sabilullah*) whose acronym is conveniently the same as that of the political party. Accoring to UMNO Kedah, membership in PAS and P.A.S. were to be construed as interchangeable, combining "political radicalism, racialism and religious fundamentalism" (*Star* 19/3/80; *Bintang Timur* 20/3/80). By laying economic and political problems at the door of "religious extremists and fanatics" without even demonstrating the validity of the accusation, UMNO once again showed how easy is the transition in Malaysia from politics to religion and back again.

Whatever religious or ideological issues are raised in election campaigns, leaders on both sides may be motivated as much by self-interest as by more esoteric or spiritual values. For all the condemnations by the PAS leaders of the UMNO brand of secular state—commitment to capitalism, material progress, and alliance with the infidel—there is no evidence that a PAS-run state, were it to come about, would be much differently balanced (cf. Chandra Muzaffar, 1979). Indeed, the enjoyment of private property, defence of trade and commerce, and even inequalities in wealth differences, are supported by PAS, so long as the mode of their acquisition and use is not in violation of Islamic principles, for example, by the exploitation and oppression of others in the manner of *gelintir capitalis* (capitalist class). On the model of Iran as an Islamic state, the PAS secretary general of Kedah is suitably evasive: Iran's attempt to create an Islamic state cannot be faulted, although as yet it has not had sufficient time to be properly implemented (*Watan* 9/5/80). What is more revealing in the Malaysian context, from Mansur's (1978) investigation of the PAS and UMNO élites of the Muda area, is that PAS leaders, as large landholders themselves, are no more in favour of land reform than are their UMNO counterparts. Areas of reform proposed tend to be confined to the rarefied and unassailable, but almost meaningless, motherhood issues pertaining to the basic rights of man as dictated by God, and the provision of an adequate living to the poor and deprived. Presumably PAS's Islamic state would merely transfer the justification for inequalities to religious principles and be more free with the use of Islamic symbols in their legitimation.

The line between religious and non-religious authority is a thin one in rural Malay Islam. At all social levels, from sultan to peasant, in most institutions—religious council, schools, political parties—and in a wide range of activities—elections, education, prayer—the two types of authority regularly confront and conflict with one another. The zone of uncertainty between the two provides a leeway for constant reinterpretation and casuistry and transfer of symbols from one domain to the other, but the basic problem remains. Historically, some ulama have proved willing to play "Brahmin" to secular and royal rulers, while others have cultivated an independence and autonomy for themselves through the manipulation of abilities, connections, and personal influence to carve out small domains in kampung and school. Threats to their nicely established status as religious élites in their local area by the encroachment of external powers have led to a kind of convergence. Those who support the political status quo, including the sultans, legitimate themselves through the appropriation of such controls as the religious council and so undermine the position of the "independent" ulama. The latter respond by turning increasingly to the tactics of open party politics to protect their position against the invaders of their territories. Meanwhile, each persists in its own self-righteousness as the ultimate claim to authority. What the implications of these events are for the future of ethnic relations and for possible radical class movements will be reserved for a later chapter. So too will an assessment of the degree to which the dakwah revival has intervened as a kind of third force.

3

The Tightening of the Screw:
The Prelude to Dakwah

Just as urbanism is a relatively recent development in Malaysia, so inevitably, is a distinctive urban religious tradition. Indeed, in differentiating rural and urban religious styles, the continuities and connections, as well as the oppositions, cannot be ignored. The distinction in the first place is made for convenience of treatment and analysis, but it becomes increasingly important in substance and content in the post-1969 period, which could be said to mark the beginnings of the contemporary religious revival in Malaysia, the so-called dakwah movement.

In order to understand the ideas and happenings of this past eventful decade, it is necessary to review the gestation period of the dakwah movement and the reasons for its birth in Malaysia at all. Once again, the trail leads back to the familiar problem of Malay identity and to contests between the different sources of power and authority. It also reflects some of the uncertainty, even disillusionment, of young Malays over new conditions, roles, and occupational requirements brought about by urbanism, economic development, and foreign contact, and the relationship of Islam to each of these problems.

One thread continuing from the past, as a focus of Malay identity, is the question of language or bahasa. It was around this issue that many of the organizations and future leaders of the emerging religious revitalization movement crystallized. Since Independence in 1957, the measure of the progress and effectiveness of the national language policy, whose more diffuse aim is "national integration," has been in the sphere of education, where the Malay language has gradually been phased in at all levels to replace both English, the colonial language, and the other vernaculars, principally Chinese.[1] Throughout the 1960's, special programmes were created for the training of Malay teachers and for the translation of school texts into Malay, but UMNO leaders have always allowed other languages (English, Chinese, and Tamil) to be used for limited official purposes, such as in the law courts and even in Parliament. Predictably, the pace of this policy was too measured and permissive for those who saw language as the main index of Malay cultural and political development, and the spirit of the times may be summed up by the rallying call of the day: *bahasa jiwa bangsa*, or "language is the soul of a people." Among those who took up the cudgels in 1969 were students at the Islamic College (Kolej Islam) in Petaling Jaya and those at the University of Malaya via the Malay Language Society, of which a certain Anwar Ibrahim was a prominent member. Like its parent body, the National Muslim Students' Association of Malaysia (*Persatuan Kebangsaan Pelajar-pelajar Islam Malaysia*, or PKPIM), the Malay Language Society was at this time more preoccupied with Malay ethnic interests than with Islam per se, for 1969 was the year of the electoral foment which culminated in the communal riots of May 13th.[2] Several leaders in the Malay Language Society played an active part in the riots, including Anwar Ibrahim.

With the New Education Policy of July 1969, in which plans for the linguistic Malayization of the education system for the following decade were first unfolded, attention turned to the task of increasing the number of secondary and tertiary level learning institutions and the percentage of Malays in them. A selective quota system for entrance and scholarship eligibility in favour of Malay students resulted in the proportion of their representation in the university student body leaping from 49.7 per cent in 1970 to 66.4 per cent in 1979. At the National University (Universiti Kebangsaan Malaysia), the pride and "showpiece" of the new centres of advanced learning, the proportion of Malay students exceeded 90 per cent.[3] Given the demographic distribution of the population, with almost 70 per cent of Malays still resident in rural areas, one consequence of the influx of Malay youth into the universities has been that there now exists a very large cohort of rural-origin students, for whom Malay (rather than the English of their immediate seniors) is the principal language. Although they fit well into the system as designed by the ideal educational policy, delays in the translation of appropriate texts and a shortage of instructors competent to lecture in Malay have created a new kind of linguistic crisis. The students are still faced with the need for a considerable facility in English, in addition to which they are often underprepared for the general academic standards required at this level. Anxiety, disillusionment, and the potential failure rate are therefore high and cause many tensions which prevade the atmosphere of student life on campus, for which other expressive and ideological outlets are now sought.

Now that the symbolic and political battle of the status of the Malay language has been won, a certain linguistic levelling process has set in. Increasingly, the entire multi-ethnic population of Malaysia, beginning with the present generation of school-age youth, will eventually be undifferentiated by language. If it is remembered that the constitutional definition of a "Malay" consists of fulfilling three conditions: habitually speaking Malay; practising Malay custom (adat); and being a Muslim, it can readily be seen that some of these crucial distinctions are quickly evaporating. Since the observance of traditional "custom" is empirically impossible to measure with any reliability (and, indeed, were it to be attempted, many elite, western-educated Malays would probably not qualify), and now that the linguistic barrier is being dismantled, it follows that the last remaining bastion of Malayness is that of religion. "Bahasa jiwa bangsa" of the 1960's is yielding to *bangsa dan agama* ("religion and race") as the new slogan of the 1970's and 1980's.

One other aspect of the New Education Policy merits comment at this point. In addition to the intensification of recruitment to university places at home, the decade of the 1970's has also witnessed the largest government-sponsored exodus ever of Malay students for overseas training, from high schools to doctoral and professional programmes. Malay students are scattered over the globe,[4] from Australia and New Zealand to the United Kingdom, North America, and many countries in the Middle East and India. Despite the diaspora, most of these students have undergone a number of common experiences. One, not totally unexpected, is cultural shock, an unpreparedness for different life-patterns, social and moral values, and academic styles, some of which actually conflict with their own. Such daily concerns as food, climate, mode of dress, male-female interaction, and availability of religious facilities become daily problems. But when these are combined with an unaccustomed degree of academic competitiveness and even aggressiveness and with standards which may prove too demanding, the fear of failure or of returning home without fulfilling expectations adds to the intense pressure. Language too, for those raised largely under the new educational policy, is often an additional handicap. As with foreign students everywhere, there are the usual bouts of loneliness, homesickness, and distaste for the new environment. On the other hand, international student communities can provide the source of a different kind of experience, which sometimes proves to be the antidote to the afflictions mentioned. It is among the students from other Muslim countries that solace and solidarity can be found, and with them, many new religious ideas, of which the current fundamentalist revival is most dominant. Religious revitalization, of course, must not be dismissed as a mere psychological "cop-out," nor yet as just another student fad, for it is much more. It is the result of a living and evolving cross-fertilization of ideas, some traditional in Islamic thought and philosophy, others less so, of the kind that occurs with the meeting of new people and minds. Malay students are learning from their new Muslim acquaintances for the first time of some of the major religious issues that their own religious education at home had never raised. Debates on religious topics challenge the views once passively accepted in the "empty vessel" method of traditional Malay religious instruction referred to in Chapter 2. Students are further exposed to the works of unfamiliar authors like the Egyptians Hassan al-Badr and al-Qutb, the Iranian Al-Shariati, and most popular and influential of all, the Pakistani Maulana al Maudoodi. The social reinforcement which accompanies this mental and ideological ferment tends to encapsulate the students into a close and intimate network of religious confrères and consoeurs who pray together and often eat and stay together in protective sub-communities. Symbolically, they assert their distinctiveness from the more "worldly" students by adopting forms of Islamic or Arab dress. Thus Malay students who leave their home shores in western dress return from the west in Arab garb, with many new ideas underneath.

One of the issues raised by the writings of the Muslim scholars by whom the student youth are most influenced is that of the status of knowledge itself. This relates to the possibility or desirability of "value-free" science and academic disciplines. Whereas westerners have generally lauded and sought a morally neutral approach to learning, modern Muslim youth, who are committed to a particular code of ethics and society, feel that science should not be shy of serving these commitments. In conscious opposition to the prevailing western intellectual environment, they propose, for example, that social science should unapologetically base itself on a set of specific moral principles, which, of course, should also be Islamic.

A second problem concerns the nature of the acquisition of knowledge. Some Muslim students question the western bias towards empiricism, especially in natural science, and are beginning to propose an alternate form of "inspirational" knowledge (wahyu), the result of divine revelation, on the assumption that all knowledge ultimately comes from God. Those not prepared to go so far as to reverse the entire scientific methodology and foundation have a different approach. Convinced of the debt of western scholarship to early Arabic civilization, they demonstrate the contributions of Arab scholars and ideas to the western tradition and assert, even further, that most of apparently recent scientific discoveries have their germs in the Koran, to which source can be traced the principles of genetics and the theory of atoms. It is also stressed that science and scholarship has always been encouraged and nurtured by religion by such Islamic scholars as Ibn Khaldun and Avicenna, a rationale for those students willing to accommodate to their courses of university study and yet remain good Muslims in the eyes of their peers. Generally, however, the emphasis today appears to be less on accommodation than on opposition. As a result of these debates, a few students have dropped out of their programmes entirely and returned home to a new life of religious commitment, in which they have rejected the material and occupational blandishments for which they are ostensibly being trained. I shall return to this in a later chapter.

YOUTH

The language policies have largely been enacted on behalf of the Malay youth through educational institutions, and it is on this segment of the population that most of its consequences have redounded. The participation of students and the Malay Language Society activists in the communal riots shows a concern with politics which has continued in various guises ever since.

Prior to 1969, one of the principal youth organizations in Malaysia was the National Muslim Students' Association of Malaysia (*Persatuan Kebangsaan Pelajar-Pelajar Islam Malaysia*, or PKPIM), founded in 1961. It drew its initial membership from various teacher and agricultural training colleges and from the Islamic College and also had contacts with Singapore and Indonesia. Before it became involved with language issues, it had a history of concern with broader social causes and a distinctly reinformist bent, consistent with the general tenor of interests everywhere in the 1960's. Among the causes espoused by the PKPIM was opposition to the repressive government of Thai premier Thanon Kittikachorn in his treatment of the Muslims of the southern part of his country, concern over the Vietnam war, and a call for an Islamic university for Malaysia. PKPIM took as its original model the Egyptian Muslim Brotherhood, *Ikhwan al-Muslimin*, and like its prototype, it became increasingly involved in political issues. From the early 1970's, PKPIM expanded its influence beyond the perimeters of college and campus through a series of extension and service programmes into the kampungs of the countryside (*Rancangan Khidmat Masyarakat*), where the students were adopted for the duration into local families. As the religious factor became more salient among the college youth, they would try to persuade their adoptive families to go to the mosque, to pray more regularly, and to provide their hosts with more "lucid explanations" (*penerangan yang jelas*) which the students somewhat presumptuously believed were not available in the village. This seems to represent the early glimmerings of what was to blossom into the dakwah movement and also illustrates the rather ambivalent relationship that was to characterize young urban "intellectuals" and villagers in matters of religion. Besides its rural service programmes, the PKPIM also began, in 1968, a "consciousness raising campaign" (*Gerakan Kempen Kesedaran*) to draw the attention of rural Malays to broader issues relating to health and economic and political problems, with the dual aims of promoting Malay development and instilling a true spirit of Islam. It was the latter which eventually prevailed, and as the 1970's progressed, speeches by PKPIM's president, Fuad Hassan, placed the focus of "development" in a moral/spiritual rather than a material framework. The most dramatic show of social consciousness by the PKPIM was undoubtedly on the occasion of the 1974 Baling demonstrations,[5] in which thousands of students from all the colleges and universities in the country, together with workers and other urban youth, participated to protest the alleged deterioration of peasant conditions in Baling, Kedah. The overlap of several organizations participating in the demonstrations make it difficult to assess precisely the role of PKPIM or how far the motive force grew out of religious ideology and a sense of Islamic justice, but the clear message of support for the "underdogs" of Malay society and the implicit criticism of government policy were sufficient to threaten the official peace of mind. One result of this event was a much-tightened Universities Act[6] in 1975, which banned all overtly political activities and organizations on campuses and prohibited university lecturers from running for public office.

In the unfolding career of the PKPIM between 1960 and 1980, two themes draw attention. The first is the progressively greater emphasis on Islam as a Malay symbol, as a mode of life, and as a guiding thread of the policy of the association. It also underlay the social causes on whose behalf it took up cudgels, for example, the plight of the Thai Muslims and the Islamic university. This was further strengthened by its ties with Islamic student bodies overseas, including, besides the Egyptian Al-Ikhwan, Pakistan's Jamaat al-Islami and the Turkish Bediuzzaman Nursi. PKPIM still maintains strong ties with Malay Muslim student organizations abroad, such as FOSIS in London, the World Association of Muslim Youth (WAMY), and the Australian Malay Students' Association. As the 1970's went on and political activities became subject to heavier official pressures, it also became expedient to stress the religious dimension in contrast to the more obviously political aspect of certain issues, particularly as religion has never been declared a "sensitive" or non-debatable topic. The second also reflects an inbuilt structural problem arising out of the natural "developmental cycle," of the changing position of individual members in an ongoing corporate body. While the body is perpetual, students eventually cease to be students, the young become older, and both are ineligible for continuing membership in PKPIM. Out of this dilemma was born the idea of a permanent body with similar objectives but with fewer membership limitations, able to accommodate the graduates in perpetuity. This body was ABIM (*Angkatan Belia Islam Malaysia*) or Malaysian League of Muslim Youth. ABIM was in fact first conceived in 1969 by many of the same individuals active in the Malay Language Society and even in PKPIM itself and who had played a part in the riots of May 13th. ABIM thus carried the interests and ideals of PKPIM into the wider world along with its graduating members, immune from the constraints of the Universities Act, although it did not exclude students from its membership. Over the course of the 1970's, not only has the absolute number of student members increased (see Chapter 4), but also the proportion engaged in religious studies.[7]

The political potential of organized youth, as the future wearers of the hats of the present leaders, lends this force a peculiar power of its own. So seriously is this taken in Malaysia that there is often competition for various youth leadership positions, particularly at the national level, which involve some of the highest-placed government elites,[8] and it has become one of the central features of Malay politics. While the university-based movements were gathering momentum on one corner of the stage, on other parts of the set parallel acts were being performed by different youth organizations. Of these, the most important was, and is, UMNO Youth, a wing of the political party, carefully nurtured, sometimes more dangerously incited, by a succession of controversial, if not charismatic, leaders. In addition to UMNO Youth, there has long been in Malaysia a series of popular grass-roots youth movements, including Boy Scouts and 4-B agricultural groups, and an assortment of clubs affiliated to specific religious and ethnic groups for example, Tamil Bell, Buddhist Youth, and so forth. In 1972, most of these were incorporated into a single, overarching, though loose, Federation of Malaysian Youth Clubs (*Majlis Belia Malaysia*) (MBM) by a government increasingly apprehensive of youthful politics. Among its twenty-five affiliated founding bodies was ABIM, whose leaders felt it expedient not to exhibit too much independence of action at this stage, but to bow to official pressure for all youth groups to unite with the MBM. Attempts by government to control MBM have at times been heavy-handed, resulting in at least one major organizational crisis following the Baling affair. Owing to the detention of some of the leaders of the demonstrations, there were several threats by affiliated clubs to withdraw from the federation altogether.

The tale of UMNO Youth is one of constant ambivalence and intrigue and struggle for leadership. On the one hand, it is officially recognized as the junior branch of the senior party in the government, and as such it has legitimacy while its membership is being scoured and groomed as future leaders. As one of its past leaders, Datuk Harun, declared, "If UMNO Youth is weak, then the whole party will be weak" (*Straits Times* 6/2/78). On the other hand, it is seen as a potential powder keg which can just as readily be ignited by the wrong direction or cause, and as such, it is sometimes referred to as a "ginger group." Among the more controversial statements emanating from UMNO Youth—whether as an official "testing of the water" by the senior party or an unsanctioned devil's advocacy by the "ginger group" is not always entirely clear—have been virulent oppositions to the Chinese university proposal, calls for discontinuation of all non-Malay schools at the primary level, a call for the exclusive use of Malay in all Immigration departments, and a rejection of aid for the Vietnamese boat-people refugees. More recently, in keeping with the tone of the times, and possibly to deflate the sails of the religious groups, generalized calls for "more attention to Islamic law" and changing the national week-end holiday from Sunday to Friday have been heard (*Straits Times* 15/9/78).

In contrast with PKPIM and ABIM. UMNO Youth represents the Bumi Malay end of the spectrum, where the narrowly ethnic rather overshadows the religious interest, following the more "ultra" ethnic orientation of some of the senior members of the party in the old Malay tradition. In this capacity, it is sometimes scathing in its criticism of other religious youth groups which presume to question government policies and are "hiding behind a religious administration to seek power" (*berselindung dibelakang tadbir agama untuk mencari ilham dan kekuatan*") (*Utusan Malaysia* 27/10/79). Almost dangerously large powers accrue to the leader of UMNO Youth, who can turn these to his own advantage in cases of upper-échelon political infighting. The glory and power of the leadership of UMNO Youth was in the hands of the capable one-time Mentri Besar of Selangor and silat patron, Datuk Harun, until he was indicted and jailed on charges of corruption in 1974.[9] So popular was he, that in 1979, 300 requests from 114 youth branches were received for his release (*Mastika* July 1979:8-25), and in 1980, even from jail, he was able to command 48 per cent of the popular vote and was only narrowly defeated by his nephew, Haji Suhaimi. It is also significant that, at the time of his initial incarceration, Datuk Harun historically compared his own situation to that of the betrayal of Hang Jebat, the quintessential Malay hero, to whose ethical tradition the youth leader clearly sees himself as heir.

THE STATE AND THE STATES

It should be recalled that, under Article 3 of the Malaysian Constitution, Islam is the official religion of the federation, but Malaysia remains a secular state. Islam also provides the validating symbols for most national ceremonies and public events. Otherwise, there is complete freedom of worship for followers of other religions, as long as they do not attempt to proselytize among Muslims. But the constitution leaves open to uncertainty (with a resulting tension) such questions as to what extent Islam belongs in national political institutions and, reciprocally, how far the federal state can control religion. This is part of the problem of the definition of the "Islamic state," so hotly debated today. Finally, ever at issue is the gnawing question as to what degree Islamic law should be imposed upon the non-Muslim population.

Malaysia allows considerable autonomy to each of its eleven states in a number of areas. Of these, the most important, for the present analysis, lies in the domain of religious affairs. As noted in Chapter 1, by early pre-Independence arrangements with the British, the sultans were confirmed in their role as Heads of Malay Religion and Custom, and these powers have not changed appreciably since that time. Islam may be the official religion of the federation, but strictly speaking, there is no Head of the Muslim faith for the entire country, and unlike Indonesia, Malaysia has no national Ministry of Religion. The King (*Yang Di-Pertuan Agong*) remains Head of Religion for his own state and also oversees religious affairs and makes religious appointments for the states of Penang, Malacca, Sabah, and Sarawak, which have no sultans of their own, and for the Federal Territory (*Wilayah Persekutuan*) of the Kuala Lumpur area. It was through the creation of the Federal Territory (in 1974), and with it the National Council of Religious Affairs (*Majlis Kebangsaan bagi Hal Ehwal Agama Islam*), that the federal government was first able to place its foot more firmly in the door of religious administration in an area not pre-empted by the royal authority of a specific state. Before this date, (from 1968 to 1974), there had existed a National Council for the Muslim Religion (*Majlis Agama Islam*) with a more limited territorial jurisdiction and powers restricted to voluntary co-operation by representatives of state religious councils, with the exceptions of Kedah and Pahang. The present national council of religious affairs administers the daily affairs of the Syari'ah court and religious properties within its domain and supports its own Grand Mufti, who, like his counterparts in the royal states, is charged with the right to issue fatwa for the Territory alone. Despite his "grand" title (besar), this mufti by no means wields any national authority, and he has no power to challenge or overrule religious council decisions in the other states, which retain complete autonomy in all such matters. Major pronouncements by the Grand Mufti, however, are often seen as a reflection of government views, in the hope that they may be taken into account in the decision-making processes of the state religious councils. Thus in the Nasrul Haq case (to be discussed below), the Grand Mufti was the first to ban the movement, and several of the states subsequently followed suit, although each one clearly had independent reasons of its own for so doing. In a few administrative areas, such as establishing the dates of the fasting month of *Ramadan*, most of the religious councils have agreed to co-operate, to ensure uniformity throughout the country, although as we have seen, Kedah has sometimes seen fit to flout even this agreement.

Given the federal/state constitutional arrangements, the central government does not have much room to manoeuvre in religious matters. This has not prevented, rather probably contributed to, the creation of a number of national agencies concerned with religious education and policy and with the prevention of "false teachings" (*ajaran sesat*). One such agency is the Centre for Islamic Education in Malaysia (*Pusat Penyelidikan Islam di Malaysia*), established in 1969, and now many government departments and ministries, including the Prime Minister's Office, have their own religious branches and educational programmes for their employees.

Also centrally administered is the Pilgrims' Savings Fund (*Lembaga Urusan dan Tabung Haji*), created in 1969, to co-ordinate the financing, travel arrangements, and welfare of Malaysian pilgrims in Mecca. Among its services is a controlled and efficient savings bank, whereby aspiring Hajis can make regular contributions according to personal means and eventually qualify for a "bonus" from the proceeds of the Fund's investments.[10] The fund also has a monopoly over the transport of pilgrims to the Holy Land, originally through the national shipping line, and later by special flights on the government airline, and requires all Malaysian pilgrims to use this service.[11] In these arrangements, the Fund has generally received the acceptance and co-operation of the state religious councils, all of which recognize this as a worthy national programme.

Finally, as will be elaborated in Chapter 6, a number of additional agencies have recently been created under the auspices of the federal government for purposes of its own dakwah or religious mission. This is intended partly as an antidote to the effects of the "spontaneous" dakwah movements, now so powerful in the country at large, but ostensibly to "control deviant practices and teaching."

NASRUL HAQ

If any youth organization could be said to epitomize the Bumi Malay spirit, of the sort of elemental *semangat* (essence/spirit) of pre-Islamic vintage, the branch of silat or martial art known as Nasrul Haq would certainly come close to this ideal type. Literally meaning "Friends of Truth" and representative of a sub-culture with deep roots in Malay history, Nasrul Haq has been described as a "form of Malay culture inherited from our Malay ancestors over hundreds of years" (*satu bentuk kebudayaan Melayu warisan nenek-moyang yang telah beratus-ratus tahun umurnya*). The connection is even more explicit when one hears of Nasrul Haq branches named for the Malacca hero, Hang Tuah (see Chapter 1). Like other silat clubs, some of the original Nasrul Haq branches were under the patronage of various sultans, and the Sultan of Perak was particularly known for his sponsorship of such activities in his capacity as patron of a popular type of martial art form, *Seni Silat Cekah Sabil*. As part of a broad and ancient Malay tradition, silat generally also has strong roots in Indonesia, with its widespread martial and mystical tradition of kebatinan.

In its brief flowering, the Nasrul Haq movement developed many branches, only to be pruned somewhat prematurely. In its bloom, it displayed a number of unique elements which make it very much a creature of its times. Generically, Nasrul Haq is directly related to the ancient Malay martial arts tradition and its many variants (for example, *silat gayong, silat pencak, silat lincah, silat cekah*), each of which involves different styles of action, techniques of self-defence, and modes of discipline. Equally important, each one is heir to a distinctive line of guru which specializes in one variety of silat only, and through personal instruction, hands down the "secrets" (*rahsia*) and esoteric lore. The tight hold of the silat tradition over a large segment of the kampung Malay population of both sexes and of all ages must be recognized. Pupils range in age from pre-pubertal youth to old men, all seeking some form of spiritual enlightenment, physical release, and special secrets, such invisibility and invincibility. Many kampungs, especially in rural areas, have active silat clubs, with a special court or arena (*gelanggang*), and, as mentioned in Chapter 2, some of the guru silat are simultaneously village ulama. Popular Malay newspapers even advertise silat courses, guaranteeing "instant results" in the form of an ability to handle weapons "within five minutes," improved bodily condition, resistance to enemies, and invulnerability. In the manner of miracle patent medicines, there is something for everyone. These advertised clubs operate on the same principles as pyramid sales organizations, forming new cells wherever demand and local leadership can be established. Delegates are then despatched from the headquarters to instruct the new recruits in return for appropriate fees (*saguhati*, or "gifts from the heart"). Some silat teachers are nationally-known and idolized figures, on a par with, and sometimes doubling as, film stars. One of the most celebrated film-star silat lincah leaders is Omar Din, whose enthusiastic fans eulogize him in both roles. Secure in his immense popularity, Omar Din is now rumoured to be turning his head towards politics, which illustrates yet another link between youth and political power. Datuk Harun, of UMNO Youth, was also known for his active sponsorship of silat gayong in his home state of Selangor, which was undoubtedly part of his appeal. Girls may also participate in silat activities and wear a female version of the male costume, which includes a short, knee-length sarung, a form of "pirate pants," and loose blouses, which leave exposed the hair, arms, and lower legs in very un-Islamic fashion. It goes without saying that this is regarded by dakwah followers as totally immodest and unacceptable.

What drew so much public attention and acrimonious debate to Nasrul Haq, which was only founded in 1977,[12] was, first, its relationship to Islam in an era of heightened sensitivity to religious niceties, and, second, its tutelage under a certain contentious cabinet minister. This minister was appropriately and strategically in charge of Youth, Culture, and Sports and the focus of a number of political intrigues and conflicts, which made his control over a large, loyal, and enthusiastic following of youth all over Malaysia a somewhat awesome political prospect with shades of another Datuk Harun scenario. By 1978, it was estimated that the membership of Nasrul Haq had reached at least 300,000, of whom 114,000 were from Kelantan, 20,000 from Perak, 40,000 from Penang, and 30,000 in Kedah.

On the first, religious, count, critics alleged that Nasrul Haq had overstepped the legitimate conventions of silat proper in a series of dubious practices wrongfully invoking Islam and by taking the name of Allah in vain. Members were accused of introducing into their self-defence sessions a form of Sufi-like chanting (zikir) in order to achieve a state of trance, somewhat in the manner of Indonesian-style mystical cults (kebatinan). Moreover, these sessions were alleged to be held in mosques, where participants were said to be quoting the Koran to their own ends. Further objections were raised when the Nasrul Haq leaders began to claim Islamic-sounding titles like *Khalifah* (Caliph), giving sermons, and demanding personal religious oaths of loyalty (*sumpah*), thereby impinging upon and insulting the true faith. In their sermons, these guru were also implying that anyone who died in the practice of Nasrul Haq could be considered a religious martyr (*mati syahid*). These practices, together with the immodest female attire were roundly denounced by religious critics and branded as evil (*syirik*) and as forms of black magic (*syihir*) (cf. *Watan* 22/2/80). On purely religious grounds, Nasrul Haq was vulnerable on several of the above counts, and it certainly placed the movement in a camp diametrically opposed to that of the dakwah youth. For while the Nasrul Haq followers were no doubt genuine in their commitment to Islam, they were also of the sincere conviction that silat in fact supports religion. It is one of the more blatant examples of the adat-influenced, syncretic Islam of the old Melayu tradition that the modern revivalists have condemned and are trying to change.

The political aspect of Nasrul Haq was its other contentious feature and both its strength and weakness. When the movement first blossomed in January of 1977, its founder had to his political credit both the Ministry of Youth, Culture, and Sports and an Indonesian pedigree, from his Negri Sembilan birth, which made him by implication heir to the mystical (kebatinan) tradition. Through the perquisites of his office and access to its financial resources and channels of communication, he was able to provide his followers with funds for elaborate costumes and to construct arenas and muster giant rallies in the capital of Kuala Lumpur, accompanied by lavish entertainment and much publicity. Initially, as in the opening ceremony for Nasrul Haq House in Kuala Lumpur early in 1978, no less a patron than the then prime minister (Tun Abdul Razak) made an official speech of welcome, praised the organization, and exhorted the members to use their art to national ends (*Watan* 6/4/78). It has been suggested by some observers that Nasrul Haq was at this time seen by UMNO leaders as an exploitable Bumi Malay counter to PAS's Islam, which, however, got out of hand.

Later in the same year (1978), the minister, as the Mahaguru and Khalifah of the movement, convened a massive rally and ceremony in Kuala Lumpur to confer diplomas (*ijazah*) on successful graduates of the Nasrul Haq course, at which a member of the Pahang royal house also officiated. To this rally were transported sixty thousand enthusiastic young followers, boys and girls, who then staged an impressive demonstration of their skills amid a rich and heady display of traditional costumes, embellished with a lavish use of incense, flowers, and traditional Malay rhymes and repartee (*pantun*) recalling the epic events and glories of the heroic Malay past (*meningatkan zaman kegemilangan pahlawan dulukala*). Amid the various speeches, the youth were exhorted by their *mahaguru* to use their skills for the sake of their "race, country and religion" (in that order), to respect their parents and families, not to use drugs, to concentrate on their own spiritual development (*pendidikan rohani*), and to "remember the greatness of God" (*Watan* 17/4/78). This event really marked the apogee of Nasrul Haq's existence, certainly at the national level. Thereafter, its leader was increasingly harassed by attacks from both religious (particularly dakwah) groups[13] and by his political rivals. First, he was forced to renounce his title of Khalifah and then to ensure that none of the less controlled regional branch members continued to misuse Koranic verses or mosque buildings for their self-defence activities. These impositions were enforced, despite the minister's protestations that another silat lincah leader, aspiring film-star Omar Din, was even allowed to take with him on the pilgrimage to Mecca (in 1979) a troupe of his star pupils to present silat performances before Arab syeikhs. This was permitted despite the well-known fact that yet another branch of silat and kebatinan cult was even then percolating deeply through the ranks of the national Armed Forces with the cognizance and participation of some of the highest officers. In this case, the guru behind it all was a more shadowy figure of Sumatran origin. Another adviser to the chief of the Armed Forces was a Javanese-born lecturer in the Faculty of Islamic Studies at the National University. Neither of the two, however, appeared to harbour any political aspirations, and the appeal of the Sumatran was initially achieved by virtue of his alleged miraculous curing of the Armed Forces' chief's sick child. In its more general self-defence/invincibility techniques, silat, of course, is not inconsistent with army ethos and morale, particularly where the majority of the soldiers are of rural Malay origin. However, this movement too had held prayer and chanting sessions in no less than the National Mosque, at which the chief imam and then Prime Minister Tun Abdul Razak had also been present. The effect of this silat movement on the rank and file soldiers was supposed to be one of inspiration and self-control in combat situations, reinforcing physical discipline with the spiritual, although it was not suggested that the army should cease to rely on bullets or other weapons entirely.

The final claim by the minister of the "conspiracy theory" against Nasrul Haq was the evidence that other kinds of silat had been made a permissable alternative option to dance in the physical education curriculum of the Islamic Training College in 1977. The political aspects of Nasrul Haq and of the potential power it could unleash, became clearer when condemnations began to roll in from the religious councils of different states. Under pressure from certain UMNO quarters, the National Council of Religious Affairs, in its capacity as spokesman for the national capital and federal/district only, was the first to condemn the movement as sinful and deviant and to impose a ban on its activities in that area. This was quickly followed by a ban in the state of Selangor, whose chief minister was close to the same UMNO interests. Later, the mufti of Perak also banned Nasrul Haq in his state, despite the fact that the sultan is honorary patron of other silat groups. In this case, the allegation by the minister of Youth, Culture, and Sports was that the Perak religious council is PAS-dominated, and the same response was elicited when Kedah too followed suit. Perlis, like Kedah, also eventually banned the movement, but in this case, the influence may have been the persistence of a strong vein of Kaum Muda ideology in religious council circles, particularly in the person of the mufti. Penang likewise, whose religious council is rather docile, and easily influenced by ex-Prime Minister Tunku Abdul Rahman, who resides in Penang, though less by UMNO interests, also subsequently prohibited the practice of Nasrul Haq. The final blow came from the leader's home state of Negri Sembilan, whose chief minister was alarmed at the political strength of a rival. Only Kelantan and Johor endorsed the movement. In the first case, Kelantan has had a long tradition of opposition to federal decisions since the days of its PAS state government (1959-78), while Johor's religious council is currently in the process of asserting a greater autonomy for itself vis-à-vis secular and other authorities. Thus the reasons vary in each case, but they appear to reflect some of the labyrinthine political interests and intrigues, interwoven with competing authorities: federal and state, royal and non-royal, religious and secular, in different combinations. Pahang alone made no explicit ruling on the matter, largely, unkind observers say, because its religious council is embarrassingly ignorant in some religious matters.[14] Finally, the complexity of the response to Nasrul Haq is underlined by the reactions of some dakwah spokesmen who, while condemning the movement from a purely scriptural perspective, nonetheless call upon the National Religious Council to justify its own stand more articulately in fairness to all the parties concerned.

As for the minister himself, his credentials and legitimacy as a guru silat seemed to be derived and supported principally from his government post, and it was upon challenge to, and subsequent loss of, this post that he also lost much of his power as a youth leader. To this extent, he could be said to have enjoyed the charisma of office. But there did remain a residue of personal appeal which did not derive from the position alone and which was able to satisfy the needs of some of his followers, as in the case of many "freelance" ulama. Despite the many official bans, Nasrul Haq branches still operate fairly openly in most states, including those where the religious councils are opposed to it, and it remains particularly strong in rural and northern areas. Membership in 1980 was estimated to be in the region of 114,000 (from a peak of 300,000 in 1978). For their part, the young followers self-righteously claim that they are being victimized unnecessarily and protest that they are willing to shed their blood for their country and faith and that Nasrul Haq is for them a means to purify their hearts from jealousy, anger, pride, and treachery (*mensucikan hati dari perasaan dengki, iri hati, sombong dan khianat*).

As a general trend, Nasrul Haq clearly represents an intensely traditional pattern of Malayness with its heroic myths and symbols, its use of the indigenous silat format, and typically syncretic and uneasy relationship with a more orthodox Islam. The leader himself, in an interview in 1979 (*Dewan Masyarakat* 15/8/79), asserted quite unapologetically that for him the most important cultural questions, (in the old spirit of the 1960's) are those of language, custom, and race, which in turn are derived from the more basic concept of Nusantara, which seeks to eliminate immigrant Chinese, Indian, and even Arab traits. The minister did not go so far as to deny the importance of Islamic, as opposed to Arabic, custom and culture, but he used this opportunity to make known his antipathy to the dakwah variety of Islam, with its Arab accretions. It is therefore not surprising to find the greatest strength of Nasrul Haq in rural Malay areas, often those in which the tradition of ulama and religious school does not play a dominant role. Although it will be recalled from Chapter 2 that some ulama are simultaneously guru silat, none to my knowledge, were ever involved in Nasrul Haq. Like dakwah participation for young urban Malays, Nasrul Haq seems to reflect a quest for shared experience and identity as a people for those rural youth whose future in a rapidly changing society appears somewhat uncertain.

THE NEW ECONOMIC POLICY

Preoccupations with problems of social roles and identities in a rapidly changing and complex society for many Malays have both shaped and been shaped by, ethnically grounded government economic policies. A number of now-familiar, special constitutional rights for Malays stemmed from the British colonial period, when the Malays were being groomed for eventual leadership, and extended to land reservations, certain occupations, and occupational licences, scholarships, and quotas for civil service posts (cf. Ratnam 1965; Means 1976; Ness 1967; Pillai 1974). During the 1960's the newly independent Malaysian government established what were to become the statutory bodies of MARA and PERNAS, both of which were intended to provide assorted loans, training schemes, and commercial experience to aspiring Malay entrepreneurs. After 1969, attempts to chart an even more unchallengeable position and direction for Malay economic development was intensified. The spirit and details of these new directions were most clearly enshrined in the New Economic Policy of the Second Malaysia Plan (1971-75). The twin goals of the Plan were an overall increase in prosperity for Malaysia as a whole and a rectification of the ethnic economic imbalance by enlarging the Malay share of the national pie, particularly through their participation in industrial, professional, and entrepreneurial activities and in the ownership of more share capital.[15]

In its first aim of increasing the global pie, Malaysian economic policy has favoured a combination of state and private capitalism, together with an open-armed approach to foreign and multinational investment firms. It has certainly succeeded in attracting a large share of the standard electronics and assembly-line investment so common in the third world today. Foreign companies are expected to comply with the Malay participation quotas, although compliance does not necessarily lead to enforcement in every case. Constant expansion of basic resources is an essential underpinning of the other goal of more general Malaysian development for all, if only to defuse local zero-sum sentiments that Malay success must necessarily be at the expense of non-Malay interests. Racial harmony is also regarded as an essential component of success, both for internal and external reasons and for the country's reputation in the international business community.

It comes as little surprise to find that the reception of the New Economic Policy by the non-Malay community has not been uniformly favourable, and its most tangible expression has been in a sharp decline in private domestic investment, especially by Chinese capital. This has meant a compensatory increase in state capitalism and investment, which only aggravates the situation. It has led, inevitably, to an overall economic and political scene in which most of the "good things of life," connected with money and power, are seen as ethnic perquisites, and, indeed, the government does not shrink from linking the two. The Malay electorate is wooed with economic incentives in the name of their "race" or bangsa, and now "religion" or agama, which have become the material and ammunition used to combat such political parties as PAS. Suggestions raised by some elements of the dakwah brigade that serious Muslims should be prepared to substitute spiritual for material values and that excoriate all forms of materialism in general, particularly when derived from the west, thus clearly strike at the very heart of the government's economic philosophy, and undermine its strategies for creating a united Malay front, and vote, as the basis of its own power. Any hint of concern over social ills or inequalities within the Malay community (such as the Baling affair), whether among dakwah followers or not, also constitutes a threat to this elusive unity. Worse still, it even raises the spectre of class differences. UMNO party and government élites are constantly on the defensive, for the entire structure and success of their consociational alliance with the non-Malay élites hinges upon the unquestioning support of the Malay grass-roots and the playing off of ethnic interests. This has the desired effect of diverting attention from the existence of rich Malays towards the wealth of other communities. Given its basic economic orientation and objectives, the UMNO party can only combat divisive tendencies within the ethnic community through the lure of employment, schools, and other material rewards for loyalty to its line. One consequence of this has been the incremental growth, over the past ten years, of a new Malay middle class. Most of this results from an ever-expanding civil service and professional community, many of the latter in the universities. Now, by the grace of MARA and PERNAS too, many more Malays are also to be found in business and commerce. By 1980, there is little sign of the oft-threatened "middle class unemployment" crisis which is beginning to impinge upon the economically unprotected non-Malays.

While middle class status, and the prosperity commensurate with it, may appear to be sufficient reward in itself, some of the new middle class Malays are discovering hidden disadvantages. Being "middle class" in the diffuse western sense means being part of a status group defined largely by a generalized bureaucratic lifestyle based on consumerism, which effectively eclipses older, more subtle and meaningful cultural distinctions between the Malays and non-Malays and, with it, some of their identity. From the other direction, as the non-Malays begin to speak Malay, graduate through the national educational system, and move into corresponding occupational positions and lifestyles, a convergence of sorts takes place. While this is admittedly an oversimplification of a more complex process, there are grounds for arguing that fear of loss of identity as a Malay, or at least failure to find any other identity equally satisfying, is part of the middle-class problem. On the surface, in the homogenized suburban housing complexes which resemble their middle-class residential counterparts elsewhere in the world, Malay and non-Malays fraternize, visit one another, and share their version of the middle-class dream. But, retreating behind closed doors, letting down their hair and putting on their sarung, secure in the privacy of family and faith, ethnic jokes and biases can prevail. Old values of kampung and religion may be resurrected, and they propel Malays into one of two possible directions. The first is towards a more militantly Bumi Malay stance, by which the special rights and preferences for Malays of the constitution and New Economic Policy are aggressively upheld and ethnic party leaders defended. Like the "feudal" loyalty of the ancient Malay, which was a virtue bringing both material rewards and a social identity, loyalty to the modern Malay élites confers similar advantages. It perpetuates the Malay domain very much along the old Malacca principles in modern dress (cf. Chandra Muzaffar 1979). Absolute loyalty in return for protection and favours is still a familiar concept to many twentieth-century members of the Malay middle class.

The other direction to which middle-class Malays may turn in the private domain, though increasingly coming into public view, is towards religion. A revitalized Islam, which, after all, remains an important element of Malay identity, is polished up as the chief symbol and guiding spirit of a new form of Malay distinctiveness, even in middle-class suburbia. This is Malayness in Muslim dress.

Among this cohort of Malays are many who trained overseas and so were caught up in the dakwah activity of their student peers and who now carry their new convictions back with them to home and office. Some observers of the Malay scene predict that in the not-too-distant future the inevitable "white-collar unemployment" typical of countries which have too rapidly expanded their higher educational opportunities will add to the problems of the expectant professional class. Already there are signs that the constant proliferation of government departments and multiplication of positions within them are straining the seams. If and when the seams burst, more disillusioned Malays may gravitate away from their absolute loyalty and ethnic Malayness, and seek an alternative, or even opposition, whose banner will be Islam. It is well known that this kind of reaction has precedents in a number of Muslim countries of the Middle East and North Africa. This question of internal Malay opposition will receive further attenton in Chapter 8.

Another area of change, stimulated by a decade of the New Economic Policy, is the intensification of rural-urban migration by Malays in search of the industrial and other occupational opportunities now available. For the unskilled, there are more mundane jobs in the factories, the fruits of the foreign investment so assiduously cultivated by the government. The assembly-line electronics factory syndrome has assaulted the major cities of West Malaysia, especially Kuala Lumpur and Penang, and many young, kampung-born Malays are being exposed for the first time to the ills of an urban, industrial, often lonely and emotionally unsatisfying existence in an unfamiliar environment. For the new factory girls in particular, the conditions and low social image of their occupation render them vulnerable to the vicious, and often over-imaginative, gossip of more self-righteous Malays with strong ideas about propriety for young women. Since many of the female workers live an "unchaperoned" life, with no male relative to supervise them or to provide an anchor to the rest of Malay society, some inevitably relieve their daily drudgery with films or discos. Whatever the circumstances, however, all workers tend to be tarred with the same slanderous brush, and they have been accorded the popular epithet, *minah karans* which carries the sense of girls who seek thrills, like an electric current, or "hot stuff." Such is their reputation that some factory girls disguise their occupation from their families back in the kampung.

The organization of the factory tends to follow highly regimented, authoritarian, even repressive lines (Lim Kah Chen 1979; Linda Lim, 1978), with the object of maintaining a docile, disciplined, and undemanding labour force and peace for the management, hence contributing to the high level of foreign investment dear to government planners. Formation of labour unions, of course, is made almost impossible, as are most attempts to represent worker interests. This particular combination of circumstances has given rise to what is now being recognized by Malaysian and non-Malaysian managers (cf. *Asian Wall Street Journal* 12/3/80) alike as a pattern or syndrome of mass hysteria,[17] which especially afflicts Malay women. What is of interest here, however, is that the frustrations of the assembly-line sub-culture have taken this particular form of release, rather than a more Islamic turn. Dakwah and religious revival have not yet hit the factory floor. Clearly this is a cautionary tale against uncritical assumptions about the relationship between dakwah and dissatisfaction in social life. Suggestions as to why events have taken this turn in the factories will have to be deferred until Chapter 5.

WOMEN

One area of Malay life in which quantum changes have been occurring over the past decade is the position of women. They are, of course, no more immune to stress, uprooting, and identity problems than the men, insofar as females are exposed to the increased educational (including overseas) and occupational changes. Women, however, undergo stresses of their own, in coming to terms with a transition from a largely rural-based Malay society, where even urban-born females tended to be judged by traditional rural values (Manderson 1980). In comparison with their Middle Eastern or Arab sisters, however, Malay women have never been rigidly secluded or veiled, and in the old Southeast Asian tradition, they have been relatively free to leave the house unaccompanied and even to engage in petty trade and marketing alone. Traditional dress, while modestly covering arms and legs, and usually including a headscarf or loose shawl (*selindang*), certainly did not approach the all enveloping folds of her Arab counterpart. In the socially explosive late 1960's and early 1970's, many university students even dared to experiment with mini-dresses and jeans or, at least, a very contour-revealing sarung with high-cut slits and fitting blouse or T-shirt. To balance this picture, however, there is in Malay society a strong undercurrent of conservatism over female roles and comportment, and authority is generally biased in the direction of males (ibid.). Although the issue may be somewhat oversimplified by equating these two antithetical strains in Malay womanhood as "Malay" and the "Islamic," it is not entirely fanciful. Any observer is struck by the contrast between the situation of Malay women in the more isolated "Malay" areas of the east coast—for example, Kelantan and Trengganu—and her cousins of the urban areas of the west coast. In the former there are many examples of the greater freedom and uninhibitedness whereby female traders travel, unaccompanied, up and down the coast in their various ventures, while their husbands remained at home with the children and rice paddies. Here too, the divorce rate is the highest in Malaysia, reaching a total of over 50 per cent. West coast Malay women are less commonly so enterprising and are almost never seen in the open marketplace. Indeed, those who do prepare items for sale generally prefer to employ an intermediary for the actual sale and contact with the public (cf. Nagata 1974b; 1979). The difference between the two styles of female behaviour here may be related to the impact on the west coast of a stricter form of Islam, emanating from the several waves of immigration from the more conservative Muslim regions of India and the Middle East, with their customary views of sex roles and propriety. Where the Islamic view prevails more strongly, so does a more fundamentalist religious attitude to women's duties and obligations. Typical of this orientation is the kind of opinion expressed by Datin Sakinah, wife of past PAS president, Datuk Asri, and once head of the women's section of PAS, the *Kaum Muslimin*. While fully endorsing women's contributions to public social life through voluntary service or as teachers, she is convinced of their lack of suitability for top leadership roles, on a par with their menfolk, and particularly where this would conflict with their roles as wives and mothers. The latter must always receive priority, and in this connection, she also supports polygyny ("God allows four wives") and even some of the traditional Islamic penalties for sexual transgressions such as stoning to death for adultery (interview reported in *Straits Times* 2/8/77). Datin Sakinah herself was an important figure in the early Malay nationalist movement in the immediate post-war years and in the founding of PAS. However, she insists on her own subordination to the "heads" of husband and children and dresses carefully, covering her entire head, save for the face, with a voluminous veil in the manner of many older Malay women. Like most women of her generation, Datin Sakinah's education was limited to Malay vernacular primary school and studies at the religious pondok of her Sumatran relatives.

Over the past fifteen to twenty years, another type of Malay woman had been emerging from the daughters of the more westernized, urban élites. These girls have often received English-medium and western-style schooling and have been trained for a broader spectrum of occupations as secretaries, teachers, and even civil service positions. Out of this small cohort have emerged a few leaders of prominence. Whereas only one female candidate ran in the first general elections in Malaya in 1955, by the late 1970's there were several female M.P.'s and even members of Senate, for example, Senator Hajjah Aishah Ghani, minister of social welfare and president of Wanita UMNO, Senator Rafidah Aziz, deputy minister of Finance and minister for Economic Development, and Puan Kontik Kamariah, head of the Officers' Loans Fund for Selangor and of the co-operative Union of Malaysia (*Angkasa Kerjasama Se-Melaysia*). Below this rarefied level, women have managed to increase their representation in non-traditional fields substantially since 1970. Whereas in 1970, there were 5,200 women in professional and technical occupations, by 1977 there were 33,900. In the field of administration the numbers rose from a bare 100 in 1970 to 2,900 in 1977. Over the same period, the number of women in sales occupations rose from 4,900 to over 25,000, and in services from 8,400 to 31,800, but it declined, from 67,000 in 1970 to 38,400 in 1977 in agriculture, traditionally a major area of female employment (*Berita Harian* 19/6/78). Women's associations have proliferated, to a current total of fifty-six, and many of these are concerned, at least in part, with women's issues and rights, for example, those relating to marriage and divorce. In this connection, there is concern that Islamic laws should be administered more in accordance with its spirit than the letter. Thus, husbands wishing to take a second wife should be required to consult the first wife and demonstrate satisfactorily their ability and intention to treat both equally. Since Muslim marriage is basically a contract (*akad*), women would also like to use this, on occasion, to make certain stipulations which, if violated, would render the contract and the marriage invalid. There is also concern over the equal division of property on divorce and a sentiment that couples or individuals should be allowed representation by secular lawyers in the Syari'ah court. In their attitudes to dress and to religious authority, women who run these associations may well be characterized by the following incident. At the 1975 Women's Congress on Muslim marriage and the family held by the Muslim Women's Welfare Association (*Pertubuhan Perempuan Kebajikan Islam*), a small constituency under pressure from certain conservative ulama, feeling threatened and embarrassed by some frank discussion and criticisms of the current Syari'ah administration, moved a motion that all delegates should be asked to modify their dress to show their genuine commitment to Islam and to appear at the conference on the third day with their heads covered by a selindang. When the third day came, however, none of the other delegates (the majority) had complied. One recalcitrant reportedly declared that they "wouldn't go to hell for not wearing the selindang" and implied that there were more important matters to occupy their attention (*Berita Harian* 28/3/75;4/4/75). Such outspokenness would be almost unthinkable in the Malaysia of the 1980's.

The implementation of the national educational and economic policies, together with the efforts to improve the overall status of the Malays as a whole, has led to a growing proportion of women in higher education institutions. Not only are more kampung girls attending non-religious schools, but many of them are also being sent to larger centres for secondary training in boarding schools in preparation for university and sometimes overseas education thereafter. Girls are uprooted from their home environments quite early in life and confronted with unfamiliar styles of living, academic standards, and authority. In the secondary schools they are still largely in an all-female environment and a highly disciplined and structured régime, but in the university, even given the slight Malay majority, they are exposed more directly to men, to members of other ethnic groups, and to a wider array of social situations. Girls and young women in these situations tend to become extremely dependent upon their immediate peer group and to form intense personal attachments for mutual social, emotional, and moral support. Physically, they move around in clusters and cliques, and this reinforces their conformity to whatever norms prevail. The effects of this on adoption of new religious practices will be apparent in Chapter 5. Finally, in occupational matters, female university graduates have to face the question of choosing a career, for their very position (by way of scholarships) is conditional upon their serving their patron, the government, for a number of years following graduation. This pressure is even stronger for those sent overseas, who are "bonded" to government employment for a minimum of seven years on their return. Women in high-ranking positions in the civil service, university faculties, and even in the armed forces and police, not to mention those who eventually enter industry and the private sector, are all faced with problems of adjusting to jobs for which there are few precedents or role models for females, as well as the inevitable reshuffling of their personal and family obligations. To this I shall return in Chapter 5.

THE WIDER MUSLIM WORLD

Although Malaysian Islam faithfully reflects many of the interests, conflicts, and cleavages of the home front, it derives much of its impetus from overseas connections, as it has done in the past. In contrast with the past, however, when most Islamic news and views were filtered almost exclusively through the ulama and a few returning hajis, today the contacts are more diverse and direct, and many individuals and groups have both physical and intellectual access to events in the religious heartland. As a result, there is a greater variety of religious interpretation and style in modern Malaysia and more opportunity for contact with Muslims from outside the country. The overseas students are a case in point.

Through their connections with the Middle East and the Arab world, Malays have become more sensitive to the curious ambivalences of modern Islam. On the one hand, the politics of oil and its economic consequences for the prosperity of many Muslim countries has led to an upsurge of confidence in their own position and identity, compensating for centuries of slights and humiliations suffered at the hands of western Christians and others, whether the fall of Baghdad in 1258, the loss of Spain in 1492, of Malacca in 1511, or of Java in 1596. On the other hand, there remains a pervasive pride in an ancient and splendid Islamic civilization, which will be revived in defiance of temporary national, political, and other barriers and of the current subordination of Islamic philosophy and science to western technology. These sentiments have led, in recent years, to an orientation among some Muslims to the past and have fed the tendency towards fundamentalism. It was in the context of such sentiments that the Muslim year 1400, ushering in the fifteenth century, 22 November 1979, was to have been the critical turning point and the dawn of a glorious new era for Islam. It was also to be a fulfilment of a prophecy dating from the time of the Hadith, that the first 700 years of an expanding faith would be followed by a 700-year "dark age," when Islam was on the wane, or at least on the defensive, after which a third glorious era (*zaman gemilang*) to parallel the first would emerge and Iran was seen as the portent of this. Many speeches and predictions were made to that effect throughout the Muslim world, including Malaysia, as the new century approached. Some of the celebration and anticipation turned to anxiety and doubt, however, as a dissident political-cum-religious[18] group chose this occasion to invade and occupy the Grand Mosque (*Masjid Il-Haram*) in Mecca. At first, Malaysian religious and government authorities were uncertain how to construe this inauspicious beginning to the anticipated new age, but fearing its revolutionary implications and the possible effects on Muslim youth, they were officially negative and classed the event along with dangerously extremist and deviant messianic rebellions that have punctuated Muslim history elsewhere (cf. *New Straits Times* 25/11/79).

Common faith for the Muslim world does not, of course, bring with it political unity, nor yet consensus over social or economic philosophy. Some areas have made experiments with socialism, as in Libya and Syria, while others such as Morocco, Saudi Arabia, and many Gulf Emirates, are conservative monarchies. Yet other variants are Pakistan's military régime, and the new Islamic state of Iran. Internal politics in these countries, as in Malaysia, reflect, or are reflected by, religious movements and the activities of the Islamic Brotherhoods. *Jamaat Islam* and *Al-Ikhwan* are now part of the political equation in Egypt, the Sudan, and Syria. All of these groups, as the Malaysian government is well aware, have their roots in youth and student movements of the kind now emergent in Malaysia, and some of the support for Ayatollah Khomeini came from this constituency. All the above are basically fundamentalist in religious orientation. Egypt's Jamaat Islam in particular closely resembles Malaysia's ABIM in its membership concentration among high-school and university students, and its self-cultivated image of a religious welfare organization, but with covert political ambitions.

Regardless of political orientation, reports from all corners of the Muslim world, from Indonesia to Morocco, comment on the rising tide of religious awareness[20] and incidence of rededication among the youth, marked publicly by high rates of mosque attendance, rejection of western and "worldly" entertainments, and greater attention to modest attire, which make some of the younger generation more conservative than their parents. In international affairs, the spirit of Islam is probably higher today than it has been for many decades, and there is pride in being Muslim. For Malays and other "peripheral" Muslims, this association provides a new, world-centred source of identity, whereby a once little-known people are now linked with people who are very well known indeed.

If there is a common thread in these assorted changes and movements across the Muslim world, it can probably be derived from the problem of authority. The age-old questions in Islam, transcending specific political parties, régimes, or philosophies, of the balance or "mix" of sacred and secular, of the role of the ulama, and of the nature of the Islamic state, constantly resurface through these various forms. Also played out are the continuing themes of fundamentalism versus modernism ("reform"), ijma versus ijtihad, and the relationship of specifically Arabic customs to the requirements of Islam. Finally, there is the common antipathy, at all levels, to the west, and the old anti-Christian crusade or jihad spirit has been rekindled. All of the above helped to shape the contemporary religious scene and to shake the status quo. It is reinforced by a constant shuttle of mutual visiting and staging of Islamic conferences within the Muslim circuit both by official and independent revivalist or dakwah bodies. In light of all this activity, it is not surprising that the Malaysian authorities are concerned with the ultimate aims of its own revivalists, for it is obvious that one of the vital issues is the political legitimacy and acceptability, not to mention moral rating, when judged by strict Islamic standards, of the authorities themselves.

Finally, on a totally different front, official Malaysia regards itself as beleaguered by another ideological and political behemoth: communism, both internal and external. Ever since the Emergency[21] (1948-60), substantial underground activity by "communists" has continued in Thai border areas. The alleged China connection of the communists has been much stressed by Malaysian government releases, in keeping with its general ethnic cosmology, although it is known that there are Malay members. Reciprocally played down is the contribution to the "terrorist/guerrilla" scene of dissident Muslim irredentists on the Thai side of the border. Acknowledgment of this problem would overcomplicate the otherwise more simple dichotomy between Chinese-communist troublemakers versus Malay-Muslim/ non-communist peasants. Communism, whether of Chinese, Vietnamese, or more recently, Soviet-in-Afghanistan provenance, has the power to mobilize Islamic sentiments as only atheism and westernism otherwise can, and all are equally seen as variants of the devil incarnate (syaitan) and enemies of the Muslim community.

Since 1969, the overall political and social climate of Malaysia has been marked by progressive "tightening of the screws," in which the federal government has created powerful and far-reaching new policies and centralized old ones, has appropriated to itself greater powers, and has reduced the autonomy of opinion and action of other institutions and bodies. Ever conscious of the fragility of National Front consociation and of the potential sources of disunity in the Malay-Muslim community itself, whether along lines of generation, class, residence, political ideology, and, now, religious orientation, the dominant party of the coalition, UMNO, must exercise all its ingenuity to create a sense of unity of purpose and identity. In this enterprise, it must face the obstacles of the constitutional strength and virtual autonomy of the state in matters of religion. Religion, as yet not a "sensitive" topic, is fast becoming the idiom in which other officially sensitive issues are expressed and debated. By its very nature and status in Malay society, religion, especially Islam, is immune from direct frontal attack and must itself be used in retaliation against those whose ammunition it has become. Islam, therefore, is now the banner under which all manner of interests and groups play out their contests of power and authority, from the sultans to the special-interest youth, student, rural, and other constituencies.

The government must wield this two-edged sword with care. On the one hand, with its Bumi Malay policies, it continues to promote the traditional Melayu culture and values and the ideals of absolute loyalty as the foundation of unity and identity. On the other hand, it self-righteously appropriates the symbols of Islam against other Malays and to its own political cause. As a result, the dakwah religious revival has become, in the 1970's and 1980's, a crucial ideological and political arena for a number of very basic problems in Malay and Malaysian society and may be the turning point of the future.

4

The Urban Religious Revival: Development of Dakwah

What is popularly referred to as the "dakwah movement" in the Malaysia of the 1970's and 1980's is by no means as monolithic, unified, or co-ordinated in ideology or organization as it may appear to outsiders. It is a loose term which, for locals, concisely sums up an aggregate of trends, activities, ideas, and associations, each of which, in its own way, promotes or nurtures the cause of Islam.

One characteristic the various dakwah elements in Malaysia have in common is the fact that they are "non-establishment" groups in that they have no traditional, legal, historical, or other institutional basis for their authority, but have risen spontaneously and independently. They are easily vulnerable to representations that they are non-legitimate by government authorities, who would prefer to keep to themselves all rights of political power in its broadest sense. Religious power and authority is likewise jealously guarded by those who have held it longer, that is, the ulama of the older rural tradition, religious councils, and sometimes even the sultans. Dakwah in Malaysia, therefore, reflects aspects of relationships and conflicts which have long existed under other names and banners.

Strictly, in the Muslim ummat at large, dakwah is intrinsic to the faith, the duty of all its followers. Every Muslim should be a *da'i* or evangelist. Dakwah as a mission can be intended as a revitalization of the flagging spirits of the lapsed Muslim or as call to non-Muslims or infidels to convert to the faith. The term *da'awat* comes from the Arabic root *da'a*, "to call" or, more delicately, "to invite," which in the religious context means a call to join the faith. There are many precedents in Islamic history for more specialized uses of dakwah, sometimes with political implications (*Encyclopaedia of Islam*

1965:168). On some occasions dakwah was invoked by parties claiming the right to both civil and spiritual authority over Muslim subjects in theocratic states as a validation of their cause and legitimacy. At other times, the religious rationale has just as readily been used by governments to brand political opponents as "false prophets." Again, the line between religion and politics is a thin one. Dakwah can be carried out in any one or a combination of three ways: by force (*paksa*), as in the constant strivings of jihad; through the art of gentle persuasion and instructional, educational, and other participatory activities; and the softest touch of all, by example, whereby the high ideals and superior moral behaviour of the faithful are sufficient to inspire others to greater dedication and zeal.

So essential to Islam is the communication of its message and spirit through instruction and other forms of revitalization that four more precisely detailed modes of dakwah are distinguished. The first of these is known as *tabligh* and consists of explaining the tenets of the faith and its virtues but without any connotations of force or pressure to follow. Those who practise tabligh, as bearers of the message, are called *muballigh*. The second, *taklim*, is concerned with teaching in order to "increase the knowledge of the learner" and is commonly used in the context of instruction on the basic religious obligations of prayer, fasting, and so on. Included in taklim is a form of instruction, popular in Malaysia, known as *tamrin*, or leadership, which involves courses for the training of new missionaries and organizers for the Muslim community. Like tabligh, taklim implies a "low-key" mission. *Tadzkir* consists of reminding the "lapsed" or forgetful members of the faith of their neglected obligations in areas of prayer, fasting, giving of alms, and charity and encouraging a general tightening up of their religious life in order to gain blessings (berkat). Finally, tasywir aims at awakening a broader religious consciousness and tries to establish a framework by which to guide the Muslim in the conduct of an exemplary daily life (cf. Ma'aruf Salleh 1979). With the exception of tadzkir, which is specifically intended to recall the "born" Muslim back to the straight and narrow path, the other three missionary or dakwah modes can be directed towards Muslims and non-Muslims alike.

Historically, dakwah in its generic sense has been associated with a wide range of expressions and meanings from an almost unspoken, but implicitly accepted duty, to identification with specific political causes. In the contemporary Middle East, there is little doubt as to the political significance of Islam, but at present, the term dakwah does not seem to be associated with these forces. This too was the situation in Malaysia until the 1960's turned into the 1970's. Before this, dakwah was a term little known or used, save by ulama familiar with religious vocabulary, but it drew little public attention and stirred no controversy. Today, by contrast, even when used in its original sense, dakwah has the power to stir many more and stronger emotions, and its use is commonly associated with some value-laden message of approval or disapproval. To label another individual as "dakwah" is to register a judgment, positive or negative, of both the individual in question and of the orientation in general.

Behaviours now labelled as dakwah are most visible and audible in sectors of public life. Overflowing attendance at the mosques, especially by the young, is particularly striking when the overflow backs up into the street, and the proliferation of public religious lectures, conferences, and special events are announced and well attended everywhere. Dress styles are among the most immediately arresting signs of the times, and for both men and women they are moving closer to the Arab pattern, with loose, body-obscuring robes for both sexes. For the men, the robe, or jubah, is usually either white or green (Islam's holy colour) and accompanied by a white or green skull-cap or turban (serban) and leather sandals. Women cover their heads with a short head-veil somewhat resembling a nun's wimple, although in Malaysia, only a minority affect a face veil too. Some of the more zealous may also hide their hands and feet with gloves and socks, although this is not strictly required by Islam even in Arabia. Some dakwah followers have rather dramatically cast away their television sets, western furniture, and other worldly items of western origin, but the number and significance of these events has probably been greatly exaggerated by the media, and the same few examples seem to be recycled on the lips of the more unsympathetic elements of the public. Dakwah influence has also made itself felt in the realm of entertainment, increasing the religious content of radio and television programmes and the arts generally and resulting in severe restrictions on "immoral" western entertainments from films to night-clubs.

In popular conversation, dakwah in Malaysia, apart from the kinds of behaviour mentioned, often refers to one or other of three nationally known organizations or movements, which for many Malaysians have become the epitome and totality of what dakwah is all about. The three organizations concerned are: ABIM (*Angkatan Belia Islam Malaysia*), or Islamic Youth League of Malaysia; Darul Arqam, "House of Arqam," (after Arqam who was one of the friends and protectors of the Prophet Mohammed); and Jemaat Tabligh (the "missionary" association).

To ask whether an individual is "into dakwah" (*berdakwah*) often first elicits a response reflecting that person's organizational affiliations or sympathies: "he/she is an ABIM person," "a member of Darul Arqam," or "he goes to Tabligh meetings," and so on. Even when specific organizational connections are not known, they are often automatically assumed to exist if the individual exhibits behaviours now generally identified with popular images of dakwah. Thus any male or female who affects strict Muslim attire (whether Arab style or not) is labelled "dakwah" and by implication linked to all that the named dakwah organizations stand for. So common are such assumptions that some individuals are intimidated from closer adherence to Muslim requirements for fear of being tarred with the dakwah brush. One man, for example, who had never been in the habit of wearing the Malay-Muslim fez (songkok), published an article in a local journal accompanied by a formal personal photograph in which he appeared in his "Friday songkok." For many weeks thereafter, it was only through vehement protestations that he was able to convince his friends that he had not, in fact, "gone over to dakwah." In the popular image, dakwah also tends to be associated with the young, intellectual urban-dweller. This has a high correspondence with reality, but, at the same time, it oversimplifies by suggesting too neat a dichotomy between urban and rural religious practices. It thus obscures any continuity and interaction between these two constituencies. These popular and official views are more or less summed up in a 1977 statement by the then minister of Youth, Culture and Sports (of Nasrul Haq fame), who regretted that so many "fanatics were misusing dakwah by refusing to watch TV or listen to the radio," and he remarked that, sadly, in this group are "our young people with the highest education, including teachers, engineers, accountants, government servants and other professionals (*Utusan Malaysia* 24/4/77). This to him was well-nigh inexplicable.

Views such as this one show up the ambivalence of many non-involved Malay Muslims towards dakwah. Whereas there is a general agreement and consensus on the importance and desirability of strong religious commitment — or possibly apprehension over public expression of sentiments which could be construed as critical of Islam —, there still exists some uncertainty among older, more traditional Malays over the extremes to which some youth are prepared to go in their religious zeal. Some parents, for example, are concerned lest their offspring throw away, in one dramatic move, all the benefits that advanced education should bring and on which their seniors at least had set their hearts. Among these are the parents of the university students who "find dakwah" while on overseas scholarships or who are introduced to it on a home campus, who then abandon the "materialistic" and secular western education and lifestyle and, with it, not only their radios and furniture, but also their job prospects and the anticipated and reflected glory for their families. Mothers too are concerned that their daughters, by adopting the more extreme forms of Arab-like dress, are embarking on something which cannot be reversed without appearing to be turning back on Islam or reneging on a commitment undertaken. The mothers feel that their daughters may be cutting themselves off not only from the vices but also some of the innocent pleasures of youth and that they might regret it later. More seriously still, parents contend that the marriage prospects of dakwah offspring may be severely curtailed, and selection of an appropriate spouse may be unnecessarily difficult. It frequently leads to a situation in which the young people are unwilling to heed their parents' choice but prefer to seek a compatible fellow dakwah practitioner. Where the dakwah commitment also leads to a rejection of non-Islamic Malay adat too, of which the marriage rituals are among the most prominent, then the parents feel a double deprivation. By failing to hold as elaborate and generous a ceremony and feast (bersanding and kenduri) as means permit, they lose in social standing and risk gossip over the propriety of the marriage or about the reputation of the spouses themselves. Whether they are urban parents, whose often material, middle-class lifestyle is the object of rejection, or kampung parents, whose adat-based social life, with its sometimes questionable Islamic orthodoxy, is under fire, dakwah helps to create or feed the generation gap. It was this factor which stirred the same minister of Youth, Culture and Sports, quoted above, to deplore the effects of dakwah on the family and household (*keruntuhan rumahtangga*). There are, too, other apparently trivial considerations, of concern to mothers, such as the tendency to skin irritations and hair problems which result from constant binding, constriction, and lack of "airing" of the Arab dress in Malaysia's tropical climate. Fired by such concerns, some parents, like their counterparts in the west whose offspring have joined esoteric cults, attempt to have their children "deprogrammed" by employing a trusted family religious teacher (ustaz) for debriefing instruction.[1]

DAKWAH ORGANIZATIONS

"Independent" Dakwah Organizations

A prominent Malay religious teacher (ustaz) has publicly commented that there are in Malaysia, and in Islam generally, three kinds of (not necessarily mutually exclusive) religious leaders: those who support the government; those who perpetuate the venerable scholarly tradition by transmission from guru to disciple; and finally, those who "arise spontaneously" (*muncul dengan tiba-tiba*) without any of the traditional bases of authority. It is into this last category that most of the leaders of the three principal urban dakwah organizations would fall, notably those in ABIM. Further, all of the three, ABIM, Darul Arqam, and Jemaat Tabligh, are independent, in the sense that they do not support, nor are they supported by, the political status quo. If anything, they are seen as a potential political thorn in official sides.

Each of these organizations differs in its mode of operation and has its own distinctive style, but ultimately, they all have similar goals. Simply put, these include the rekindling of the religious spirit and entrenchment of

Islamic values in Malay society. Their target is invariably the "born" Muslim — principally Malay — population, and with the partial exception of Jemaat Tabligh, they make little attempt to recruit or interest non-Malays, despite the intent of the original spirit of dakwah. Dakwah in Malaysia is particularistic, not universalistic and aims at a remobilization of Malay interests and consciousness as a distinctive community, one which may create models, but not brothers, for the non-Malays. Beyond their ethnic and national boundaries, the only ties these organizations cultivate are with Muslims in other countries and associations.

A prominent feature shared by all three organizations, albeit to different degrees, along with most of their confrères in other parts of the Muslim world, is a strong streak of fundamentalism, which in the case of some spokesmen and members manifests itself as an extreme dedication to atavistic forms of Arabism, some of whose connections with Islam are tenuous and the result more of historical coincidence than theological requirement. The tone of all three organizations is decidedly traditional with considerable emphasis on the past. Without pressing the parallel too closely, the dakwah movements call to mind the "back to the primitive church" of Christian sectarians, relying heavily on the authority and literal interpretation of the scriptures. They favour an unquestioning acceptance of the religious tradition and scholarship as it had crystallized by the twelfth-century early Islamic period (ijma) without further exegesis or reinterpretation. Not for them the redefining of Islamic goals in the light of unfolding conditions and times (ijtihad). Rather, their quest is for an authority whose venerability cannot be doubted. Given that many of the "spontaneous" new leaders are not in the direct line of intellectual descent (isnad) from past scholars as "heirs of the Prophet" (*pewaris Nabi*), it is particularly important for them to create a convincing and unchallengeable tie through other means. This orientation is in marked contrast to the approach of such reformist movements as Indonesia's *Muhammadiyah*. As described by Geertz (1963) and Peacock (1978 a and b), Muhammadiyah encouraged innovations (*bida'ah*) conducive to the requirements of a rising merchant class with modern educational and economic needs. Despite close Malay-Indonesian ties in the earlier Melayu Raya and Nusantara contexts, neither Muhammadiyah nor its spirit ever really took hold in Malaysia.[2] Similarly, the free interpretation which allows, on the basis of reason and analogy (*al-urf*), that certain actions, whether or not specifically sanctioned by the Koran, are acceptable, receives little attention by exegesists. In this respect, Malay dakwah followers espouse the views of the Maulana al-Maudoodi, one of their principal mentors and heroes. Maudoodi, who died in 1980, was a Pakistani whose voluminous writings (many in English) have probably inspired more Muslim youth on the international scene than any other commentator in recent years. Maudoodi's application of the Koran to modern life leads him to conclude, for example, that women are unsuited to leadership roles and that popular elections are un-Islamic. It is but a short step from such fundamentalism to a form of anti-westernism as representative of a culture of decadence, supporting a lifestyle in conflict with the principles of Islam. Anti-western sentiments thus fuel and justify a number of the religious fires of young dakwah followers. To the extent that the dakwah followers (and al-Maudoodi) extol the pristine virtues of seventh-century Arabic culture and take refuge in the authority of the scriptures, they are less disposed to debate more profound philosophical or theological issues such as the meaning of life, suffering, or even the question of revelation itself. Their approach to the Prophet Mohammed is as to a "tape-recorder," whose message is played over again and again but can never be adapted to circumstances as they arise. Yet even this conservatism or caution does not insulate the scripturalists entirely from charges of heresy, if only for political reasons.

The modern dakwah organizations tend to be critical of the syncretic and frankly non-Islamic elements of Malay adat, on grounds that such customs are not mentioned in, and some even discouraged by, the Koran (see above, Chapter 3). This attitude has led to a reinforcement of a number of old dichotomies, adat/Islam, rural/urban, old/young, more/less educated and forms the basis of the discussion in Chapter 5.

Finally, if dakwah protagonists are not in total agreement among themselves over specific goals or unified politically and organizationally, they find it relatively easy to define common enemies. Aside from "communists" and "socialists" and the generalized unbeliever (*jahiliyyah*; kafir), the principal enemy is clearly the west. Whether for its aggressive educational system and scientific practices, for its materialism and moral decadence, for its "godlessness," for particular political policies such as its alleged support of Zionism against the Arabs, or for its various colonial and neo-colonial roles, the west is the arch-villain, even the devil incarnate (syaitan). Many dakwah commentators attribute most of the evils of contemporary Malaysian society to the invidious influence of the west, through its schools, technology, and economic interests in the country. This cultural opposition is symbolized by calls for a struggle more ideological than physical between the two systems.

ABIM

When dakwah is mentioned or discussed in Malaysia, many minds turn first to ABIM, the Muslim Youth League of Malaysia. ABIM was an outgrowth of the PKPIM, providing those leaving their youth and student status behind with an associational basis for activity without contravening the Universities

Act. As an organization, ABIM's membership is not clearly defined as in a truly corporate group or exclusive religious sect. While it has a definite, committee-style leadership and a network of branches at state and local levels, its following tends to "fade out" on the fringes. Many individuals sympathize without formally joining, and university students have to be particularly circumspect in this regard, owing to the ban on "political" activities on campuses. Despite the problem of defining membership, ABIM's leaders estimate its numerical strength to be in the region of 35,000 (in 1980), with a steady annual growth from the 153 charter members present at its inception to approximately 9,000 in 1972, 11,000 in 1974, and 20,000 in 1977. Of the current 35,000, 90 per cent are estimated to be between fifteen and forty years of age, with about 11 per cent female representation.

Leadership and Membership

Recalling ABIM's origins, the founders and first leaders were many of the same individuals active in the student organizations which preceded them, notably the Malay Language Society at the University of Malaya and PKPIM. At its official inauguration, in the Faculty of Islamic Studies at the National University in 1971, ABIM received official approval from the presence of the minister of Youth, Culture, and Sports (presumably in his first capacity), the predecessor of the minister of Nasrul Haq fame. It was duly registered as a voluntary association under the Societies Act in 1972. ABIM's best known president, Anwar Ibrahim, whose name is now a household word among most Malays, was initially ABIM's public relations officer, later its secretary, and its president from 1974 to 1982. In the days before ABIM, he had been president of both the Malay Language Society and of PKPIM. There was an uneasy hiatus between 1974 and 1975 when Anwar was in detention for his part in the Baling affair, but he rapidly became firmly entrenched as the core and leading light of ABIM, whose authority derived, not from a traditional isnad, nor yet from formal religious training or connection with ulama families, and certainly not from venerability of age, but exclusively from an intensely personal appeal.

With his formidable combination of qualities, Anwar was long sought after by various organizations and causes, including at least two prime ministers. The first overture, by Tun Abdul Razak, was rejected, but the second, by Dr. Mahathir in 1982, he surprisingly accepted, as he did an invitation to run for an UMNO seat in the general election of that year, which he won. This, of course, was the end of Anwar's career with ABIM. Whatever his cause or affiliation, Anwar can only be placed in the category of "spontaneously arisen" leaders, and like most of his kind, he has the gift of touching the interests and sensitivities and of gauging the level of sophistication of his audience with great skill. For example, when speaking to students, he makes liberal use of academic references and peppers his language with English expressions—despite the history of his campaigns through the Malay Language Society—and he can be appealingly humorous. When addressing soldiers, he tends to play up the element of "struggle" (*perjuangan*; jihad) in both the symbolic and physical senses, but he appears less comfortable with rural audiences. His greatest appeal is undoubtedly to the set from which he "spontaneously arose," namely, the young, urban, middle-class Malay with higher education. It is clear that part of his "charisma" (as with traditional rural ulama) lies in the fortuitousness of the timing of his entry onto the Islamic stage in Malaysia when the urban educational explosion affecting Malay youth was beginning to create the problems of adjustment and identity described in the previous chapter.

Anwar himself was born in the late 1940's into a middle-class urban Malay family in the northern town of Bukit Mertajam, where his father was once a UMNO official. Despite the fact that Bukit Mertajam is noted for its many religious schools, both pondok and madrasah, Anwar went to none of these, and his early schooling was entirely secular. His secondary training was completed at the prestigious Malay College in Kuala Kangsar,[3] and this was followed by a B.A. in Malay Studies at the University of Malaya in 1971. Old classmates recall that he displayed qualities of leadership even while at the Malay College and joined the PKPIM while still in Sixth Form, although at that time, he was not particularly noted for any marked religiosity. His early career as an activist centred far more upon issues of Malayness, and his shift to use of religious idiom only came with the birth of ABIM and with the growing problems of overt political expression.

Of the thirteen original leaders and office-holders of ABIM, Anwar included, the oldest was born in 1937, and most of the others in the mid-1940's. Given the structure of the educational system during their childhood, these leaders invariably had primary schooling in Malay, followed by a transfer to an English-medium secondary school, via a transitional "remove" class, usually in a larger urban centre. Finally, all of them underwent some kind of tertiary education of special training, either in a university, polytechnic, or training college. Fewer of these young men had been exposed to the intensive Koranic instruction than the older generation or their more rural cousins, however, and today, this deficiency is deplored both by them and by other commentators on the educational and leadership scene (cf. Ismail Ibrahim 1977). The orientation of their advanced training, however, divides the ABIM leadership into two distinct cohorts. The first, a total of seven, received a typical western education or diploma in such fields as language and literature, engineering, management and accountancy, or administration and diplomatic training, while the second, six in all, were trained in religious institutions of higher learning, such as the Islamic College in Malaysia or Al-Azhar University in Cairo. More recently, an increasing number of ABIM leaders and lecturers have been products of the National University's Faculty of Islamic Studies, whose first graduates only emerged in 1974.[4] All of ABIM's leaders, like Anwar, had been active in a variety of associations since their secondary school days, although in that era the organizations' focus was more commonly on Malay than Islamic interests. All of those who went overseas held office in their local Malay Students' associations and were thus already socialized into leadership roles. Now that they are no longer students, their current occupations range through university lecturers, accountants, engineers, to administrators. A number of sympathizers in the civil service and other government employ, however, have dropped their formal membership for fear of reprisals or "blacklisting," as one of them put it, and the possible loss of their jobs. Some ABIM members in Kelantan state posts were reportedly "replaced" with only twenty-four hours' notice because of their affiliation (*Risalah*, April 1978:8). Of the original thirteen leaders, only one was a woman, with a B.A. from the National University, after earlier training in the Islamic College and with a sequence of Malay primary and English secondary schooling and associational activity parallel to that of the males. Predictably, she was the first head of the women's section of ABIM, HELWA (*Hal Ehwal Wanita ABIM*).

Detractors of ABIM frequently call attention to the lack of depth of religious experience and learning of so many of its leaders and complain that very young overseas ABIM followers are presuming to lead the prayers and giving sermons "like an imam" for which they are allegedly ill-prepared (*Watan* 16/5/80). In face of this constant battle for legitimacy and in the absence of a convincing isnad, ABIM members have tried to cultivate the "service" of already established and commanding religious figures with a reputation of independence from any other constituency or interest. One of those most frequently invoked is Syed Naguib al-Attas, now a hero of the organization, both in his capacity as professor and dean at the National University and as a noted Islamic historian and religious scholar. Syed Naguib stems from an illustrious family of Arab descent and is distinguished for his studies of Sufism and for his anti-westernism. Whenever possible, other well-known scholars and professors are also called upon to speak on behalf of ABIM, for example, Deliar Noer, an Indonesian with a Cornell Ph.D., now teaching in Australia, and as a recent dakwah "convert" himself also vehemently anti-western. Another anti-western firebrand is Professor Ismail al Faruqi of Lebanese origin, who holds a permanent post in a university in the United States. Both of the latter are examples of scholars who use western science against itself, who travel international circuits on their newly discovered dakwah trail, and who exert substantial influence on overseas Muslim students in their areas.

Of the original ABIM membership, based on an early list (later ones were allegedly destroyed by insects), 32 per cent were drawn from white-collar office-workers, 26 per cent from teachers, 13 per cent from students, 8 per cent were self-employed workers, with 21 per cent assorted "others" (Harun Haji Salieh 1976). ABIM now has branches in all states of West Malaysia, although its greatest strength still lies in the larger towns and the universities. Probably only a small minority are familiar with and clearly understand the goals and principles of ABIM or have any conscious plan to serve it personally before joining the organization. Many more, as is evident from local seminars around the country, join ABIM for reasons of nationalism or to lobby for Malay interests (where prohibited from political activity by the Universities Act), while some members, according to suspicious insiders, are government infiltrators, or "enemies in the blanket." An example of the latter is a member of one of the minority political parties, Kemas, whose platform is avowedly multi-racial and supportive of social reforms. This individual feels he can "work" more effectively covertly from within ABIM to subvert what he considers to be the chauvinism and excesses of the movement. To date, ABIM has few followers in rural areas, save for some returned students and administrators. As will be seen, some traditional ulama feel threatened by, or are antagonistic to, these youthful self-proclaimed religious zealots and missionaries.

Aims and Activities

For a confraternity of Malay youth, without a legitimate outlet for political causes and interests, the religious banner remained the only one available, and thus it became strategically, as well as ideologically central. The kinds of ethnic and social issues which motivated and mobilized the PKPIM and Language Society continued under the Islamic rubric, and this generated a need for a much deeper investment in Islamic studies and civilization for credibility. Now one of ABIM's principal concerns is to provide intensive information and training through a perpetual round of lectures, conferences, seminars, and leadership and cadre training courses (*tamrin kader*) all over the country. Those who have been overseas have often found themselves religiously "exposed" in comparison with fellow Muslims from elsewhere and have tried to compensate by reading the texts and publications circulated by Pakistanis and others attending their religious activities and by attempting to learn Arabic. Through these contacts, many Malays have discovered the works of al-Maudoodi and become aware of the fundamental religious and political issues faced by contemporary Muslims everywhere. Under these pressures, the adoption of Arab dress may be at worst a cover for inner theological and spiritual uncertainty, but in any case, it is an outward manifestation of a renewed religious commitment and self-realization.

The level of theological and philosophical debate among the newly conscious Muslims, overseas or at home, is not always profound, but it tends to settle more on issues of Muslim identity and relations with non-Muslims, whether as "foreign students" or on the international political stage. Nevertheless, on the home front, ABIM members give the impression of a certain religious and moral superiority, at times even arrogance, in their goal of eradicating what they perceive as ignorance and misunderstanding of the "true Islam" by most Malays. Dakwah is thus aimed squarely at Muslims in a form of spiritual rehabilitation and as an attempt to convince Malays that there are more desirable alternatives to the western materialist approach to life. This is just one of several reasons why ABIM is less popular in rural areas, where the principal aspirations of many peasants is for the urban amenities and luxuries promised by modernization, development schemes, and five-year plans, a goal not to be surrendered too lightly. Anwar himself recognized this problem (personal communication). This perceived arrogance towards rural-dwellers is reinforced by ABIM's attacks on Malay adat which forms the basis of kampung social life, including marriage customs, silat, some folk curing and, of course, Nasrul Haq.

Since 1973, ABIM has published its own journal, *Risalah*,[5] as well as a voluminous flow of tracts and pamphlets, many of them translations and imports from other Muslim countries.

Among the more impressive achievements of ABIM is the series of independent schools it has established in five urban centres of West Malaysia offering an alternate form of education to the present ministry secondary school system. The goal of these schools, which operate only at the secondary level, is to combine religious and secular education patterns in such a way that pupils can both sit for the national promotional examinations which open the doors of occupational opportunity to government and private sector and receive a solid religious and moral foundation for life as good Muslims. In this respect they are not unlike the better nizami-madrasah schools of the older tradition. This arrangement has the advantage that in the event that a pupil fails the government exams,[6] he or she can be reassured that the exams are not to be taken so seriously in the broader scheme of things and that God obviously has other plans for the failed candidate. These pupils can then be channelled into other occupations, such as working for ABIM, or as religious teachers (ustaz). Most of the (approximately forty) ABIM schoolteachers are dedicated ABIM members, who either "moonlight" from other jobs—

many are lecturers at the local universities—or are willing to devote themselves, part- or full-time, to the enterprise, despite a salary far below government rates. At present, several eager young women graduates from MARA Institute of Technology seem particularly prominent among the staff, although cynics have unkindly and unverifiably suggested that this is because they failed to graduate or get better jobs, or even, originally, were fascinated with Anwar as an attractive male.

The schools cover all the main academic subjects which occupy about 60 per cent of the curriculum, while religious law, jurisprudence, ethics, and Arabic are compulsory. Even the academic subjects have a distinctive Islamic flavour. Geography, for example, is taught from the standpoint of man's misuse of God's well-designed environment, while history emphasizes a divine plan, including the unfolding of Islam, and even major scientific theories, whether in the realm of atoms, astronomy or genetics can be proven to have their germs in a Koranic base. ABIM's view is that science is part of a legitimate Islamic tradition, and insofar as it does not conflict with religious values, it may be pursued, as it was by such Muslim luminaries as Avicenna. It is only the western "abuse" of science which should be avoided, for the disastrous consequences that have sometimes resulted from it. The unique ABIM slant on academic subjects is presented in its two monthly journals for high schools, *Diskusi* and *Potensi*.

By 1980 the number of pupils at ABIM's Kuala Lumpur branch, *Yayasan Anda* (literally, "your institution") had reached 1,300, many of them from outside the capital, residing in an attached hostel. The other four branches are in Bukit Mertajam, Ipoh, Kuala Trengganu and Kota Bharu, and they also have large student enrolments. Among modern Malays, the lure of education is very strong, particularly as a means to occupational mobility, and for which many Malay parents are willing to make substantial sacrifice.[7] When pupils fail government exams, they are frequently despatched to one of a number of flourishing "cram" or rehabilitation schools for a second try. Part of the appeal of Yayasan Anda lies in this second function, and undoubtedly many of its pupils are drop-outs or failures from ministry schools, looking for a second—or even third—opportunity in the religious option. Just as some poorer rural parents continue to "feed" the pondok religious schools with pupils who have failed the secular stream, so those with more means "feed" Yayasan Anda. The built-in religious option is, however, an added incentive, for many parents still value religious education and find the combination attractive. The schools foster an Islamic way of life in all daily activities, including full Muslim dress, segregated seating by sex in class, lack of emphasis on sports, and recreation hours filled with extra religious lectures. Whatever the formal curriculum, the ethos that emanates informally from

Yayasan Anda schools tends to be one of a strong sense of Malay exclusiveness, reinforced by the intensity and solidarity of close physical and social accommodation. By the time they leave the schools, many pupils are attached to ABIM, and the most promising have been recruited to represent their schools at university religious conferences where they are encouraged to spread further the word (dakwah) among friends and acquaintances.

In the case of the ABIM school in Bukit Mertajam, home of Anwar and of many traditional religious schools, ABIM has formed an alliance with an existing, once highly prestigious madrasah. The latter provides the religious content of the curriculum and guides for its teachers while ABIM takes care of the secular side. This is an example of a successful adaptation by one of the older religious institutions under pressures described in Chapter 2 which prevents their "going out of business" completely.

One other early activity of ABIM was an attempt at a co-operative economic enterprise (*Syamelin*, or *Syarikat Melayu Internasional Malaysia*). First registered in 1971, it is now virtually defunct. Its underlying rationale was both religious and ethnic in its goal of raising the economic level of the Malay through the provision of an exclusively Malay trade and marketing network, although based on strictly Islamic principles (*"berlandaskan kepada perjuangan ummat Islam, khususnya bagi bangsa Melayu"*). Once again, Syamelin was the brain-child of eager young students, whose idealism somewhat exceeded their funds, economic experience, and sophistication. It was optimistically launched with an initial basic capital of M$493, provided by PKPIM. A subsequent government loan through MARA provided the foundation for two or three years of training for its members and aspiring shareholders who were mostly students (including high-school pupils), a few government servants, and policemen. This was sufficient for them to open a few private shops and supply centres for the marketing of goods produced exclusively by Malays such as spices, coffee, cooking oil, noodles, and so on, with the aim of by-passing the "non-Muslim" (Chinese) domestic market. Syamelin concentrated on the more traditional Malay areas of North Malaysia, especially Kedah, Kelantan, Trengganu, Negri Sembilan, and not too surprisingly, Anwar's home area around Bukit Mertajam in Province Wellesley. At its peak (ca. 1973), Syamelin had over eight thousand members and about thirty shops. Lack of co-operation by major commodity suppliers including such foreign companies as Nestlé and severe transport problems eventually reduced Syamelin to a ghost enterprise, and ABIM turned its attention to other issues. However, the theme of religious and ethnic independence and the goal of raising the economic participation of the Malays is a recurring one, which comes up again in other organizations and dakwah contexts.

Social Attitudes and Issues of ABIM

In their public theology, the leaders of ABIM are the least chauvinistic of all the dakwah elements in Malaysia, and indeed they have espoused a number of reform issues that cut across ethnic boundaries. As we shall see in Chapter 7, however, these enlightened messages can become somewhat distorted in their passage down the ranks.

In one of his most widely reported speeches, at the eighth annual general meeting of ABIM (*Muktamar Senawi*) in 1979, Anwar made the strongest statement of his career on Islam's, and his own, distaste for "racism" (*'asabiyah*) and its tragic potential for such complex societies as Malaysia. Quoting from such western social scientists as Furnivall, Rex, and Banton, particularly the parts where they are most uncharitable to the racial and colonial policies of their own society, Anwar attributed the source of Malaysia's racial friction to the west itself, a colonial import. All racism and colonialism are alien to Islamic principles. This is the same Anwar who, ten years previously, was literally fighting the Malay cause in the streets of the capital and, more intellectually, through the Malay Language Society. Thus, Anwar turned the tables, and used western science against itself, a typical reversal by Malays and other Muslims trained in western disciplines and methods. Invoking the Muslim principle of the Unity of God (Tauhid), Anwar generalizes to the unity of all mankind (*"kesatuan dan persamaan manusia"*) and reiterates Islam's aversion to discrimination. While decrying narrow racial and nationalist sentiment as socially destructive, however, Anwar does not rule out forms of nationalism based on Islam (*nasionalis agama* or *wa'i Islami*), as opposed to *wa'i qawmi*, which is "racial nationalism." Thus, he subtly leaves open the door to a form of religious-based ethnicity. At the end of his Muktamar speech, Anwar enigmatically concluded that the war on poverty (*"peperangan bagi memberentas kemiskinan"*) should take priority over racial wars, a statement which, remembering Baling, is of possible far-reaching significance for Malaysia.

This speech illustrates the rather ambivalent nature of ABIM's social philosophy. On the one hand, there is evidence of a social conscience trancending "race," but this is balanced by many countervailing attitudes among its followers, especially at local levels. The active involvement of Anwar and his supporters in the Baling demonstrations, which clearly cut across ethnic lines, in the urban connection, implicitly raised class-like issues of exploitation of workers and peasants alike. This suggests a commitment to more universalistic reforms. Yet detractors argue that, for all its surface class-like character, Baling was essentially in defence of the Malay peasant, who was both its source and symbol. In keeping with the Baling precedent, at various times Anwar spoke out against corruption, especially of the élites and ruling class, although he always avoided mentioning specific cases or names. When he finally joined UMNO in his surprise move of April 1982, he made it clear that he believed Prime Minister Mahathir's anti-corruption campaigns were working. In January 1980, *Risalah* published a short statement in favour of land reform, which, given the nature of land-holding in Malaysia, could only be an oblique tilt at the Malay landowning class (including royalty). ABIM also verbally, if not actively, supported the goals of the Alor Setar demonstration of January 1980, which, like Baling, was a mobilization of Malay peasants against an allegedly callous marketing policy towards rice-producers (see Chapter 8). Here again, the ethnic and class elements cannot be easily disentangled and neither can the attitudes of ABIM as an organization. Another widely publicized case in the fall of 1979 was a statement by dakwah Malay students in the United Kingdom expressing opposition to the government's new economic policies. Among other things, the bias in favour of Malays was declared inappropriate for the success and harmony of a multi-ethnic society such as Malaysia (*Watan* 13/3/80). Not unnaturally, this was construed by UMNO as "biting the hand that fed them," as rank ingratitude, and a threat to the government itself. One immediate response was a noticeable increase in the number of visiting government representatives to foreign shores, from cabinet ministers to religious ustazes, to investigate the "deviance and misunderstanding," and to explain the policies from the official point of view.

This statement of hostility to ethnic policies, however, is counterbalanced by the nature of campus politics and the communal factions of student government in Malaysia itself, especially at the National University and the University of Malaya, where ABIM members are most heavily concentrated. It is particularly marked at the latter institution, where one of the two principal student bodies, the *Gabungan Mahasiswa*, is openly and militantly anti-Chinese, as opposed to the more ethnically neutral *Barisan Mahasiswa*, whose members the former accuse of "socialism." On most campuses too, comments and opinions expressed in seminars indicate a more narrowly Malay interpretation of dakwah and a strong support for the direction of government policies and Malay rights, sometimes combined with unabashed anti-Chinese sentiments. Whether the rationale be the indigenousness of the former or the "godlessness" and "greed" of the latter, it is now invariably couched in the language of religion, as a conflict between Muslim and non-Muslim, In closed, all-Malay gatherings and at religious meetings, some comments are unashamedly chauvinistic, along the lines that "all Chinese should be kicked out of Malaysia" (as infidels) or, worse still, should be "treated as Hitler treated the Jews." These tendencies are labelled by some observers as "Islamic Bumiputeraism." Finally, the moral impact of ABIM and other dakwah influences on the universities has had the effect of segregating the social activities of Muslim and non-Muslim or Malay and non-Malay, since the former will no longer tolerate or attend the films, dances, and other campus recreations which once provided arenas of inter-ethnic social interaction.

Perceptions of the Islamic State

On the question of the Islamic state, ABIM is cautious. To ABIM, like other dakwah groups (and also to PAS), the Islamic state is a motherhood issue, but its definition and mode of implementation are far from clear. In private discussions, Anwar confided that he dislikes the term "state" and that the emphasis should be on Islam per se, on the symbol rather than the content. The implications of an Islamic state in the fields of law, economic institutions, royalty, and, above all, for the almost 50 per cent non-Muslim "minority" in Malaysia, have yet to be worked out in detail. ABIM leaders declare their admiration and moral support for the Iranian revolution and their close ties with some of its protagonists, and ABIM representatives were among the first foreign Muslim observers to visit Iran after the February 1979 coup. However, they are equally swift to deny any intention of importing the revolution to Malaysia, and Anwar was always very sensitive to any comparison of himself and Khomeini. Nor do they see Pakistan's military régime, or Libya's and Syria's socialisms, as suitable models. Obviously, ABIM is careful to avoid political confrontation with UMNO by avoiding identification with "revolutionaries," "armies," or "socialists," all anathema to the latter. Without specifically rejecting the authority of the present Malaysian government or of the sultans, a generalized Dar-al-Islam is proposed, together with a more complete implementation of Islamic law to replace the British court system. This would involve expanding the role of the Syari'ah courts from the personal/private domain to public and criminal justice, and as in most debates of this kind, the question of the historic Muslim penalties of cutting the hands of thieves, stoning of adulterers, and so forth is a delicate topic which has not been squarely confronted. Skirting the organizational issues, ABIM spokesmen deflect attention to the positive features of "Islamic justice" as a universalistic ethical system and claim that under a Dar-al-Islam there would be fewer inequalities to lead to crimes or corrective measures in the first place. They assert that the separation of church and state in Christian countries has led to a moral decline, which justifies their appeal for greater involvement of religion in all areas of life. ABIM is on safer ground in attacking the obvious vices of abuse of drugs and alcohol, nightclubs, and the general moral laxity (*maksiat*) of modern city life, which they would have outlawed. Such bans would clearly have implications for the lifestyle of the present rulers of the country. Their reactions to the prospects of an Islamic legal system are uneasy, they attempt to retreat gracefully without appearing un-Islamic. In a 1980 statement, Syeikh Mokhsein, one of the government's religious spokesmen in the National Religious Council of the Federal Territory, put it this way: an Islamic state is an all-or-nothing matter, which he supports in principle, but since it would be precipitous and irresponsible to try to tackle so awesome a task without substantial preparation and since few Muslim states in the world have historically ever succeeded in its full implementation, Malaysia must wait a little longer and meanwhile be content to strive towards that ultimate goal (cf. Hj. Dusuki Ahmad 1980:28).

ABIM must therefore always tread carefully. Wary of offending any major constituency, whether government, the sultans, rural people, ulama, or even non-Muslims, Anwar and his successors constantly referred to ideals but rarely the details. Anwar was always quick to point out that a "good and just ruler" (khalifah or sultan) can have a legitimate place in an Islamic state and cited the rule of the second Caliph, Omar, as an example of a régime based on the Koran, which gave him the title "Commander of the Faithful (*Amirul Mumirin*). Omar ruled through a consultative council (syura), attacked corruption, and even (significantly) refused to cut off the hand of a thief who was the victim of poverty. Omar's rule was also instructive for the administration of a multi-ethnic society, for his realm comprised many non-Muslims (*dhimmi*), and his policy was to allow complete freedom of worship, guaranteeing their protection in return for their obedience and a poll tax (*jazia*) in lieu of a religious tax (zakat). Recent calls in Malaysia, however, by some dakwah enthusiasts in ABIM, for the inclusion of non-Muslims in the jurisdiction of the Syari'ah, have disturbed the non-Malays. They remain unmoved by arguments to the effect that justice is a universal good, transcending specific creeds and peoples, or that all religions equally deplore the same sins of fornication, theft, murder, and so on, by which non-Muslim fears are supposed to be allayed.

Economic Institutions

Following the demise of Syamelin, most of ABIM's economic interest has been purely theoretical. Predictably, it appeals for banks which operate without the use of interest (riba), although one such bank with headquarters in Kuwait, has already been approved for operation in Malaysia by the government which recently launched in 1983, a comparable bank of its own. Yet ABIM refuses to label itself either "capitalist" or "socialist." Extreme forms of either, it is assumed, are equally undesirable, for both involve the exploitation of the little man by a totalitarian government and limit individual freedoms, especially the religious. Once again, colonialism and communism conveniently come under fire. On the other hand, ABIM followers, as disciples of Maulana al-Maudoodi, see no harm in private property or personal wealth, so long as it is acquired by religiously acceptable means and does not involve the oppression of others (*Dakwah* 1980:25-26). The important consideration is that each individual earn his own economic privileges and status, rather than by passively inheriting property and goods, thus eliminating a "frozen" stratification system and allowing for the mobility of all members of society. Moreover, in a true Islamic state, the correct use of the obligatory religious taxes, zakat and fitrah, for the assistance of the poor would contribute to a more even distribution of wealth. In this respect, the generalized economic idealism is reminiscent of the PAS platform which equally vaguely promises to eradicate poverty and the need for begging, again without providing details about how this will be achieved. The brief Syamelin experiment was an attempt by ABIM to create, on a small scale, an economic system based on religious principles (or at least, not in contravention of them), but because of organizational problems it did not prove to be a strong vindication of the theory or ideals behind it.

Women

One area in which ABIM's commitment to fundamentalism is most apparent is in its attitude to women. Despite the fact that most of its female supporters are women who have been exposed to the freedoms of higher, and often overseas, education and opportunities for professional occupations, like some Iranian women, they have chosen to return to the modest, unrevealing attire (half-purdah) required by their faith. That is, they must at all times cover the parts of the body deemed "immodest" (*aurat*), permitting the exposure of the face, but not of the hair, soles of feet, or palms of hands. Although Anwar himself insists that Islamic dress is not necessarily Arabic dress, most of the dakwah women are now enveloped in loose robes, derived from the Malay loose-fitting *baju kurung*,[8] and wear a shoulder-length mini-veil (mini-telekung), which frames the face and hangs from a tight headband that binds the hair in place. On the other hand, *Risalah* is full of bitter comments on the cases of young women who, because of their Muslim attire, have been turned away from jobs by potential employers who fear the negative impact of the costume on their clients and customers, for example, in car rental firms or travel agencies. In the 1980's, however, even these attitudes by employers are beginning to change.

In matters of occupation, ABIM recognizes the value of education and the role women can play in certain professions, as long as the job does not compromise their primary roles as wives and mothers. ABIM members are fond of the Koranic quotation that "paradise lies under the feet of a mother" (*"syurga terletak dibawah tapak kaki ibu"*), and most dakwah women also quote this line with approval. In most conferences and lectures convened by HELWA, ABIM's female branch, this is always stressed, along with a verbal distaste for western-style women's liberation excesses. The themes of most of HELWA's meetings revolve around the role of good Muslim women in education, child-rearing, and in creating a social conscience in general. A case in point is Anwar's own wife (married in 1980), who is a practising medical doctor, trained in Ireland, but who observes the strict dress requirements of her faith and follows Anwar in his belief that female doctors should only treat female patients. Likewise, in schools, Anwar favours segregation of the sexes in most activities and feels that sports are inappropriate for women, since the uniforms reveal too much of the body. There is no reason to believe that his move to UMNO will necessarily affect his attitudes to his wife and women. Indeed his subsequent political career has co-incided with, if not partly determined, a noticeable shift in government policies and life-styles too towards a more Islamic orientation. Female ABIM followers whom I came to know all seemed pleased and proud to adopt full Muslim attire "for the sake of God" ("kerana Allah") and to show their sacrifice and commitment to the faith.

Finally, the popular heroine of most of today's young ABIM women is, intriguingly, a New York Jewish convert to Islam now known as Mariam Jameela, who like many converts is more zealous than the "born" members. She lives in Pakistan and writes books almost embarrassingly anti-western in praise of her new faith and its worldwide re-awakening.

Political Interests and Aspirations

Unlike Christianity, Islam has never made any pretence over separation of "church" and "state," and political involvement has always been central to membership in a Muslim community. Religion, *al-Din*, is a total way of life and must be lived as such. It is surprising indeed that for several years, until the late 1970's, Anwar was persistently able to deny any political interests or ambitions for himself or his organization. Presumably, the Universities Act and other pressures made this a matter of expedience. By the end of 1979, however, Anwar was publicly admitting that in Islam there can be no retreating from political reality or avoidance of social issues. At this time too, it became common knowledge that a few ABIM members, who had prudently taken the precaution of resigning their formal affiliation first, were even running for political office in certain Kedah constituencies on the PAS ticket. Of the five candidates who have run, only one, Ustaz Nakhaie Haji Ahmad, has been successful, in a constituency in the Baling area. Ustaz Nakhaie is actually not a "typical" ABIM member of the younger, overseas-trained generation; he is in his late forties, comes from a traditional Kedah ulama family, and was himself trained as a religious teacher. He left Malay school early and later, on his own initiative, put himself through the Higher School Certificate and university entrance as a mature student in his thirties. This put him in the category of the so-called *mahasitua*, a play on words conveying the idea of an "older" student, representing a generation who matured too soon to take advantage of the university explosion of the 1970's. During his schooldays in Kedah, he was, however, a member of an older, peninsula-wide student body with strong nationalist learnings (*Gabungan Pelajaran Semenanjung Malaysia*). It is likely that Ustaz Nakhaie won his seat for his more traditional rather than his ABIM connections, for in most respects, ABIM has received little interest or support in these rural areas. Attempts by ABIM leaders to create a local branch in Baling have made virtually no impact, and Ustaz Nakhaie, to protect his standing with older, influential voters in the district does not press his ABIM connections too strongly either. In another, highly publicized Kedah by-election in Bukit Raya in 1980, the losing PAS candidate was also an ex-founder-member of ABIM. Like Nakhaie, in his campaign he did not advertise or make use of his ABIM affiliations, nor did ABIM provide any visible support or assistance. Once again, this was undoubtedly because such ties would have conferred little advantage—possibly the reverse—in the eyes of the kampung electorate.

The very existence of the relationship between ABIM and PAS as well as its mysteriously covert nature raises questions about the motives of members of both parties. In many respects, the "constituencies" of ABIM and PAS are totally different. PAS has traditionally drawn its strength from the rural, older, and more conservative kampung Malay, including from many rural ulama, who are often at odds with ABIM's youthful, urban and overseas-oriented, non-traditional support base. ABIM dakwah missionaries have been accorded but lukewarm receptions in the villages, especially as some of the adat has come under fire from ABIM. Yet at a more general level, some of their interests do converge, in their promotion of the cause of religion and, more cautiously, of Malay interests and in their common opposition to UMNO and the present system of government. It could therefore be argued, cynically, that the alliance is little more than a temporary marriage of convenience, of strategic advantage to both. Through ABIM, PAS may be able to increase its foothold among urban Malays, where it has never previously gathered much strength, while ABIM, through the graces of PAS, is attempting to establish a firmer political base and legitimacy in the rural sector, possibly as a preliminary to moving in a more independent direction. To date, this has not been particularly successful, and as of 1981, to add to

ABIM's discouraging election record, severe new restrictions on its publications and activities were imposed, including prohibitions on campus lectures, the principal recruiting ground for the movement.[9] In other ways too, local authorities have created obstacles and obstructions to roving ABIM lecturers in the countryside, in the form of road blocks and sudden "closures," or refusals to provide speakers' licences or entry to public lecture halls. In 1979 Anwar himself was formally barred from giving a religious address in Kampung Besut, a hotbed of PAS/UMNO kafir-mengafir (see Chapter 2). Such restrictions make it unlikely that, in the near future at least, ABIM will achieve the level of independence and influence of say, the early Indonesian Muhammadiyah, or of other religious-based parties such as Darul Islam or Masjumi, or even of the Egyptian Al-Ikhwan. Finally, with Anwar's precipitation into UMNO electoral politics in April 1982, which involved him in an unprecedented direct conflict with the PAS candidate, events took a more unpredictable turn. Without Anwar, however, ABIM may continue its present relationship with PAS, although the emergence of new young and attractive PAS leaders in Trengganu may steal some of the thunder of ABIM sans Anwar and reduce one appeal of the old arrangement.

In order to defend himself and his organization against opposition, Anwar always cautiously refrained from direct attacks on any important constituency in Malaysian society, whether government, royalty, or rural ulama and, significantly, on occasion even made positive overtures to these groups to keep the peace. Thus the Ministry of Education's moves to increase the amount and intensity of religious instruction and to reintroduce the Jawi script as compulsory in all schools, elicited swift and public praise from ABIM. Anwar, together with some of his committee members, regularly participated in meetings of ulama associations at local and national levels. In 1980 too, Anwar joined a new, national Dakwah Committee (*Majlis Syura Dakwah Malaysia*) under government auspices. Watched with a mixture of admiration and apprehension on all sides, Anwar was approached by Tunku Abdul Rahman, in 1980 in his capacity as Head of Perkim, the government approved missionary society (see Chapter 6), to join forces with that organization. Co-operation with Perkim would undoubtedly, and intentionally, have diluted some of ABIM's strength, but while Anwar diplomatically expressed interest in public, he referred to the discussions as "preliminary" and left open his final decision. At the time, several ABIM insiders felt that Anwar would never tolerate such a compromise and that his interview with the Tunku was only to be treated as a "friendly tea-party with an old father." The event of 1982 was therefore the more startling and unpredicted.

In public addresses, Anwar always tried to appear moderate, whether in matters of ethnic or religious tolerance or in his references to official bodies. He was a model of rationality in defending his attitudes to women, supporting the wearing of Muslim attire on the basis of the Koran on the grounds that any Muslim woman seriously concerned about dakwah could not be convincing and genuine were she to be lax in such basic personal matters. Likewise, he deplored the "extreme" acts of a tiny minority of ABIM and other dakwah enthusiasts of throwing televisions into rivers, emphasizing that attention to the afterlife (akhirat) must be balanced by responsibility to society in this world (*dunia*). In other matters, however, Anwar could be as literal or parochial as any of the rural ulama he used to criticize, as when he objected to the use of the term "Allah" in a Malay translation for "God" in publications relating to Christianity or insisted that only in Arabic can Islamic ideas be fully and correctly rendered.

Possibly Anwar's most emotional public speech as ABIM president concerned the Soviet invasion of Afghanistan in 1979, a speech which culminated in excited cries of "Allah Akhbar!" ("God is great") from his audience and calls for a jihad (holy war), whereafter Anwar was bodily carried out on the shoulders of his supporters from the mosque where he made his address. At the time, none of them anticipated his future change in strategy and career.

Overseas Connections

ABIM's links with, and support for, overseas Muslim bodies are extensive. Many were initially established through student connections, and ABIM is heavily involved in Malay and other Muslim student associations in most western countries. Certain foreign Muslim governments, notably Libya and Saudi Arabia, have now stepped in with financial aid, and many of ABIM's funds, especially those for its schools and other projects—including Syamelin at one point[1] are said to come from such sources. They also help to sponsor a ceaseless round of visits and exchanges with other Muslim countries and lubricate the circuit along which move such international academics as Deliar Noer and Ismail al Faruqi, mentioned above. Anwar was the one of the first foreign observers to visit Iran following the revolution, and he was Malaysia's delegate to the World Association of Muslim Youth (WAMY) and other Islamic bodies and conferences. As a result of his close ties with, and admiration for Iran, Anwar had taken to minimizing the differences separating the Sunni and Shi'ah branches of Islam, the latter being the one to which the Iranian Muslims belong. In turn, this is countered by government religious spokesmen, who to the contrary, play up the distinctions, in fear of the revolutionary baggage that could conceivably accompany ideas imported from Iran. In Malaysian government eyes, Libya is also viewed with some apprehension, owing to Ghaddafi's reputation for interference in the internal affairs of other countries. ABIM, however, has little love for Egypt, whom, in a sort of international "kafir-mengafir," it accuses of selling out to Zionism and betraying the faith.

Summary

ABIM may be characterized as a fairly "this-worldly," universalistic religious organization, transcending national and some ethnic boundaries at the level of its leadership. At grass-roots levels, however, it frequently takes on the colouring of a more ethnically Malay movement and is certainly perceived in this light by non-Malays.

The tenuous legitimacy of ABIM's leaders, without the traditional isnad or salasilah, kinship connections or customary age and experience normally associated with religious leaders, makes it difficult for them to claim the status of ulama, yet this is in effect the role they are trying to play. Like the ulama throughout Islamic history, ABIM's leaders are concerned with broader social issues, which ultimately brings them into the political arena, in a tense, if not overtly oppositional, relationship to the government.

DARUL ARQAM

Darul Arqam, or "House of Arqam," named for a friend of the Prophet who, according to the Hadith, sheltered him on one of his journeys, arose about the same time and amid the same general social conditions of the late 1960's which gave rise to ABIM. In several important respects, however, Darul Arqam has developed in very different directions, despite a declared similarity of goals.

Out of the flux and confusion, coming and going of members in the early days of student associations and ABIM, there emerged one or two individuals who, for personal reasons, did not agree with the leaders and who wished to develop their own ideas independently. Among them was Ustaz Ashaari Mohammed, a slightly older man, originally from Negri Sembilan and a more conventional pondok religious school background, but who, because of the secularizing educational trends and financial problems adversely affecting the rural religious schools, was unable to establish a school of his own. It was only through the collaboration of some new-found friends in the emerging dakwah movement that Ustaz Ashaari was able to build the nucleus of what was to become, in 1971, a residential commune in Sungei Pencala, on the fringes of the capital of Kuala Lumpur. This eventually grew into the present community of about forty permanent houses on eight acres of land, together with its own prayer house (surau), school (madrasah), and several small workshops and "factories."

Leadership and Membership

Unlike Ustaz Ashaari himself, who is also something of a mystic and a poet, most of his closest associates and followers are from the same urban, highly-educated, university background as the members of ABIM, with a particularly high representation from the National University's Faculty of Islamic Studies, whose products are now coming to be known as the "modern ulama." In retrospect, it may well turn out that this faculty becomes the university equivalent of the old, lower-level madrasah, equally able to train the urban and rural-origin student. As more of the latter join the university ranks, bringing with them the heritage of a residual religious tradition, they find it natural to gravitate to an academic form of religious study, a religious option in an otherwise secular and urban environment. When they emerge from the faculty, however, these graduates have more in common with other university graduates than with the traditional ulama class, particularly in their capacity as self-conscious young intellectual élites in their country and as members of a larger youth cohort, national and international, with problems and interests of its own. Besides the Islamic faculty followers, Darul Arqam numbers among its permanent residents a few highly placed civil servants who, in the office, are western-like bureaucrats, but at home and in the religious community are transformed into plain-living religious devotees in Arab dress. At home too, many of them reject western-style furnishings, televisions, radios, fans, and other amenities (although they invariably drive cars to work), and this has fed the often exaggerated stereotype of a community of otherworldly "fanatics," concerned more with the afterlife than with this world. The occupants of the Darul Arqam commune appear to have no social interaction with the surrounding "natural" community of Sungei Pencala, many of whose inhabitants are of Javanese extraction. Indeed, the entire community presents an air of a "siege mentality," and patrols at the entrance screen all comers with some suspicion and many questions. Members tend to be extremely defensive about themselves and their community, accustomed as they are to curiosity-seekers and, more seriously, to religious and political criticism. They are convinced that there is a constant danger of infiltration by hostile government authorities.

In addition to the "professional" members, who live there with their families in private typically Malay-style houses, there is a growing residential cohort of young, unattached people, principally males, who live in clusters in other houses of the commune, or in the school dormitory, and usually cook and care for themselves in the old pondok spirit. Most of the young men are involved in labour in the Darul Arqam craft and cottage industries and in selling their products on circuit all over the Malay peninsula. Between tasks, they engage in intensive religious studies or instruction, depending on their competence, and help to maintain such community facilities as paths, buildings, and so on. Young women may also assist in some of the "industrial" enterprises (see below) and also help in supervision of the school.

The combined efforts and contributions of these members and leaders has enabled Darul Arqam to establish a large and successful school, with an enrolment in 1980 of over eight hundred pupils, most from outside the commune, and indeed from all over West Malaysia and South Thailand. The outsiders are boarded in a hostel, where, much as in the old pondok system again, they perform many of the daily chores for themselves.[10] They also eat "Arab style," that is, squatting on the floor in a circle around a common metal dish (*talam*) taking food with the first three fingers only, and sometimes, it is said, even colouring the rice green, the holy colour of Islam. Several of the twenty-seven teachers are part-time volunteers from local campuses, representing various departments from religious studies to engineering and animal sciences. Other teachers are advanced students from the same sources. The curriculum reflects and promotes the overall goals and philosophy of Darul Arqam as a whole. Essentially, this community resembles a sort of latter-day, urban pondok, which aims to provide a sound religious education with a strong emphasis on Arabic language and culture, the inculcation of religious duties (*fardhu khifayah*), and role behaviour appropriate to sex, age, and status (*ibadat*) in a Muslim community. The concept of the religious community as providing an integrated and complete way of life (al-Din), where religious and social goals complement one another, is reflected in the "academic" side of the school curriculum, which concentrates heavily on training in such practical, community-serving skills as carpentry, mechanics, and electrical skills, and for the girls, the arts of cookery and sewing. The effectiveness of this kind of instruction may be gauged from the level of the kindergarten, where four- and five-year olds, demurely clad in Arab costume appropriate to their sex, give voice to their aspirations for the future. Most of the little girls want to become nurses or religious teachers (ustazah), while the boys have set their sights on being doctors or businessmen. At the school, and in most activities, segregation of boys and girls is enforced, beginning with the kindergarten. Everyone in the commune adopts full Islamic dress, namely, the telekung (head veil) and loose baju kurung for females, and a white or green robe and turban for males. Part-time visitors, of all ages, from outside are accepted as students for regular weekend retreats and also donate their labour to the commune's enterprises.

Economic Goals and Organization

Darul Arqam's most distinctive feature is its cultivation of an economic organization based entirely on strict Islamic principles. It is to these ends that most of the practical, "academic" training of the members and its workshops are oriented. Financially, its "treasury" (*baitul-mal*) depends for the bulk of its funds on members' contributions, in the form of a tithe, as a percentage of the monthly salary, in the spirit of the original Muslim religious taxes and charities (zakat and sedekah). One member, who is a pilot with the national airline, reputedly contributes up to M$500 per month, which must be in the region of one-sixth to one-quarter of his salary. Other funds come from the fruits of Darul Arqam's enterprises.

Darul Arqam's second economic goal is for total independence from non-Muslim control. As in the case of Syamelin, from which Ustaz Ashaari may have drawn some of his ideas,[11] there runs a strong desire to shake off the yoke of Chinese and foreign dominance of the Malaysian economy and to "stand on their own feet" (*berdikari*). Although the term "non-Muslim" is more often judiciously used, it is clear that the business side of Darul Arqam has an ethnic as well as a religious dimension. Since the early 1970's, Arqam has gradually built up a series of manufacturing, agricultural, and trading enterprises throughout West Malaysia, aimed first at the most elemental self-sufficiency for members and second at promoting the economic autonomy and prosperity of the Malays as a whole. What the government strives for in its New Economic Policy, Arqam hopes to achieve through the strength of its religious commitment and organization alone. For Darul Arqam, the most illustrious precedent of all is that of the Prophet Mohammed himself, who, as is well known, was a successful businessman, as was his first wife, Aishah.

The commune's "factories," which are in reality small shops or sheds or converted terrace houses—the latter in another suburb of Kuala Lumpur—are equipped with simple machines capable of manipulation with a minimum of training. Production is concentrated mostly on foodstuffs and other daily needs, such as noodles, pickles, jam, soy sauce, fish crackers, toothpaste, talcum powder, some medication, and notebooks. Self-sufficiency has the added advantage of eliminating all shadow of doubt as to the purity of food and personal products as *bersih*, *halal*, which is always open to question by the fastidious when the products come from non-Muslim (for example, Chinese) factories. It is often rumoured, for example, that the Chinese roast or fry their coffee beans in lard. Arqam's commodities are produced largely by the volunteer labour of the young, single members of the commune, and each factory is manned by four operators, usually working in day and night shifts for three or four days per week. This leaves Fridays and the weekends free for religious obligations and activities. Somewhat paradoxically, for all the stress placed on religious purity, purity of another kind may receive rather less attention. Dirty hands in the noodle or bread dough apparently are considered less polluting than lard in the coffee beans or than items processed during the times of compulsory prayer. Furthermore, there is little control over the ultimate source of raw materials, since soybeans, flour, and vegetables are purchased at wholesale markets or, alternatively, from the government marketing agency, FAMA. Containers, such as bottles and tins which are bought from non-Muslims are subjected to a ritual cleansing process (*samak*), which involves seven successive washings, the first time with mud. Darul Arqam's products are distributed and sold under its own labels and in its own retail shops, staffed by at least one of its full-time members and other volunteer assistants. From the thirty or so shops, eight of which are in the vicinity of the capital (with only two in Kedah), an average profit of 9 per cent of sales is claimed by the operators. However, both operators and the consuming public frequently complain of erratic distribution and unpredictable inventories, partly the result of their dependence on private cars and motorbicycles of members. Sometimes there are also complaints of uncertain quality control in different "batches" of the same product.

Ideally, of course, the marketing network is designed to draw in all those Malays who desire to "uplift themselves" and their "race" through trade and commerce, and any Malay with a product to sell is encouraged to join the network, allowing Darul Arqam to handle the distribution. A substantial number of Malay petty-traders—largely proprietors of small, dry-goods, general purpose shops or stalls—all over West Malaysia have expressed interest in the Arqam scheme but have found, or heard, like other retailers, that the transport and other services are unreliable as yet. Regardless of these problems, other Malays affiliate purely on principle. Thus one chicken-seller in the main Kuala Lumpur market, still has to buy his birds from non-Bumi (as he phrased it) suppliers, but then he slaughters them in the ritually correct way (*sembelih*) as his personal contribution to dakwah. Many non-Darul Arqam Malay consumers likewise approve in principle the idea of the ready availability of "pure" Bumiputera and halal products, as long as supplies can be assured, even when taste quality is not up to expectations in comparison with commercial goods. Arqam has recently taken to staging large regional exhibitions of its products in conjunction with sales promotion tours by way of advertisement. These are usually held in university campuses or in local mosques. At one Kelantan sale in 1980, a member claimed total sales to the value of M$20,000 gross over four days and said that they could not satisfy the enthusiastic demand for some of their products. The young men who operate the sales circuit are normally members of the commune, who often initially joined the movement through dissatisfaction with their own personal life and who were seeking fulfilment and a place in a society "suitable" (*"sesuai"*) to their own needs. A profit motive may also intervene, for according to the claims of some of the itinerant salesmen, the monthly commission they receive on sales (the actual percentage was not specified, varying somewhat with the community's financial situation) amounted to more than the M$250 monthly wage they had received from factory jobs in pre-Arqam days. Fixed wages as such, however, are not paid by Arqam and appear to be subject to a sometimes haphazard reshuffling of funds between various divisions of the organization. Thus investment funds may be channelled from the lucrative publications section to subsidize transportation needs. When a critical shortage of ready cash is experienced, appeals are usually made to members for extra donations. It is therefore difficult to assess how far the enterprises are profitable in a strictly market sense.

Other Darul Arqam projects include motor-mechanical training, which has enabled one or two Arqam "graduates" to open their own repair shops and garages outside the community, while their owners/operators remain affiliated to the organization and donate a proportion of their earnings to it. More recently too, Arqam has diversified into cattle-raising projects for meat and milk and is planning further agricultural rice-growing schemes, to which the young males are despatched as workers. Finally, the publications section, responsible for the dissemination of religious literature, in the form of a monthly bulletin, tracts, and pamphlets galore, as well as a steady stream of tapes and cassettes of Ashaari's speeches, is said to be better organized and more profitable than its general store network, and its profits are ploughed back into the general dakwah mission.

The Clinic

Darul Arqam's other distinctive enterprise is its medical clinic, first opened in 1978. Again, this reflects an attempt to marry harmoniously religious principles and the best of modern medicine by providing patients with a choice or combination of "scientific," traditional, or spiritual therapy. Women can give birth either under anaesthesia or with a traditional midwife (*bidan*) in a "holy" (*suci*) atmosphere, in which the word "Allah" is immediately whispered into the right ear of the newborn. The mother then may receive all the traditional ministrations of herbal infusions, restricted bathing, and dietary taboos normally accorded to kampung mothers.

The clinic is served by both western-trained doctors and nurses and several Malay curers (bomohs) who make extensive use of Koranic incantations, traditional herbs, and such homeopathic techniques as massage and forms of chiropractic, which again have the advantage of being uncontaminated by non-Muslim hands. A preoccupation with health and healing is not uncommon in religious and revivalist movements, for physical and spiritual well-being are regarded as mutually reinforcing. This sentiment is epitomized in a favourite quotation, "health for a pious person is more valuable than wealth."

One full-time doctor is on salary ($300 per month) and several of the nurses and midwives are paid $120 per month to ensure staff stability, although this is but a fraction of what they would receive in government service. Others are part-time volunteers from local hospitals, sympathetic to the movement. One of the keenest of the latter, also a graduate of the University of Malaya, was a girl who eventually became Ustaz Ashaari's second wife.

A special interest of the Arqam clinic is the rehabilitation of drug addicts, now acknowledged to be a major problem among modern Malay youth. The clinic's onslaught on drugs has a two-pronged approach. First, it avowedly attempts to upgrade those of their "race and religion" who have degraded themselves and their community and, second, to garner more recruits or supporters. A large part of the therapy consists of intensive religious study and re-education, mental and spiritual treatment, which promotes the virtues of the Arqam way of life and simultaneously generates some new members. Some concerned families travel long distances to the Arqam clinic seeking a cure for kin with drug problems, and they are sometimes asked to pay as much as M$120 per month for treatment. Arqam leaders stress that neither the clinic nor the school is restricted to full Darul Arqam members, but since there are no established definitions as to membership, save for those few who actually live in the commune, "membership" is more accurately a question of a very diffuse influence and sympathy, which educational and medical services can undoubtedly create or turn to their advantage. As part of the wider business enterprise, the clinic charges approximately M$7 per outpatient consultation, M$100 per childbirth, but otherwise claims to operate on the principle of a "means test," adjusted in favour of the poor. Funds are also supplemented by sale of Arqam's own patent medicines.

Commune Administration

Administration of the commune, both in specific economic and other domains, is designed to conform to the leaders' perceptions of an Islamic social system. It is conducted through a series of committees (syura) in mutual consultation. Committees exist for education, economic organization, religion, and publications, and these are further sub-divided into special departments. Thus a retailing committee is subordinate to the general economic syura, which in turn is responsible to an overarching syura for Darul Arqam as a whole. Ashaari himself remains the ultimate co-ordinator and source of decisions or "appeals," however. Each system has its own financial allocations or treasury (baitul-mal), modelled on the idea of the public purse of traditional Islamic societies. The egalitarian ideal of the community as a whole is fostered by a number of economic levelling mechanisms, achieved mainly by the graded levying of religious taxes and contributions, thus guaranteeing support for the poorer members. None of the property in the commune remains under individual ownership; it is deeded over to the group in an attempt to maintain some facsimile of a non-stratified society and the basis of a non-capitalist Islamic state. It goes without saying that there is total avoidance by Arqam of any investment or savings in commercial banks, or receipt of interest, as examples of the forbidden usury (riba).

Considerable funds are expended upon the active part of the mission, the propagation of dakwah, Arqam's ultimate goal. This involves an ambitious programme of rotating lectures and study sessions, many led by Ustaz Ashaari himself and aided by a steady stream of volunteer lecturers from the universities, particularly the Faculty of Islamic Studies of the National University. An even wider public is reached through the bulletin and tape-recordings of Ashaari's sermons, which are often mailed to such strategic targets as youth clubs, schools, and universities. Unlike those of Anwar Ibrahim, Ashaari's speeches tend to be more earthy and homely in style and example. Extreme reliance on extensive scriptural quotation casts Darul Arqam in a more fundamentalist light even than ABIM. Ashaari customarily takes the peasant's or "little man's" perspective and concentrates on matters which strike immediate chords, such as the errant wife who fails to have the rice cooked when her husband returns home or leaves the house unnecessarily without her husband's permission, as a means of urging all Muslims to know their role and duties in society. The message is often put over with considerable humour, as when Ashaari comically mimics the husband's shock in arriving home and finding his meal not yet ready. Another common theme is a brand of asceticism or frugality, and it encourages Muslims to eschew unnecessary pleasures and luxuries in a spirit of sacrifice as one means of attacking the ills of modern society. His speeches usually build up to a climax in which he exhorts audience to "change their ways" (*ubah hati*), not to shy away from a life of sacrifice and struggle (*perjuangan untuk hidup*), culminating in the cry: "*mahu mati Allah hidupkan, mahu hidup, Allah matikan*" ("if you desire death, God will give you life, but if you desire life too much, God will put an end to it"). Finally, Ashaari poses rhetorical questions, about "who owns all the biscuit and sauce factories in Malaysia?" to which he provides an immediate answer, with a dramatically intoned:

"orang lain" (others, that is, non-Malays). In public, he is quite careful to use the term *"kita orang Islam"* ("we Muslims"), but it is usually clear that such references are really to the Malay/non-Malay dichotomy. The burden of the total message then is transparently that the Malays should rouse themselves from their sleep and make an all-out effort to do everything for themselves, once again, the emphasis being on struggle and independence. Outside the lecture hall, displays of Darul Arqam products provide visible and tangible testimony to what can be achieved by way of illustration of Ashaari's words, and sales are usually brisk enough to take care of most problems of dismantling at the end. On the whole, Ashaari sets more store by the symbolic and social importance of strict Islamic standards of dress, of visible respect by children for their elders (for example, in kissing their parents' hands before leaving the house), and Arabic customs, such as the eating styles mentioned, than do most of ABIM's leaders. Urban audiences at off-campus lectures comprise a wider crosssection of the public than do those for most ABIM meetings. They include many more older people, although since they are often accompanied by younger family members, it is possible they were "brought along" by their enthusiastic juniors in some cases. Also in evidence are young office girls, members of youth groups, many children with their parents, and the usual university contingent. Few are in the complete Muslim or Arab style attire that the more committed followers affect, but merely dress modestly, the women with a headscarf and the men wearing a songkok (fez). Many attend more out of curiosity, on the recommendation of friends, or as an acceptable way of spending an evening, rather than out of prior knowledge of the Arqam movement or of particular sympathy with it.

Some of Darul Arqam's practices, for example their sacrifice of western luxuries, ascetic mode of dress, and so on, are responsible for the popular view of the organization as overly oriented towards the afterlife (akhirat), despite their business interests. Recently, in order to correct the balance a little, Darul Arqam has taken pains to demonstrate its commitment to society and the "world" (dunia), although sometimes with a barely disguised chauvinism in matters already referred to. Like ABIM's leaders, Arqam is trying to modify the image of the movement as hostile to the government, if only for reasons of expedience. In the beginning, Arqam ostentatiously and self-righteously refrained from accepting any assistance or co-operation from the government for its economic projects, but since 1978, it has gracefully agreed to register as a business corporation and has also begun to purchase some supplies from such government marketing agencies as FAMA and Majuikan, while opening one or two retail outlets in the new mini-markets provided for Malay entrepreneurs by the Urban Development Authority (UDA). Arqam still refuses, however, to accept direct financial aid.

Despite the fact that, unlike ABIM, Darul Arqam has no affiliation to any political party, nor any obvious political platform of its own, in a more subtle way, the movement does carry political implications. First, Arqam's economic policies, with their emphasis on self-sufficiency and autonomy from not only non-Muslims and foreigners, but also largely from government agencies, have been seen as an indirect challenge to the integrity of the New Economic Policy and its commitment to a western/capitalist pattern of modernization.

Although magnified by the media and other observers, incidents involving Arqam's physical rejection of "items of progress" and the "anti-social" withdrawal of members into either the commune or just into a life of religious seclusion in lieu of taking a job for which they have been trained, only combine to reinforce this image.

Second, Darul Arqam's acknowledged influence, both among youth in the nerve-centres of the country's capital and universities, as well as a growing strength in certain rural sectors, especially in Kelantan, Trengganu, Selangor, and Negri Sembilan, could become the nucleus of a powerful force, to be mobilized for other purposes at other times. It is just such potential political mobilization, with an underpinning of powerful personal and religious loyalties, which causes the greatest apprehension in official circles, as it did with the followers of Datuk Harun and of Nasrul Haq.

Finally, Arqam's sense of moral superiority and authoritarianism, exaggerated by its siege mentality, has sometimes been cited as a cause for suspicion. In the isolation of the commune, to which streams of young people make regular retreats, they are accused of refusing permission for parents to visit their sequestered offspring or to allow them only verbal access through a window grille. They are said to insult even Muslim/Malay visitors by suggestive references to their inadequate (by Darul Arqam standards) dress or head-covering or by criticizing them for arriving for a visit at the time of prayer. Their religious superiority is shown in their belittling of well-intentioned questions by visiting non-members attending a lecture, by giving as their reason for insistence on Arab attire, for example, the contemptuous answer "to keep away the mosquitoes," suggesting that the questioners are not to be taken seriously. Its bulletin, too, cavalierly relegates the entire outside world (that is, non-Arqam) as a collective "syaitan" (evil). Some other Muslims consider such behaviour as not only impolite and un-Malay, but also as un-Islamic, both of which value harmonious personal relations, etiquette, and a concern for the feelings of others.

Evidence and "leaks" from within suggest that the administration of Darul Arqam does not always run smoothly, and recently several instances of dissension in both the ranks and the leadership have been reported.

One of these involved the establishment of a second Darul Arqam school in one Kedah community, initially on the invitation of an interested religious teacher there, whose own traditional school was suffering under the combined pressures of modernization, secularization, and religious council control, as described in Chapter 2. Impressed from afar by Arqam's philosophy, and its apparent power to draw people back to the path of the true faith, this guru saw in the organization a possible source of renewal for the fortunes of his own school, and he went into partnership with a number of Arqam teachers. He also allowed one of Arqam's shops to be set up in the school compound, under the management of one of his pupils, now an ardent Arqam disciple. Initially, the new "hybrid" school seemed a success. Its advertised curriculum combining intensive religious instruction along with practical and "academic" subjects was one which appealed to many kampung parents, and since the latter have a deep respect for the resident guru who had invited Arqam in, their support was assured. At one point, near the beginning, the parents were even using their kinship networks in other towns and villages to encourage high-school children in government schools to come and spend week-long retreats under Arqam tutelage. Their confidence, however, was short-lived. The parents soon discovered that the "academic" side of the curriculum largely consisted of carpentry, making chili sauce, and even "stealing" home recipes and remedies for use in Arqam commercial enterprises and that the children were being channelled into the organization's business activities, at the expense of subjects which could lead to the path of the civil service. This was not the "balanced" education they had expected. Their ambivalence grew when the new teachers threw out all the desks and chairs and even the fans and insisted on full Arab dress for their pupils. Allegedly, they even refused to open the windows of the now fan-less classrooms, to prevent the observation of the girl pupils by the boys. Finally, in keeping with their policy of self-sufficiency and independence from official bodies, Arqam's leaders refused to allow the original guru to continue receiving his usual financial allocation for the school from the state religious council, and at this point, there were appeals from all quarters for the guru to restore the "old régime." This he finally did, after an experience of barely a year, although a small minority of parents, who had apparently been won over by Arqam, withdrew their children and recommitted them to the school in the Sungei Pencala commune. The shop, however, was permitted to remain at the gate of the school compound and it still does a strong trade locally. Its operator claims to support Arqam still, although this in no way affects his loyalty to his original guru. In order to cover some of his embarrassment, the original guru justified his own reversal of policy and unfortunate judgement by claiming that Ustaz Ashaari was a bit too much of a "ladies man," who encouraged his close colleagues—among whom the guru was one—to take extra wives, one in each Arqam centre, for "convenience" when travelling on service, and of this the guru claimed to disapprove. The fact that the co-operative experiment occurred at all, however, indicates that rural ulama are well aware of, and open to, changes and new ideas from other sources. And just as the teachers of the Al-Masriyyah school in Bukit Mertajam made the decision to protect their own ailing institution from similar pressures by making the alliance with ABIM's Yayasan Anda, so this guru had hoped to solve some of his problems by this creative approach. It also illustrates the importance of the school as an institution in Islam more generally, not merely for its role in socialization, but also as a revered social institution, with significance for the wider community, along the lines of the pesantren in Indonesia.

Serious rifts in the leadership of the Sungei Pencala commune have also reportedly occurred. The first outward manifestations came in the publicized expulsion of four young factory workers and one young man on the cattle project without reason given. Disagreements were said to have arisen over increasing tendencies by Ashaari and a coterie of his closest associates towards mystical, Sufi-like observances in a movement called Muhammadiyah (which bears no relationship to the Indonesian organization of the same name). Allegedly, Ashaari was resurrecting an old personal connection with a venerable alim and guru, Sheikh Muhammed Suhaimi, who died in Kelang in 1925, predicting that a successor, who would be an Imam Mahdi, or messianic leader, would emerge from one of his pupils in the future. By implication, this was to be none other than Ustaz Ashaari himself, invoking an isnad and a legitimacy of a more traditional kind, powerful ammunition in what appears to be a conflict over leadership. This very claim, however, laid Ashaari open to accusations of "doubtful practices" by some of the university-trained members, who uncovered all manner of "secret" silat and mystical activities going on in villages close to Ashaari's Negri Sembilan birthplace. Once again, controversy reigned over questions of religious syncretism, reminiscent of the Nasrul Haq affair, although entirely within the Arqam community. Basically, however, the affair seems to relate to authority and leadership and to be a contest between a more dynamic, young, university-educated faction challenging the more traditional incumbents and, in the process, raising the possibility of redefining somewhat the character and image of the whole movement. Some of the young challengers, who now accuse Ashaari's contingent of "heresy" (syirik), are more concerned with the success of the business enterprises and with rectifying the production and distribution problems. In this cohort, a strong vein of "Malayness" clearly persists. There are among them, however, others who are not averse to greater co-operation with government agencies for the viability of their enterprises and for a more positive public image.

Significantly, support for this latter category has been expressed by the Kedah guru of the failed school experiment, who still maintains a personal interest in Arqam and some of its principles. The conflict was sharpened and publicized when the expelled young men, who had surrendered all their worldly possessions to the commune on joining, now demanded their return. One university lecturer, who had given up his job to work on an Arqam chicken farm in Johor state, also wished to reverse his decision and claim compensation. On the other side, some of Ashaari's supporters threatened that, if instructed by their leader, they would kill the members of the opposition. The opposition countered with further attacks on Ashaari's personality and attitudes, to his authoritarianism in breaking the rules of his own syura, or retiring from a debate in a huff, thus earning him the pejorative title of "syeikh." Finally, the expelled opposition called into question Ashaari's messianic "illusions," of his ambitions as a "khalifah muda" (young Caliph) planning a take-over à la Khomeini, and even of the secret training of young henchmen dressed in Turkish uniforms, culminating in "mess-nights in which the activities were less than Islamic." Amid all this flurry of unverifiable accusations between the factions, it seems evident that the younger, anti-Ashaari group upholds views closer in line to those of ABIM (for example, in its rejection of traditional adat and syncretic Islam), although using these as rationales for seeking a larger political role within the organization.

JEMAAT TABLIGH

The meaning of Tabligh, as one of the four original varieties of dakwah, is derived from *Tafrigh-i-Waqt*, "to spare time," that is, for the service of God. The principal burden of this service consists of conveying the religious message, although today, some followers prefer the term *usaha* (works) to convey the idea of greater social responsibility. Unlike ABIM and Darul Arqam, Jemaat Tabligh was not born on Malaysian soil but was in fact founded as far back as 1925 in India, and its nucleus still resides in Delhi. Its founder was Raizul Muballighim Allama Maulana Ilyas, who, on returning from the pilgrimage (haj) and praying at the Prophet's tomb, had come to the conclusion that the Muslims of his day were too apathetic and were in need of spiritual revitalization. Accordingly, he embarked upon his own missionary programme with incredible international success, for the Tabligh network now covers the world, including many areas not normally regarded as "Muslim." It supports, for example, large quarters in places as diverse as South Africa and Chicago.

Of all the "spontaneous" dakwah movements now active in Malaysia, Jemaat Tabligh is the least structured. It operates largely through a cadre system, or ever-ramifying network of missionaries (muballigh), who first penetrated Malaysia and Singapore in the early 1950's.

Organization and Membership

Tabligh's basic goal is to renew the spirit of Islam on the strength of the personal contacts and example of its missionaries, who move from place to place to replant the seeds of dedication. In spreading the message, Tabligh relies entirely on volunteers, who, at their own expense, are encouraged to travel as far as they can afford, sometimes locally, sometimes to other countries. This is said to be the manner by which the Islam of the Prophet Mohammed's day was originally spread from tribe to tribe in Arabia. Its "organization" is best likened to a chain in which new links are ever being forged or to an open-ended network, with intermittent nodes in the form of cells of followers clustered in certain locations. On arrival in a new place, missionaries, who usually travel in pairs, will seek out a local Muslim in good standing in the community, usually an imam or religious teacher, but occasionally a respected secular leader, such as a village headman, from whom to borrow an initial fund of legitimacy. Having established a base in a local mosque or prayer house,[12] they then circulate from door to door around the community, inviting males to attend their lectures and retreats in the mosque. Reception can be mixed, as in any door-to-door salesmanship, but most Malays are by custom courteous and usually several are sufficiently curious or interested to attend at least one meeting, particularly when apparently endorsed by local high-status members of the community. Should the local imam happen to disapprove of Tabligh, he may adopt a personal solution, as did one kampung imam, who permitted Tabligh to convene in the mosque, but avoided direct confrontation by scheduling another meeting simultaneously, one with equal drawing power (for example, an UMNO committee) requiring his own presence and that of other prominent members of the community. Recently, another fruitful recruiting ground has been through the universities, both in Malaysia and overseas, as in the case of the other dakwah organizations. Once new cells are formed, further missionaries are despatched to open up new areas following the same procedures. Although the missionaries claim to use only "soft" (*lembut*) techniques of persuasion, in Malaysia they have the reputation of accosting Malay males in the streets, pressing them to commit themselves then and there to Islam and to dakwah, to "remember Allah," and, reportedly, sometimes carrying them almost bodily off to the nearest mosque for a meeting.

Tabligh is an exclusively male organization, and wives of followers are encouraged to hold prayer and discussion meetings (*usrah*) in their homes for like-minded friends. They are also counselled to refrain from placing any obstacles in the path of their menfolk who wish to attend Tabligh activities or to undertake duties as missionaries away from home. If indeed all these prescriptions are faithfully carried out, it puts a premium, as some followers have recognized, both on the women's not working outside the home and on an extended family unit, whereby "substitute" males are always available to take care of the females whose husbands are absent on duty. Women are also expected to adopt the full Islamic dress of most other dakwah females and only to communicate with non-related males through intermediaries or, at least, by averting the head and avoiding eye-to-eye contact. (Such behaviour, on university campuses, between lecturers and students is somewhat limiting for effective advising and discussion sessions.) Among the highly (and even overseas) educated, urban, middle-class Malay females who become involved in Tabligh through their husbands, the above-mentioned restrictions pose a dilemma when occupational choices must be made, and some women so caught, admit considerable problems of personal adjustment. Even the husbands themselves, though committed to the movement, will find justifications for not fulfilling the ultimate requirement of itinerant missionary work, most frequently because it conflicts with employment duties.

Retreats

In order to remain in good standing, even those men who do not volunteer for missions are obliged to attend a retreat (*i'tikaaf* or *jemaat*) sponsored by Tabligh in the mosque to a total of either one day a week, three days per month, forty days per year, or four months in a lifetime, and, if possible, to include a visit to the Delhi headquarters, which is said to receive almost as much emphasis as Mecca. The pattern of the retreats, inspired by the Prophet's own precedent of seclusion in the cave at the time of his revelation, usually revolves around a series of readings and expositions from the Koran (taklim) and the prescribed prayers. These are supplemented by lectures (*ceramah*), either by local members or visiting missionaries, and open discussions in which participants give voice to their personal questions, and moral, religious, and ethical dilemmas encountered in daily life. What seems to impress most regular attenders, however, is the sense of confraternity and solidarity which develops in the train of these meetings and sharing of common experiences. Whether closer to a form of "group therapy" or mere camaraderie, the intensity of these effects are heightened by the sharing of meals and overnight accommodation, which in some cases may even approach a spirit of *communitas* (Turner 1967). In such a state, everyday, secular roles are suspended, and a mood of ecstatic communion takes over. Each participant contributes one item to the communal meal, which is eaten Arab-style, from a single central tray (talam), and all wear the flowing white or green Arab robes (jubah). In the longer retreats, all sleep, dormitory fashion, on the floor and often punctuate the night with extra, non-obligatory prayers and vigils, bringing additional merit. No contact with the "outside" is allowed for the duration.

These sessions have become particularly popular among certain segments of unmarried urban youth between twelve and twenty-five years of age and could be regarded as a religious alternative to other forms of youth culture and groups. In Tabligh, the mosque replaces the coffeeshop as the convening place, Arab dress has become the alternative to jeans and T-shirt, and almost a fashion in itself, worn with a certain flair and panache. The common meals and discussion sessions are substitutes, and sometimes even antidotes for, the coffee and drug-taking and other group activities of otherwise aimless and wayward urban Malay youth. Older Tabligh followers perceive the value of some of these effects and encourage young men and boys to spend their leisure hours in and around the mosque (as is done in rural kampungs), even when not in retreat. Some of the older men consciously see Tabligh as one mechanism for reducing delinquency among the "excitable" (*gelisah*) young, particularly among the unemployed who are not in school or university. As in other forms of youth group and culture, however, Tabligh participation for some of this category of males may end abruptly on marriage, for reasons of family pressure mentioned above and detachment from the immediate sanctions of the peer group.

Sympathetic observers of the Tabligh movement attribute to it other social benefits, such as an increase in personal integrity and trust among its followers. They cite transformations in personal character, for example, that Tabligh merchants will leave their stalls unattended while they go to pray at the mosque or opt to cut prices and reduce their profit (*untung*). Whether verifiable or not, stories like these seem to carry a certain ethos, which may be the spirit of Tabligh at its best, one intended, if not invariably achieved.

Although Tabligh followers claim that theirs is the most democratic of all the dakwah movements, with no formal hierarchy, leadership, or even committee structure, inevitably informal leaders do develop in specific localities. Sometimes these are already respected guru, with an established isnad and position in the local community who then come to adopt Tabligh ideals and form the nucleus of a permanent and active disseminating centre. One such man is the tacitly acknowledged "leader" of the Penang Tabligh movement, a hafiz (a man who can recite the entire Koran from memory), who lives in, and presides over, the so-called "Pakistani mosque." As the imam, he draws the usual Friday congregation, but in his more personal capacity, he is the guru to a number of devoted disciples, and in addition he conducts more intensive discussion groups and retreats along the lines described. He also maintains a small dormitory for visiting missionaries. The Pakistani mosque itself has historically been associated with a lively and intellectual religious tradition somewhat apart from the mainstream of Islam in the city. Its first manifestation was through its Kaum Muda connections in the 1930's, when the (then) Indian imam had a loyal following, which continued in private long after the main core of Kaum Muda had withered away. The present hafiz is a successor to the earlier guru, though from a different background. During the retreats, although ideally egalitarian, the agenda tends to result from the decision of one or two of the same individuals, who often guide or dominate the "open" discussions. According to insiders, these decision-makers can in fact become quite authoritarian, both in details of the retreat format and in determining the circuits and strategies of missionaries. Independent action is generally not encouraged, and for a democratic organization, there is much in Tabligh ideology encouraging "obedience," of the followers to their teachers and of women to men, using a favourite metaphor of obeying the "captain of the ship" for all such relationships. Some young men indeed claim to have left Tabligh for reasons of its authoritarianism.

Since Tabligh deliberately maintains a relatively low social profile and publishes no literature, its views on social and theological issues are harder to assess. Individual followers express a broad range of opinions. Some oppose traditional Islamic penalties, such as cutting off the hands of thieves as too harsh (*keras*), whereas others support it, as an essential requirement of the Islamic state. Some accept the extreme subordination of women; others try to get around it, particularly when there is a job at stake. Some meekly submit to the commands of missionary service; others resist on grounds of occupational priorities. Some militantly oppose traditional Malay adat; others are more tolerant. Some stress individual responsibility and decision-making; others enforce group conformity and obedience to what one lapsed follower described as misleading "fairy-tale" tactics and rituals and threats of retributions in the "horn of doomsday, at the hands of angels and devils," which create excessive anxiety in some minds. Some Tabligh activities stress a rational exegesis of the Koran, and others, a more Sufi-like mysticism, depending on the personal orientation of individual leaders. Among the mystical element, there runs a strong tendency to belief in miracles, such as that a travelling missionary is invulnerable to "dirty water" and that God will intervene in difficult cases of obtaining entry visas to foreign or hostile countries, including the Soviet Union, and protect His messenger from suspicious immigration authorities for the sake of the cause.

Ethnic Aspects of Tabligh

Consistent with its Indian origins, the earliest Tabligh affiliation in Malaysia and Singapore in the 1950's and 1960's was drawn almost exclusively from the Indian Muslim community. Because of the locus of much of the Indian population, Tabligh was urban-centred and tended to cluster around mosques popularly identified as "Indian" or "Pakistani," as were their imams and guru. The language of discourse (and of Friday prayer and sermon) was often Urdu, Tamil, Arabic, or even English, but rarely Malay. In these early days, Tabligh did not have much success in recruiting Malays, many of whom still took seriously the distinction, pervasive in urban areas, between "pure Malays" (Melayu jati) and Muslims of mixed descent (Jawi Peranakan). They were not prepared at this time to unite with Indians, even within their common faith. There were also criticisms to the effect that Tabligh followers revered Delhi at the expense of Mecca as a place of pilgrimage. The recent surge of religious fervour in dakwah seems to have put an end to the exclusive association of Tabligh with Indians, and there is no doubt that Tabligh is now attracting recruits from Malay rural kampungs, particularly in the "Malay" states of Kedah and Kelantan, even when it is necessary to use interpreters, for example, from Urdu to Malay. Tabligh followers indeed seem to be attempting to shift the crucial ethnic dichotomy away from that of Melayu jati/Jawi Peranakan to Malay/Indian Muslim. For there still exist a number of Indian Muslim religious organizations which are unequivocally and uncompromisingly "Indian" and make no attempt to identify as Malay under any circumstances, nor do they claim to be part of the dakwah movement. The Indian element in Tabligh seems to represent that segment of the population which is anxious to improve, and even change, its ethnic status through greater association with, and acceptance by, the Malays. As they move more closely into the Malay orbit, they necessarily draw further apart and dissociate themselves from the Indian community (see Chapter 7).

Not surprisingly, current Tabligh teaching makes a virtue of non-racism within Islam, and one of its most respected guru in Penang is in fact a Chinese convert (now known as Haji Hussein), who studied extensively in the Middle East, married a Malay girl, and became attached to the Pakistani mosque.

In rural areas, Tabligh probably has greater appeal than either ABIM or Darul Arqam, if only for its low-key approach and lack of controversial political or economic associations. Even the most suspicious and conservative rural ulama are less reluctant to host Tabligh meetings without fear of compromise. Further, rural Malays have not been so exposed to the image of the "greedy and aggressive" Indian Muslim trader which has alienated so many urban Malays in the past. Overall, Tabligh elicits less negative comments from ulama than do the other dakwah movements.

Some Tabligh missionaries come directly from India to rural Malaysia, thus avoiding the stigma of identification with the traders, and they are regarded as religious representatives of just another important Muslim country. Meanwhile, other Malays are finding Tabligh from other sources, such as through the ubiquitous international student associations on foreign campuses, where the rather specific image of the Malaysian Indian has no meaning. Despite its increasing inroads into rural areas, Tabligh must still be seen as a predominantly urban movement with a following of young, often well-educated youth, that is, of the same contingent that forms the backbone of ABIM and Darul Arqam.

With the current trend towards bi-purpose schools, combining religious and secular options, at least one enterprising young university graduate, who is also a native of rural Kedah and was once active in PAS, has opened a private school of his own in which Tabligh principles are emphasized. It is in the tradition of the line of other "rehabilitation" schools for pupils retaking failed Ministry of Education exams, but its religious component involves invited lectures by Tabligh colleagues in the university and other professions. At this school, history, for example, is taught as a series of migrations of Muslim populations from India to Malaysia, with a transparent bias towards the movement of Tabligh missionaries and ideas.

For obvious reasons, it is impossible to estimate the number of Tabligh followers in Malaysia. With the exception of the few excessively zealous followers who assail and harangue potential recruits in the streets or who journey to rural kampungs with the express purpose of making aggressive verbal attacks on syncretic Malay customs, they are perceived both by government and other religious council authorities as least threatening, among the dakwah elements, to the political and religious status quo.

ALIRAN

It is not altogether clear whether the Aliran movement should be regarded as a manifestation of the overall dakwah spirit or not, for in several major respects it differs from the three dakwah organizations described. First, Aliran is not an all-Malay, nor even an all-Muslim body, and second, its explicit aims and activities extend beyond the strictly religious. Third, it is defiantly anti-fundamentalist, but rather more close to the reform tradition; by self-appellation, it avoids the term dakwah, preferring "progressive Islam." On the other hand, Aliran promotes Islam, not only as a great faith in its own right, but also, optimistically, as one of the few possible sources of unity in Malaysia's multi-ethnic society. To achieve this last aim, Aliran's spokesmen find it necessary to correct some common misconceptions about Islam prevalent both in other dakwah organizations and in the non-Muslim population at large. As such, no discussion of dakwah organizations, or of the responses elicited by them, would be complete without reference to Aliran.

The Aliran organization, founded in 1978 by a university lecturer, is numerically small, with less than a hundred members, almost entirely drawn from Penang and Kuala Lumpur. Its members, who must formally join the organization, rather than hovering on the fringes as undecided sympathizers, are drawn from the multi-ethnic ranks of university lecturers, civil servants, doctors, lawyers, trade union leaders, and some workers. It is towards trade union activities that much of Aliran's social conscience has been directed to date.

Aliran's ideals and goals probably demand a level of commitment, sophistication, and even of political risk beyond that of most dakwah affiliations. Its central focus consists of raising the consciousness of all thinking and concerned Malaysians, not just Malays or Muslims, about the essential nature and direction of their society and, more concretely, about problems of workers and peasants and social injustices. It also plays a devil's advocate role in drawing attention to élite corruption and to the unwarranted ethnic friction it feels is perpetuated by these élites in their quest for power. Particular aspects of the problems and ills of Malaysian society are studied individually and in depth at regular meetings and seminars, and often efforts are made to bring in "witnesses" in the form of representatives of the oppressed constituencies being discussed, from factory-workers to fishermen and trishaw drivers, to add authenticity to the proceedings. Partly in order to be taken seriously by Malays and other Muslims, Aliran finds it expedient to use the language of Islam, particularly in its dialogues with other dakwah movements. The leader, who is himself a Muslim convert from a Hindu background and married to a Malay, possibly reflects his own somewhat marginal status in the brand of Islam promoted by Aliran in its publications and policies. It is a plea for greater universalism, emphasising the elemental virtues, moral values, and justice of the pristine faith, uncontaminated by ethnic particularisms and divisions, along the lines of such scholars as the Indian Muslim, Muhd. Iqbal. Ethnic chauvinism within Islam and communalism across religious lines are equally condemned by Aliran on the grounds that the essential spirit and moral tone of all the major religions are very similar: all advocate brotherly love, universal justice and compassion, tolerance, honesty, patience, and so on. At this abstract level, few would dispute such statements, and it is Aliran's self-appointed task to attempt to translate some of these ideas into empirical propositions and action for real (that is, Malaysian) society (cf. Chandra Muzaffar 1979:1-11). The successful administration of a multi-ethnic/multi-religious state by Caliph Omar II of Damascus is, like ABIM's, Aliran's favourite example as a possible model for Malaysia and for the peaceful co-existence of Muslim with non-Muslim. On these grounds, Aliran is particularly critical of the use of Islam in support of the

Bumiputera brand of Malayness and of both the Malay élites and the dakwah leaders who contribute to and perpetuate this bias.

In contrast with the fundamentalism of the three dakwah movements, Aliran's approach to Islam favours the practice of muzakharah, or open theological debate, and of ijtihad, to accommodate religious values to the needs of changing eras and societies. Aliran's Islam comprises a set of basic principles which can be applied creatively in different situations as necessary (for example, by the principle of al-Urf, see Chapter 1), rather than as a body of rigid unchanging laws of the blind acceptance (*takhlid buta* / ijma) variety (cf. *Utusan Malaysia* 20/12/79). Thus innovations, whether or not from the west, should not be discouraged for their provenance alone, but should be judged according to their inherent merits, regardless of any specific mention in the Koran.

Conversely, Aliran argues against the uncritical acceptance of Arab customs, through an erroneous confusion of these with Islam. Thus the principle of justice and the spirit rather than the letter of the law should prevail in punishments of thieves, rather than a literal application of an ancient Arab penalty. In this respect, Aliran is closer to the reformist bent of the Indonesian Muhammadiyah than to any other Malaysian movement.

In Aliran's view, the inner religious commitment and spirit (keimanan) are more important than outward symbols such as dress, the more so as these symbols can be socially divisive by reinforcing the cleavage between Malay and non-Malay. Likewise, its attitude towards women does not involve the extreme segregation or subordination of, say, Arqam or Tabligh. In view of Aliran's president's own recent entry into Islam, his non-Malay origin (which inevitably provide grounds for criticism by his detractors), and the self-taught character of his theology, the problem of legitimacy looms large, and his potential influence is correspondingly small. In fact, the president's self-acquired knowledge is impressive, and he is able to support all his statements and views with detailed references and quotations from Koran, Hadith, and the writings of an illustrious line of Muslim scholars, as his own intellectual "isnad." Aliran's heroes, however, tend to be the modernist thinkers such as Mohd. Abduh and al-Afghani, rather than ABIM's Maulana al-Maudoodi. The latter, indeed, represents all that is anathema to Aliran in its literalist interpretations of the scriptures over the status of women, democratic elections, and uncritical support for ruling élites regardless of their morality. Aliran in fact is rashly critical of both Malay royalty and UMNO élites for their alleged corruption and un-Islamic character, adding that it is an insult to refer to the Prophet by the Malay/Sanskrit royal title, *Baginda*, with all its autocratic, feudal connotations. It is only Aliran too, which has the courage to draw attention publicly to the persistence of the socially dangerous strand of feudal protectionism and patronage that still pervades the relationship between the élites, royal and bureaucratic, and their grass-roots subjects, heedless of more universalistic canons of morality (cf. Chandra Muzaffar 1979).

Superficially, all the dakwah movements, including Aliran, may seem to be concerned with some form of social justice. The differences lie less in their normative concerns than in the manner of their implementation, which in turn reflects their attitude to change and to reinterpretation in Islam. While Aliran looks outward and attempts to meet non-Muslims on common ground, the fundamentalists and dakwah protagonists will only relate to outsiders on their own terms and within their own frame and prefer to concentrate on "born" and reborn Muslims.

On the level of personalities, there is in fact, a close association, even friendship, between the president of Aliran and ABIM's past president. They are old acquaintances from university days, and privately the two seem to have more in common (for example, their opposition to unbridled "racism" and commitment to social reforms) than the public image of their movements might suggest. As noted, however, ABIM's following lags somewhat behind its leadership in intellectual sophistication and even sophistry, and Aliran's membership is insignificantly small. Thus two intellectuals, with somewhat convergent interests, engage in frequent and amicable personal meetings and dialogues, but the external tone and tenor of their followings often appear radically different. The question of the centrality and consistency of ideology in relation to organizational conformity and to social pressures will be further explored below.

COMMON FEATURES OF CONTEMPORARY MALAYSIAN DAKWAH:
A SUMMARY

With the exception of Aliran, whose somewhat unique position has just been described, ABIM, Darul Arqam, and Jemaat Tabligh have a number of common features. Ultimately all are committed to the goal of revitalizing the faith of "born" Muslims, of "promoting the good and eradicating the unjust," and as such, they claim to transcend the mazahab or "sectarian" divisions of Shafie, Hanafi, Hambali and Maliki, or even of Sunni and Shi'ah. All three tend to find their strongest followings among the more educated, high-school, university, and professional, urban-and-middle-class young. To some degree, they constitute an alternate "youth culture," but with Islamic symbols and rationales, and in this respect they have parallels across the Muslim world, from Tunisia to Indonesia. Yet all dakwah spokesmen take pains to stress the serious nature and responsibilities involved in embracing dakwah and resent one popular image of themselves as "failed

students," "cop-outs," neurotics, or the "garbage-dump of their generation," sometimes propagated by the media.

Given the looseness of the organizations and overlapping loyalties, "membership" is not easy to pin down or define, and probably not an appropriate
term by which to describe the followers. Malays themselves use such expressions as *bersimpati* (to be sympathetic), *juru-dakwah* (dakwah experts), and
berdakwah (to be or do dakwah), while support is often described as *menjadi
bahu* ("lending a shoulder") to the movements.

Although each dakwah movement has its own distinctive public character
and profile—ABIM's growing political commitment and ties to PAS, Darul
Arqam's "shadow economy" and entrepreneurial activities, and Tabligh's
Indian connections—they are all decidedly fundamentalist in outlook and
depend heavily on the scriptures and their perception of seventh-century
Arab customs as their models. This has led to a tightening up, not only of
attitudes to dress, but to relations between the sexes and public and personal
morals, such as in the newly enforced *khalwat* law, which prohibits "close
proximity" between unrelated males and females.[13] Critics of extreme fundamentalism, such as Aliran, accuse the latter of a preoccupation with trivia
(remeh-temeh) and suggest that they should pay greater attention to more
basic religious principles and problems, such as the nature of suffering, social
injustices, and elimination of corruption. In such respects then, dakwah
behaviour can be almost as ritualistic as the syncretic, Indic "rituals" it so
virulently opposes, particularly as some of the local dakwah cliques have
their own form of private initiation rites. Fundamentalist and revivalist
though they be, they are hardly millenarian. With the exception of a few of
the more isolated and independent rural cults, where there is sometimes talk
of a mahdi (for example, the Johor group), the current dakwah movements
are rational-social rather than thaumaturgical or millenarian in orientation.

The three major dakwah organizations are uniformly anti-western and
also anti-socialist and anti-Zionist, and all of these segments of the world's
population are included in a collective "infidel" category (jahiliyah) or else
seen as manifestations of the devil (syaitan). This attitude prevails despite
the Prophet's well-known tolerance of Christians and Jews in the Arabia of
his day. Dakwah followers can always counter this with some appropriate
quotation from the Koran, to the effect that they should not be "yoked
together with unbelievers." A somewhat unexpected spin-off from this dual
anti-western/anti-Zionist bias has been in the virulent attacks made by dakwah organizations against the Order of Freemasons, whom they accuse of
being a conspiratorial Zionist secret society. The ambivalence over western,
scientific and inspirational forms of knowledge has also overcome all the
dakwah revivalists, and in a few cases, it has immobilized them from making
occupational decisions. Some of this ambivalence is communicated by lectur-

ers and teachers to their students. Required by their profession to convey western forms of knowledge and judge by western standards, their religious commitment intervenes. Thus, a teacher of linguistics is persuaded that it is inappropriate to discuss structural linguistics, or a social scientist considers it wrong to discuss Marxism. Yet their preoccupation with the status of knowledge and education and their place in society is a serious one, illustrated by the emphasis of all the Muslim revivalists on the role of the teacher and of the school. Both have historically been fundamental to the transmission and organization of Islam, in every Muslim community, rural and urban, from Morocco to Indonesia. In this sense, the modern dakwah groups continue the tradition, although their concepts of the form and function of the school and of the legitimacy of the teacher have been adjusted to their own goals and conditions.

Dakwah "fanaticism," an accusation commonly levelled at the movements by both popular stereotype and government critics, has received unfavourable publicity in a variety of contexts. Although much has been made of the destruction of material goods, it is possible to argue that such acts are comparable to a sort of defiant but symbolic breaking with a past way of life, a rejection of a life without religion, in preparation for the rebirth and a new identity. Such radical acts and crossings, marked by similar, apparently destructive acts, have been noted in many religious and other crises, both on the level of the individual and group. Other, more disturbing acts of violence included a series of incidents, in 1976 and 1977, involving assaults by masked Muslims in Arab attire on a number of Hindu temples, and destruction of their "idols" (*patung*). Such campaigns against idolatry were supposed to guarantee for their perpetrators a sure place in paradise, and there was even believed to be a formula by which one's term in paradise could be calculated by the number of idols vanquished. One hundred thousand was considered necessary for residence in perpetuity. This particular series of events, many of which seem to have been perpetrated by either teachers or overseas-trained students of dakwah persuasion, was effectively put to an end with the defensive killing of four out of five of the Muslim attackers by the guards at the Hindu temple of Kerling in September 1977.[14] The slain assailants were thought by dakwah sympathizers to have died a martyr's death (*mati syahid*).

Although the terminology used is religious and the symbols Islamic, there is little doubt that the interests of dakwah have a strong, if latent, ethnic component. All promote Malay interests in some form, whether ABIM's ties with PAS, Darul Arqam's programme for economic independence, or Tabligh's concern with the status of "marginal" Indian Muslims. Yet dakwah supporters are not alone in their Malay chauvinism. In their own way, UMNO supporters, with their emphasis on Bumiputera policies and special

Malay rights, are equally communal. This opposition is particularly salient among Malay students overseas, where, in most communities, two distinct cohorts co-exist but do not co-operate (cf. Mohd. Taib Abdullah 1978). The dakwah Malays are scrupulous about religious observances, whatever the obstacles presented by western campus life, and interact but minimally with either local students or non-dakwah Malays, preferring the company of Muslim students from other countries. By secluding themselves as far as possible from alien influences and temptations, they try to preserve the religious customs, orientations, and social contacts that will enable them to reintegrate into Malay-Muslim life on their return home. The Bumi Malays on the other hand, are prepared to accept many western offerings from the modernization programmes of the New Economic Policy, including collaboration with non-Malays in political and economic alliances where necessary. The social gap between the Bumi and the dakwah Malays on foreign campuses is further widened when the former schedule social and other events at what are the hours of prayer for the practising Muslim (particularly midday and about seven o'clock in the evening), which prevents the latter from participating in common activities, even should they so wish. Thus Malay cultural shows staged overseas are usually produced by the Bumi contingent, for these invariably make much of the visual and sensory richness of that part of "Malay" tradition and adat which is more Indic and less Islamic. The two groups even tend to reside separately, where options are available, and this helps to reinforce their distinctiveness and encapsulation (ibid. 1978).

One of the biggest problems faced by all the new dakwah leaders lies in the creation of a legitimacy for their authority in the absence of a more traditional isnad or salasilah. As noted above, only Ustaz Ashaari has any direct ties with the pondok tradition, while the rest are either self-taught or "spontaneously arisen" and attempt to translate the role of secular guru to a religious one. Those trained at the National University's Faculty of Islamic Studies are finding that this degree is slowly becoming recognized as a modern or latter-day source of legitimacy in Malaysia, although by no means on a par with the kind enjoyed by the established ulama. Further, dakwah leaders are young by traditional ulama standards. This is a major obstacle to their ready acceptance in rural areas, particularly when contraposed to the authority of more venerable local teachers and scholars. Even though their religious zeal and dedication are respected, the new young dakwah leaders are sometimes regarded by rural Malays as either arrogant or shallow in their knowledge of Islam, and, moreover, as poor in experience, not having "tasted the salt of life." What is more, their adoption of Arab dress is seen as presumptuous, for by the standards of their elders, this is the prerogative of those who have made the pilgrimage, a reward for religious status and merit. Probably the question of authority is as important as the ideological and theological controversies raised, whether over Malay adat or the style of kampung religious education. For once a village alim feels his personal control is slipping or threatened, he becomes defensive and reluctant to show support for dakwah ideas, as in the case of the Darul Arqam experiment in Kedah. To the extent that dakwah can reinforce the authority of an alim, however, it is more open to acceptance, as are some Tabligh activities and the joint school ventures between ABIM and a more traditional madrasah enabling the latter to cope with some of the pressures of social change. It is possible that in the future the rise of dakwah could prove to be the saviour of some of the now-threatened religious schools and turn the educational tide once more from secularism to religion.

At one level, dakwah leaders affirm similar goals, especially in opposition to outsiders. On other occasions, however, they take care to preserve their respective boundaries and power domains, sometimes by mutual criticism. Thus Darul Arqam's excessive "otherworldliness" and Tabligh's sometimes aggressive recruitment tactics have come under fire from the other groups. Behind the scenes, there is in fact considerable personal interaction, and even co-operation, among the leaders of the various organizations, who visit and discuss problems with one another and sometimes even attend each others' lectures. Likewise, their followers are often eclectic, rather than exclusive, in their loyalties, so that in practice organizational boundaries are by no means clear-cut. As we shall see in the next chapter, this very fluidity is one of the strengths of dakwah, although it makes any structural definition hard to pin down.

Meanwhile, back in the rural areas, where it is to their own advantage, and where it can be controlled or put to an enhancement of their legitimacy, traditional religious authorities are willing to lift ideas selectively from the modern dakwah movements and even to co-operate with them in limited ways. A case in point (already described), is the Bukit Mertajam madrasah which joined forces with the ABIM school network. The religious teacher clearly felt that the arrangement breathed new life into an otherwise doomed institution, hence the concessions would ultimately buttress his own position. Financially, the school was relatively secure from the investments of another branch of the family in a bus company and bookstore, but the guru was also concerned about keeping abreast of the rapidly changing ideological and social climate and not being left stranded by the religious ferment engulfing his potential "clientele." He still retains complete control over the religious section of the school, which meets in the mornings, and leaves the academic and examination side to ABIM's teachers in the afternoons. In 1980-81, plans were reportedly afoot for a similar alliance between ABIM and another religious school in Alor Setar, Kedah. Most of the "traditional" ulama interviewed in fact showed substantial flexibility of opinion, at least verbally, and receptivity to new religious ideas from other sources. In support of this, most of the pondok and madrasah guru interviewed had, at one time or another, allowed urban dakwah lecturers to speak to their pupils or had themselves attended dakwah lectures elsewhere. Most recognize and respect the genuine commitment of the dakwah leaders and find it gratifying in modern, urban youth. But again, the crucial issue for the older leaders is to retain their own position locally. To go along with some of the new trends is to bow to the inevitable. On the other hand, where association with ABIM, and its PAS connections, is liable to compromise him with the state religious council or local UMNO authorities, a guru will reject out of hand any formal ties with that organization. Likewise, too close a sympathy with Darul Arqam can create an undesirable reputation for "fanaticism," which conflicts with the rural population's desire to achieve more "urban" material levels of comfort and standard of living and economic development. One religious guru in Kedah admitted to being a personal friend and admirer of Arqam's Ustaz Ashaari, but he would not reveal this to his pupils or congregation or try to introduce Arqam ideas for fear of compromising his own authority and credibility. Because of its freedom from political bias or other interests, Tabligh is the movement to which many prudent rural ulama are willing to lend their support. Finally, the ritualistic forms of Arabism practised by many dakwah followers, such as the practice of stepping into the latrine with the left foot and out again with the right, their dress and eating customs, are regarded by rural people as excessive and unsuited or impossible for villagers to follow. Some rural guru too, who have spent long years in the lands whence these customs supposedly originate, have a more earthy, less idealistic view of Arab behaviour. One guru described with great gusto the avidity with which Arabs eat, their enormous appetites for large quantities of meat, and their habit of wiping their greasy hands on their beards. Others criticize the wealthier Arabs for their gambling and other spending excesses from their oil profits, which they feel should be redistributed, according to religious principles, to the poor and needy. By contrast, the urban dakwah idealists, many of whom have never visited the Arab homeland, place all Arabs on a pedestal, on grounds of origins alone. Ironically, just as urban dakwah enthusiasts denounce old-fashioned kampung religion as "ritualism," so their own attitudes to Arab custom are considered equally ritualistic by the villagers looking from the other side.

The fundamental concern of the rural authorities, then, is to protect their own position and reputation. As long as they retain their followings, they can afford some flexibility. Like the classic "big man" they must constantly be on their toes, be able to gauge the climate of the time and the needs and interests of their "constituents" and, if necessary, to renegotiate the "bargain" that maintains the established relationship and authority.

5

The Medium is the Message:
Modes of Transmission of Dakwah
in Malay-Muslim Society

So far, little attention has been paid to the question of how and why particular individuals become involved in dakwah at all. How far do ideological convictions alone determine participation, and to what extent do social pressures intervene? Must there be some pre-existing normative consensus over the goals, ideals, and meanings of dakwah, or is this an ex post facto creation of shared activities and social interaction? Are questions of theology and social conscience paramount, or does the shared experience of solidarity, and sometimes even communitas, override such concerns?

The very term "ideology"[1] conveys a notion of intensity, a conviction and independent pattern of thought, with a power and strength of its own. Ideas can reach a pitch sufficient to override, and sometimes control, the groups which bear the message, overcome by the fervour which engulfs them. The fever of ideological excitement and motivation, in this view, may be capable of dissolving old social boundaries, if only temporarily, into an unstructured and unabashed communitas (cf. Turner 1968). Implicit in the notion of ideological determinacy is the power of intellectual principles and other shared beliefs and norms to create the kind of strong mutual attachments and bonds to which Shils gave the name "ideological Bund." The obverse of this stand, however, is that the appeal of an ideology, or the reinforcement of ideas and norms already held, is as much dependent on the nature of the support groups as on the ideas themselves. Thus, the degree of acceptance, the sustaining and transmission of an ideology, may follow previously established groups and networks as much as create new ones. It is through the pressures of prior attachments and the sanctions of regular social interaction that normative consensus is achieved.

In Shils' pioneering study of German and American soldiers in wartime, he found that perception and attachment to grand causes and principles for which their countries were ostensibly fighting was in fact largely a function of platoon loyalty and comradely obligations. The effective group controlling these "national" sentiments was in fact a small, face-to-face unit of a primary or peer group variety. For these soldiers, the reason for their association was less compelling than the association itself, and the most immediate reality was an immediate fear of "letting their comrades down" rather than a more abstract loyalty to the values of the central system. Pressures such as these may be exerted either "horizontally," through the action of the relatively equal status peer group, or "vertically," via the emulation of respected authorities, either by virtue of their role or personality.

In the study of an entire ideological movement, we also confront the question of communication into broader domains, the channels along which ideas are carried, and particularly the roles and individuals which link the smaller units. These may be seen as nodes in a wider network (cf. Epstein 1973; Kapferer 1975). Structurally, the form of an ideological (or any social) movement may be hard to pin down. Far from being a unified entity with a well-defined shape or boundary or with an easily identifiable membership, a social movement, especially in the pre-routinized, developmental stage, is usually rather amorphous. Rarely will it correspond with any other formal structural group or constituency. To the contrary, it may thrive in the interstices or on the margins of such groups. In the event of a need for mass mobilization or demonstration, the groundwork is laid through the activity of the lesser units referred to as the bearers and transmitters, and sometimes decoders of, the ideology. In the jargon of members of many mass movements themselves, such units are more often known as "cells" and the actors in the communications network as a cadre system. In other words, the "movement" consists of a series of more or less interconnected smaller sub-sets, each with its own local variations, idiosyncracies, unique personal ties, and obligations. An understanding of the movement thus entails an analysis of these sets as well as the connections between them. Although from a distance, social movements may appear to have a distinctive form and structure and an equally identifiable ideological platform, on closer scrutiny, their apparent unity frequently dissolves into a diffuse assemblage of uncertainly linked fragments, each by itself somewhat fragile and ephemeral in a social-structural sense. In movements of this type, the communications network is particularly vulnerable to disjunctions and to modifications in the information transmitted from cell to cell. The links themselves are tenuous, and the interpretations often fallible and oriented towards the immediate, rather than the general, audience. Even where the symbols are the same, their meaning for each unit may undergo substantial modification.

Malaysian dakwah provides a good case of an ideological movement whose strengths lie heavily in the informal and personal relationships of other social ties and groupings. The movement as a whole, however, has only a weak structural autonomy of its own and proves particularly elusive to classical modes of institutional analysis. Even to use the term "movement" has its hazards, for this may suggest a greater unity, singleness of purpose, and concentration of activity than is actually the case. Adherence to dakwah lies more in patterns of behaviour or lifestyle, which, for individual participants, is normally embedded in the context of their more immediate social environment and relationships. Basically, this pattern is consistent with the fundamental meaning of "dakwah" ("a call to the faith"), which enjoins all Muslims to rededicate themselves to the faith in accordance with their own station in life. For "born" Muslims, this is a renewal of a commitment and can be expressed through a variety of behaviours, some highly visible, others more private. Interpretation and practice of dakwah therefore varies widely from individual to individual and can encompass any one or a combination of the following behaviours: to become consciously more "religious" or to be a good Muslim in the broadest sense (*beriman, beribadat*); to show good character (*peribadi*) and be respectful of others. More specifically, this may be expanded to a more meticulous observance of the pillars of Islam, such as praying, fasting, charity, and where possible, the haj, and may also include active participation in spreading the message more widely. For other dakwah followers it additionally means particular attention to Arabic rituals, symbols of dress, and eating styles. The more fastidious ostentatiously avoid all foods not cooked by Muslims or even not "traditionally" Malay or Arabic, for example, beancurd, bread. Finally, there are the most dramatic and defiant behaviours of all, those which may be said to mark a deliberate and calculated break with their less observant past, and which may involve rejection of all items symbolic of westernism and of jobs in secular society.

SOME BASIC SOCIAL RELATIONSHIPS IN MALAY SOCIETY

In order to place in proper perspective the role played by social support groups in the modern dakwah movement, it is necessary to understand the social relationships fundamental to traditional Malay society. These may be divided into two principal types: "horizontal" and more or less equal status; and "vertical" and of unequal status.

I. Horizontal

a) *Age and generation sets* (*golongan selapis*). In traditional Malay society, cleavages along lines of age and generation were apparent in most kampung activities, whether economic, mutual aid, religious, ritual, administrative, or recreational. Work groups, coffee-shop or mosque-lounging cliques, co-preparers of feasts (kenduri), various committees, and so forth, all tended to be recruited from the same age cohorts within their respective sex. This principle extended from informal to the most formal realms of activity and even determined terms of personal address. This is further reflected in kinship terminology—which is basically of the generational Hawaiian type— with a meticulous attention to sub-divisions by age within the generation sets.[2] Such terms are of importance too in determining categories of "appropriate" marriage partners. In practice, there often occurs a marked "generation gap" between parents and offspring, in contrast to the greater solidarity of the sibling group (*adek-beradek*). This peer pattern now tends to be carried over into the modern, urban and educational system, within such institutions as schools, universities, and hostels, in youth clubs and among the rank and file of army and police barracks, as well as in more marginal and ephemeral formations as gangs and coffee-shop cliques. Within the age or peer group, smaller clusters of a more personally based nature are usually more significant for the individual, and these are generally of a span of between ten and twenty persons.

b) *Kinship and Residence.* In Malay villages, it is often difficult in practice to separate the principles of kinship and neighbourhood for the two may coincide. Where they do not, however, neighbours frequently take precedence over kin in many co-operative activities, from the mundane work group to the ceremonials and rituals attending weddings and other rites of passage. The bonds of residential propinquity, important in themselves, are immeasurably strengthened when combined with membership in the same age and generation set and generate a double solidarity of great durability. Neighbours should under no circumstances be passed over in any events involving more than a single household, and their presence will be requested before invitations are issued to relatives residing at a greater distance. Neighbours should also be the first to render assistance in times of need, again, before the more distant kin may appear on the scene. The ties of neighbourliness are nowadays carried over into the less traditional contexts of dormitories, hostels, barracks, and other workers' "quarters," permitting the development of strong and intimate bonds of loyalty between those in such association. Physical proximity and neighbourhood thus have the power to eclipse the influence of the family, whose importance in the life of the individual proportionally recedes. From a historical perspective, no doubt the relatively high degree of geographical mobility in situations of adequate available land, encouraged the cultivation of neighbourly relations when true kin were not readily accessible. Once again, Malay society could be said to be "on the move," this time to the towns and larger centres, where regroupment in new secondary schools, universities, housing developments, police and army quarters, and even land schemes, simultaneously draw kinsmen apart and create new neighbours and colleagues. In many institutions, of course, we see a combination of the peer and neighbour principles, particularly in educational institutions, whether the traditional religious pondok or the modern university.

II. Vertical Relations

Traditional Malay society was both authoritarian and hierarchical and characterized by the existence of several distinct strata from royalty to slaves. At the level of the kampung, aside from the penghulu or headmen, or occasionally some other *orang besar*, representing the lowest ranks of the political hierarchy, the other major stratum with some claim to élite status was that of the religious teachers and ulama. Not only do they qualify as an alternate to the secular local élite; these scholars also set the style for teacher-pupil relationships of modern, secular, Malay society, even in urban educational institutions.

Characteristic of the traditional guru/disciple relationship, which was normally cross-generational, was the extreme respect, although not necessarily personal affection, shown by the pupil in conjunction with a passive-imitative mode of learning. Discipline was strict, and questions not encouraged. The pupil was compared to the "empty vessel" waiting to be filled from the fountain of wisdom and knowledge which was imparted in a one-way flow. Modern teachers and even university lecturers share many of the same general characteristics of the traditional guru, whose methods and authority, in the eyes of rural-origin Malays at least, they are expected to display. In place of the religious/intellectual genealogy (isnad), however, are now substituted western-derived academic credentials. Like their traditional counterparts, modern teachers and lecturers often bring back new ideas from overseas, and they are in a particularly strong position to mould their students' attitudes, through their manner of presentation of academic material and the possibilities of alternate sources of knowledge and values. Unquestionably, one almost certain way to gain respect in Malay society and often, by extension, to serve as a role model for the young is to become recognized as a teacher, whether by founding one's own school, by joining the ranks of the more bureaucratized educational institutions of the government, or even by becoming accepted as the personal mentor of special-interest groups such as poetry circles or silat clubs. The status, and both personal and social gratifications, of the teacher-as-a-role also contributes to the immense appeal of the burgeoning crop of "alternate" schools for rehabilitating examination dropouts, cramming students for examinations, or for some other special religious purpose or tutorial function.

Vertical relationships with a strong authoritarian bent are also familiar in other domains of Malay society, notably the army and police forces. The position of the commanding officer is one requiring great loyalty, again, as much to the role as to its occupant or person. Malays are a majority in their country's armed forces, and they customarily live in hierarchically organized barracks, where not only the men, but also their wives and families, are subject to the influences and emulation of rank.

The sense of "knowing one's place" in the vertical scheme of things is, for Malays, more than a logical or technical product of administrative necessity. It is a much more pervasive ranking of inherent personal worth, as much an element in a system of honour and prestige as of a bureaucracy alone. In the ever-expanding web of the civil service these subtleties are reflected in personal behaviours, especially between status senior and junior. Thus it is only on reaching a certain level in the hierarchy that a civil servant knows, for example, that he may run a Volvo, for there are unwritten, but tacitly understood, agreements as to the appropriate range of car models for each rank. No civil servant is expected to violate the ideal order and equation and "jump the gun" by purchasing a Volvo prematurely. Ultimately, of course, such patterns of behaviour can be related back to the old "protector" ethos, which is still a dominant principle in modern Malay government, whether in the formal civil service bureaucracy, in Party UMNO or in other political-appointive positions. Like Hang Tuah and Hang Jebat before them, the civil servant supports but does not try to outdo, his master.

THE PATHS OF DAKWAH

a) Horizontal Ties

The genesis of much of the dakwah activity and ideology in student communities, both at home and overseas, highlights the importance of modern transformations of the horizontal peer group or golongan selapis. Outside Malaysia, its effectiveness is frequently enhanced by the enclave, even siege-like existence of some "foreign" students, who turn inward on their own resources or else join forces with others in a like situation, such as fellow Muslims from other countries. In this case, psychic support and social resources are contributed by networks of Muslim students and buttressed by their common faith. Religious ideology is the consummation of the social needs which thrust them together in the first place. Even in the absence of the more formal structure of Islamic associations or else within them, smaller and more informal groups and cliques tend to emerge for a variety of social, recreational, problem-solving, and advisory purposes. These are the active cells which co-opt new members, particularly those arriving fresh from home, by meeting them from the plane, finding the new arrival a place to live, usually within their own enclave, and by providing extensive informational and support services which most neophytes sorely need. In so doing, the "patrons" generate a sense of obligation to their own group or organization and so to its religious observances. As many overseas students who have involuntarily enjoyed such welcomes testify, once they are involved or identified with one of these networks, it is progressively more difficult with time to become detached. By the same "serendipity" factor, should the newcomer happen to be met or inducted into campus society by other kinds of students, for example, the Bumi Malay group, then he or she has an equal chance of being co-opted into that sub-community and to subscribe to its lifestyle and tenets (cf. Abdullah Taib 1978). In some ways, the newcomers are the "empty vessels," ready to be filled by whatever source first encounters them. Normative or ideological consensus will then follow.

Although all the major overseas Muslim student communities support an impressive number of well-organized Islamic associations, with large memberships from all parts of the Muslim world, the really effective and meaningful group for most day-to-day activities and personal contact is a smaller unit, usually centred on a residential cluster, for example, neighbours in a hostel or dormitory, room- or flat-mates, or, alternatively, those in the same academic faculty or class. It is always a single-sex group only. When such units also function as discussion groups, particularly for religious and moral or for personal problems, they are commonly known as usrah. Usrah may be regarded as the basic cells on which the dakwah movement both in Malaysia and overseas is built. In their sessions, usrah may debate such questions as how science students, being taught by non-Muslims who do not base their teachings on the Koran nor on the religious values and premises of Islam, nor yet recognize non-empirical, inspirational sources of knowledge, can come to terms with their disciplines, scientific, and spiritual. To this particular problem, a typical solution might be along the following lines: "since God is great, God can also be a scientist, therefore science must also be good, and good for one's country, as long as it does not lose sight of Islam." The point for these students is that they should be selective in their adoption of western customs and try to use their religion to guide their choices, in this case as future science teachers and practising Muslims simultaneously. Some students face serious health problems, which they often attribute as much to moral and spiritual as to physical or climatic causes, and their usrah discussions focus on improving their health through personal commitment to the faith by extra prayers and Koran reading, sometimes at the expense of their secular studies. Usrah are now found in schools and campuses everywhere, and they are also beginning to be held in some middle-class neighbourhoods as an acceptable new form of social activity for people of the same sex and age group, in keeping with the current religious climate. Neighbourhood usrah commonly select a passage from the scriptures and spend about an hour debating its implications and meaning for modern Muslims, with the accompaniment of refreshments. In these meetings, the level of theological sophistication varies with the participants, as does the choice of topic.

In some cases, especially where the degree of isolation, encapsulation, or even sense of deprivation, as among some student bodies, is high, the pitch of emotional involvement with the usrah clique and the solidarity engendered qualifies it as a situation for the experience of communitas. Here, everyday realities, roles, problems, and obligations can be temporarily cast aside, and this release lends extra energy to the emotion with which to vent their feelings. Some write or quote poetry, others give thanks to Allah for guiding their decisions and experiences, from the most mundane "luck" in finding a convenient parking spot to the most severe of identity crises. So mutually dependent are some of these students on their usrah, that social disengagement becomes progressively more difficult, as does disengagement from the ideology which accompanies it. Shared experience leads to the shared idea. As noted above, the ideological option between the categories of Bumi and dakwah Malays, especially overseas, is often determined by the initial contacts of the newcomer, rather than by the latter's conscious reflection and choice, and once established, is well-nigh irreversible.

Like the classic "*huis clos*," some of these groups are so all-encapsulating as to encompass and control the individual's entire life. Members may impose an almost vigilante-like watchfulness over each other, as well as providing support in times of distress. Although usrah memberships are normally of a single sex, associations between two usrah of the opposite sex frequently lead to early marriages, since a rigid observance of Muslim sexual propriety through dakwah so severely restricts inter-sexual contacts that marriage is the only acceptable solution to the desire for a more sustained relationship. There can be no "dating" outside of matrimony. It is thus becoming a familiar practice in dakwah circles for young people, particularly overseas, to marry while still in high school, and this causes some anguish to the authorities who have provided their scholarships in anticipation of future years of service under the terms of their contract or "bond."

Similar pressures exist in Malaysia itself, both in universities and in high schools, and they are particularly evident in the hostels where most Malay students reside. In every modern university dormitory there is at least one usrah, usually of about eight to ten persons, based either on the residence principle or else on line of study. The mode of "launching" dakwah into an existing or potential clique may be through the lone activity or pressures of a single individual, but it is more often achieved through a growing awareness and familiarity with one another's sentiments and problems and interests. Given that there is a foundation of apparent sympathy in a dakwah direction, a decision to make a formal commitment to it may then be quite conscious and calculated. Indeed, most new dakwah followers are quite articulate about their choice and about the lifestyle changes and restrictions it will entail. Verbal reasons given tend to follow one or other of a limited number of pro forma statements, such as "kerana Allah" (for the sake of God), a personal test (*percubaan sendiri*), to give meaning to an empty life (*jiwa kosong*), or words to the effect that everyone should follow the Koran and Islamic law as far as they are able. Those contemplating a change in lifestyle to more dakwah will often undergo a "preparation" period, during which they gradually adjust their behaviour in line with dakwah requirements. This may be helped along by taking a weekend retreat (*jemaah*) offered by one of the organizations, ABIM, Darul Arqam (or in the case of men, Tabligh). Or initially they may make a vow (*niat*) that if, for example, they pass a particular exam, they will conform to full Islamic dress requirements. In the interim, a girl may begin just by wearing a headscarf, covering all her hair, and eventually graduating to the full mini-telekung. During this trial period, she will constantly discuss the problems and prospects of her decision at length with friends in the same situation, or with those who have made the pact together for mutual support. They are aware that once full Islamic attire is adopted, it will no longer be proper to attend films or other entertainment, to travel alone, or to be seen in doubtful company, situations, or places. Once begun, to backslide will mean a loss of face. It also has implications for the kind of friends of the opposite sex or potential spouses who will be attracted. Dakwah followers will often avoid direct contact with members of the opposite sex or at least communicate by more indirect means, for example, by averting the head.

Pressures to find a like-minded spouse will often alienate young people from their parents and their choice of partner, and this pushes the dakwah followers deeper into dependence on each other. In dakwah circles the only acceptable forms of male-female interaction take place within the circuit of religious lectures, seminars, and conferences which bring the members of the smaller usrah together and which become the effective arbiters and guardians of reputations, particularly of the women. Girls who wish to preserve their reputation or to win the approval or attention of certain boys feel constrained to cover themselves and to observe dakwah principles, sometimes in self-defence, in order to avoid being labelled loose or "evil women" (*perempuan jahat*). However, the desire of boys and girls to see each other helps to increase attendance at religious events. Some boys too ingratiate themselves with girls by claiming to be "dakwah," so that any advances are regarded with less suspicion.

The initial "point of entry" of an individual into a dakwah clique or usrah may be through one of the horizontal ties of a close friend, a fellow student, or possibly a sibling, along the lines of the golongan selapis, or, alternatively, under the influence of a respected teacher, student leader, or religious lecturer. The timing of the initial appeal can also be important. Many young people make the final decision following such personal crises as failing an exam, falling in love, or experiencing the confusion of adjusting to a rapidly changing life situation, whether overseas or on returning home from abroad. The psychological dimension of dakwah goes beyond the capacity of this writer to assess reliably, but these impressions are strong.

Another situation which may propel potential followers into dakwah activity is a desire to dissociate themselves from, and to show opposition to, specific other groups, such as those identified with drug-taking. In the school and university environment, the "pariah" groups avoided by the dakwah-oriented students are those involved in sports and in drama. Both of these activities permit an un-Islamic exposure of the body, mixing of the sexes, and in the case of drama, the presentation of often risqué themes, frequently of western origin. On campuses, the polarization of these two cohorts, drama and dakwah, both Malay, manifests itself in all possible dimensions, from style of dress to recreational preferences, modes of sexual interaction, and, of course, choice of company. In class they never collaborate, they sit at different tables in the canteen, and they have different "heroes" among the faculty.

Solidarity of usrah groups, once formed, is reinforced by the sharing of a number of activities, beginning with the dawn prayer (subur), to which they rouse each other by knocking on doors while it is still dark. Ablutions are performed quickly; one girl will help her companion push a forbidden strand of hair out of sight under her prayer veil all amid whispers, so as not to awaken their less religiously observant neighbours. Prayer will often be followed by a special, non-obligatory religious talk by one of the more zealous lecturers or dormitory supervisors, and then the "secular" day begins. Prayers throughout the day are also performed together whenever possible, and prayer garments are constantly carried from room to room or in briefcases around campus for ready use. The students await the sound of the call to prayer and begin to pray in perfect unison. Such activity has the obvious effect of increasing the social distance between dakwah and non-dakwah students and erecting barriers which become progressively more divisive. Morality and piety thus become very much the function of social interaction within the small group or set whose members also eat together, study together, walk in clusters, and accompany each other everywhere. In the usrah too may sometimes be found something of the communitas, for its members temporarily abrogate daily and non-religious social distinctions and concerns in the collective euphoria of discovering new interests and meanings and even a renewed strength in their ethnic identity through Islam amidst the emotional support of familiar faces, close personal bonds, and sharing activities and experiences.

The strength of the usrah lies in a number of features. First, its size is crucial. It must obviously be small enough for everyone to know everyone else, directly and personally, independent of any intermediate linkage; hence it is extremely close-knit. Second, and consequent upon the first, the degree of role transparency is extremely high, so that individual deviations or behavioural inconsistencies are made exceedingly difficult, particularly when reinforced by residential closeness and the shared daily round. The multiplexity of the roles played, simultaneously as friends, fellow students, neighbours, Malays, and Muslims together, within the usrah, creates a heavy investment in the relationships involved, and the sanctions each can exert upon the other in their own circumscribed personal, mutually appraising little world can be truly devastating. Verbally, the in-group ethos is sometimes sustained by the use of Arabic personal pronouns (*ane*; *anté*), and the Muslim greeting, *as salamualaikum*, among themselves, but only selectively extended to outsiders. To neglect one's religious or dakwah obligation is thus to deny this close bond and to risk the overturning of the protective shell which mediates between the vulnerable individual and the wider, more anonymous structures of the campus, town, or alien ethnic and religious groups. For roommates not involved in the usrah of their neighbour, denial of usrah membership is equally difficult. It can only be achieved in such close physical quarters by evasive tactics, for example, one non-participant "taking a nap" at the crucial prayer times, lying prone on the bed, facing the wall, while in the same small room a cohort of roommates and friends perform their rituals, their faces towards Mecca.

Peer group conformity sometimes leads to an almost competitive "holier than thou" syndrome with obsessive concern over the minutiae of presentation of self in matters of dress, prayer, eating habits, and other semi-public rituals. Inevitably, a few real zealots, among them some of the dormitory counsellors, take an almost prurient delight in patrolling the rooms in search of any deviations from the straight and narrow, and they may receive the collaboration of the more competitive dakwah residents. There is always the fear among usrah group members of revealing their innermost weaknesses to the others. One girl, for example, confessed to a morbid fear of being called upon to read a passage from the scriptures in Arabic at a religious celebration she had been invited to attend in honour of the successful completion of his first reading of the Koran by the younger brother of a friend. Afraid that her inability to perform in accordance with her public image as "dakwah," would stigmatize her forever as a "false dakwah" to the world, she made an excuse to leave the ceremony before it began.

Ultimately, all of these religious activities have the effect of highlighting the exclusive Malay character of the bond. Not just the obvious exclusion of non-Muslims from various esoteric religious practices, but also the curtailment of a broader social life are consequences of dakwah observance. The fact that many additional recreational activities, especially those involving non-Muslims, invariably conflict with prayer times and/or Islamic morality and may also involve "doubtful" foods makes them off-limits to the faithful. Further, increasingly preoccupied and turning inwards to their own interests and numerous obligations, they draw apart and so the ethnic gap grows wider.

The kind of mutual influence among peers which operates among clusters of friends in educational institutions is also found in other segments of Malay society. Youth clubs, of which Malays have a particularly large number, and tend to join with greater frequency than non-Malays (see Chapter 3), are often the vehicles of new ideas and comparable social pressures. For example, should one or two members develop an interest in ABIM, this interest will spread throughout the entire branch, from friend to friend, until it may become known as an "ABIM Youth Club." ABIM lecturers may then be invited to address the members, and individual members will find it increasingly difficult to avoid attendance or its dictates. One urban youth club, which became identified with ABIM in this manner, adopted its own "uniform" of green Arab robe for men and the "half-purdah" with mini-telekung for girls, which made them distinctive in the kampung where the youth club was centred. This affectation of dress angered many of their parents and older residents, whose view of such costume is that it should be reserved for those who have already made the pilgrimage. Several of the youth leaders were called to account for their "presumptuousness" by the chief of UMNO in the kampung and by the local imam, but in their own defence, the youth claimed that they should not be judged by their attire, rather by their behaviour. On the latter score, the kampung elders had to acknowledge that since their "conversion" to ABIM, they had indeed been active in providing extra-curricular tuition to the younger children and, in the process, acting as "child-minders" for the Malay equivalent of "latch-key" children, those left unattended by working mothers. On the other hand, the content of some of the tuition was also suspect, on the grounds that it was carrying a rather transparent ABIM message and teaching its academic subjects in ABIM's Yayasan Anda style. Once again, in their own defence, the young people claimed that by creating a solidary membership with a sense of common purpose, they had managed to draw in and "cure" a number of young drug addicts, who were now claimed to be models of youthful virtue. The confrontation continued for many months and became particularly acrimonious on the part of the UMNO leaders, who read political meanings into the youth club's activities and saw it as a threat to the membership of the local branch of UMNO Youth. By way of retaliation, UMNO Youth was also rallied into a flurry of sudden activity and began to organize a variety of events, including carnivals (*pesta*), containing many elements such as popular religious songs (*nasyid*), which they hoped would deflate some of the moral superiority of the other youth club. Eventually, kampung life settled down to an existence of mutual toleration and a form of routinization set in. Similar generational conflicts have occurred in other urban kampungs, and among the issues have been suspicion on the part of the elders of the excessive popularity of tape cassettes of the speeches of Darul Arqam's Ustaz Ashaari, now widely circulating through the youth club network. In another case, a local youth club was famous throughout the city for its sponsorship and as perennial champions of the Boria[3] dance and musical comedy routine which had long delighted many fans beyond their home kampung. When the members of the Boria team suddenly renounced all connection with or participation in Boria, as "inappropriate" (*tak sesuai*) to Islam, great was the disappointment and even resentment among many townspeople over this latest religious "deprivation," and it received headline treatment in the local media. Once again, the powerful influence of the peer group can be seen at work and, along with it, the tendency to polarize the different generations. It should be noted that most youth clubs caught up in the dakwah ferment have members with direct contacts with colleges and universities or are themselves students.

Finally, the same principles of peer group pressure fostering the sweep of new religious ideas through the ranks seem to occur in police and army barracks and quarters. Here, the residential/neighbour and equal status factors are reinforced by the already present emphasis on codes of discipline and group conformity central to these professions. Even the wives are similarly affected and develop their own parallel dakwah activities and usrah groupings.

Although encompassed by their peer groups, cliques, and networks while at school and on campus, when rural students in particular return home to their kampungs, they inevitably revive old relationships both with members of their golongan selapis and with kin. Some students confess quite frankly that they are drawn inexorably back into more relaxed kampung styles of interaction for the peer pressures here operate on the same principles and with the same imperativeness as those at school. Some claim that full dakwah observances are difficult to sustain in the kampung setting. For example, the relatively open structure of the rural Malay house and the custom of constant, unannounced neighbourly visiting makes it difficult for a girl committed to Islamic personal modesty even to relax in her own home. Normally, the full religious attire is only required in public or in the presence of males in a potentially marriageable category (*muhrim*). While in the security of the home, a woman may take off her veils and relax or do housework in a simple sarung and literally let down her hair. While it is true that most Malay women do typically spend more time in the back regions of the kitchen, this is more from domesticity than from modesty per se, and since Malay homes, unlike those in the Middle East, are not designed to seclude, they are still frequently visible by visitors. Such compromises to religious convictions distress some dakwah followers, who try to rearrange their family's domestic life and post their brothers as "gate-keepers" to the house to warn them of impending visits. Probably the most critical test is aroused by the prospects of marriage. Whereas their dakwah teachings have led them to condemn as alien and un-Islamic all Hindu-origin rituals attending the customary Malay wedding, the followers are faced with a personal choice of pleasing the elders or of remaining loyal to their peer and religious loyalties. Even when questioned away from home and from the direct influence of their relatives, some dakwah students allow that in practice they may have to be prepared to undergo the traditional adat rites. The recidivists are usually armed with defensible religious rationales for their decision in succumbing to parental and kampung pressure. One is that if no public bersanding is held, "people will think that I have been secretly married before" or that the bride and groom must have "lived together first," and that this could create an undesirable image for the couple, the family, and for the dakwah movement. Such rationales may then be clinched with the oft-quoted Koranic injunction (by both dakwah and non-dakwah alike), to respect one's mother, under whose feet heaven lies (*syurga letak dibawah tapak kaki ibu*), and who, presumably, favours the adat way of doing things. By this, dakwah followers, both male and female, indicate that they may be prepared to accept parental selection of spouses according to Malay custom, for "parents have their children's best interests at heart." Knowing the religious inclinations of their offspring, they can therefore be trusted to find a suitable mate, that is, sympathetic to dakwah, for those inclined in that direction. Such statements, however, sometimes fly in the face of reality, for "old people are bound by what others say, and are hard to change" and may, on the contrary, try to defuse that dakwah orientation by arranging an "anti-dakwah" marriage.

Others, more militant and intransigent, return home with the aim of active religious "consciousness-raising," either informally, or else as part of the PKPIM's organized campaigns (see Chapter 3). Intent on propagating the dakwah message, they try to influence the attitudes of their seniors through personal example and gentle hints, urging them to pray more regularly, attend the mosque, and sometimes they bring in ABIM or Darul Arqam lecturers. Among their peers and juniors, especially younger siblings, they provide tuition and school assistance, ever welcome in the kampung, to which are attached a variety of subliminal religious messages as well as more overt moral education (*ahklak*) classes. When the community mounts even a secular festival (pesta), such as those often staged by the UMNO political party, these enthusiasts work to substitute choirs of religious songs (nasyid) for the old-style Boria or modern pop music and entertainment. Obviously, the decisions and solutions of each dakwah follower will vary with the individual and the situation. But in each case, the crucial variables to consider will revolve around the relative strengths and effectiveness of the various networks, peer and inter-generational, and the nature of, and commitment to the home community. Upon these social pressures religious ideology may rise and fall.

Moving out of the small, nucleated usrah, friendship cliques and residential ties, a more extended network takes over without clear limits or boundaries. At its widest, it may be equated with the entire ABIM or Darul Arqam following, or even with the whole "dakwah movement." Even this network, however, is based ultimately on peer group ties and depends on these for its effectiveness. Many high school students, for example, are first exposed to, and encouraged to follow the activities of, ABIM through university friends (slightly older members of essentially the same peer group) or by older siblings or the younger friends of older siblings. For example, one high school student decided to join ABIM under the influence of an older cousin at the university, who was writing his honours thesis on a religious topic. The younger cousin started to pray regularly, attended the mosque, and spent his summer vacations working in ABIM's book department. He also preferred ABIM over Arqam, in his words, because they allow him to do some sports, and he is something of a badminton champion. Sometimes exposure to dakwah occurs through special programmes organized by the latter. Among these are programmes whereby university students "adopt" (angkat) fifth or sixth form high school pupils to introduce them to campus and hostel life on the assumption that they will eventually enter university. Often their introduction to the university will coincide with a religious conference, with follow-up sessions arranged. Other projects such as the vacation "consciousness-raising" campaigns have already been mentioned. Here again, the principal and most accessible target is the kampung youth, and the most effective medium is tuition. Along with the new, often close, relationships so generated goes an exposure to the dakwah way of life, which, of course, is reinforced if and when these young people enter university. Whether or not an individual adopts ABIM, Darul Arqam, or Tabligh ideas depends very much on the orientation of his or her particular network and the overlap of its membership with those already involved. It is entirely possible for two siblings, whose networks, other than those of kinship, involve separate schools, clubs, and sets of friends, to develop different dakwah loyalties, for example, one to ABIM, another to Arqam. Many rural Malay children are taken from the kampung at a relatively early age to attend secondary schools in town with the result that their effective friendship networks are centred there and may even result in their spending weekends in religious retreats rather than at home. Once dakwah ideas enter an institution, it is only a matter of time before they spread more widely along the paths of personal ties and associations, from class to class, room to room, friend to friend. Only when some more deep or unbridgeable social division is encountered, such as the gulf "outcasting" the university drama students, then dakwah cannot leap the gap, and the limits of ideological transmission are reached.

It should be noted that the mode of transmission of the religious message via such personal networks, and the exclusivist nature of some usrah discussion groups often results in subtle changes of that message as it travels down the line. The ideology "at the top," for example, as propounded by the president of ABIM or by Arqam's Ashaari, may be otherwise interpreted as it moves away from the centre to followers on the periphery. Where the president or leaders may preach the transcendence of Islam over racial or ethnic divisions, rank and file followers, to the contrary, may use their religious identity to provide them and their immediate social circle with reinforcement of ethnic identity and to merge Islam and Malayness in opposition to the non-Malays. Both points of view can be supported with appropriate quotations from the Koran, taken as isolated passages, as the basis for usrah discussions. Factual information also varies at different levels of the organizations, to the extent that some self-proclaimed religious devotees had barely heard of Anwar Ibrahim or else knew nothing about him or what he stood for. As a mode of communication, therefore, the religious network can sometimes be less than reliable and not always capable of replicating faithfully the input at one level with the output at another. In part, this accounts for the variability of belief ("ideology") and practice in different segments of the dakwah community and the easy fluidity of "membership" or followings. On the other hand, the resulting lack of specificity permits the affiliation and interest of a wide variety of individuals whose varying interpretations may never become overt nor come into confrontation.

b) Vertical Ties of Authority

Apart from the importance of the peer group and other "horizontal" links in the transmission of dakwah, the other prerequisite for its acceptability by other Malays is the example and stimulus of a high status and respected authority with credible religious connections. In the modern, urban-based dakwah movements, a new pattern or religious authority has been substituted for the more traditional alim or guru, in which the teacher's credentials are often derived from a western university or other academic background rather than the traditional isnad. Despite his youth and lack of deep immersion in an old religious tradition or school, the modern teacher inherits the generally high status and aura associated with the established guru role. The modern guru tends to compensate for traditional qualifications by a greater "intellectualism,"—a stress on rationality as opposed to the "ritualism" of adat—combined with a calculated appeal to the authority of the past through a fundamentalist emphasis on the original scriptures and acceptance of Arabic customs and precedents. Once the modern teacher is accepted as a religious role model, he/she will generally be accorded the same respect as the more traditional guru. At the high school level in particular, pupils tend not to question either the material or the authority and may even be rather passive (*secara penerimaan*), sometimes even in the face of personal dislikes. Popular teachers with religious messages, however, are often the most influential figures in the lives of impressionable young pupils, who may accept the message out of respect and admiration for the guru as much as for the message's content. Many ABIM members are now on the staffs of high schools throughout Malaysia and are making their influence felt in this way. Some use formal tactics and found religious associations in the school, which reflect the ABIM philosophy; others get their message across by the more informal means of personal example and opinions. For every teacher with a dakwah message, however, there is usually another with an alternate approach, and frequently this is the official religious teacher of the school, a ministry-appointed ustaz. Few of these ustaz are part of the dakwah movement since they are expected to follow ministry-approved religious curricula and to be faithful to the interests of their employer. Somewhat paradoxically, therefore, the official religious teacher may be far more permissive in matters, say, of sports participation for girls than a teacher of mathematics who is sympathetic to ABIM. Both kinds of teacher will have their own followings and favourites, and upon this will depend to a great extent the religious "ideological" bent of different contingents of pupils.

Malaysian education generally, like its Islamic precedents, is noted for its tendency towards authoritarianism, although when this is excessive, some resistance or reaction may be ignited. This may take the form of the "mass hysteria" syndrome, described in Chapter 3. The Ministry of Education considers that the ideal teacher-pupil relationship resembles that between father and child with an emphasis on obedience and respect by the child and responsibility and firmness, tempered by a touch of paternal kindness, as the "fatherly touch" (*bersifat bapak*), without being overly harsh (*tidak terlalu kejam*) (*Bintang Timur*, 10/4/80). College and university students, with more exposure to the aggressive academic tactics of western education, however, may be more willing to challenge their teachers, although not always directly. On some occasions of disagreement, they have been known to circulate anonymous letters, like the *surat layang*[4] of rural peasant protesters, framing their grievances. This occurred on one occasion when a class of dakwah university students, dissatisfied with a course on Islamic history being offered by a certain professor, despatched a series of anonymous missives to the dean, justifying their position by quoting liberally from the works of an admired guru and religious leader at another university, thus, symbolically at least, pitting one "authority" against another. At no time, however, did the dissatisfied students confront the unpopular lecturer openly, largely out of respect for his pedagogic rank. Lecturers in subjects other than religion can also trade on their high status and authority as teachers and can make an impression with their religious views along with the academic instruction. Sometimes this is done directly, as an adjunct to the principal theme; at other times, it is more subliminally interwoven as part of the academic message itself. For example, in a social science course dealing with economic development, materialist interpretations may be discarded in favour of more "spiritual" kinds of development, Marxism may be rejected on overtly religious grounds, and students may be made to understand that, before any meaningful programme of national development can be achieved, they must first be satisfied as to their own identity and sure of their "roots" (*akar umbi*). They may also be told that, whatever the deficiencies in man's planning, ultimately "God will provide." Some lecturers, newly returned from overseas, are often rehearsing aloud their own confusions and conflicts, and in one case, an instructor fresh from a western university began his course with a Marxist bang but concluded the course by exhorting his students to "trust in Allah," to pray for success in their exams, but if they failed, to take consolation in the fact that knowledge is better "in the heart" (*ilmu disiarakan dalam hati, itu yang baik*). One MARA social science lecturer claims that western sociological theories are so disparate and contradictory that it is more satisfying to substitute a deliberately Koranic base for social studies and to provide the students with a clear sense of purpose and direction. Quite a number of dakwah lecturers admit to counselling their students not to set too much store by exam results or even by particular kinds of jobs, suggesting that should they fail in one or both, then this must be construed as God's challenge and plan for them. No individual, they advise, should struggle against his/her fate (*rezeki*), and in the case of women, they should always give priority to their future roles as wives and mothers.

Insofar as many of the rotating lecturers and recruiters for ABIM, Darul Arqam, and to a lesser extent, Tabligh are also secular teachers or lecturers, in some other field, in their own right, what they lack in traditional religious legitimacy they make up in their high secular guru status. By their fundamentalist orientations and constant appeals to the past, they attempt to re-traditionalize new roles, transferring the "halo" of one to the other. Now too they conduct conferences and "leadership training" courses (tamrin kader) for their most promising followers to spread the message more widely still. It is instructive to note the use of the term "cadre" (kader) here; it is a tacit acknowledgment of the way in which the network operates, for it places this kind of religious organization in a broader category along with other types of political and social movement.

A similar pattern of religious authority based on a social status differential derived from a secular role is found in such institutions as the police and armed forces. It has been observed that in barracks where the chief commanding officer had adopted a form of dakwah (or, in the case of the supreme chief of the Armed Forces, a more traditional form of Malay mysticism fused with silat elements), his own men tend to follow his example while the wives follow that of an officer's wife. Thus, when one city police chief, concerned with the eradication of corruption in his jurisdiction, became known as a "dakwah man," most of the police cadets in his quarters followed suit. There is no denying that the influence of the peer group may also be operating simultaneously, thus compounding the effect, but the initial catalyst had to come from a respected authority figure above it. Most usrah and other small groups each have their own personal "hero," mentor, or counsellor as a permanent role model, inspiration, and *animateur*.

One traditional authority relationship which does not appear to be instrumental in mobilizing an appeal to dakwah is that of parents. Partly this may be a function of age and generation, for, given the history of the contemporary revival, they have not been exposed to the same influences and experiences, especially in education, under the "new breed" of lecturer, teacher, officer, and so forth. Many older people too, parents or not, feel that it is not seemly to emulate the young. Rather, a classic form of "generation gap" seems to colour the relationship between parents of the urban, middle-class, UMNO-supporting variety in particular, and their religiously radical offspring from the foreign-educated set of the 1970s. Many parents actively disapprove of dakwah tendencies among their children. They sometimes fear that their daughters may be unnecessarily committing themselves to a life of restrictions and restraints, marked by seclusion from public events and retreating to the back of the house when visitors arrive. Their middle-class standards of progress and mobility are also disturbed by sons who neglect their exams or turn down good jobs and material advantages. Other parents fear possible political repercussions of dakwah association, with the result that some attempt to have overzealous offspring "deprogrammed." Here, they take pains to find another convincing authority figure capable of counteracting the influence of the one responsible for the initial conversion, usually another guru or alim. For their part, the dakwah offspring feel that their parents are too materialistic, too little concerned with religion, or alternatively, too "ritualistic" about it, in the sense that it adds no meaning to their lives. These young people may resist their parents' opposition and take pride in such epithets as "fanatics for Islam," for to them it is the highest form of praise. Until the present dakwah generation gets older and raises children of its own, as is beginning to happen in the commune of Darul Arqam, it can only be a matter of speculation whether this generation gap will persist or whether the new generation will follow in their dakwah footsteps. To date, the most common pattern of intra-familial dakwah influence is between siblings, from older to younger. Today, some unschooled and intellectually insecure rural parents who are impressed by the high academic status of the dakwah enthusiasts, especially in their role as teachers, refrain from following their religious example on grounds of their own inadequacy, claiming that they are not sufficiently "advanced" (maju) educationally. This is the reverse of the self-righteous religious superiority of other members of the older generation who are returned pilgrims or retired pondok dwellers.

INFLUENCE OF DAKWAH IN OTHER DOMAINS

Various combinations of the two principles of peer group and authority as influences in dakwah dissemination can be observed in other areas of Malay life. One is the civil service, although, apprehensive of official repercussions, officials often disguise their dakwah sympathies. Again, it is principally among the younger, overseas-trained civil servants that dakwah is strongest, and these individuals may still have like-minded friends in the universities. Indeed, given the scale of Malaysian society, and the small numbers of the earliest cohort of university- and foreign-educated Malays who graduated before 1972, most of them are so closely acquainted personally that a dense and multiplex set of relationships still links them in their subsequent careers. This helps to explain the apparent incongruity of the personal friendships of the presidents of ABIM and of Aliran and the relationships in turn of these two men to a number of important army officers, civil servants, and even a few well-known "leftists." These multiplex ties also span the Darul Arqam/ABIM boundaries, so that some ABIM leaders are willing to spend weekend retreats at Sungei Pencala, through personal connections with Arqam residents, some of whom were originally members of the fledgling ABIM movement before Arqam's birth. Dakwah sympathizers in the civil service frequently claim that their brand of dakwah does not involve distinctive dress or Arab customs nor a total rejection of modern technology and occupations. In practice, it is difficult to reconcile the two lifestyles, since the nature of government service requires forms of entertaining and other social activities not compatible with fundamentalist Islam. Female civil servants claim they are not encouraged to appear bertudung in the office. Committed dakwah followers in government service often prefer to operate as "loners," in the interstices of the established cliques, or just as links in the network. They may take advantage, however, of their high status positions to convey their ideas subtly and covertly and to cultivate new lines of transmission. Thus, in his capacity as an agricultural officer, an ABIM sympathizer giving advice in rural kampungs may be able to get across a message to the effect that some peasant woes may be caused by a government which has neglected some basic Islamic principles or even by wrongful practice of the faith by the peasants themselves. One civil servant uses his "inside information" as a basis for counsel to his old, ex-university friends in Darul Arqam, on the strength of which some of Arqam's militant anti-government policies, at least publicly, were modified in favour of more compromise and co-operation. By heeding this advice, Darul Arqam was able to soften some of the hard feeling growing up around it. Even when dakwah convictions do not run as deep as this, the overall religious climate has penetrated government offices sufficiently that collegial pressures make it desirable to be seen in department surau at prayer time, and small prayer rooms are now provided for this purpose in all government departments.

One or two other professionals are also dakwah sympathizers, including one judge, who upheld the rights of a dakwah motorbike rider accused of riding without a crash-helmet, in place of which he was wearing his religious turban. The verdict in favour of the "religious rights" of the defendant made many dakwah youth jubilant for months afterwards.

Another domain of dakwah influence is in the FELDA schemes. Although each land settlement has its own state religious council-appointed imam, the peripatetic circuit of the dakwah lecturer has not penetrated directly to FELDA inhabitants. Sometimes, as in other rural areas, this is done with the permission of the local imam, but at other times he is bypassed. One FELDA director, who also emerged from the graduating cohort of the early 1970's, claims that the mode of dakwah penetration is once again attempted through the personal network of old school friends of Anwar Ibrahim and other ABIM leaders, now employed as FELDA officers. In this director's estimation, as many as 10 per cent of the inhabitants of some FELDA settlements have been affected by dakwah, with the result that some "extremists" have lost their commitment to the worldly goals of economic development, which is what FELDA is all about. One or two younger parents are now demanding separate classes at school for their children and are refusing to allow them to ride together in the same school bus, while a few children have been taken out of school altogether. It will be remembered that it was from one of the FELDA schemes that the Kampuchean-led militants who attacked the Johor police station were drawn. Not surprisingly, few FELDA administrators approve of dakwah "invasion" of their schemes, and as individuals they are also resistant to overtures made by their ex-colleagues.

One area of Malay activity which does not appear to have been penetrated by dakwah is the factory. This is significant if only because of the growing number of young Malay factory workers in urban areas who might be expected to be obvious recruits for the movement. The factory would also seem to provide a suitable peer group network, particularly given the social and task clustering of the mostly female Malay workers, who are often separated, by inclination and management policy, from non-Malay employees (cf. Mohd. Razha Rashid 1978; Lim 1978). Studies in three major urban areas, including Alor Setar (Mohd. Razha Rashid, ibid.) and Kuala Lumpur (Ackerman, personal communication), confirm a very low incidence of dakwah. This is not to be attributed, as has been done by some cynics, to the waywardness or immorality of urban "minah karan" (see Chapter 3). What apparently is lacking is the existence of an appropriate and effective religious authority to serve as role model and catalyst. Surprisingly, the dakwah movements do not seem to have sent their representatives into this area, and this, in turn, may be partly related to the lack of personal network ties or common background between these leaders and any factory personnel. The majority of the factory managers who control access to the workers are non-Malay and non-Muslim, and, if Malay, are strongly resistant to the idea of their employees' work, dress, and attitudes succumbing to the requirements of a strict Islamic code. Further, as noted by Mohd. Razha, Lim and Ackerman above, the deliberate disjunctions in the Malay worker network often created by management policy, along the lines of divide and rule, would also weaken the horizontal bonds of unity which have proven so "contagious" in universities, schools, and army barracks.

SUMMARY

Despite their outward and public differences in orientation and style and distinct external images and character, upon closer inspection, the principal dakwah movements show a number of similarities. First, in their structure — or lack of it: beyond the inner core of acknowledged leaders and spokesmen, the movements dissolve into a somewhat amorphous series of informal cells, based largely on pre-existing personal connections, in which there is already a considerable social investment on other counts. As noted, its mode of expansion could be compared to the cadre system of some communist movements elsewhere, and the use of the term "kader" has now even been incorporated into a course in the Faculty of Islamic Studies, entitled *Perkaderan Darul Islam*. Many of these effective network ties seem to follow patterns of relationship with an established strength in Malay society whether of equal or unequal status. Dakwah norms are thus partly adapted to the character and needs of the group or set, whether more or less Malay or of the Islamic Bumiputera style. None of the movements follows a truly hierarchical, pyramidal, or bureaucratic pattern of organization with formal branches and committees at national, state, and local levels, in the manner of some youth clubs or other voluntary associations. When reference is made to say, the "Kedah/Perak branch" of ABIM, it means little more than just that: a loose aggregate of declared sympathizers in the state, which lacks any headquarters, buildings, formal committees, or distinctive enterprises. Volunteers describe their role as "to help a little" (*tolong sedikit*) by such activities as lecturing, helping to organize conferences, or collecting contributions, but they do not hold formal offices or grades and are unlikely to be "card-carrying" members in any strict sense. Jemaat Tabligh, of course, is the least structured of all, its cells multiplying like hydra, mechanically adding more units but without changing its organizational complexity. Even in the schools and universities, activities are organized on an ad hoc basis by individuals and informal groups rather than in the name of an official club or branch. It must be recalled here that, under the Universities Act, all group events are regarded with some apprehension by the authorities, which imposes constraints of its own. Most university and school "religious associations" are therefore not identified with specific dakwah affiliations but contain followers of each one, as well as some who follow none of them.

For different individuals, dakwah may provide: a solution to academic, professional, or intellectual conflicts (for example, science and Islam); the creation of economic or trade contacts, as in Darul Arqam; a mode of expressing opposition to, or disassociation from, disapproved groups (drug addicts, drama enthusiasts); or a means of maintaining favour with role superiors, such as army officers, teachers, or even members of the opposite sex. These are the units and relationships that determine which movement or activities individuals will support and with what degree of exclusiveness. Thus, in some years, the "trend" on certain campuses, depending on personal contacts and personalities, will be more in the direction of Tabligh, while in others, when the Tabligh followers have graduated, ABIM and Arqam ties may flourish. But none of these organizations are exclusive or totally encompassing groups (save possibly for Darul Arqam's commune) in a Christian sectarian sense, and total commitment to a named organization is not necessarily part of the normative expectation in dakwah. Unlike the traditional, theologically oriented approach to Christian sectarianism, defined in terms of doctrinal orthodoxy and ideological consistence (cf. Troeltsch 1931; Niebuhr 1929; Wilson 1959; 1961), Islam presents a difficult case. For reasons given in Chapter 1, "orthodoxy" in Islam is often established de facto, by acceptance of ideas appropriate to specific local contexts and constituencies. For all its legalism, Islam never developed the obsessive preoccupation of Christianity with hierarchy or with institutional boundaries and forms. Nor does Islam emulate Christianity's predilection for exclusiveness of membership, in such a way that acceptance of one set of beliefs necessarily precludes or invalidates all others. Finally, in the west, the term "sect" has frequently had derogatory connotations, a manifestation of something "less than ideal," a deviation. In Islam, despite universal acceptance of the ultimate authority of the Koran and Hadith and a recognition of the canons established by the ijma, the technically present possibilities of ijtihad (particularly strong, as noted, in Shi'ite and reform Islam), leave open the doors of reinterpretation or personal fatwa as a legitimate theological exercise for those who wish to take advantage of it with obvious social consequences. Differences of theological opinion therefore have to be assessed not as degrees of deviation or heresy, but as fulfilling the needs of particular Muslim communities in different situations. Islamic dakwah movements may thus more profitably be analysed in terms of political (in its broadest sense) or factional perspective (cf. Mendelssohn 1978), which ultimately reflects a constant struggle for, and effort to retain, religious legitimacy by spokesmen of the movements. And in the case of the traditional ulama, for all their individual differences and idiosyncracies, each one had, by definition, established an acceptable interpretation and modus vivendi in his own kampung. The leaders of the various dakwah movements have, by the same logic, acquired legitimacy for their views among their own followings. Finally, given that the effective domain covered by any religious leader tends to be restricted to the constituency or community to which he has tied his professional fortunes and by the number of people he is able to sway by his personality and skills, his influence may be as narrow as half a parish or as wide as the span of an international movement.

Just as it is presumptuous and misleading for Christians or westerners to imply a lack of doctrinal "quality control" or consistency or lack of any absolute standards in Islam, it is also possible to overestimate the utility — or even existence of — undisputed canons of Christian orthodoxy as a yardstick for measuring all its myriad of sectarian variations. Indeed, most of the "major" religions of the world, when subjected to the more intensive scrutiny of the social scientist's microscope, appear to dissolve more diffusely into a kaleidoscope of ever-shifting fragments, rather than to emerge as solid patterns with fixed points of reference. Probably the Islamic mode is more the rule than the exception. The myths associated with the unity of Christianity or Islam of, say, the era of the Crusades, with its protective historical and social distance, help to obscure this lower-level fragmentation and, more important, the processes by which the fragments come into being. The sectarian problem therefore has both an ideological and a political dimension, whereby micro-political interests of both leaders and followers, as the instruments by which ideas are interpreted and pressed into service, must equally be considered. Such has been the history of many Christian schisms and sectarian formations, for example, the Older Order Amish, Mennonites, and Hutterites[5] (cf. Nagata 1974b). This is not to be construed as suggesting that all theological and ideological principles have some calculated, Machiavellian character or political platform in the narrow sense. Rather, just as other cultural items may be used to symbolize particular social interests and items, for example, ethnic identity, so religious ideas become the hallmarks, rationales, myths, and charters of certain groups and interests too. In these respects, at least as seen through the eyes of a western social scientist, Christianity and Islam may have more in common than some Muslim observers would be willing to concede.

To return to the terminology and ideas of Shils, in Malay dakwah, what initially appears to be a form of ideological Bund, in fact more closely resembles a primordial Bund, or, at least, the two coincide to such a degree that they are, in some contexts, almost indistinguishable. In this respect, dakwah cliques or usrah function much like Shils' small military platoons, in which the underlying relations and loyalty to the unit and one's comrades are what sustain the power of the ideology and endow it with an immediate and compelling urgency and meaning at the grass-roots level. Social interaction thus precedes normative consensus rather than the reverse. Again, the argument could be reinforced with comparisons from other areas, showing that the spread of dakwah in Malaysia is by no means unique in the broader scheme of either religious or other social movements. A recent study of the influence and acceptance of the Indonesian Darul Islam movement in three Javanese villages (Jackson 1980) illustrates the primacy of the leader-follower dyad and the dependence on traditional village authority over strictly ideological considerations. Thus, according to Jackson, sympathy with Darul Islam could be predicted by no cultural or theological orientation other than that mediated through the local leaders (*lurah, kiyayi*) and their relationship with their "*anak buah*" (villagers). Although there is rather scanty evidence generally on the actual process of transmission of ideas in religious or other cults at the grass-roots level, a clear parallel to dakwah exists in the Buddhist *nikaya* of Sri Lanka (Kemper 1980). These small, community-like groups of monks, almost independent of formal attachment to the main sangha, are usually adapted, ulama-like, to specific villages in which the monks and *bhikkus* already have personal and kinship ties with the local lay population, and they recruit new members on the basis of these. Ideological or ritual questions play only a minor role in selection of a nikaya for layman or monk and are very secondary even as a justification for differentiating one nikaya from another. Yet collectively, viewed from afar, these nikaya constitute the "structure" of the Sri Lanka monkhood (sangha).

To this extent, it may be argued that the "medium is the message," in that it is the group or network which provides the nurturing host or environment for the message to grow or to be cultivated to its own needs. It also accounts for the already mentioned fact that the message, as articulated in different groups or levels, may vary. The analogy is the classic party game in which a message is whispered around a circle becoming increasingly diluted or distorted in the process, so that it emerges at the end of its passage substantially different from its original form. Generally, at the level of the "lowest common denominator," most messages become somewhat homogenized and lose subtlety, and sophisticated intellectual arguments can be reduced to a more diffuse or crude form of ethnic expression. As Simmel remarked (Wolff 1964:37-38), at the "lower level of the collective capacity... morality becomes personalized and assumes an imperative character in small groups." This provides only a partial parallel, however, for it obscures the creative adaptation which occurs in different times and places. In this fluidity probably lie both the strengths and weaknesses of dakwah. It ensures sufficient ideological flexibility to draw in a wide spectrum of followers, but it also tends to make dakwah movements difficult to define in formal structural or institutional terms alone. This fluidity is compounded by the high degree of role transparency of Malay society, which is small in scale and numbers, and the high incidence of multiplex ties linking dakwah leaders across apparent religious, social, and ideological boundaries. This makes for considerable individual flexibility (or as some would have it, inconsistency) and, on occasion, even for some "unholy alliances" as one declared dakwah follower who saw "nothing wrong with Nasrul Haq." Finally, it is not my intention to diminish or underplay the serious commitments to religious and social issues which undoubtedly motivate many dakwah followers, but it is equally important to recognize the strength of the supporting social infrastructure. Certain kinds of role models are crucial in drawing attention, stimulating initial religious awareness, and providing a new kind of meaning to the lives of young Malays for whom the latent needs already exist.

The structure and organization of Malay society, the strength of informal age and generation sets, the premium placed on certain kinds of authority and roles as well as the pressures towards social conformity, it is argued, probably account for much of the current pattern of distribution of dakwah. It is not thus simply a question of a clear rural-urban dichotomy, for even some rural ulama are receptive to certain elements of "urban" dakwah, while many urban parents are somewhat hostile to its adoption by their offspring. The determining or predisposing factors in dakwah receptivity seem to lie partly in the complex interaction of these various horizontal and vertical relationships, the intensity of peer group bonds, and the type of authority most respected and emulated, which inevitably span the rural-urban divide.

6

Anti-Dakwah and Alternative to Dakwah: Responses to the Dakwah Movement

For all the "rising tide of Islam" and of dakwah revivalism in Malaysia, there is also a significant body of opinion and bodies with personal or political interests that are not entirely sympathetic. Militant opposition is rare; the more common response is a somewhat cautious and diplomatic approach in the form of alternative propositions, ideologies, or organizations, some religious, some not. There is now even an official alternative variety of dakwah, widely known as "government dakwah," which is an exercise in the use of the same Islamic symbols but to different ends from that of the "spontaneous" dakwah movements and designed partly to counter their effects.

THE OFFICIAL RESPONSE

It would be misleading and an oversimplification to suggest there is a single "government" response to dakwah revivalism beyond the generalized apprehension of its potential appeal among a volatile youth and the fear of its impact on Malay unity and the UMNO vote.

This is clearly not the decade in Malaysia for any official, whether of Party UMNO, civil service bureaucrat, politician, or appointed office-holder, to give any appearance of resistance to Islam. Any form of political challenge or defence which uses Islam in its platform or philosophy must be expressed circumspectly. It presents delicate problems of terminology and use of symbolism, for having cast the gauntlet down in an Islamic arena, the challenge must be taken up in those same terms. The antidote to an "excess" of religious zeal then, is paradoxically more of the same. Thus, to counter such religious organizations as ABIM, Darul Arqam, and Tabligh, and to some extent, Aliran, which are believed to be co-opting too many young Malays and inculcating ideas of social and political change, however subtly, that do not accord with UMNO policy, the government has now begun to establish a number of competing dakwah institutions of its own. Increasingly, since Mahathir's incumbency, the ethos and orientation of official policies has been in more Islamic direction. The presence of Anwar Ibrahim as a deputy minister in the Prime Minister's Department has reinforced this effect.

As we saw in Chapter 3, the first real impact of the potential strength of the new religious forces emerging throughout the land probably came with the Baling events of 1974. In the same year, the new Religious Council of the Federal District (*Majlis Ugama Islam*) was created to supplement the old National Council for Religious Affairs (*Majlis Kebangsaan Bagi Hal Ehwal Ugama Islam Malaysia*). By this move, the new council acquired a territorial base and area of jurisdiction, whereas the previous council was merely a voice without much of a constituency or domain. On many occasions since 1974 use has been made of both councils to air government views on religious matters, and attempts have been made to recommend "national" religious policies to the state religious councils. As we saw in Chapter 3, however, co-operation of the state councils is entirely dependent upon the latter's goodwill or self-interest, since they are supreme in their own domains. Thus Sheikh Mokhsein, in his capacity as Grand Mufti of the Federal District Religious council has variously been pressed into service by government interests to try to persuade the states to declare Nasrul Haq as un-Islamic and to participate in the national Dakwah month. He also intervened in one of the Kedah by-elections in which the opposition candidate was an ABIM follower by adding his weight to the credentials of the UMNO candidate. He has confirmed the government's commitment in principle to an Islamic system of justice, while conveniently providing reasons for its inability to implement such at this time, as noted in Chapter 3. Equally important, the National Religious Council has sprouted numerous programmes and projects of its own, carrying on the backs of these its own, or the official, messages about Islam and dakwah. These programmes include informational and educational services in all the media from national religious broadcasts, dissemination of texts for Friday sermons, books and pamphlets galore, supervision of the religious curricula in National schools, and now the assembly of a body of materials to expose and counteract the "false teachings" in Islam in Malaysia today. Finally, in conjunction with its counterparts in Singapore and Indonesia, the Council has tried to establish a uniform standard calendar to fix the dates of the fasting month and other religious holidays for the entire country.

In addition, there has existed since 1969 the national-level Islamic Educational Centre. Of late, this centre has intensified its activities to keep pace with those of dakwah in other quarters, particularly in areas of publications, instructional aids, and information programmes. One of its aims is to co-opt the "information market" by introducing its own projects and services before the dakwah groups can move in with theirs, and there is now a very real competition for an audience on both sides. Being first on the scene, however, does not necessarily guarantee success for the government body, for rather ironically, by its initiation of religious programmes, it may sensitize a local population to religion sufficiently for them to become more receptive to other kinds of dakwah such as those of ABIM, Arqam, or Tabligh. One difference, however, is that the Educational Centre directs its attention also to non-Malays and non-Muslims and in other languages, including Chinese and English. This represents yet another instrument of government policy in attempting to centralize all religious education in Malaysia and supplements the Ministry of Education curriculum whose effect is now being felt so keenly in the rural religious schools. The ministry collaborates with the Islamic Educational Centre in despatching to all Malaysian National schools a contingent of official religious teachers (ustaz), part of whose responsibility is to counter the influence of other dakwah ideas through their classes and religious clubs.

As dakwah interest steadily gathered momentum throughout the 1970's, the government felt increasingly constrained to prove its commitment to Islam with its own version of dakwah. This led to the creation of two new institutes specifically designed to propagate the "true" Islam and a society imbued with spiritual values. Thus were born the *Institut Dakwah dan Latehan Islam* and the *Yayasan Dakwah*, for the implementation of, and training in, the Muslim faith. Significantly, the first institute is dedicated to a "progressive" and "dynamic" Muslim society, which is the government code for a society which supports economic development and modernization through the New Economic Policy, the basis of UMNO's power. While there is considerable overlap between the functions of the Institute, the Islamic Education Centre, and religious council programmes, the Institute offers the most comprehensive series of training courses and retreats at its own hostel in Kuala Lumpur and now also sends its own lecturers out on circuit throughout the country, in an obvious attempt to duplicate the influence and activities of the other dakwah groups. This institute is also the agency which tries to encourage "unity," or at least a public image of co-operation, between all the dakwah groups in Malaysia and regularly invites representatives from ABIM, Arqam, and Tabligh to sit on grand councils (syura), which the latter diplomatically rarely refuse. In all of these government programmes could be sown the seeds of their own downfall; their own interpretation of religion, could also be blazing a trail for the very groups they are trying to discredit and dislodge.

The *Yayasan Dakwah* (Dakwah Foundation) is a semi-autonomous institution, founded in 1975 with government approval, under the leadership of a man in the Prime Minister's Office, a minister without portfolio. The foundation now publishes a widely circulated, Malay language journal, *Dakwah*, which is carefully orchestrated to cover a broad range of religious viewpoints, strategically combining articles with a definable ABIM and even Arqam slant with others more clearly oriented towards official varieties of Islam. Its editors claim that the articles it publishes do not necessarily reflect the foundation's own views, and the overall selection, while seemingly eclectic, succeeds in leaving an impression favourable towards government policies. The journal also reports favourably on the sultans and their activities, particularly where these can be related to religion, thus adding another voice to support for the legitimacy of the role of royalty in a Muslim state. The head of the foundation's education section, and one of the most frequent and articulate contributors to *Dakwah* magazine, is a man whose personal network connects him strategically with both ends of the dakwah spectrum. Originally an active member of the PKPIM and an old friend and colleague of Anwar Ibrahim, he later graduated in Islamic law from Al-Azhar University in Cairo and entered UMNO politics in Kelantan. After losing a local by-election there, he joined the religious bureau of UMNO Youth, whence began his career in free-lance writing. He is a good example of some of the more "free-floating" individuals or intellectual loners, deeply committed to the principle of religious revitalization, but not exclusively co-opted by any single dakwah movement or orientation. The breadth of his own personal network, which spans several of the dakwah groups as well as the pressure points of party and government, is his strength. He is regarded with respect and as a potential resource person speaking for the interests of all sides. Certainly, his writings tend to reflect the more universalistic views of ABIM's leadership, many of whom are his personal friends, for example, in his rejection of "racial" chauvinism, and in his pleas for more Islamic content in the legal system, in education, and in daily life. In his writing, he uses a sufficiently generalized level of argument to avoid being directly offensive or challenging to the government. In steering this precarious middle course, he distinguishes, for example, between dakwah and politics. Dakwah should transcend politics and not be limited by its conflicts, for the sole aim of dakwah is to Islamize (*Berita Harian* 20/5/77). But he cautions his audience not to confuse politics and political parties, thereby leaving ambiguously open the critical question as to how far dakwah, and Islam generally, can go along the political path. His overall conclusions may be distilled into the view expressed in *Dakwah* journal (April 1980:10-13) that unity among Muslims is crucial and that they should not wash their dirty linen in public, which gives irresponsible journalists the opportunity to exploit their differences and divide them further.

There is now, in addition to this editor of *Dakwah*, an important minority of young men who are managing to steer a personal path between the various religious factions without being identified with any single one, and who are yet maintaining a reputation for religious integrity and dedication. Another such man is a lecturer in the National University's Faculty of Islamic Studies, a close friend of the leaders of both ABIM and Aliran and, with government approval, a lecturer on religious programmes on television, as well as a freelance writer on religious topics. On occasion, he can sound like Anwar, in criticizing corrupt government officials, luxuriating as if in a "date garden given by Allah," while at other times he becomes a defender of the status quo, as in his television statements. Publicly, however, he is always a scrupulous supporter of the universalism of Islam in racial and ethnic matters. These are men for whom the commitment to an independent ideology transcends the constraints of any narrow network or peer group and who, by their very social and intellectual agility, are able to effect rather than follow changes in Malaysian Islam.

In their anxiety to demonstrate an impeccable Muslim character and a religious commitment as deep as any spontaneous dakwah body, all branches of government have now spawned religious bureaus and sections of their own. Nowadays, all government departments and army quarters have at least one prayer room, and no official or social meetings are permitted to coincide with the Friday noon prayer. Despite considerable duplication, most departments sponsor a variety of religious classes and lectures, although they do not encourage employees to wear full Islamic dress to work, paradoxically because it might create an image of "backwardness" (*kolot*) to outsiders and foreigners. With the same concerns in mind, a number of peripatetic religious teachers representing government scholarship bodies have now been despatched to various points both at home and overseas, instructing both foreign civil servants and students not to mix religion and politics and in all things to maintain moderation (*sederhana*). Finally, these teachers purport to correct any deviant ideas and to move back to the true course of Islam. Some of these government dakwah missionaries have not been entirely without their miscalculations, mésalliances, and faux pas. Kampung dwellers tell stories of the gauche behaviour of some government emissaries who arrive to launch a tea-party at the moment of the afternoon prayer (*asa*), who inadvertently insult or bypass the resident imam and ulama, or who pepper their talks with exhortations for an election with appeals for loyalty to Allah and UMNO.

Most of the mass media, which are dependent on government approval for their programming and/or licences, show the imprint of official dakwah. Programme breaks are made for each of the five daily prayers, and there is now a noticeable emphasis on religious content, in the form of discussions, forums, lectures, and music. The most popular variety of religious music is nasyid, the unaccompanied singing of religious songs, said to be of Arab origin, and usually performed by a choir of girls, who wear a loose baju kurung, but a less restrictive headscarf in place of the telekung. Nasyid competitions have now joined Koran-reading contests in popularity, both among government sponsors as "safe" religious projects and among the public at large.

Finally, to add to the restrictions of the Universities Act and the monitoring of students overseas, other rearrangements on the home front have been implemented by government to reduce the impact of dakwah. One or two well-known dakwah-sympathizing lecturers from MARA and the National University have been transferred to the remoter and more inaccessible campus in Sabah, East Malaysia. In 1980 too, the Ministry of Education recommended the creation of a separate campus of the University of Malaya out of the erstwhile Nilam Puri Religious College in Kelantan, at which all religious programmes and courses are henceforth to be concentrated. This policy will in effect keep "at arm's length" the centres of religious activity and potential dakwah strength, away from the main campus and larger student body. The Nilam Puri campus will thereby become a form of intercalary institution, whose function is simultaneously to unite and divide, but ultimately allows the authorities a greater measure of control. Whether in the universities or in the state at large, party and government favour increased compartmentalization of the "religious" and "secular" along lines more familiar to modern Christianity, whereby ulama and other religious figures and religious councils would be relegated to a lesser position. The aim of the dakwah revivalists, however, is quite the reverse, and in the present religious climate, theirs is the more morally defensible position to which the government cannot afford to yield. This is where the war of words and careful use of rhetoric comes into its own.

In 1982, a new proposal was unveiled by Prime Minister Mahathir for the launching of a new international Islamic university in Malaysia, whose languages of operation are to be Arabic and English. This is the fulfilment of demands made for over a decade by PKPIM, ABIM, and other bodies.

Since both sides, government and other dakwah bodies, equally claim to espouse the cause of Islam, the restoration of religious and moral values, and the promotion of a harmonious and just society, nothing would appear to separate them at this level of generality. Neither side of course wishes to expose its baser, political self-preservation interests, and the language of conflict remains very much in the rarefied and irreproachable realm of religious symbolism. In response to the suggestion by dakwah groups that they are infidels, government leaders, among them the deputy prime minister, retaliate by hurling the epithets of "deviant" and "heretical" and an extended litany of insults (songsang, menyeleweng, *sesat*, salah), now familiar to the dakwah contingent and media watchers alike. Datuk Hussein Onn, past prime minister of Malaysia, was once quoted as admitting quite frankly: "You may wonder why we spend so much money on Islam...if we don't, PAS will get us. The Party will, and does claim that we are not religious, and the people will lose faith" (*Berita Harian* 21/10/79). In government circles, expressions to the effect that if this "sickness" grows, we shall be destroyed are heard, and warnings are constantly issued about the people's being misled by those who "behave as if their salary comes direct from God." Imams representing PAS and UMNO are regularly pitted against one another, attacking the legitimacy of their political opponents in the rites attending the slaughtering of animals for meat, in validating marriages, and accusing them of "twisting the Koran to their own ends" in elaborate exercises in casuistry. For its part, Darul Arqam advises its followers not to read certain national Malay language newspapers, for example, *Utusan Malaysia*, on the grounds that they are not written in the Arabic script (jawi). Of late, the Ministry of Education has decided to re-introduce jawi into the compulsory school curriculum, for non-Muslim as well as Muslim students, and now Arqam is making pleas for compulsory Arabic language classes. Overtones of a national-level "kafir-mengafir," combine with a government penchant for timely references to such forms of "extremism" as the desecration of the Hindu temples and television- and furniture-throwing incidents as antithetical to the "true Islam." Great care is taken not to relate any of these epithets to specific individuals or groups by name, and the usual term is "certain groups" (*golongan tertentu*) or similar euphemisms. It is clear, however, what inferences the public is expected to draw. Use is frequently made of forms of "closed codes" or enthymeme (cf. Paine 1981), whereby the premise is not overtly stated or spelled out, but implicitly assumed, so as to avoid any direct responsibility for any associations made by the audience. This practice maintains sufficient ambiguity for personal recriminations and hostilities to be deflected, although the subtleties of the restricted codes are well enough understood within the symbolic "privacy" of the Malay-Muslim community. Thus, all Malays are aware of the identity of the "certain groups" and "deviants," although in translating out to non-Malays, they may insist on keeping the literal, unglossed meaning at its face value. Politicians also use restricted codes to control some of the internal disjunctions within an ideally united community. Unable to "throw out" entirely the dakwah contingent from the Malay-Muslim community either politically or socially, the cracks have to be papered over by a clever and convincing use of symbols, with Islam as the common element. Deviants must be corrected or take the consequences for dividing the Muslim ummat and driving a wedge between groups of their own people. In the cause of their "market mentality Islam," government spokesmen and ustaz are fond of reminding the religious community—which for them is really the Malay electorate—that the Prophet himself was a businessman and always encouraged his followers to do their duty to the world (dunia) as well as to the after-world (akhirat), hence justifying UMNO's New Economic Policy of development with Islam as consistent with religious teachings. It is also quite possible, they argue, to be a good Muslim without wearing Arab clothes, practising Arab customs, or "going back to the seventh century." They are cautious enough to reassure the public that western technology is only being used for the public good and social justice, although the opposition dakwah groups accuse senior government officials of enjoying the more questionable fruits of western influence in the form of entertainment, luxury travel, hotels, and other material benefits. The latter retort that dakwah critics should not be "side-tracked" by issues of night-clubs, but turn their attention to social welfare instead. The government is now busy building up its own cohort of ustaz and religious authorities, whose legitimacy is based on their graduation from the National University's Faculty of Islamic Studies, the new intellectual isnad serving both officials, who provide most of the funds, and many of the "spontaneous" dakwah interests alike. In turn, these developments have vastly increased the rate of employment for graduates with religious degrees, resulting in the expansion of the Islamic Faculty even further. Probably the ultimate accolade of legitimacy of the government position sought is by the successful co-optation of Hamka, one of the most illustrious and well-known Indonesian ulama of this century (he died in 1981). Until his death, Hamka was a regular visitor at religious conferences and celebrations at the invitation of the Malaysian government as the counterpoint to dakwah's peripatetic lecturers or of the more popular rural ulama. Originally a protagonist of the modernist Kaum Muda movement in the 1920's, Hamka subsequently mellowed theologically somewhat, and until his death was the Indonesian Minister for Religion. With his unique combination of qualities and reputation for religious reform, as representative of a national religious body and government, and, above all, as a "neutral" outsider, yet able to communicate in Malay, Hamka was the perfect choice as a symbol of government dakwah, with something intended to appeal to everyone. Needless to say, some non-government dakwah critics saw Hamka as a "sell-out" to officialdom, despite his illustrious religious credentials. For his part, Hamka's praise for the religious zeal of even his dakwah critics was always generous, although invariably tempered with cautions over unnecessary extremism.

When government officials themselves are suspected of being dakwah sympathizers, they are first given every opportunity to "correct their wrongdoings" (*New Straits Times* 30/10/80), and the public is advised to report people propagating "false teachings." Thus orthodoxy is prejudged and has become the rationale by which political enemies are measured or possibly even created. Both sides follow the same logical process, whereby those in the other political camp are automatically stigmatized as not being "true Muslims." So strong has the pressure become for leaders of all segments of Malay society to demonstrate their religious worthiness, that even Datuk Harun, past head of UMNO Youth, when convicted of corruption in 1974, immediately donned his songkok and elected to play the role of ustaz or religious teacher, in an attempt to deflect some of the criticisms of his behaviour and character, although, as it transpired, to no avail.

It is clear that the role of Islam in the modern Malaysian state is in an active process of reappraisal and that the issue underlying much of the dakwah activity, "spontaneous" or official, is ultimately one of power and authority. It is but the latest phase in the age-old conflict, not only in the Malay states, but in other Muslim states since the inception of Islam.

The power and authority issue is further complicated, as described in Chapter 3, by the existence of different levels of jurisdiction between the federal and state religious councils. While it is not possible here to review the policies of every state in Malaysia, one or two points capture the essence of the overall religious scene. Dakwah has become one of today's most important vehicles for trials of strength between these different authorities over the political status of Islam. The "obstructionism" or lack of co-operation of the states of Kedah and Pahang in certain national religious endeavours such as the Dakwah Month of 1978 have already been noted as reflecting some differences of viewpoint over the powers of the respective sultans and the federal government. Several state religious councils were also persuaded that Nasrul Haq was a potentially dangerous and politically subversive force at the state level, hence they were willing to bow to federal interest and brand it as anti-Islamic. Some councils have now been infected by the government's concern over the activities of the smaller, rural Sufi cults, and these too are relegated to the "deviant" category. By contrast, certain states, for example, Johor and Malacca, have actually made concessions to strong dakwah (especially ABIM) constituencies and lobbies, by banning such "undesirable" practices as mandi safar (see Chapter 2), the material consumption and showy display of parades for the Prophet's Birthday, and the appearance of women in such parades, or in any public religious event. Politically speaking, it should be remarked that the chief minister and some of the religious council officials in Malaccca are young and not unsympathetic to some of the newer developments on the religious front, while both Johor's chief minister and its senior religious council members are involved in a number of disputes with the federal centre. The political make-up of the state religious council also had a bearing on the treatment of a well-known alim and teacher in Trengganu in his home base of Kampung Besut, an area renowned for its old pondok school tradition since the last century. The alim in question was brought to the Syari'ah court on charges of incorporating anti-government propaganda into his religious messages. In his defence, this alim concentrated on "proving" that the majority of the Syari'ah officials are also UMNO Party members and that some are even senators, which impeded his chances for a fair trial. In fact, the trial scene resembled more a political election rally, in which an excited crowd of observers made audible and critical comments against government sympathizers for their "infiltration" of the guru's lectures and disputed the accuracy of their memories over what he had actually said. For its duration, the trial became something of a vigil in which the spectators remained rooted for the entire proceedings, praying on the premises and causing such congestion that there was not enough water available for the ritual pre-prayer ablutions. Because of its defiantly independent reputation and longstanding willingness to experiment with alternate religious ideas, this same Kampung Besut once invited ABIM's Anwar Ibrahim to address the local population, but it was here too that Anwar was prevented, on some technical grounds presented by the local district officer, from making his appearance. This is also the area where ABIM is considering the establishment of its next Yayasan Anda school, along the lines of the alliances in Bukit Mertajam and in Kedah. Indeed, in various states, religious councils, in conjunction with district officers uneasy at the activities of religious leaders, whether of the traditional guru or urban dakwah variety, claim that they are upsetting the local population, and are refusing to provide the requisite permits to speak publicly and allegedly even setting up roadblocks along crucial access roads. Would-be lecturers, however, have their own means of circumventing some of these obstacles manage to "get invited" to the house of a sympathizer who "happens" to be holding a kenduri of several hundred people. Likewise, the administrators of most FELDA settlements have also taken steps to prevent outside religious visitors without permission.

One particularly delicate issue has surfaced in recent years in Sabah, East Malaysia, which has a reputation for making its own immigration policies. Sabah has been freely admitting emigrants from the Sulu and Mindanao areas of the Muslim South Philippines (Moros), up to an estimated total of between 50,000 and 100,000 to date (*Watan*, 11/4/80). Non-Muslims are not included among the preferred immigrants.

It should be apparent that the number and potential combination of factors entering into the relationship between federal and state religious authorities, political centre and periphery, varying political and religious ideologies and interests, traditional and modern representatives of Islam is indeed complex. Where local state policies are not acceptable to the federal centre, the latter may try to provide its own "antidote" in the form of its various educational programmes and school curricula, religious teachers (ustaz), and by representatives of its own dakwah organizations. In all cases, every effort is made to avoid direct confrontation, with a preference for indirect allusions and rationales in the elliptical language of "deviance," "orthodoxy," and parables from Koran and Hadith. Only in the last resort does the conflict become overtly political and the celebrated kafir-mengafir break out.

MUSLIM WELFARE LEAGUE (PERKIM)

Probably the most important and influential agency the federal government has in its arsenal against the new dakwah movements is the ageing, but revitalized Islamic Welfare and Missionary Association (*Pertubuhan Kebajikan Islam Malaysia*) or PERKIM. PERKIM was the original, national-level, religious and missionary institution, operating directly out of the Prime Minister's Department, unconnected with any state religious council. The organization was founded and given its missionary purpose by Malaysia's first prime minister, Tunku Abdul Rahman as early as 1960. Its symbolic head is a Chinese Muslim by descent, Haji Ibrahim Ma, of an ancient and well-known lineage of traditional Muslims from China itself.[1]

PERKIM's principal goals include the provision of material welfare and assistance to needy Muslims, promotion of the faith through instruction and education, co-ordination of activities with other Islamic associations, strengthening of national unity and loyalty through the official religion, and, finally, the propagation of the faith, particularly the conversion of non-Muslims. Its welfare and educational activities have largely been concentrated in kindergartens and medical clinics, which cater to Muslims and non-Muslims alike. There are also adult education programmes, and special instruction is available for new converts, while ambitious new agricultural and construction projects have recently been conceived, partly to finance the basic programmes. In marked contrast to the dakwah organizations, PERKIM is particularly receptive to non-Malays, and in its proselytization and welfare programmes actively seeks them out. Indeed, the primary target for PERKIM's conversion campaigns has long been the Chinese community and its main operating languages are the Chinese dialects of Mandarin, Cantonese, and Hokkien, as well as English, rather than Malay, and for this purpose, PERKIM employs a small full-time team of Chinese-speaking missionaries (muballigh). The organization also provides accommodation in hostels and funds[2] for the further training of new converts where required, helps them in finding new jobs where necessary and in adjusting to their new life as Muslims. PERKIM publishes a number of regular journals and informational booklets in several languages, Malay, English, and Chinese, for example, *Nur Islam*, *Suara Perkim*, and the Islamic Herald. Like other religious organizations, it also sponsors a variety of conferences, lectures, and forms of dialogue with other religious bodies, including attempts, as noted, to engineer an alliance with ABIM. Apart from a small government budget, most of PERKIM's funds are derived either from its own investments or from the substantial contributions made by a number of other Muslim countries, notably Saudi Arabia, Kuwait, and Libya.[3] In this respect, Tunku Abdul Rahman has made the most of his personal connections with the leaders of these countries through his many years on the executive committee of the world Islamic Secretariat. They have also encouraged PERKIM to expand its missionary activities to the Far East, where it has succeeded in obtaining numerous converts in Korea, Taiwan and Japan. Recently too, PERKIM expended considerable resources and efforts in aiding Muslim refugees from Kampuchea following the Vietnamese invasion, reputedly spending as much as $4,000 per day in order to charter boats to bring the Kampucheans to Kelantan and to house them in special camps there (*Berita Harian* 16/6/78; *Islamic Herald* 4(5-6):24, 1979). No such aid was forthcoming, however, for the non-Muslim "boat-people."

The founding chapter and headquarters of PERKIM is in Kuala Lumpur, where its newest building, the Balai Islam, is largely the product of financing by a Libyan donation of M$12 million. Over the years, PERKIM has gradually established about fifty branches throughout West Malaysia, mostly in the state capitals and larger urban areas. In East Malaysia, it has branches in Sabah (USIA) and Sarawak (BINA), which are particularly active among the non-Muslim aboriginal population. Each branch has had to develop its own working relationship with the local state religious council, and although relations are normally co-operative and cordial, co-ordination frequently leaves something to be desired, particularly in matters of record-keeping, for example, in registration of new converts. In theory, new Muslims should first register with the state religious council in order to be eligible for the monthly "instruction allowance" and for marriage with other Muslims and then also with PERKIM for the purposes of obtaining that instruction and other services. Converts not contemplating a Muslim marriage, however, will often bypass the council, and those who do marry into the Muslim community may dispense with the assistance of PERKIM.

Despite its role as a missionary organization, PERKIM has never been particularly aggressive in this direction until recently. From about the mid-1970's, when dakwah began to gather momentum, the association started publishing its own conversion statistics and making ambitious projections as to its goals in terms of "body count." In this it was clearly urged on by the government as an antidote to the "rising tide" of dakwah in other quarters. In 1976, PERKIM declared a Five-Year Plan (until 1981) of a target of a quarter of a million new converts, but long before the completion date was reached, it was admitted that these goals were unlikely to be achieved. Certainly, if past records are to be considered any guide to the future, such figures are entirely unrealistic. By compiling totals kept by each local PER-KIM office of its annual registration of converts between 1967 and 1978 — unfortunately these are not centralized by the Balai Islam in Kuala Lumpur — only a rather disappointing 11,370 (see Table below) can be demonstrated. This conflicts with PERKIM's grandiose claims of 30,000 since 1967, made in other contexts (cf. *Straits Times* 29/9/77). As noted however, these figures, periodically blazoned in media headlines to impress the public, tend to be unreliable for a number of reasons. Aside from the lack of an accurate referral system between PERKIM and the religious councils and poor record-keeping generally, there is a high incidence of recidivism, regretfully acknowledged by PERKIM officials, but rarely accounted for in their statistics. This means that an uncounted number of converts are lost by default (*murtad*) or, in some cases, that they are brought back into the fold for a second time, and registered once more as "new" converts.

PERKIM has been particularly active among the aboriginal tribal peoples (*orang asli*) both in West and East Malaysia, for which it received a special grant from Kuwait in 1978. As a result, it claims to have converted over 800 orang asli in Perak alone in the past few years, although once again, some of these figures may be misleading. In East Malaysia, a man with a mission, the past chief minister of Sabah, Datuk Tun Mustapha, was legendary for his aggressive conversion campaigns among the large tribal population, followed by "total immersion" training programmes in especially isolated communities with PERKIM's co-operation. Between 1970 and 1973, they jointly declared a total of 75,000 converts (*Utusan Malaysia* 19/9/73), followed by claims of weekly additions by the hundred. Thus a *Berita Harian* news report for 23/2/74 announced the induction of 2,000 new converts, while two days later (25/2/74), according to the same paper, the number had risen to 2,300. Information as to the "durability" of these new recruits, however, is not available, and the mode whereby the conversion is initially obtained may bear the seeds of its own limits. In many cases, subtle pressures, often with economic bait attached, are exerted on popular community leaders and M.P.'s to lead their flock into the Islamic fold. After intensive training, sometimes of several months in impressive new religious centres, the neophytes are sent back to their home communities to spread the message more widely, with apparent numerical success. In Sarawak by contrast, neither PERKIM nor the other dakwah bodies are as strong (and nor is the chief minister so zealous) as in Sabah. PERKIM's branch, BINA, is less active than USIA in Sabah, and apart from a few returning students, ABIM, Darul Arqam, and Tabligh do not seem to have gained a secure foothold. This may be accounted for partly by distance from the centre, but more effectively by lack of the necessary social support groups and networks for the maintenance of the

Number of New Converts to Islam in W. Malaysia,
1967-1978*

1967	541	1973	944
1968	539	1974	1844
1969	677	1975	1977
1970	773	1976	809
1971	884	1977	411
1972	1563	1978	408
		Total	11,370

* (Compiled from separate statistics of local PERKIM offices
by year.)

dakwah way of life for those returning. Sarawak also has a smaller Malay population than other states (18.7 per cent in 1970), and lacking the commanding leadership of a Tun Mustapha, it has not yet been launched into the world of the Islamic revival.

In keeping with its general identification with government religious policy and underscoring its differences from the dakwah orientation, PERKIM's missionary activities essentially employ the "soft" touch. Little emphasis is placed on such outward forms or rituals as Arab dress or customs or on excessive preoccupation with food origins, and certainly there is no objection to things modern or western. In the case of male converts, even circumcision is not necessarily enforced, for as one PERKIM official rather aptly put it, "it is the heart that counts." Some of the dakwah people have criticized PERKIM for its lack of teeth in imposing more stringent religious observances, and especially for its tolerance of the "sins" of the country's élites, as patrons of night-clubs and race-tracks, which represent barely veiled attacks on PERKIM's president, Tunku Abdul Rahman himself. In lively retaliation, the Tunku retorts that members of ABIM and other organizations should spend less time worrying about night-clubs and concentrate on more important problems instead, for example, on social welfare (*Utusan Malaysia* 22/6/76). Tunku Abdul Rahman also takes the dakwah followers to task for uncritically eulogizing all things Arabic, trenchantly pointing out that many Arab élites are wasting more millions of oil dollars than is any Malaysian leader on very non-Islamic entertainment and high living. He is also quite explicit in his view of the traditional Islamic legal penalties, which he considers excessive. As a western-trained lawyer himself, he remains a firm advocate of the existing court system in Malaysia, with the Syari'ah taking care of civil aspects of Muslim law. As mentioned in Chapter 4, Anwar Ibrahim was not very receptive to a proposal by the Tunku for a merger or other co-operative enterprises between PERKIM and ABIM, for he clearly felt that their goals were incompatible.

In the case of the Islamicization of the orang asli, PERKIM, in its characteristically flexible manner, is tolerant of the continuing taste of the tribal peoples for their delicacy of wild boar and other "doubtful" foods. It is recognized that there is often a lack of alternatives and that prohibition would not only cause severe deprivation and hardship (*kepahitan*), but might also endanger their commitment to their new faith. Insofar as the orang asli, as true indigenes, are accorded the status of Bumiputera (see Chapters 1 & 7), their Islamicization makes them potentially eligible for full Malayness, which may reduce some of the present status incongruence, but it raises more thorny questions over the limits of the extension of "Malay" privileges. As shown by some of its religiously non-exclusive education and welfare programmes and its concentration on converts from among the ranks of non-Muslims, PERKIM is known to be relatively generous in its interpretation of the definition of Malayness or of who is eligible for certain privileges normally reserved for Malays, for example, scholarships or taxi licences. PERKIM's reputation in assisting new converts to find jobs in either the restricted "Malay" sectors or others has generally been good, and PERKIM has also remained a reliable broker for the M$30 monthly allowances allotted by the religious councils for the converts. The question of the ethnic status of non-Malay converts to Islam will receive further attention in Chapter 7.

In some of its special projects, PERKIM consciously tries to promote co-operation and balance between "born Muslims" and new converts, (mua'laf or saudara baru), or Malays and non-Malays, although not always with the greatest success. While its clinics and kindergartens have long been open to non-Muslims, "without obligation" (to convert), in view of the association's principal goals, it is clear where its interests lie. Recently, PERKIM launched an even more ambitious 170-acre settlement scheme in Selangor to provide new housing lots to needy Muslims of all races, with a planned complement of approximately 20 per cent "born" Muslims, who would help and advise their neighbouring settlers, converts ali, about the ritual and social aspects of their new faith. To date, recruits for this project have yet to be found. In Penang, a new training complex provides job training for new Muslims in such skills as bookkeeping, stenography, accountancy, and mechanics. Shopping complexes to accommodate Muslims of all ethnic origins are also planned for Kuala Lumpur.

PERKIM is clearly the most broadly ramified of all the missionary bodies, particularly in view of its approach to non-Malays, and it has only recently begun to use the term "dakwah" to enhance its appeal more widely in the direction of "born" Muslims and Malays. More than the other dakwah organizations, however, PERKIM makes much more of the issue of universalism in Islam and of the necessity of eliminating age-old perceptions of "race," language, and culture as obstacles to religious and social unity. The overall tenor of PERKIM's social philosophy therefore closely parallels the government's own, both in its appeal to the "average" Muslim, as opposed to any extremes, and in its tolerance of minor deviations, concessions to westernism, and so on. The other dakwah bodies prefer to see the perpetuation of Malaysia's complex society in its present combination of Muslims and non-Muslims, partly to preserve Malay privileges, and for them religious unity must be on the terms and conditions laid down uncompromisingly by Islam and an Islamic state, regardless of conversion. PERKIM's approach, on the other hand, is one of increasing the absolute proportion of Muslims in the total population, which in principle should eliminate many social problems, but insofar as the New Muslims would not be Malay by origin while claiming Malay constitutional rights, Malaysia's economic policies and political games would clearly have to be reconsidered. To this I shall return in the next two chapters. Probably PERKIM's orientation can most accurately be contained in the statement made by Malaysia's King (*Yang Di-Pertuan Agong*) on the occasion of his address to open a major PERKIM conference in 1980 to expand the Muslim mission to the Far East and the Pacific. In his capacity as the representative of both government and national interests, the King stressed his conviction of dakwah's importance as a principle and model for world Islam, but at the same time he counselled a cautious approach to overly militant or "fanatical" groups with "deviant" ideas. Noting that Islam was not brought to Malaysia by the sword but to the accompaniment of the peace and prosperity of trade, the King advocated uniting all dakwah bodies into a single organization to demonstrate Islam's universalism and to concentrate on spreading the faith more widely into more distant parts of the world, including East Asia and the Pacific. Subsequent to the King's speech, a joint council of several prominent religious leaders and organizations (syura) was convened, from which the dakwah groups could not diplomatically shy away. The remarks about spreading the message beyond Malaysia were probably intended to direct some of the local religious energies and passions to less immediate and less dangerous situations overseas.

The question may be raised as to whether the Malaysian government and PERKIM are trying to make Islam do double duty as a "civil religion" (cf. Apter 1963; Bellah 1968; Aronoff 1981). In the case of Malaysia, this could be described as a revitalized symbolic system derived from a sort of "secular" Islam, which is being pressed into service as a justification and charter for its political and development policies. The idea is to make the symbols sufficiently multi-purpose and general to make them acceptable, "motherhood style," to a broad crosssection of the population, Muslim and non-Muslim alike, and to mobilize them to national unity and goals. Paradoxically, while government spokesmen have chided the youth and dakwah followers for mixing politics and religion, many official political and economic issues are now phrased in religious and moral terms and are so presented to the public. Through the efforts of the Ministry of Education, too, new courses, a sort of combination of ethics, religious principles, and civics (ahklak) are being taught in all national schools with the burden being on unity and loyalty to "religion and country." To somewhat different ends, and by different means, Aliran also attempts to generalize its interpretation of Islam to a level sufficiently diffuse to accommodate the needs of all Malaysians and to provide even non-Muslims with a moral/ethical guide to conduct, independent of actual conversion.

Yet it takes little reflection to recognize that in a plural society such as Malaysia, there are few enough common elements, Islamic or other, to serve as a foundation for a truly successful civil religion or as a unitary model for society. It would seem to require the prior existence of a certain level of consensus or integration that can be elevated to a more rarefied symbolic and religious plane. Either Islam will have to be extended to larger segments of the population, PERKIM-style, or else it will have to be stretched to its highest levels of generality and milked of its specific content, in order to accommodate notions of social justice acceptable to non-Muslims. The use of Islamic prayers at national celebrations, such as Independence Day (*Hari Merdeka*) or at the installation of the King, tend to be regarded by non-Muslims as forms of Malay culture, rather than as truly national symbols or as examples of a civil religious tradition.

Clearly, Islam at present both unites and divides, and it is invoked by all sides. Even within the Malay community, dakwah has created divisions. Some, though not all, of these cracks can be papered over in order to present a united Malay front to non-Malays. And neither Islam nor any other ideology or set of principles, it seems, are yet capable of uniting the entire population of Malaysia into a single civil polity or of endowing the ruling élites with undisputed legitimacy, acceptable to all.

RESPONSES IN THE CHINESE COMMUNITY

Predictably, some of the greatest impact in the wake of dakwah has been felt in the Chinese community. In Malaysia today, there does appear to be a connection between the rise of dakwah religious activity and a general resinification process in both culture and religion. Religious developments in the Chinese community, as they pertain to ethnic status, will be discussed in the next chapter.

To the extent that the development programmes of the New Economic Policy have been designed for the improvement of Malay fortunes relative to the non-Malays and insofar as even Chinese Muslims, with or without the assistance of PERKIM, are finding themselves ineligible for Malay constitutional privileges, the Chinese are being increasingly thrown back on to their own resources for economic survival. Education has always been a central institution in Chinese life, as a means both of transmitting the ancestral cultural and religious heritage and of succeeding in the non-Chinese professional world. Both of these goals are frustrated by the contemporary Malaysian educational policies and by UMNO's continuing rejection of the Chinese community's perennial attempts, via the MCA, to establish their own Chinese-language university[4] (see Chapter 3), and this has led to considerable bitterness. A growing number of Chinese who can afford it are now attending universities overseas, and it is said informally that at least 10 per cent of all available university places are reserved for the "Malaysian Chinese quota" in the University of Singapore.

At the primary school level, where the national educational policy still permits streaming in the vernacular languages (Chinese, Tamil, and Malay), trends in enrolment seem to reflect broader Chinese concerns over their status in Malaysian society. Prior to 1969, a progressive Malayanization had in fact been occurring, marked by a decline in the percentage of Chinese children attending Chinese primary schools, from 33.9 per cent in 1960, to 27.2 per cent in 1967. The revived ethnic polarization created by the events of 1969, however, was signalled by a renewed increase in enrolment in Chinese-medium schools, up to 30.3 per cent by 1974 (Inglis 1977:121). Although, as a "sensitive" issue, educational statistics by "race" are no longer revealed to the public, figures reported for primary school enrolments in 1980 indicated that for all the supposed social and political advantages of a mastery of the Malay language, the number of Chinese pupils in national language schools was only 63,991 out of a total of 501,156, or approximately 12 per cent of all enrolments. To put it another way, 87.8 per cent of all Chinese pupils are in Chinese schools, and given that 36 per cent of the overall Malaysian population is Chinese, that the English-medium option no longer exists, and that the Tamil option is unlikely in the extreme, then the evidence for a strong Chinese cultural reversal seems persuasive. It is common knowledge locally that there has been a recent resurgence of interest in Chinese education and culture among parents in all segments of the Chinese community. This is found equally in all income and status groups, among Christians and non-Christians, and, particularly revealing, among English-educated as well as among Chinese-educated[5] parents. Even locally, this is acknowledged as a form of cultural "backlash." Most parents justify a seemingly "irrational" choice from the standpoint of their children's future prospects on the grounds that they will eventually learn sufficient Malay at secondary school, but that it is important to receive a thorough grounding in their ancestral culture first, while they are still impressionable. Further, this strategy prepares the individual for entry into a more personal Chinese business community later in life, where language and social contacts are essential. This also suggests a declining confidence in prospects for employment in the public sectors of the Malaysian economy. Sentiments such as these help to account for the financial support also being given to private Chinese schools, some of which are run under the auspices of various Buddhist institutions and others by Confucian and Taoist religious foundations.

At the secondary level, government-supported Chinese-medium schools no longer exist, and since 1976, English too has been progressively phased out at that level. Chinese parents concerned with their own culture are thus faced with two options. The most obvious, and least expensive, is to allow their offspring to attend a national language school. In this event, however, many parents take great pains to secure a place for their children in schools converted from previously Chinese-medium as opposed to those which were already operating in Malay before the conversion.[6] By this strategy they are assured that a majority of the teachers will also be Chinese, and since their Malay is frequently still poorer than their mother tongue, in the unsupervised privacy of the classroom, where most of the pupils are also Chinese, they often revert informally to the vernacular, if only to make more effective communication possible. The alternative is the private Chinese school, which must be financed entirely by the Chinese community, and some wealthy businessmen and Chinese associations (*kongsi*) occasionally sponsor $100-a-plate dinners for their support. A general lack of funds, however, has limited the number of alternate facilities offered, and they can rarely compete with ministry-financed institutions in these respects. In 1980 it was estimated that approximately fifty-one such schools now exist in the whole of West Malaysia and that the enrolment rose from 29,791 in 1976 to 35,110 in 1979 (Loh et al. 1981:60). In practice, however, given the unreliability of the funding, poor co-ordination of curricula, and their declining competitiveness in relation to government institutions, these schools now tend to be associated with drop-outs or failures from ministry schools. Like some of the alternate Malay religious schools, therefore, the creation of such institutions reflects deeply held cultural and religious convictions and principles valued by their respective communities. Yet these are not entirely able to eradicate an underlying strand of pragmatism in the desire to preserve a more "mainline" national secular option and reserve the alternate stream for those unsuccessful in the first.

INDIVIDUAL RESPONSES TO DAKWAH

The power and penetration of dakwah into almost every area of Malay life over the past decade should not be allowed to obscure the fact that there still exists a large number of individuals who consider themselves "religious" (beriman), though not dakwah, and some few who take neither very seriously. In fact the visible, and audible, dakwah followers, the ones who make a public impact on Malaysian society at large, are probably smaller in number than the waves they create. In the universities, where they are most concentrated, they involve approximately 20 per cent of the students of the University of Malaya, 40 per cent at the National University, 10 per cent at the Agricultural and Technological Universities, and barely 10 per cent at the Science University.

The first category of Malay, describing themselves as religious but not dakwah, includes the traditional kampung dweller, with his or her own brand of religion, heavily subsidized by Malay adat. Basically, rural Islam tends to be earthy, practical, and this-worldly in a solid peasant style, grounded in a social community which the adat also reinforces. Aspirations to the material benefits of urbanism from clothing to TV are also common. In later years, the orientation becomes increasingly other-worldly, with attention to the pilgrimage, the pondok religious school and community, and the after-life. At this stage only is it considered legitimate to adopt more Arab-style clothes, as a reward for virtue. In keeping with their combined this- and other-worldly aspirations, support for the newer, dual-purpose secular-cum-religious schools, whether madrasah, pondok converted to nizami style, or for the people's religious schools is logical and consistent. For them, neither form of extremism is desirable. While PAS's rhetoric for the upgrading and greater role of Islam in general is endorsed, the specifics of the more hair-splitting details of the dakwah requirements are less so. As well, the youth of the dakwah leaders is to their disadvantage.

In the urban areas too, the new sweep of religious consciousness has claimed a number of the younger, educated set, who nevertheless explicitly resist being identified with dakwah, save in its broadest, original sense. For these individuals, religion is a private matter and may entail scrupulous attention to prayer and cleanliness, a solid religious education for their children, contributions to charity, and so on, yet without the conspicuous and obsessive accompaniments and other behavioural minutiae (remeh-temeh) of the stereotype dakwah follower. Some of these people deliberately resist assuming Arab dress or wearing songkok to which they have not been accustomed in order to avoid being classified with the dakwah contingent. Such individuals consider the outward forms to be so much "window-dressing" and claim that what counts is in the heart. Other individuals, conscious of the "platoon" mentality or power of peer-group control involved in much of the current religious revival, are determined to resist this loss of personal autonomy or to surrender to group rituals. Some speak in a quite uncomplimentary fashion of "crowd psychology" and "bizarre Arab customs," of a "mindless" approach to what should be seminal and serious theological and social issues. They belittle the students, who are sometimes unflatteringly referred to as "psychos," caught in the idolization of mediocre teachers and officers and their weak religious legitimacy and exegesis. Throwing up their hands in gestures of mock surrender, these critics recommend that those fundamentalists who set so much store by seventh-century Arabia should take a camel instead of flying to Mecca for the pilgrimage. Such commentators also hold the opinion that even PAS, were it to come to power, would probably become almost as corrupt as UMNO. Yet for all the vituperativeness of their comments, even the cynics cited above would not reject Islam and the authority of the scriptures per se, they only dispute the interpretations and the uses to which they are put.

Among the non-dakwah religious individuals are some schoolteachers who have to confront pupils refusing to take sports classes, either because they are too aggressive and competitive or because they require non-Islamic clothing. Some teachers compromise by allowing girls to wear slacks under their dress, although others counter religious objections with religious responses. Thus, it is frequently pointed out, on the basis of both the Koran and the Hadith, that the Prophet himself advocated the practice of physical exercise and bodily health through sports, although in his case, the preferences were for horse-riding and camel-racing. Such is the casuistry of daily life.

Some overseas Malay students face a similar situation of not wishing to become engulfed in dakwah enclaves and obligations social or ideological. One girl, studying in the United Kingdom, who (by pre-dakwah standards) had always regarded herself as more religious than the average and had even been in the habit of organizing small prayer and discussion groups for fellow Malays in her university was suddenly disenchanted when the "dakwah fever" erupted there. She refused, however, to be pressured into the exclusivist, isolationist social life of the new dakwah contingent, to don the new "uniform," or to cut herself off from friendships with non-Malays and non-Muslims. She thus remained on the outside of the new Malay community and its usrah, only to be labelled by the dakwah people as "loose, like the drama students," the only other Malay reference category in their social universe. Thus, she was declassified from religious to loose and irreligious in a single stroke.

These more outspoken individuals on matters of dakwah, courageous or not, tend to be "loners," who, for personal or other reasons, have fewer close emotional commitments to specific groups or networks, who may have become detached from an effective golongan selapis, and who can steer an individual path of their own. While religious beliefs and ideology for many dakwah participants is largely a product of social interaction, for these loners, their relative freedom is the result of a lack of such interaction. The principle is the same in both cases: religious attitudes depend partly on the wider social environment. Among the more independent religious thinkers are one or two well-known writers, who can give voice, if only a minority one, to this brand of Islam. While declaring themselves steadfastly committed to Islam, their approach is to the universalistic faith, with its foundation in social justice and humanitarianism, transcending petty local ethnic and political divisions. Some of them are even reform-oriented, promoters of Islam as a body of ethics and morals rather than defenders of a rigid law or ancient customs. The best-known and most articulate proponent of this approach, a speaker sought by dakwah and non-dakwah organizations alike, is Syed Hussein Alatas, a brother of the ABIM hero, whose views diverge somewhat from those of his sibling. Physically detached from the immediate Malay scene by his Singapore residence, Alatas is, like Hamka, immune from, and able to transcend, some of its internal divisions, and thus to speak convincingly for a more generalized, albeit revitalized, Islam. Alatas can find in dakwah things to praise—it espouses social justice for example—but he excoriates its tendencies towards an uncritical de facto identification of Islam with Malay interests. While Islam has undoubtedly contributed much of the best in contemporary Malay culture, as he has documented historically, it is not totally isomorphic with it, and it must not be used as an ethnic prop nor as the charter for special privileges. Alatas is critical of élite corruption, drawing on the old, and regrettable, values of autocratic, ancient Malay kingship and its Hang Tuah mentality. He does, however, support modern technology and economic development, as long as they are dedicated to the general welfare. In this he differs from the fundamentalists and particularly from their hero, Al-Maudoodi, whom he often singles out for criticism in his writings. Like the leaders of Aliran, with whom Alatas has some personal connections, he favours "opening the doors of ijtihad" (1979:2) and a creative reinterpretation of the scriptures to accommodate changing social conditions and times.

Finally and inevitably, there is a small minority of Malay Muslims, whose numbers and influence cannot be easily gauged, owing to the delicacy of the issue, who are implacably opposed to the entire spectrum of the religious revival in whatever form. There are those who, somewhat improbably, see dakwah as part either of a "Zionist" or Chinese conspiracy to undermine

Malay attempts to uplift themselves—a brand of an ethnic, if not Islamic, interpretation—others regard dakwah as a somewhat irrational aberration, and the trend is seen as having the same regrettable effects of impeding progress and the modernization of a developing society, hence as regressive. In this category are found a number of government officials, although few would openly proclaim such sentiments. In public, they either conform to the current linguistic and rhetorical devices, by which Islam can be shown to be more progressive than normally portrayed in dakwah circles, or else they avoid the issues. Needless to say, all are concerned with the future of their children and with the problem of finding educational institutions, either at home or abroad, immune from dakwah's influence.

Among the anti-dakwah contingent are those overseas students who become the core of the Bumiputera Malay group. In many respects, the Bumis can be just as isolationist or withdrawn from the host society as the dakwah groups, looking inward to their own resources, and sharing similar academic and social problems. Whereas the Islamic group only interacts with other Muslim students for religious purposes, the Bumi Malay is more likely to co-operate with non-Muslim Malaysians in "cultural events," in celebration of national holidays and of the religious holidays of Chinese New Year, Hindu *Deepavali*, and so on, which the dakwah Malays conspicuously shun. Bumi Malays are also more willing to experiment with discos, dances, and movies, in general preparing for the lifestyle many of them will probably follow, as relatively prosperous élites, on their return home (cf. Taib Abdullah 1978).

ISLAM AND THE ARTS

One domain of Malaysian life which has recently been buffeted by the winds of religious change, is that which is broadly defined as "the arts." Dakwah has had the effect of creating a deep cleavage in the artistic community between those who have entered into the new Islamic spirit and those who feel constrained or betrayed by it. In this area, it appears particularly difficult to maintain a neutral or middle-range position. Only two alternatives exist: those in favour of Islamic art and those not. Thus phrased, the agony of decision is acute.

Over the past two or three generations, since the first flowering of the Indonesian novel and the writings of the Kaum Muda literati of the early part of the present century, a substantial body of Malay literature has accumulated. Today, there are many young Malay writers and poets, some free-lance, but increasingly becoming linked to the universities as writers-in-residence. Many other writers are also schoolteachers by profession, and they, together with their fellow-writers in other occupations, have created a number of literary associations where ideas are exchanged at regular workshops and conferences. The National Writers' Association, GAPENA (*Gabungan Penulis Nasionalis*), has several branches in each state. Since the advent of dakwah, GAPENA members have come under increasing pressure to sponsor the development of a new "Islamic literature." So severe has the rift become that, all compromise finally abandoned, the dakwah supporters have launched a new Islamic Writer's Association, GAPIM (*Gabungan Penulis Islam Malaysia*), under the leadership of Ustaz Nakhaie, the ABIM M.P. for Baling, who is also a writer. Members of the new group, however, have not relinquished their membership in GAPENA and persist in trying to imbue it with a more Islamic character. Much discussion time is now devoted to clarifying just what "Islamic literature" consists of, to nobody's complete satisfaction. Among the various prescriptions for this elusive creation are plays and novels with religious themes and explicit dakwah goals, where, predictably, the virtuous always triumph over the evil. An example of this genre is Othman Kelantan's story of a religious teacher who successfully resisted temptation in the form of the charms of a young girl entrusted to him to study the Koran and the vindication of the trust placed in him by the girl's parents. Recognizing that all human behaviour worth writing about is not of the religious variety, some writers propose that any theme is acceptable, as long as vice, corruption, and other sins of the flesh are portrayed in such a way as to underline their undesirability and that they are never rewarded or upheld as worthy of emulation by others. Yet other writers, particularly poets, assess the quality of a good Islamic poem by the proportion of Arabic-origin words used and the cultivation of the Arabic model quatrain style of Sya'ir. This represents a complete reversal of a pre-dakwah (1954) statement by Hamka, himself a much respected writer in his own right, to the effect that Arabic words should be consciously avoided in Malay/Indonesian on the grounds that changes in the spelling and meaning in the process of transmission from the parent language can lead to confusion and misunderstanding.[7]

One of the leading lights of the pro-Islamic surge of Malay literature is Shahnon Ahmad, now one of the country's most esteemed novelists and also dean of the Faculty of Fine Arts at a local university. Writers, like others in the university environment, also tend to become infected with the reigning dakwah ideology, through colleagues and, to some extent, through the students. As a result, Shahnon has renounced all his early, pre-dakwah novels, the works by which he was first acknowledged as a master of his craft, as "worthless," as he publicly enters his new Islamic phase. He is now concentrating on novels with themes of corruption among government and city élites, with much moralizing about their irreligious lifestyle which bears the seeds of its own destruction. He openly condemns urban writers without any religious background or philosophy as well as those who write for financial reward, although he is swift to defend certain comforts, such as his own Mercedes. Shahnon further contends that in order to produce high quality works, an author must himself be religious and pure in spirit, for this will shine through in his writing. Thus, the good artist should avoid sinful and immoral activities in his own life and work only for dakwah and for God. While Shahnon has a substantial following in GAPENA, other members privately confess that they and some of their colleagues are dismayed at the turn of events, but that they fear to speak out in the current religious climate. Other highly respected writers appear ambivalent: they give an appearance of supporting the new trend, but seem to lack conviction. For example, two brothers from Kedah, both nationally acclaimed Malay novelists with an early history of involvement in the wartime, socialist-inclined pan-Malay nationalist movement with Indonesia (of the Melayu Raya and Nusantara days), now write articles in national literary journals praising the new dakwah developments in literature. In these pieces, they publicly "regret" their own weak religious background, as if in anticipation of criticism. But as if to answer the criticism expected, they then proceed to assert that Islam is more than just the outward signs (for example, prayers over the front door or on the desk) and that must be demonstrated in every personal endeavour (cf. Abdullah Hussein 1979:34-36). The new literary trend has not been lost on government officials, who see yet another non-threatening way to become involved in religion and who have now launched, through the prestigious Institute of Language and Literature (*Dewan Bahasa dan Pustaka*), an annual prize for the "best Islamic novel."

The close-knit, face-to-face, small group, "transparent" nature of the writers' personal ties, whose professional reputation lies in investment in each others' approval and support, resembles the situation of many of the student and other peer groups in their usrah and other group activities. So pervasive has the dakwah pressure become that some small and clandestine groups prefer to meet privately and unobtrusively in private homes. One such is a small poetry circle which meets in the home of an Aliran member, where its members are able to express their fears that their works are not being published because they are not Islamic enough and their resentment of the confusion of art and politics, as they see it. Yet they need to devise a compromise strategy to gain access to publishers without totally violating their principles. To these poets, a compromiser like Hamka is viewed negatively as the Al-Maudoodi of Southeast Asia.

The dakwah spirit has also invaded other areas of the arts. Attacks are now being directed at such traditional Malay art forms as the shadow puppet plays (*wayang kulit*) and dance dramas (*bangsawan* and *Ma'yong*) on the grounds that like much of Malay adat they contain non-Islamic, that is, Buddhist or

Hindu, elements and themes. Further, those performances involving humans allow for an unacceptably "close proximity" of males and females, with the latter not suitably covered. As a result, the content of performances sponsored and staged by the Fine Arts Department on certain campuses are strictly controlled, particularly where the dean of the faculty is also a dakwah supporter. Control is effected largely by informal pressure, rather than by direct fiat. Lecturers and directors of these programmes themselves—few of whom seem very sympathetic to dakwah—have taken great pains to purge non-Islamic elements from the plots and even to insert extra comments favourable to Islam where feasible. Nevertheless, it goes without saying that no dakwah student will either take part in or attend the performances, and some have even petitioned to have the drama programme terminated. Those Malay[8] students who support the traditional art forms are invariably an entirely different cohort and move in separate social circles from the dakwah followers. They form their own cliques, partly in opposition to, or in self-defence from, the dakwah usrah, for mutual support and to defend themselves from the sometimes vicious criticism they receive from their more "religious" peers. The most devastating blow the drama group received came when the dakwah protagonists successfully petitioned the Fine Arts dean to impose a ban on a university Malay language production of Hamlet for the national television network, TV Malaysia, alleging that it would reflect the university in a "bad," that is, un-Islamic, light. Outside the universities, too, there is growing pressure against the traditional wayang performances, even in places where these were once popular. Some zealous or cautious district officers in rural areas now refuse permission for wayang to take place for fear of repercussions from unpredictable religious authorities. For the same reasons, the government-sponsored television service, becoming known as a latter-day patron and reviver of some of the traditional Malay arts, is also sensitive to the changing climate and is vigilant about excising from its national programmes any elements which might offend the religious groups.

Similar opposition has arisen to the visual arts—painting, sculpture, and photography—although these have always laboured under certain constraints in Islamic culture. As in the case of literature, pleas for Islamic themes are the order of the day, and damning remarks about iconography abound. Dakwah university students do not take such courses and relegate all human representations, especially sculpture, to the "garbage dump of idolatry" (patung), in keeping with longstanding Muslim conventions. The effect of these attitudes on a number of practising artists of late has been to persuade some of them to seek a livelihood outside Malaysia. There is now some question as to the fate of arts departments in various educational institutions, including MARA, save for those dealing exclusively with graphics, calligraphy, and abstract design.

Popular art, as presented on television, tries to satisfy the religious public by providing regular doses of nasyid, although even this does not always please the dakwah purists. Some of them claim that the singer should adopt the telekung to replace the customary head scarf and should ideally only perform before members of the same sex, for even a sweet voice can seduce men from the path of righteousness.[9] Finally, the martial art of silat, as noted, has been questioned in several dakwah quarters, particularly when it involves the invocation of spirits or the use of Hindu or "pagan" rituals as a prelude to the performance.

In all of the above—in the political and government responses to dakwah, in the reactions of non-Malays, in the more personal responses of individuals who have alternate modes of religious expression, and in the reorientation of the artistic community—Islam is showing in Malaysia what it has shown elsewhere, namely, that it has a role to play in every facet of life. What is at stake ultimately is a definition of the boundaries of Islam in other domains of social life. It is a test of the limits of religious jurisdiction in an officially non-Islamic state and particularly of the rival claims of various religious authorities whose legitimacy comes from different sources, secular, political, traditional/religious, Bumi Malay, and dakwah. Given that Islam considers the social and political arena its own domain and that the current political élites find it expedient to defend their present bureaucratic, constitutional, and ethnic authority with a unique blend of ancient Malay autocracy backed by more transcendental religious symbols, the prognosis is for continuing friction.

Islam, moreover, is divided within itself, not only over matters of legitimate sources of authority, but also over the definition of "orthodoxy." One message which can be culled from this situation is that, from a comparative world perspective, Islam, like so many other major religions, is not a single, monolithic entity with unambiguous canons of belief and orthodoxy, but is in reality a vast, widely ramified congeries of disparate groups, each specialized and adapted to particular local settings and constituencies. Any distinctive ideological and theological variations develop as part of that adaptation, and in this fact probably also lies much of its strength and versatility. Where social and political involvement are strong, inter-group friction may be as much factional as ideological, although the language and issues are attuned to a religious vocabulary, even to the extent of propelling political foes outside the religious fold altogether. The final accolade is the application of the labels of "unbeliever," "deviant," "renegade", and so forth by which the co-operative door is closed ever more firmly.

7

Born Again Muslim or Born Again Malay?
Dakwah and the Search for Ethnic Identity

THE UNIVERSALISM OF ISLAM

The transformation of so-called universalistic religions into more particularistic forms is not an uncommon process, especially in the context of multi-religious and multi-ethnic societies where the two attributes may become fused or confused. The Sinhalese of Sri Lanka define themselves in terms of their Buddhism, in opposition to Tamil Hindus or Muslims, and even reject Christian converts as genuine Sinhalese (Obeyesekere 1975). The Dutch in Indonesia were identified by their Christianity to the extent that local Christian converts were said to have "become Dutch" (*masuk Belanda*). By a parallel process of identification, the Malays in Malaysia have come to equate Malayness and Islam. We saw in Chapter 1 how the spread of Islam gave a new shape, character, and unity to the previously amorphous concept of Melayu, as well as contributing important new elements of Malay culture. Today, it is also a political and legal fact that Islam is written into the constitutional definition of who is a Malay and that, officially, all Malays are Muslim. It is also increasingly obvious that, as other components of the "constitutional Malay" (notably language and custom) are either unreliable or being eroded as distinctions, Islam has begun to shoulder the full burden of Malay identity as the dakwah movement attests. We have also seen how, historically, becoming Muslim was tantamount to "becoming Malay" a possibility epigrammatically summed up by the oft-quoted equation (masuk Islam/ masuk Melayu), along the same principles mentioned above.

The gradual appropriation of Islam as a feature exclusive to the Malays in the local context raises a number of fundamental taxonomic problems for

Malaysia's complex ethnic and religious population structure. The first concerns the status of Muslims, born or converted, who either do not wish to identify with or, alternatively, are not accepted, as Malays. A second is the discrepancy sometimes caused by applying only cultural (religious) criteria (by a literal interpretation of the constitution), as opposed to ethnic/racial ones (bangsa) to define the subject. A third arises out of the ever-present demographic problem of ethnic proportions. Should the boundaries of Malayness be allowed to expand, as through widespread conversion policies such as those of PERKIM, it will inevitably bring in its wake economic and political implications for the Malay special position and the NEP. Finally, there is the ongoing political and administrative problem of the relationship—legal, as well as social and cultural—of Muslims and non-Muslims in a single state, where Islam is culturally dominant and the force which shapes the moral and ethical climate.

In the easy, early days of the late nineteenth century, before the period of heavy foreign immigration began, any Muslim in the Malay states was theoretically considered eligible for Malay ethnic status (Nagata 1974a; 1979). In practice, there were at that time only a few non-Malay Muslims, and of them, most were either Indians, Arabs, or groups from the Indonesian archipelago, who often married and, within a generation, assimilated into the Malay community. In those days too, no outstanding political or economic privileges attached to being Malay. Few obstacles would therefore be raised when immigrant Muslims took local spouses (usually wives), Malay names and customs, and became parents of a new Malay-Muslim generation.

The question ignored by this simple cultural/religious concept of Malayness, like the constitutional definition which succeeded it, was that of "race" or bangsa (cf. Nagata 1979). As long as the number of converts or inmarrying non-Malay Muslims remained small and their subsequent lifestyle congruent with that of the local Malay community, the issue of bangsa rarely obtruded as a distinct or even conflicting source of identity. Gradually, however, the pressure of growing immigration forced the bangsa question out into the open. It was first recognized taxonomically under conditions in which successive waves of Indian Muslims, especially in urban Singapore and Penang, intermarried over several generations with local Malay women, creating a physically identifiable type. Regardless of culture and religion, acknowledgment of their separate origins (bangsa) intruded and was permanently registered in the form of a new hybrid term *Jawi Peranakan* (Roff 1967; Nagata 1974a; 1979). The Jawi Peranakan were in practice held in somewhat lower esteem than Malays of uninterrupted descent or "pure" race, and a new term, Melayu jati (pure Malays) was coined at that time by way of opposition. In contrast, a higher measure of esteem was accorded to the offshoots of another kind of inter-ethnic but intra-religious union, namely, that between Malays and Arabs. By virtue of their connection with the Holy Land and bearing genealogies which were conveniently remote and immune to inspection or verifiability, many Arabs claimed descent from the Prophet and adopted the titles Syed and Syarifah. In neither case did the old Islam-Malay equation quite work. For even while the religious factor held constant, a degree of status differentiation was measured by the source of the "blood" or ethnic input, that is, Indian or Arab. Implicitly, therefore, bangsa was being entered into the equation as the growing preoccupations with the refinements of purity (jati) and indigenousness (asli) attest.[1] Two conclusions may be drawn from the above. First, the boundaries of Malayness are multiple and not quite isomorphic, which inevitably creates ambiguities in some contexts, but which also allows for flexibility in others and for the possibility of marginal situations leading to social and political manipulation. Second, masuk Islam / masuk Melayu notwithstanding, the existence of non-Malay Muslims is implicitly recognized and, with it, the universalistic aspect of Islam as a faith transcending ethnic (bangsa) lines. This realization was entrenched when increasing immigration gradually built up a distinctive cohort of Muslim Indians who preferred to maintain their Indian identity and evinced no desire to be regarded as Malay. Later, whenever the latter wished to stress their Muslim-ness (as opposed, for example, to Hindu Indians), they adopted the label "Pakistani," for its Islamic connections, even though most were born long before the creation of that state.

A second factor to drive a wedge between the one-to-one identity between Malay and Muslim status was the trend, beginning in the late 1960's and early 1970's, for a small but significant number of Chinese to convert to Islam, partly through the efforts and assistance of PERKIM. Not only are the Chinese clearly of a separate descent line or bangsa from Malays and other Muslims in Malaysia, but they are not "born Muslims" (hence cannot be "born-again" Muslims either), and this gives them something of a second-class taint in the minds of many Malays. Probably just as important is their perceived economic dominance in Malaysian society, where they are often depicted as the proverbial controllers of the purse-strings at the expense of non-Chinese. Justifiably or not, this perception has caused the economically less successful, but now politically more powerful, Malays to retaliate by selectively introducing special advantages to enable their community to "catch up," as under the provisions of the NEP. All of this understandably makes the Malays reluctant to receive Chinese Muslim converts into the community as full-status Malays (cf. Nagata 1978). Nor are the converts encouraged to adopt Malay names, dress, customs, or any other hallmarks of Malay identity. Instead, the Chinese Muslim is relegated to a separate category and urged to remain culturally Chinese, where this does not directly conflict with the requirements of their new faith. To this I shall return.

What is happening here is somewhat paradoxical. On the one hand, the universalism of Islam, transcending ethnic, local, or national boundaries, is in some contexts allowed, as in the solidarity expressed between the Malays and their Middle Eastern brethren as members of the wider Muslim community (ummat). On the other hand, a particularistic thread can also be discerned in the defensive way in which Islam is being used to define and protect Malay status. This is a more subtle process, involving the use of religious symbolism as a sort of code and rhetorical device to refer to Malays and to Malay interests, as in the speeches of some of the religious and dakwah leaders noted above. Furthermore, to the extent that the revivalism of dakwah is directed exclusively towards the Malays, only they can have the distinction of becoming "born-again" Muslims, so that, Brahmin-like, they appear in a superior "twice-born" relationship to their "new associates." To change the metaphor, boundaries which have lost their tightness can be reaffirmed through constant refinements to eliminate the "undesirables" and to ensure, once again, that Malays are distinctive in "their" religion, at least in the Malaysian context.

In public life too, frequent references by politicians to "religion, race, and country" (*agama, bangsa, dan tanahair*), as a sort of indivisible holy trinity, persist in the rhetoric of both UMNO and PAS leaders. This triad is often pithily referred to nowadays as the "Malay ABC," a popular, if rather crude, rendering of the acronym Alif, Ba, Ta, the first three letters of the Arabic alphabet. In election campaigns, when Malays are warned of the dangers of lack of Muslim unity, of "dividing the Muslim community," the target is those revivalists who would, by their efforts, create two kinds of Muslim, dakwah and non-dakwah. So too would they destroy the comfortable one-to-one identity between the Malays and "their" Islam and encourage the splitting of the Malay vote. All this is reinforced by a renewed stress on the role of Islam in Malay culture, again from two opposing perspectives. At one extreme there are the dakwah enthusiasts who would purge non-Islamic elements from Malay social life and custom. But even the less zealous, middle-of-the-road politicians are giving more attention to those Muslim rituals which solidify the Malay community and increase its distance from the non-Malays, on occasions of the Prophet's Birthday, Hari Raya Puasa celebrations at the end of the fasting month, public prayers and Koran-reading competitions, and now they are also encouraging greater Islamic content in the arts and sponsoring an Islamic university. The latter are also supporting attention to more religious education in the schools, including a reintroduction of the Arabic (jawi) script. On matters of adat, however, most politicians with the kampung vote in mind, remain silent. Finally, in a context where open discussion of racial or ethnic issues is officially sensitive or taboo, religion provides a suitable cover for the old political and other disputes to be carried on in a different idiom.

As we saw in the last chapter, the particularistic bias in their use of Islam towards the interests of the Malay community distinguishes the dakwah followers and politicians alike from the orientation of PERKIM. In its evangelistic overtures to the non-Malays, PERKIM is moving towards the reduction of the particularistic identification of a religion and a people.

There are, however, some differences over the nature of the relationship between religion and Malay identity between some of the dakwah groups, and even within them. ABIM's top leaders, especially Anwar in the past, have publicly, if cautiously, been known to criticize the extreme chauvinism (*semangat perkauman*) still present in Malaysia as it is regrettably exploited by some zealous Muslims. In his now famous speech given on the occasion of the Eighth Mukhtamar (ABIM General Meeting) of January 1979, Anwar explicitly rejected any form of prejudice in the name of Islam or of Allah, a faith which enjoins religious tolerance. Anwar quoted Mohammed as rejecting 'asabiyah or racial fanaticism (*golongan kefanatkian/golongan kebangsaan sempit*) and exhorted his followers to transfer their "struggle" (perjuangan) to poverty rather than people, in the true spirit of Islam. Predictably, Anwar attributed the source of all ethnic consciousness in Malaysia to the western presence, which presided over the decline of religious faith in the colonial period and introduced many non-Islamic practices, including the resurrection of the pre-Islamic "Malay" ideas under the guise of "national" culture. This was accompanied by the sponsored immigration of non-Muslims, whose separateness from the local Malays was a hallmark of colonial policy and interest.

In an exercise of casuistry and a refinement of religious argument, however, Anwar was able to rationalize and even support manifestations of nationalism in some parts of the Middle East, for example, the cause of the Palestinians and the Iranian revolutionaries. These movements and sentiments, Anwar maintained, are not motivated by ethnic chauvinism, but rather by principles of justice, whose original violation can also usually be laid at the door of western interference and exploitation. Anwar thus took the tack, as do several of his colleagues still, writing in the ABIM journal, *Risalah* (for example, Kamaruddin Jaffar, 1980:24-28), that it is the obligation of every sincere Muslim to support just causes, including ethnic ones. Moreover, if only to make the distinction more pointed, Anwar claimed that, unlike Christianity, Islam is not a "secular religion" but enters into the spirit of all causes of freedom and justice, even for non-Muslims. Here he noted the tolerance of the Prophet for Christians and Jews in seventh-century Arabia and the liberal administrative policies of such enlightened Muslim rulers as the fabled Caliph Omar II and the several Moghul emperors in India towards their non-Muslim subjects, *al-dhimmi*, a more positive label than the infidel/unbeliever, kafir/jahiliyah, epithets.

On the other hand, all Muslim writers, including those of ABIM, are swift to deny that loyalty to one's own descent group is wrong or even prohibited by Islam or that ancestral customs, insofar as they do not contravene religious laws, should be abandoned. Indeed, loyalty to a people or a country (*qawmiah, wataniah*) within the bounds of Islam is commendable, as long as the faith takes priority in the last resort. Here Anwar closely followed the liberal interpretations of the Egyptian scholar, Hassan Al-Banna. Islam thus condones love of country and birthplace (*wataniah al-Hanin*) and, with it, movements to free them from unjust, non-Muslim repression (*wataniah hurriah al-izzah*) and to unite the Islamic community into a broader society (*wataniah al-mujtamak*). Islam also respects the right of peoples to venerate traditional noble leaders, as long as they are religiously virtuous (*qawmiah al-majdu*), and even to use force to achieve freedom from dominance by non-Muslims (*qawmiah al-tamzin*). Conversely, Islam rejects forms of nationalism which divide the religious community (*wataniah hizbiah*) or which promote one people's interests through the oppression of others (*qawmiah al-udwan*) or by resurrecting pre-Islamic cultural elements, as did Turkey under Ataturk (*qawmiah jahiliyah*). ABIM leaders are also willing to admit that Islam is not exclusively an Arab religion (*al-qaba'il al-Arabiyyah*), although, as noted, not all their followers maintain this distinction.

On closer analysis, despite this apparently courageous stand, Anwar really affirmed little more than safe, uncontrovertible "motherhood" issues, to which few could object on principle, whether UMNO, PAS, or the Malays generally. ABIM's statements by no means preclude pride and loyalty to Malay interests and causes within Islam, and this is followed up by their policies of concentrating their dakwah revitalization on their own community.[2] By perpetuating this de facto identification of Islam and Malayness, they promote particularism and, moreover, give grounds for theologically less sophisticated or knowledgeable followers to interpret dakwah as a Malay movement. As we have noted, this is most frequently heard in usrah and other private sessions, for example, when questions are raised over economic resources and the rights of non-Muslims (which usually means "Chinese"). As it travels down the line, the message tends to be transformed and take on a tone and import somewhat different from those originally intended at source (see Chapter 5). Thus the charitable and aid contributions to victims of floods and other disasters which form the backbone of the activities of HELWA, ABIM's female branch, are invariably directed in practice towards needy Malays. Further, in its continued association with PAS, ABIM must inevitably share some of the burden of that party's ideology.

Even though PAS, which has always run on a platform of Malay and Islam, has now reversed the priority to Islam and Malay, the equation remains. Given this connection too, when PAS or ABIM make pleas for an Islamic state, it must be interpreted as an appeal partly for more Malay rights and the elevation of the Malay community to truly national status and dominance.

Aliran's stated goals are even more outspoken and courageous than those of ABIM. Aliran explicitly relates the cultivation of ethnic sentiments to élite political and economic interests which exploit ethnic divisions to divert attention from any common inter-ethnic cause. On this basis, Aliran main- tains, UMNO perpetuates its power. In its own membership too, Aliran is ethnically non-exclusive, and it is largely devoted to causes promoting ethnic unity.

At the opposite end of the spectrum, Darul Arqam is more detectably chauvinistic. In its language "we Muslims" (kami orang Islam) readily trans- lates as "we Malays." For example, in justifying its business policies, Arqam speaks of defending the interests of "Muslims" against those of "others" (*orang lain*), where the Malay-Chinese opposition is usually quite trans- parent. To Darul Arqam, the "enemy in the blanket" may be described as the "non-Muslim," but its followers understand, by the enthymeme princi- ple, who is meant. Ashaari's attempt to establish a "state within a state," rather than to transform the existing state, is a clear ethnic defensive move and show of resistance. Its recent and somewhat tentative acceptance of the measure of co-operation with some government enterprises has been under- taken reluctantly, on the prudent advice of sympathetic civil servants, as a means of improving its public image.

In matters of Islamic universalism, Jemaat Tabligh provides yet another variation. Tabligh's Indian origins and early base in the Indian Muslim com- munity of Malaysia (and initial lack of appeal to Malay Muslims) made it a particularistic movement in practice, if not in ideal. Some of the negative aspects of this identification still persist in certain Malay quarters, where objections are voiced to Tabligh's alleged over-veneration of Delhi, to its widespread use of Indian languages (for example, Urdu and Hindi), and to its identification with "Indian," "Pakistani," or "Kling" mosques. Even Tabligh's green robes are sometimes described as an "Indian" rather than the Islamic holy colour. In one or two urban areas, Tabligh is still associated with Indians or Klings or at least with the Jawi Peranakan, hence not accept- able to "pure Malays." At worst, Malay critics of Tabligh see the movement as an insidious attempt to gain Malay status. For example, some Malay office workers were privately cynical over the adoption of dakwah by one of their colleagues, dismissing it as part of a strategy of changing from being Jawi Peranakan to Malay. In rural areas by contrast, mention has been made of the warmth with which Tabligh messengers have been received by some traditional ulama and others. Here, the negative associations of the urban Indians are less familiar or immediate, while Tabligh's political and economic neutrality have considerable appeal to individuals wishing to keep a low profile vis-à-vis political parties, religious councils, and so on. Certainly, Tabligh's operations, both Malaysian and international, show greater openness to Muslims of all origins. One of Tabligh's most prominent lecturers in Penang is a Chinese convert, to whom Tabligh Malays defer in religious matters. Tabligh also encourages a continuous circulation of missionaries (muballigh) of all racial and national origins, from country to country, using whatever lingua franca—Urdu, Arabic, English—, is most effective or appropriate. Yet the principal thrust of Tabligh in Malaysia now appears towards the "born" Muslims and the Malay community. While not excluding other converts, neither does it make strong overtures in their direction, which tends to reinforce the impression that one of the Tabligh's more covert aims is the reduction of the marginality of Malaysian Indian Muslims and the legitimation of their status as Malays. This may also be seen as a final "divorce" from other Indian Muslims, many of whom reject the dakwah identification and prefer to retain the "Indian" label (see below).

The relationship of Arab custom to Islam and, in turn, to Malay adat, raises another point for casuistry in the modern dakwah dialogue. For all their cautioning against identifying Islam too narrowly with Malay or any other ethnic interest, many ABIM followers and others tend, in practice, to favour Arab custom because of its connection with the "original Islam." Once again, the individious process of particularism has invaded the universalist faith and has led to the paradoxical situation whereby dakwah followers critical of Malay custom on the grounds that it is non-Islamic will uncritically accept Arab custom (also known as adat), despite the fact that there is no a priori connection between Arab adat and the faith as propounded by Mohammed, as a number of Aliran spokesmen point out. These attitudes are consistent with the high status usually accorded to Arabs in Malaysia and with the fundamentalist, conservative orientations of dakwah generally. Although even dakwah people recognize the weaknesses of some of the wealthy Arab leaders, who abandon themselves to the pleasures of life in most un-Islamic ways, there remains an ingrained respect for the Arabs as the Prophet's people that even these indiscretions cannot easily erase. Further, the influence and respect recently achieved by the Arab world through the politics of oil as well as religion, provides a "halo-effect" for Malays by association, and enhances their status on the world scene. In matters of inter-ethnic brotherhood within Islam, there seems to be more kindred spirit between Malays and Arabs, both in Malaysia and across the continents, than between Malays and non-Malay Muslims in their own homeland. The position of these Muslims will be described more fully below.

Provisionally, it may be concluded at this point that Islam in Malaysia has lost many of its universalistic qualities and, in the local context at least, has come to represent Malay identity and interests. Intellectually and theologically, many Malays, dakwah or not, concede this fusion of the two identities as contrary to Islamic principles, but take few steps to correct it.

A NON-ISLAMIC VIEW OF THE MALAY: THE BUMIPUTERA

The knotty question of the relationship between Islam and Malayness is compounded by the fact that the Malay bangsa itself contains a number of sub-groups, especially those of Javanese, Boyanese, Minangkabau, Bugis, and Rawa origins, although they were born in Malaysia and are culturally Malay in most major respects. Further, it leaves open the question as to where to place the non-Muslim, but undeniably indigenous, tribal population, including the orang asli of the Malay peninsula and the myriad groups of East Malaysia, for example, the Iban, Murut, Kadazan, Melanau, Bajau, and so on. One basically "secular" solution to this problem, adopted largely by official agencies, has been to stress the "indigenous" (asli) element in the creation of the synthetic category of Bumiputera ("sons of the soil"). This raises yet another boundary of identity, which, however, partly crosscuts those of religion and bangsa. Non-Muslim indigenes are thus Bumiputera, whereas Muslims of "non-indigenous" races are not. Put another way, all Malays are Bumiputera, but not all Bumiputera are Malay. Bumiputeraism represents a brand of non-religious Malayness, with a strong appeal to the non-dakwah, but chauvinistic Malay. It is typical of the youth attracted to the Nasrul Haq movement, as well as those loyal to the UMNO line, whose ideal Malayness is unencumbered by religious restrictions on economic development, technological innovations, modernization, or western influence, and is exemplified by the non- or anti-dakwah, Bumi Malay factions of overseas university students.

Although the term Bumiputera (like its Indonesian counterpart, *pribumi*), can be traced back to the 1930's, it has only really come into its own since the political aspects of Malay identity have assumed priority. Since the early 1970's, most of the government's economic development policies, especially the Second and Third Malaysia Plans, have been phrased with reference to the Bumiputera and non-Bumiputera dichotomy, and they form the basis of the NEP. With recent dakwah developments, however, what began as a plan to improve the Bumiputera share of the national economy is now being revalidated in terms of Islamic symbols, in response to dakwah challenges and a rephrasing of the ethnic terms of reference. To resolve the incompatibility, this has sometimes led to rather tortuous and laboured statements by civil servants, who declare that it is first necessary to develop Malay unity and nationalism before Islamic consciousness can be meaningful. Many of their supporters are more direct. Letters to the editors of respectable and otherwise balanced national news magazines still seriously accuse the "immigrants" (*kaum pendatang*) of merely using Malaysia to further their own interests (cf. *Dewan Masyarakat*, 15/1/80:3). A surprising number of young people aggressively defend the need for preferential policies to protect Malay land, employment, and educational interests against the "alien races" (bangsa *asing*). Elsewhere, equally vituperative responses erupt from non-Malays, as on some wall posters in the capital, which have blazoned forth the bitter message: "when Indian clerks are given notice, Malays take over; Malays become postal clerks, the Indians and Chinese common labourers" (*Bintang Timur* 23/1/80). Some imaginative apologists even blame the sins of their own community on non-Malays, for example, the explanation that Malay factory girls may spend the night with their boyfriends is attributed to the laxity of their Chinese landlord. (*Bintang Timur* 3/1/80).

In a sense, both the Bumi and dakwah interpretations of Malayness, while starting from different premises and using different symbols, arrive at the same crossroads. They often converge in the priority given by each to Malay interests, if not always for the same reasons. Further, each has its own unique stance on ethnic boundaries in some combination of religion, "race," and origin, not entirely or satisfactorily resolved by either one.

NON-MALAY MUSLIMS

Converts to Islam

We have seen that, whatever its validity in the pre-twentieth century period, masuk Islam no longer predicates masuk Melayu. Indeed the chief minister of the State of Pahang once remarked that it is easier to "Islamicize a man than to make him a Malay" (*mengislamkan orang bukan Islam dari memelayukan orang*) (*Dakwah* 3/12/79).

The experience of converts to Islam over the decade of the 1970's indicates that the likelihood of their being accepted into the Malay community as full status Malays is becoming more remote. This, despite the fact that most converts fulfil the constitutional requirements for Malay status, including the practice of as much "Malay custom" as many urban, westernized Malays. Whether this situation reflects the converts' own desire to retain their ancestral identity and culture or the reluctance of the Malays themselves to receive them into their community, the fact remains that in Malaysia, there exists a small, but significant body of Muslims without any clear-cut ethnic identity or community affiliation, cut off from their parent group but not assimilated into any other. In part, this is the consequence of the Malay failure to resolve the dilemma of whether or not to increase the size and composition of the Malay community by encouraging and incorporating all converts. Clearly the decision has implications for Malay access to certain resources and privileges, and in a different way for the census, by swelling the Malay component of the population to above the psychologically important 50 per cent level.[3] Potentially too, it could promote the strength and feasibility of an Islamic state by reducing the size of the non-Muslim minority. These considerations have not been ignored by PERKIM in its evangelistic policies (see Chapter 6), although the evidence suggests that even PERKIM is reconsidering the question of the ethnic status of the converts.

The disadvantages of what some see as a potential flood of "converts of convenience" are, of course, apparent. This possibility was first raised in the early 1970's when it was suspected that many unemployed urban Chinese were converting to Islam mainly to qualify for Malay "special rights," which raised anew the perennial zero-sum perception of resource distribution by "race." As a result, the current tendency is for the Malays to tighten the bangsa boundary over and above that of religion. This has the added effect of preventing non-indigenes from slipping through the net into the Bumiputera category. Whether the Chinese and other non-Muslims remain as unassimilated, unconverted aliens or whether they try to follow the conversion route to a new Malay status, the reaction in the Malay community is one of defensiveness, of which one of the manifestations is the dakwah revival as a reactionary, inward-looking fundamentalist expression of Malayness.

The Status of Converts According to PERKIM

Whatever doubts and ambiguities exist as to the ultimate or ideal ethnic and religious composition of Malaysian society, one of PERKIM's continuing missions has been the conversion of non-Muslims, particularly the Chinese, as we saw in Chapter 6. What PERKIM has never totally resolved is the problem of the ethnic placement of its converts. To date, its policy has been somewhat haphazard, and individual cases have been treated on an ad hoc basis, often varying from place to place and from official to official. The pace of events during the 1970's made it increasingly evident to PERKIM that the number of "conversions of expedience" appeared to be growing and that the organization's policy of trying to accommodate them all within a Malay framework was counter-productive.

The statistics provided by PERKIM, corroborated by religious council records, indicate that approximately 75 per cent of all new converts (mu'alaf) are Chinese, and most of the balance are Hindu. While the age of over 60 per cent of the converts is less than thirty, PERKIM officials claim to have observed an increase in average age at time of conversion by the mid-1970's, when a larger number of unemployed, middle-aged, male Chinese began to join the association. It was generally assumed that the principal reason for this rash of conversions was for occupational benefits, in the anticipation of "Malay" privileges. In this connection, it may be recalled from Table 1 (Chapter 6), that the overall number of conversions of all ages and both sexes peaked in the early 1970's. This, significantly, was the period when the NEP, with its elaborate roster of preferential quotas for Malays in occupational and educational fields, was first being implemented, thus investing the constitutional definition of Malayness with new significance. The generally low educational, income, and employment status of many of the converts of these years (for example, factory workers, hawkers, rubber-tappers, and fishermen), often with a monolingual Chinese background, would tend to support the "Malay benefit" theory of conversion, with the subsequent decline in numbers as a sign that the theory was not working as smoothly as had been anticipated.

Initially, some PERKIM officials not only provided material and moral support in obtaining employment and other benefits where needed for new recruits, but even appeared willing to accept them as Malays. Each PERKIM branch had its own policy on this touchy issue, and some, for example, Penang, were more liberal than others. Tunku Abdul Rahman, its president, was magnanimously open to a broader interpretation of "Malay" and "Bumiputera"' in the pre-1969 days, and he had publicly asserted that, "since it [the term Bumiputera] had no legal meaning, anyone is entitled to call himself 'Bumiputera'...for that matter, those Chinese and Indians who have been here for several generations are entitled to call themselves 'Bumi'" (Party Debates, Dewan Rakayat, Official Report, Second Session of the Second Parliament of Malaysia, vol. 2, 1965-1966, 13 Nov. 1965), although not all other ministers agreed. Even as late as 1977, Tunku Abdul Rahman was in favour of giving new converts the benefit of the doubt: "these new converts should be given the same rights as the Malays...and the word 'Malay' should be defined to include these new converts" (Tunku Abdul Rahman Putra Al-Haj 1977:248). This plea has periodically appeared in print in the PERKIM publications by way of exhortation to less accommodating officials to follow their president's lead (cf. *Islamic Herald* 12/8/75). Not surprisingly, the most virulent opposition to this view emanates from the ranks of UMNO, who claim that conversion to Islam is only for a "particular goal" (*tujuan tertentu*) and not for God (*bukan kerana Allah*) (cf. *Akhbar Suara Ra'ayat*, 22/11/75:7). The growing strength of the latter view, of a tighter policy of allocating Malay or Bumi status and benefits, both in and out of PERKIM, has led to some disillusionment and undoubtedly contributed to the decline in conversion and increase in recidivism of late. This same period has also seen the full flowering of dakwah, with its heady appeals to Malay interests, and this too has raised doubts among the Chinese as to the wisdom of converting to Islam.

Reports from branches of PERKIM in various parts of West Malaysia suggest a few other, sometimes idiosyncratic, situations in which Chinese conversions to Islam occur. In Perak, for example, substantial numbers of converts without intermarriage have been reported from some New Villages.[4] Again, the bulk of these conversions took place in the early 1970's, largely for economic reasons, under the encouragement of roving PERKIM missionaries. As in the case of the spread of dakwah, peer group and social pressures also played a role here, for the conversion of a local notable in the community or a number of friends or colleagues launched the necessary social support groups to make future conversions more socially acceptable. Converts in some of these areas are reported (by PERKIM missionaries) as giving as their principal reason for their decision the fact that their "friends had converted." There may also have been some covert pressures on the part of the Malay authorities leading to the impression that conversion could remove any hint of suspicion about the political loyalties of Chinese, who are still often seen as potential Communist sympathizers or subversives in the oversimplified political cosmology of the centre. Similar motives, of political and social "rehabilitation" and reassurance of "good faith," were allegedly responsible for the conversion in rural Johor (another area of past Communist activity) of a cohort of Chinese once indicted and convicted of crimes under the Emergency. This conversion then was to be the visible, outward sign of contrition and grace and atonement for sins past. In other cases, groups of ex-convicts and chronic drug offenders have also been inducted into Islam as the result of their treatment at a PERKIM clinic. As in the case of Darul Arqam, the healing of the body, mind, and soul seem to hold a strong affinity for one another in the aetiological ideas of PERKIM.

Lest the above give the impression that all Chinese conversions to Islam are entirely the result of economic expedience or of the "politics of ethnicity," interviews with the small core of converts also serving as missionaries (muballigh) at PERKIM centres, provide as strong a testimony as any social scientist daring enough to judge motivations should require. The sense of deep religious commitment of some of these converts is conveyed in their often fumbling, but convincingly earnest expressions of a "search for meaning and self-realization" (*kesedaraan sendiri*) for their lives. Several of them indicate that, in their religious quest, they have "tried" other religions, for example, Christianity and other forms of Buddhism, first but without satisfaction or that they experimented with "free-thinking" (the local term for "atheism") before "finding Islam." Most of these converts of conscience are young (under thirty years), of middle-range educational and occupational status, for example, bank clerks, mechanics, insurance agents, primary school teachers, airline engineers, soldiers, and one or two high school students, who speak both Malay and English. Significantly too, most of them appear to have many Malay friends or were raised in, or close to, a Malay community or residential area. Thus the peer / social pressure factor may also have played its part in the ultimate decision. These people are willing to submit to intensive courses of religious study, and some spend several weeks or months in PERKIM quarters, followed by time in the Middle East, to deepen their knowledge of Islam. Subsequently, some of them serve as PERKIM missionaries or as assistants in the publications and educational departments (at PERKIM's expense). The number of individuals actively undergoing such training at the PERKIM headquarters at any one time is small, however (compared to the ambitious numerical targets reported by PERKIM's public relations departments to the press, see Chapter 6), averaging between thirty and forty in the late 1970's. At one count in 1979, out of thirty-three in residence in the Kuala Lumpur PERKIM branch, sixteen were Chinese, six were Indians, ten East Malaysian "tribal" peoples from Sabah, and one was Australian. All were between fourteen and thirty years of age, and seven were women.

Further evidence of genuinely "religious" motivations for conversion may be extrapolated from an informal "control" case study from Singapore. In this predominantly Chinese city (approximately 75 per cent), where to be Muslim conveys no advantage, the Muslim Converts' Association appears to be thriving, as of the late 1970's and early 1980's. This Association estimates, for the past decade, a total of about six to seven thousand new converts (mu'alaf), and although the date of conversion for each individual is not on their records, it does claim to have administered written religious tests to 282 converts in 1976, to 285 in 1977, and to 311 in 1978. In Singapore, where there is no advantage to claiming Muslim or Malay identity, in the form of economic, occupational, or status benefits (possibly even the reverse), the motivations for conversion can be narrowed down to intermarriage, the influence of Muslim / Malay friends, and to a personal search and spiritual commitment of the type mentioned for some of the Malaysian youth above. Like the latter, many of the Singapore new Muslims also experimented with a variety of other religious and philosophical ideas, ranging from socialism to Mormonism, but finally felt that they had found their solution with Islam.[5] Certainly, at the time of the interviews, these converts gave every impression of being deeply moved and committed to their new faith, and spent most of their free hours in classes and discussion with their peers. The majority are young and unmarried and in the same general educational, occupational, and income levels as their Malaysian counterparts. Once again, it seems to reflect a trend in the youth sub-culture, in which a need for self-realization and identity, particularly when reinforced by exposure to the "right" social set or influences, seem to lead in the direction of a form of religious quest.

As in Malaysia, many of the Chinese converts in Singapore confess to a rejection by their original family and friends as a result of their conversion, as a "betrayal" of their heritage and identity, although there is evidence to suggest that these may have initially been weak for these individuals. Others merely refrain from informing their families of their change and practise "avoidance" techniques in matters of eating and ritual occasions. Thus the headquarters of the Converts' Association tends to become a "home from home" or refuge (with a dormitory attached for "emergency" cases) for those with insoluble problems, as well as a sympathetic and convivial place to seek others with similar problems and interests. The Singapore Association maintains close contacts with its counterparts in Malaysia, via PERKIM.

Aside from economic pressures, the most important reason for conversion to Islam is for marriage to a Muslim / Malay. In the nineteenth century, some unattached male Chinese immigrants who took Malay wives did not in fact convert, for their progeny were required as recruits to continue the all-important patriline as the core and charter of Chinese identity. The offspring of these marriages, whose lifestyle, including language, was heavily infused with Malay as well as Chinese culture, became the founders of the so-called Baba Chinese community (cf. Nagata, 1979; Tan 1981). Today, that is, from the early 1960's until the present, the direction of intermarriage seems to be between Malay males and Chinese females. One of the reasons most commonly given is that daughters are "lost" to the lineage on marriage in any case, and since they are not responsible for the continuation of a family name or ancestral cult, there is less resistance to this than the loss of a son to a faith inimical to the cultural expressions of their ancestral identity.

Although both Hindus and Chinese who marry Malays and convert to Islam are technically in the same position religiously, the Chinese in general seem to be considered more "different" as a community, than Indians, Arabs, or Indonesians. The size of the Chinese population, together with their perceived dominance and control in economic affairs at the expense of other groups have historically contributed to this sentiment. By contrast too, there exist greater cultural similarities and historical affinities between the Malays and Indians through their Indian-derived adat and early immigration experience. Information[6] from PERKIM and the religious councils now suggests a recent increase in the number of Malay-Hindu unions at the expense of the Malay-Chinese, at lease in Penang and Kedah, although the absolute incidence of intermarriage remains low and may be further declining.

The ambiguities of the ethnic status of Malaysian new Muslims, especially those of Chinese origin, has already been mentioned. And althouth a definitive official ruling has still to be made, it is becoming evident that the convert is eligible neither for Malay or Bumi status nor for their benefits, Tunku Abdul Rahman notwithstanding. Now engraved in the new public lexicon is a surrogate new status, the "saudara baru" or "new associates" by which new converts are designated, thus avoiding any ethnic commitment or identity at all. Relegated to a permanent "hybrid" category, they are kept at arm's length from "born" Muslims and often abandoned by their own hereditary kin group, who ironically see them as "selling out to the Malays." For their part, however, the Malays are often critical of the saudara baru as "converts of convenience" and allege that they refuse to study their new religion properly, that it is "too easy" for outsiders to convert to Islam,[7] and that some testing of knowledge and faith should be administered. Some dakwah Malays would now like to see the introduction of the Singapore Converts' Association practice of requiring the completion of a series of written tests before a new recruit is formally accepted. Nowadays, there is even a tendency to regard conversions for reasons of intermarriage as "self-interested," and, again, several critical dakwah followers accuse many inmarried spouses of "still living like Chinese," of secretly eating pork, and of not praying regularly. Recently, even the Johor religious council voiced a public objection to "marriages of convenience," by which was meant alliances between rich non-Malays with Malay girls for alleged access to Malay reservation land (*Berita Harian*, 1/5/80).

In striking contrast to the traditional particularistic view, in current Malay thinking there is no longer any anomaly in being Muslim, yet remaining Chinese or Indian too, for "Islam admits all races." This conveniently universalistic interpretation thus relieves the potential pressure on Malay resources and simultaneously reinforces the ethnic boundary. It also redefines the ethnic boundary and resurrects instead the alternate idea of bangsa. Nowadays, at major religious conferences, saudara baru are referred to as members of "*masyarakat Islam*" (Muslim society), distinct from the Malay delegates.

Culturally, converts are now encouraged to retain their ancestral customs insofar as these do not contravene the rules of their new faith, while the adoption of Malay names, dress, food, and other practices is not longer recommended. Although a convert is ritually given a Muslim name, care is taken to differentiate this from a Malay name (even though they often are identical), and the family surname is less often changed. Thus on their identity cards, Chinese Muslims will inscribe names on the pattern of Abdullah Tan Boon Siew, and the section designating "race" (bangsa) is still marked as "Chinese" (*Cina*), to show that it is possible to be simultaneously a Chinese and a Muslim. This is the style adopted, for example, by one high-ranking Chinese convert, who often serves as a sort of official ideal type and role model both in PERKIM publications and by dakwah Malays who want to keep the saudara baru at arm's length. This man, a cabinet minister, is also a leader in the MCA political party, indicating once again that he is still firmly rooted in the ethnic Chinese community. It is also the custom of those few "born" Muslims of Chinese descent (from certain western regions of China), several of whom are active in PERKIM and in the Chinese Muslim Association, to retain their ancestral surname, for example, Haji Burhan Beh and Haji Ibrahim Ma, who point out that fifty million Muslims have lived in China for generations without losing their Chineseness. Rather perversely, there are some dakwah Malays who see in the refusal of converts to change their names evidence of their lack of commitment to Islam. Among the saudara baru themselves there also exists a divergence of opinion. Some continue to try to "pass" as Malays, insist on adopting Malay names and dress, always make a point of speaking Malay, and conspicuously dissociate themselves from all things Chinese. For a small minority, there is even an emergent reactionary feeling that "Islam does not belong to the Malays alone," and on this basis they are frustrated that they should be arbitrarily debarred from Malay identity.

Most Chinese saudara baru, however, make compromises. They will attend Chinese New Year and other traditional celebrations, but refrain from consuming the festive pork or wine and stand aside during the "idol-wor-shipping" events of ancestor veneration. Some converts are clearly ambivalent about such situations, which they may exacerbate by returning clad in Malay ceremonial dress, as if to "protest" their new role too much. Others hover indecisively at the fringes of the festivities, nervously abstaining from proffered food, while others, as if to fulfil the judgment they feel is already passed on them by suspicious Malays, participate fully as Chinese. In effect, most of these converts are, in the eyes of local society, neither Chinese nor Malay, but remain suspended in the permanent marginality of the saudara baru status in a kind of ethnic limbo.

In the view of some of the PERKIM officials in Penang (who are not necessarily representative of those in other parts of the country), Hindu converts are regarded as "more reliable" in terms of honouring their new religious obligations, and even while residing with or revisiting their natal families, they are less likely to "get lost" or revert to their former faith. PERKIM's overall inconsistencies, or ad hoc approaches to the whole question, are even reflected in some of the speeches of Tunku Abdul Rahman, who, on occasion, displays an unexpected and disturbing arrogance or lack of understanding about non-Malays and non-Muslims. He once commented, for example, that because of their background, the saudara baru "do not have a tradition of spiritual practices, meditation and prayer, and for them, moral and spiritual matters are not important." In the same speech, he even imputed the conversion of some Chinese to the "high cost of their funerals" (*Berita Harian*, 6/10/76).

It is in the formal social sphere that the separation of the saudara baru from mainstream Muslim society and the Malays is most apparent. Despite PERKIM's missionary, educational, and welfare goals and its early efforts to secure Malay benefits and other assistance for its protégés, it does not succeed in uniting the two types of Muslim and even maintains separate institutional arrangements for each group. Under the auspices of, but formally separate from, the main PERKIM body itself has arisen a distinct Chinese Muslim Association (CMA), with its own internal leadership and membership drawn exclusively from converts of Chinese descent. As a kind of intercalary organization, the CMA simultaneously manages to unite and divide. By its association with (and funding from) PERKIM, its members receive religious instruction, financial assistance, social support, and ceremonial sponsorship on religious holidays. But by confining these activities within the limits of the CMA, the result is a minimum of meaningful interaction with other Muslims, especially the Malays. In Penang particularly, alongside the declining rate of conversion already documented, the last few years have seen a gradual deterioration of relations between the CMA and PERKIM. This is most manifest in the rate of attendance of the Chinese at religious classes for saudara baru from over one hundred in the mid-1970's to a mere three or four in 1978, at which point the classes had to be discontinued. There was a growing feeling among the saudara baru that PERKIM no longer had their best interests at heart, and the eventual result was an abrupt secession of the CMA from its foster parent and its total disappearance from PERKIM's social map. PERKIM officials, who seemed both sad and embarrassed at the turn of events, now profess not to know whether the CMA has finally disbanded or secretly found new premises independently. It was even reported by some Penang religious council officials that PERKIM had approached them to "find the lost saudara baru," with requests for more personal information and addresses. In fact, the CMA had initially just removed itself to other quarters, although most of its remaining members seem to follow a more Chinese than Malay lifestyle (food, language, family, politics). Most social interaction also tends to be with other Chinese, and they use the CMA association for recreational rather than religious functions.

One lone "survivor" of the original CMA remains a permanent member of PERKIM, in whose office he serves as a janitor. Otherwise, PERKIM, in Penang at least, is almost exclusively a Malay organization, with lectures and activities catering to religious-minded Malays, principally older ladies, who stop short of full dakwah. In fact, it has become something of a Malay social club, with rounds of tea parties and other convivial events, interspersed with non-dakwah religious lectures. Its committees consist of middle-class and professional men and women, under the patronage of local élites and royalty, including the Sultan of Perak and the Tunku himself. Some Indian converts have remained with Penang PERKIM, but even they feel that their life as Muslims is artificially restricted to the institutional setting of PERKIM itself and to other *saudara baru*. Finally, there are in Penang even some Malays, with Chinese wives, who independently find fault with PERKIM, both over its "social club" atmosphere and for its "pushiness" and lack of sympathy or understanding of the *saudara baru*. On these counts, they refuse to allow the wives to go near the association, preferring to instruct them in religious matters themselves within their family. Most *saudara baru* do not feel qualified to pass judgment on dakwah forms of Islam and often claim to be confused by it. The principal reason given is that "dakwah is as Malay matter," thus underscoring once again the separation of two cohorts of Muslims along ethnic lines. It also shows up in the double meaning of dakwah, its original sense and that which it has uniquely acquired in Malaysia. PERKIM claims to practise the first kind of dakwah by proselytizing among non-Muslims. But the brand of dakwah familiar to most Malaysians is the more restricted kind, a form of religious affirmation of Malay identity. As an organization, PERKIM has no defined policy towards the more restricted dakwah. Most of its officials approve of the religious zeal now evident among Malay youth, and sometimes even allow ABIM or Darul Arqam followers to deliver lectures at PERKIM functions, as long as they do not advocate extremist of "deviant" ideas. Tunku Abdul Rahman's own overtures to Anwar, for some form of co-operation between their respective two bodies are suggestive of this flexibility. Of all the dakwah movements, PERKIM officers tend to see Tabligh as the least desirable, on the grounds of its aggressive tactics in some urban areas, their "taking over of mosques," and "always asking for money" (soliciting of contributions) from house to house. Again, this represents the view of individual officers and not PERKIM as an organization.

Overall, not only does the incidence of conversion to Islam appear to remain low and be further declining, both among Chinese and Hindus, but such mediating associations as PERKIM also seem to be losing whatever effectiveness they once had. Once again, Islam is de facto reverting to its original particularistic (in Malaysia) position as the preserve of the Malays. Where the existence of non-Malay Muslims cannot be denied or ignored, a form of "backhanded" universalism is restored in encouraging them to retain their separate ethnic identity. Thus the Malays try to maintain a double standard, by restricting full religious interaction, and especially dakwah, to their own community, and keeping their non-Malay co-religionists at bay.

Indian Muslims

In urban Malaysia, there has long been a solid, if small, community of Indian Muslims by birth, amounting to approximately 6.7 per cent of the total Indian population (Chandler, 1974:452). Dating from the time before the ethnic barrier between the Malays and non-Malays began to tighten, with a change in emphasis from religion to bangsa and/or indigenousness, some Indians have successfully managed to play the field or manipulate their identity (between "Indian" and "Malay") according to the situation as I have described in detail elsewhere (cf. Nagata 1974a). As in the case of converts, there are clearly advantages to being regarded as Malay for some purposes, whereas for some personal and business connections, ties with the Indian community are still desirable. Indian Muslims who are still interested in moving into the Malay community are now finding the shortest route is through the dakwah movement, partibularly Tabligh. This strategy is recognized and resented in some Malay quarters, and it is one of the reasons why Tabligh was viewed rather negatively in earlier years. As dakwah has grown stronger in the wider Malay community, however, Tabligh's respectability and appeal has also grown, and many of its original Indian followers are even defining themselves (and becoming accepted as) Bumi, although not Melayu jati, that is, local-born, sharing a common religion, but not of Malay descent or bangsa. Aware of the fragility of its position, Tabligh now plays down its India/Delhi orientation, and increasingly dissociates itself from the local-born, but self-defined Indian Muslims of Malaysia (see below). Yet Malay opposition to alleged Indian Muslim ethnic expediency does persist, as expressed in objections to the latter's attempts to join UMNO, while continuing to use the Tamil language at its meetings (Yahya Ismail 1978:38; *Star*, 28/2/80).

There remains a core Indian Muslim community, however, which has never attempted to manipulate, change, or adapt its ethnic identity or claim Malay status, even situationally. They have no doubts or reservations as to their Indianness, and Islam is not seen as a reason or strategy for attempted Malay assimilation. As such, these Indians maintain their own Muslim religious associations, for example, Iqbal, Kadayanalur, the Muslim League, the Tamil Anjuman Himayatul Islam Club, United Muslim Association, and so on. They also tend to frequent and support separate mosques, often popularly labelled "Indian" or "Pakistani," where the Friday sermon (*khutbah*) is still given in Urdu or Tamil on alternative weeks. Many of their religious organizations resemble social clubs or business associations, and while religious lectures and celebrations are regular items among their activities, their explicit interest or participation in the dakwah movement, as associations, is minimal. Some members, as individuals, may independently attend Tabligh lectures elsewhere, but in general, most "born" Indian Muslims seem to regard dakwah as a distinctively Malay phenomenon.

Ethnic Polarization Through Religion

It should be evident that current trends in Islamic revivalism, and even in the PERKIM brand of evangelism, do not appear to be conducive to any reduction of ethnic differences within the frame of a shared religion. To the contrary, a sharpened sense of ethnic differentiation seems to be taking place. Not only are the Malays looking inward, whether as Bumi or in cultivating their own dakwah, which draws them apart from both non-Muslims and non-Malays, but parallel forms of religious revitalization are now observable in the other major ethnic communities. Inasmuch as these revivals are concentrated in specific communities, the lines of ethnic cleavage are that much reinforced. For many of the reasons discussed above, the Chinese community in particular is now showing a less-disguised impatience with national government policies and institutions, especially in the fields of education and the economy and is beginning to emphasize parallel and independent organizations and responses of its own.

The Buddhist Revival

In the Chinese community at large, there has recently been a noticeable revival of interest in Buddhism, both the more traditional Chinese variety of Mahayana Buddhism, as well as a more innovative cultivation of a canonical form of Theravada Buddhism.

The Theravada interest is striking, for, historically, it has only rarely been associated with any of the Chinese religions or with Malaysia.[8] Indeed, the Theravada followers are largely dependent on personnel and resources derived from neighbouring Theravada countries, principally Thailand, Burma, and Sri Lanka, and in Penang and Kuala Lumpur, they use the temples run by Malaysian residents from those countries. The appeal of Theravada Buddhism is mainly to the middle-class, urban, educated Chinese youth, or the segment of Chinese society corresponding to that most heavily involved in dakwah among the Malays and for much the same reasons. Many of the young Malaysian Chinese are undergoing personal crises of their own, both in accommodating to the difficult and often frustrating changes in the educational system and to their reduced opportunities in it. Those who cannot afford the costs of overseas education but who do manage to secure a university place at home are still faced with uncertain employment after graduation, and, indeed, the entire future of the Chinese community as a whole is clouded with uncertainty. As the Malays turn inwards and sharpen the boundaries with the non-Malays, so the Chinese respond with a greater awareness of their own distinct identity and religious traditions and seek security in these. For some of the young, educated Chinese, like their Malay counterparts, their search takes them beyond the faith (or lack of it) and practices of their parents and families into a more esoteric world of "rational" religion characterized by a more intense and personal commitment. Traditional Chinese religion, like the syncretic Islam of the traditional Malay, is variously said by young Chinese, to be "primitive," "incomprehensible," "superstitious," and "ritualistic"—some even use the English term "mumbo jumbo"—while others, from their own personal recollections, find it intimidating to children. Here, references are made to the more dramatic and gruesome practices and bodily mutilations surrounding some of the spirit medium cults and the frightening impact of masked and costumed dancers and monstrous apparitions so prominent in many Chinese temple events. Chinese religion is also characterized, by those who reject it, as overly materialistic, self-seeking, magical (for example, the burning of paper money to ensure prosperity in a future life), and further, as noisy, crowded, and generally aesthetically and intellectually unsatisfactory. Like Malay adat, it is merely an adjunct to the social round, according to these young people, and provides no insight into more fundamental religious questions and even debases them. The teachings provided by visiting Theravada monks, constantly circulating in the Buddhist countries adjacent to Malaysia and now making regular detours into Malaysia itself are said to be more rational, to be able to tackle such basic problems, and to provide a more realistic guide to life. Furthermore, they provide opportunities for peace and meditation, in total contrast to the raucous exuberance of Chinese folk celebrations. Typical of the lectures given by the visiting Theravada speakers are such topics as "the Buddhist view of a stable economy," drawing liberally and unapologetically on Schumacher's concept of "small is beautiful" and on his chapter on "Buddhist economics." Somewhat defensively, Theravada adherents claim that Buddhism does not, unlike some extreme forms of dakwah, reject all material interests out of hand but channels these into socially constructive ways. It encourages perseverance and productivity in conjunction with spiritual development and stresses more international co-operation for the welfare of everyone. Unlike dakwah, this Buddhist revival is less fundamentalistic and also far less anti-western in its attempts to reconcile a renewed moral and spiritual path with the needs of modern life. To a greater extent than even the more enlightened dakwah proponents, however, these Theravada Buddhists emphasize that the basic tenets of their faith are universalistic and applicable to all members of Malaysia's multi-ethnic society and beyond.

Like dakwah too, this form of Buddhism condemns such vices as lotteries, corruption, excessive drinking, and drug-taking, as well as the behaviour of self-interested élites.

The current Theravada Buddhist revitalization movement has substantial followings among both Chinese students and lecturers on at least two Malaysian university campuses, and their meditation and public meetings are focused, as mentioned, on the Thai, Burmese, and Sri Lankan temples and on a Buddhist Meditation Centre. At present, most of the lectures and discussions are in English, although the prayers and chants are in the original Pali (which few actually understand, as in the case of some of the dakwah chanters of Arabic). However, just as some of the more dedicated and conscientious dakwah followers are taking up the formal study of Arabic, so some of the "new" or "born-again" Buddhists are beginning to learn Pali too. Given the numerous dialects of Chinese and the partial dependence of the Malaysian Theravada congregation on foreign lecturers and monks, an effective common language is essential. In view of the educational level and background of most of the followers, English has proven the most appropriate to date, although some followers anticipate switching to Malay (in accordance with the national language policy) in the future. Although universalistic in ideal, in practice the current Theravada revival is restricted to the Chinese community, and so in the local context at least, it becomes a particularistic feature of that community and is associated with Chinese identity (following the pattern of Sinhalese Buddhism in Sri Lanka). In much the same way that the Malays recognize a spiritual kinship with a wider ummat, including especially the Arabs beyond Malaysia, so the Chinese Theravada Buddhists extend their religious reach to Thais, Burmese, Sri Lankans, and others outside the Chinese community. For most purposes, and probably also the immediate stimulus, the oppositional relationship of Chinese / Malay is the operating principle. Yet even in the Malaysian context modern, rational Buddhism has succeeded in eroding some of the narrower and more traditional particularisms along lines of regional, dialect and clan identities. Many older Chinese religious associations and sects (cf. Topley 1967), whether spirit medium cults, temple and shrine cults, "long life" burial societies, or self-improvement movements, recruited their membership exclusively from one or other territorial or family origin group, which made even "Chineseness" a level of unity rarely achieved in practice. The particularist-universalist tension which beclouds the relationship between Islam and Malayness finds its mirror image in the dilemma of Buddhist-Chinese identity. Local and ethnic fragmentations of nominally monolithic and universalistic world religions may be more general than sometimes supposed. Unlike dakwah, followers of the Theravada revival are not markedly anti-western and indeed endorse selective technical and other forms of modernization, for example, in the "small is beautiful" vein. In these respects, their orientation is solidly "this-worldly."

The Mahayana revival is stronger among older Chinese and is more concerned with re-asserting traditional Chinese values and customs (as practised in Malaysia). Its institutional focus is frequently the privately funded Chinese school, which still teaches the old Confucian virtues and analects in Mandarin. These schools are often associated with adult education and religious centres, for example the Por Tay (Mahayana) Religious Association. Many Chinese parents are apprehensive lest the encroachment of the Malay language and educational system will divorce their children ever from their heritage and are reacting against what they see as an increase in Malay assertiveness, politically, economically, and now in religious matters. As noted in Chapter 6, even some English-educated Chinese are reverting to the original Chinese culture in apparent defiance of their western upbringing. Finally, alongside the resurrection of the more traditionalist Mahayana / Confucianist elements in Chinese life is a more intense recultivation in recent years of some of the old calendrical festivals, for example, the feast of the Hungry Ghosts, of the Nine Emperor Gods, which in some of the more "Chinese" cities, such as Penang, are now celebrated with greater intensity, expense, and elaborateness than in the past (cf. Loh 1981:71).

Christian Revivalism

Although only 3.5 per cent of the Chinese in Malaysia are Christian, 49.5 per cent of all Malaysian Christians are Chinese, and Christian Chinese too have not been immune to the recent surge of religious revival. It has been particularly striking in the swelling of the charismatic Christian movement both in the form of such "established" Christian sects as the Pentecostalists and Seventh Day Adventists and in more syncretic combinations of Christianity and traditional Chinese elements. It has even invaded some Catholic churches, where priests have been given formal dispensations to practise exorcism of spirits.

In contrast with the "intellectualist" approach of the Theravada Buddhists, the charismatic Christians are closer to traditional Mahayana practice in spirit and indulge in a total physical and spiritual immersion, even communitas in their rituals. Many of these encourage speaking in tongues to the tune of rich musical accompaniments and making public testimonies and affirmations of faith. Others have incorporated healing rites, through prayer and the laying on of hands, and have even introduced such Chinese elements as the use of joss sticks and the exorcism of spirits. In their meetings and discussions, the emphasis tends to be on such traditional Chinese preoccupations as health, prosperity, and the family, that is, a looking inward rather than outward to a wider more universalistic community.

The Christian membership appears to span all status levels of the Chinese community. Revival meetings are held in the large, suburban mansions of the rich *taukeh*,[9] where English is customarily spoken until speaking in tongues takes over. Here, westernized, impeccably dressed housewives and businessmen of all ages, who, an hour previously were discussing their latest shopping spree in Hong Kong over a sumptuous dinner, are abruptly transformed into a congregation of hysterical, weeping, fainting devotees practising glossolalia and highly emotional confessions of faith, of personal problems, and transgressions, in which all uninhibitedly participate. To their meetings, they invite both visiting missionaries (if there is a foreign parent church) from overseas, as well as local ministers. Meetings of poorer Christians are held either in churches or rented buildings, and since most of the poor are still monolingual, the language medium is Hokkien, the local Chinese dialect. Again, similar behaviours and rituals prevail, including the invocation of more familiar Chinese spirits.

A striking feature of the Christian revival is the nature of the symbolism by which some members place themselves in the overall Malaysian cosmology. Many fundamentalist Chinese Christians have explicitly compared their condition to that of the Jews and the latter's diaspora from Israel to the Chinese separation from China. This analogy is made even more potent when the counterpoint of the Muslim / Arab opposition is introduced, whether in Palestine or Malaysia, particularly given the Malays' strong antipathy to "Zionism."

Finally, there are the truly syncretic, even messianic, movements, which in classic form combine a Christian millennial expectation with many indigenous (Chinese) religious and thaumaturgical practices. One of these movements, the "Five Realizations Society" (Ackerman & Lee 1981), has a large following of lower middle class Chinese in Kuala Lumpur under the leadership of an ex-primary schoolteacher who was a failure in his profession. His principal source of appeal was derived from his fabled and miraculous healing powers through the control of spirit mediums, from the effectiveness of his personal oratory, trances, exorcism, and other public "performances." At the height of his powers, these gifts drew to the leader a personal following of about two thousand, both traditional Taoists and (Mahayana) Buddhists, as well as Christians. Pursuing a rather nebulous goal of personal fulfilment, health, and morality, the collective rituals make liberal use of Chinese symbolism, as in the imagery of ancient Chinese warriors and kings, the manipulation of the elements of earth, fire, wood, metal, and water, and the constant invocation of spirit mediums. On the other hand, the leader has also condemned some aspects of Chinese polytheism and even upheld Islam as an example of a "perfect" monotheistic religion (which could also be a shrewd political move). His followers are encouraged to cultivate a sense of self as a means of reaching God, as do Muslims and Christians.

Although little is known of the background of most of the movement's followers, they are predominantly urban, from the ranks of bus drivers, teachers, petty businessmen, clerks, and so on, and the language of communication is English. The success of the movement shows that the leader has been able, like the ulama, to establish his legitimacy through the satisfaction of the needs of a particular constituency, although, like some of the dakwah followings, it is hard to give it any clear structural shape.

It is difficult to estimate how far these religious trends in the Chinese community are related, if at all, to the Islamic revival among the Malays. On the one hand, Chinese society has always been religiously eclectic and experimental, and it has had a long history of millenarian and other cult movements, in China and overseas, both within "Chinese religion" and, later, in Christianity. (Even in the People's Republic today, there is evidence of a resurgence of such religious activity.) The current religious ferment in Malaysia may thus be a response to symptoms of the same general underlying conditions and needs that assail some members of the Malay community: a search for identity and for meaning in life, especially among the youth and urban elements. Among the more highly educated there is a profound dissatisfaction with the religion of their parents. There may be some other parallels too with the situation among the Malays, where rapid changes in lifestyle and occupational prospects, resulting from government policies, have created uncertainties and a rethinking of priorities. Yet for all the growing convergence of occupational and economic interests and goals, identities are not so easily abandoned or forsaken. It may not be surprising therefore that some Chinese MCA leaders (for example, the deputy minister of Finance), along with their Malay counterparts, exhort their constituents each to cleave to their own religion, the Malays to Islam and the Chinese to the religion of their choice, in order to create a more harmonious and stable society. This would seem to suggest a view of religious revitalization as a form of parallel adjustment of the two communities rather than a sense of "backlash."

Occasionally, however, direct abrasiveness on the part of the Malays/ Muslims irritates and widens the religious/ethnic wound. One case in point was the decision by the Penang State Religious Council to prohibit the construction of a statue of the Chinese Goddess of Mercy (*Kwan Yin*) on the grounds that its lofty elevation on a hill would allow it to tower over the new state mosque. Thinly-veiled innuendoes about "idol-worship" and the attacks on Hindu temples have reinforced the tension and kept both sides in a state of nervousness and uncertainty.

When asked to comment on dakwah as a movement, some Chinese claim to admire the Malays for their new-found ability to organize themselves so effectively and to draw in so many young people to the mosque and the cause of religion. But many more seem apprehensive at the ethnic and political implications of dakwah, and they are particularly fearful of the fanatical fringe and of the prospects of an Islamic state. Ultimately, they recognize that current dakwah developments can only result in drawing the "races" farther apart.

The Indian Community

Less evidence exists to indicate that the Indian community is undergoing a religious revival comparable in impact to that of the Malays and Chinese. At the level of educated, urban youth and the high school and university contingents, there are parallels to the concerns of the Malays and Chinese for a more intellectual and enlightened "rational" variety of religion, one capable of giving meaning to the new kind of lifestyle of today's growing middle class which feels alienated from the religious traditionalism of the parental generation. Some Hindu university students are now conducting special classes to explain the history and philosophy of Hinduism to those who have either lost touch with its practices or who have, like many urban young Malays, never been deeply schooled in the tradition at all. The emphasis in these teachings is to extend the relevance of Hinduism to modern life, in a more universalistic outreach, less narrowly preoccupied with the ritualism of popular cults. There may also be a certain sensitivity among the more educated Indians of the "irrational," "superstitious" and "idolatrous" elements of the folk Hindu tradition (the same criticisms levelled at Chinese Mahayana Buddhism by the youth), which were forcefully brought home to the Indian community during the cycle of dakwah-inspired assaults on Indian temples in 1977. Yet this revival too, though limited in scope, manifests a concern with identity in a society where convergence and common interests in occupational and educational spheres are eroding other cultural distinctions.

The other area of heightened Indian religious awareness is in the Sai Baba movement, whose appeal is no longer confined to Indians alone, but is growing on a worldwide scale. Even in Malaysia, there is a growing number of Chinese followers, who form their own separate congregations. Sai Baba is a South Indian mystic and guru with a reputation for a variety of miraculous performances and healing powers, and he is the object of veneration by a steady stream of devoted pilgrims from many countries. Still the majority of his followers are drawn from the Malaysian Indian and other overseas Indian communities. In Malaysia, most of the Sai Baba devotees appear to be in the ranks of the urban professional classes, who, like the Chinese charismatic Christians, hold Sai Baba meetings in their homes, which helps to preserve the exclusiveness of the cult to that stratum. To the outsider, the transformation of a western-trained, English-speaking lawyer or doctor into an ecstatic defender of his guru, testifying to the magical appearance overnight of the mystical "Om" sign on a portrait of the guru in his home or to the materialization of wrist-watches from "thin air," may be somewhat startling, although abundant parallels to such "dichotomous" beliefs exist in western fundamentalist sects. Once again, these professionals, although not highly visible or audible as a national constituency, are the ones most affected by and sensitive to contemporary changes in Malaysian society, through Malayanization in education and other quotas. A recent legal restriction on the hitherto relatively easy immigration and eligibility for citizenship of India-born wives has also disturbed members of the Indian community who still seek wives at "home" (*Asiaweek*, 22/2/80:13-14).

Unquestionably, religious identity and religious change in Malaysia are sensitive indicators of broader changes in the delicate ethnic balance. Extrapolating from the above material, there appear to be three principal ways by which non-Malays and non-Muslims react to the religio-ethnic revitalization in the Malay community. The first is an attempt to assimilate by means of religious conversion, in anticipation, at best, of full Malay identity or, at least, of some economic and political advantages. This is the route chosen by those who convert to Islam, such as the saudara baru, but one which is proving to be less integrative than expected. The second mode is a form of reaction against Malay-Muslim dominance and its expression both in the dakwah movement and in the cult of the Bumiputera. This response is manifest in the multiplicity of revivals among non-Muslims, whether in the form of charismatic Christianity, a newly assertive direction in Mahayana Buddhism, or the emergence of various millennial cults. If not intended as a direct backlash against dakwah, these movements certainly present a form of opposition to it, both on the taxonomic level and in satisfying similar problems of identity and of access to power and resources. The third response takes the form of an internal revitalization within the Chinese and Indian (Hindu) communities parallel to that of dakwah, each one responding to the same basic problems afflicting all Malaysians simultaneously. Into this category would fall those movements with large followings among the urban, educated youth, an interpretation which would place many ABIM followers in closer company with their Chinese counterparts in the canonical Theravada Buddhist movement and also with those young Hindus attempting the rationalization of their faith. These movements are not so much reactive or oppositional, as seeking solutions to common problems, but within the bounds of their separate respective communities.

CONCLUSION

To come full circle, whatever the historical ambiguities and changes over the definitions of Malayness and relationships between it and Islam, there is little doubt that the Malays of today see dakwah as part of the ethnic arsenal and as instrumental in elevating the role of Islam as a major symbol of the Malay community, both locally and internationally. Islam not only "supports Malay customs, such as co-operative labour" (*gotong royong*), but also unites them "against the unbeliever" (jahiliyyah), while religious deviance is the work of "wicked outsiders" (to the Malay community), who are attempting to divide it.

The union of Malay identity and affiliation to Islam has historically had a checkered career. Malay Islam has always manifested a strong particularistic strain, in arrogating the faith to the people, from the "masuk Islam / masuk Melayu" days to the present, when the tone of dakwah is one of revitalization of born into born-again Muslims among Malays only. The antithesis to this is the implicit recognition of Islam's universalism, of its transcending ethnic and "racial" boundaries, of the existence of non-Malay Muslims, such as Indians and even Chinese. Ironically, this very universalism has led to a marginalization of some of the latter, particularly the saudara baru, and to a clear dichotomy between categories of religion and descent in determination of identity. On one level this is entirely logical: common religion need not necessarily presuppose common community or identity nor yet race, but in Malaysia's unique ethnic and political situation, it merely reinforces the deep social cleavages already present. And even as Malays cleave apart from their religious confrères in their home country, they are coming closer to their Muslim brothers in the Middle East, particularly the Arabs. Finally, as it is becoming increasingly obvious that conversion to Islam does not automatically confer Malay or Bumi status, PERKIM's evangelism notwithstanding, attempts at assimilation by the religious route slowly come to a standstill.

From the standpoint of the Malay political élites, it is also desirable, and simpler taxonomically, for the identification of Malay and Islam (and also Bumi) to be kept congruent and, if possible, exclusive. Excessive expansion of the Muslim community along the lines envisioned by PERKIM would threaten its economic policies and possibly even the delicate ethnic balance of power on which its own legitimacy depends. To this extent, it is convenient to use Islam to political ends, for mobilization of the electorate. But when it reaches the point where dakwah threatens to divide the Malay community and vote, moves are made to curb any excess of religious zeal, and the Bumi label is a safer symbol of ethnic unity. The ideal Malay represents a trinity of race, religion, and political loyalty to UMNO and each one must serve the others.

Finally, when the parallel religious revivals in the Chinese and Indian communities are viewed in the context of the wider Malaysian canvas, there is a strong case for interpreting religious revitalization in Malaysia as at least a reflection of the ethnic and political condition and even as an index of increasing polarization, although to assign any definite causative sequence might be premature.

8

The Roots of the New Radical:
Class and Religious Ideology

The invasion of religion into most domains of Malay and Malaysian life inevitably reveals the major lines of unity and disunity, cohesion and conflict, strengths and weakness in the society as a whole. Some of these divisions, such as the ethnic one, require no further comment. Others are more covert, but are made overt through religious action. Finally, there are some areas where religion appears to offer little by way of reinforcement. In Malaysia, one of the latter is the cleavage that might provisionally be labelled "class," although this is not a concept with wide currency or meaning in Malaysia (cf. Nagata 1975, 1979; Kessler 1978). The fact that the idea of class as a political and ideological force has not yet come does not mean that class interests and potential class conflicts in Malaysian society cannot be perceived by outside observers. Nor does it mean that some segments of the local population do not perceive certain grievances of their own, some of which, objectively, may be of a class nature.

In this chapter, I attempt to delve beneath the surface and to probe how far religion in Malaysia, particularly in its revitalistic form, shows signs of becoming a conscious and active vehicle for issues of reform and social justice, and if so, to act on these convictions. Of concern too is the question as to whether specific constituencies in Malaysia, with covert class interests of their own (for example, peasants, urban labour), perceive a natural ally in religion and view it as a potential midwife to their cause.

It is well known that religious ideology, in other times and places, has served a multitude of social and political causes, particularly in anti-colonial and nativistic movements, although it is doubtful that these could be regarded as "class movements" in a strict Marxian sense. In colonial Indonesia of the 1930's there was some sense of identification of the oppressed native population vis-à-vis their western exploiters with a worker/capitalist dichotomy as embedded in the ideology of *Sarekat Islam*, articulated by Tjokroaminoto. This could be compared to the contemporary view of the populations of the third world as a collective oppressed class. Otherwise, the anti-colonial struggle was carried on by a series of explicitly religious movements. In addition to Sarekat Islam, there was Darul Islam and Muhammadiyah, neither of which had a clearly definable class base. Paradoxically, the non-religious agitators with socialist connections, such as the Nationalist Party (PNI), concentrated more on problems of regional identity and cultural unity (the Melayu Raya and Nusantara) than on either religious or class issues. But as Wertheim has shown (1959), the dominant identification of the Indonesian population, whatever their perception of western capitalism, still travelled in the established grooves of traditional society. Vertical ties of patrons and clients, landlords and tenants, lords and peasants, *prijaji* and *abangan* overrode most horizontal alliances of those with potential common class interests, so that even the communist vote (PKI) reflected old patronage relationships in a social formation known in Indonesian as *aliran* (stream or current).

In Burma too, the anti-colonial struggle saw a brief alliance of the Buddhist sangha with Marxist elements (cf. Von der Mehden 1963), but again, this union never materialized into a meaningful movement of peasant and proletarian Burmese against the combined oppressors of colonials and local élites as a class acting in the name of religious justice.

Malaya's own anti-colonial movements started in the 1920's (Roff 1967; Stockwell 1979), spanning a couple of generations during which a number of different ideological elements came and went, rose and fell. An ever-present religious strand was interwoven throughout all these movements, beginning with the Kaum Muda in the 1920's, and continuing through to MATA of the 1940's (*Majlis Agama Tertinggi Se-Malaya*, or Pan-Malayan Supreme Islamic Council) and its offshoot, the *Hizbul Muslimin* or Islamic Party (see Chapter 2). Another element was the Indonesian influence in the form of the Malay Nationalist Party, the League of Malay Youth (*Kesatuan Melayu Muda*), and the League of Concerned Youth (*Angkatan Pemuda Insaf*), many of whose members were radical peasants and/or socialist-inclined, Malay-educated youth (cf. Funston 1976). As in Indonesia, however, most of the issues at this stage had to do with problems of identity, of crystallizing a sense of "peoplehood" or nationality, rather than of class. The idiom and issues of exploitation by western capitalism and industrialism in collaboration with local comprador élites were at best but subsidiary strands in a broader search for a collective and national identity. Nor did "socialism" create any movement across ethnic or religious lines. It began in a defence of Malayness, but later, during the Emergency (1948-60), it came to be identified largely with a Chinese constituency, itself another type of nationalist movement.

In its most recent incarnations, socialist and class interests in Malaysia have been formally confined to such political parties as the Socialist Front and its successor, the People's Socialist Party (*Partai Sosialis Rakyat Malaysia*), neither of which have been particularly successful at the polls. Although in 1977, at the height of the dakwah ferment, the PSRM formally rejected a proposition to launch its struggle in the name of Islam (*Watan* 7/77; Ismail Kassim 1979:33), by the early 1980's two of its most prominent leaders have been openly displaying more religious sentiments. The president has declared that Islam can be a progressive force in the world (*salah satu tenaga dunia yang progressif*), yet can still be integrated with Marxism in its stress on moral over materialistic values (*Utusan Malaysia* 22/10/75). One PSRM leader, who is also a university lecturer and writer, now explicitly promotes the role of religion in economic development and recognizes the religious component of a people's sense of identity, overriding that of class. In this context, religion is seen as the "flesh and blood" (*darah daging*) of a community, Malay or other, a statement made without a flicker of a concession to "false consciousness" or "mystification."

To date there has been no development in Malaysia parallel to the experiments in Islamic socialism of some North African states, for example, Libya's Jamahiyah, or "rule by the people" through a system of communes. Under the Libyan system, it is accepted that all ownership is vested in God alone and that man only holds resources "in trust" (which thus provides a loophole for the continuation of some private property). Interest (riba) is permitted so long as it is the increment of genuine economic growth. In Tunisia, advocates of an active trade union movement place it on a firm religious foundation (for example, Al-Tahir al-Haddad). While they reject the atheism of Marxism, they do accept an economic interpretation of history and the principle of the class struggle. The Algerian experience is one of the clearest examples of a class struggle which was successfully transmuted into a combined religious and nationalist movement in dislodging the French colonists. Here, Islam became the banner simultaneously of a "people," a "class," and of progress (cf. Fazhur Rahman 1974: 247). The Egyptian idea of Islamic socialism, on the other hand, is something of a hybrid between capitalism and full communism, both of which, individually, were rejected by the Charter of 1962 (*al-Mithraq*), and, again, private ownership is not proscribed. Concessions, often more symbolic than real, have been made to the forces of Islam in the granting of a cabinet post to the rector of Al-Azhar University and the offer of three more to members of the numerous and powerful Muslim Brotherhood (Al-Ikhwan).[1] In the past few years, two more militant Muslim bodies have emerged in Egypt, the Jamaat Islami and the Takfir wal Hegira, both of which share the Brotherhood's religious fundamentalism and mistrust of communism. Recent events in Egypt, however, have triggered a new apprehension of political concessions to religious elements, which are becoming increasingly an underground or illegal counterforce. In Zia's Pakistan, Islam represents a legitimation for the power of the army, which uses religious values to turn the hearts of the otherwise remote and inaccessible villagers. To this end, Zia assiduously cultivates the support of the ulama. Zia's Islam, however, is less genuinely socialistic than the kinds of programmes attempted by the failed Bhutto "Nationalist" régime (Richter 1979). Pakistan's domestic Muslim movement, the Jama'at Islami, seems to have the greatest appeal to a mixture of students, urban youth, peasantry, and some segments of the army, thus cross-cutting the interests of any single class. Its ideology resembles that of ABIM in its basic fundamentalism and strong commitment to the conservatism of Maulana Al-Maudoodi. And insofar as the Jama'at once represented an expanded constituency of Bhutto's class-based, "leftist" party, the ideology of class has been pre-empted by that of religion alone.

Finally, in Iran, although the political leadership is now firmly entrenched in the hands of the ulama (*rohaniyat*), in addition to their personal power as ayatollahs, the sense of social causes and economic justice seems to have been directed more at the régime of the Shah and his western associates. For all its attention to Islamic banks and other economic institutions, the evidence is less convincing for fundamental social reorganization or attacks on basic inequalities, class, rural-urban, or other. The status of indigenous capitalism (for example, that of the bazaari merchants, among the most ardent supporters of the revolution) remains somewhat unclear.

The above examples are sketched merely to suggest some of the ways in which Islam has been invoked to serve other social causes and to underline its constant predilection for political involvement. Islam has been widely used to bolster the legitimacy of political élites in a wide assortment of arrangements from monarchist Saudi Arabia, Morocco, and various emirates to the avowedly "socialist" régimes mentioned. In practice, however, Islam's involvement in genuine class struggles, unless also allied to anticolonialist or nationalist movements, appears limited. Rather than identifying with class interests in a Marxist sense, Islam more commonly appears to represent a consortium of different alignments of the aliran type, which cut across classes. Even where Islam claims to support just social causes, these are not necessarily socialist, and often religion and Marxism oppose one another as competing, or even incompatible, ideologies. Before looking more closely at the Malaysian situation, it should be noted that on logical grounds alone, a religion such as Islam, which claims on principle to be concerned with the governance of the community and the right to legitimate and judge political authority, can only be rendered impotent by secularization. Thus a wholesale substitution of Marxist or secular class terminologies would ipso facto undermine any residual religious commitment and pull the ideological rug from under its feet. It is not quite vain, however, to seek situations where Islam adds a religious flavour to economic issues and where social grievances and emerging class interests contribute a social egalitarian content to an otherwise fundamentalist worldview.

In one of the few detailed studies addressing this kind of question, Kessler has made a case (1978) for interpreting the history of PAS in Kelantan as a covert form of class expression, articulated in religious language. To Kessler, PAS is the party of the peasant class and its religious and ethnic rhetoric merely a false consciousness. In some respects, as Kessler points out, Kelantan is unique in Malaysia, in that it is home to the smallest non-Malay population, which means that there is less reason and opportunity to deflect the grievances of dispossesed or dissatisfied Malays on to another ethnic community. It also means that there has been room for the development of an indigenous Malay bourgeoisie. Thus intra-Malay inequalities are more blatantly exposed. PAS in Kelantan has generally become the arm of the "less equal" in opposition to the more advantaged bourgeoisie, landowners, aristocracy, and royalty, most of whom are associated with UMNO. While the objective class situation in Kelantan is thus less disguised by "racial politics," this is not to say that class ideologies are the normal language of peasant social discourse or widely invoked in political campaigns. Any incipient class consciousness is still largely embedded in other ideologies and played out under other banners.

It does not necessarily follow from Kessler's argument that the PAS leaders themselves should be regarded as members of a dispossessed class. Inasmuch as PAS is essentially a religious-based party and many of its leaders are ulama, they do not share the same life chances as the poorer peasantry or urban proletarians and thus have somewhat different objective class interests of their own. Nor do the ulama political leaders claim to have any fully developed blueprint for a new social order of their own in which the oppressed lower classes would ultimately be free of exploitation. Religious social theory is far from explicit on such matters, as in the case of the Islamic state. The "class" interpretation of Kelantanese politics therefore does not reflect the ideological bent or emic perceptions of any of the constituencies involved. Conflict exists and has its mode of expression. But its language is religious, and even where religion fades into "pure" politics, the idiom of "class" still fails to emerge.

While the Kelantan case is in some respects unique, the overall position of the traditional ulama in local kampung society is comparable to that elsewhere in West Malaysia. As we saw in Chapter 2, their generally superior wealth, landholdings, education, kinship, and affinal connections place them in a distinctive élite status group. Their relationship with kampung dwellers, for whom they are informal leaders who set the moral tone of society, can create an uneasy balance or even competition with the formal leadership of penghulu and headman, whose material status they often share. In extreme cases, as obviously occurred in Kelantan and also in many Kedah kampungs today, this competition can become politicized along the PAS/UMNO party line. Further, as some of the traditional religious schools have lost their strength, one of the foundations of power and authority of the ulama has begun to crumble. The appointment of mosque officials by religious councils provides a challenge from yet another quarter. Under the threat of loss of personal and economic status, entry into the arena of more blatant party politics represents for some guru a compensation for power lost in one sphere and a quest for a new legitimacy. For others, it is but a logical continuation an updating of a traditional authority and the customary extension of Islam into the "secular" domain, familiar throughout its history.

Kessler's identification of PAS and peasant class interests obviously cannot be taken uncritically. Many of the PAS leaders have more in common economically and in their position in the social formation with their UMNO opposite numbers than with the average kampung dweller. What is more, they are determined to preserve their privilege at all costs, and by all means, including the political. Indeed, some Kedah ulama have preferred to surrender their schools in order to devote more time to politics, rather than to suffer the inevitable loss of financial base and personal authority brought about by the declining fortunes of the religious school.

While it could be argued that even the privileged ulama still hold peasant interests close to their hearts and direct their political ambitions to these ends, as agitators from outside the class itself, there are equally other religious leaders who do not appear to be devoted to any social cause or constituency, whether through PAS or other organization. To the contrary, as described in Chapter 2, many have historically sought social and political legitimacy through alliances with various royal and aristocratic houses, which rendered them even more formidable competitors to the secular headmen and penghulu. Whether they elect to take the "royal route" or political party (PAS) route, their ultimate goal cannot be distinguished from that of the secular élites: power and authority. As such, the ulama may be regarded as a parallel élite, or "class fraction" (cf. Poulantzas 1973). Though personal religious styles and practices may vary from individual to individual, this fact alone does not negate the fundamentally similar class base. Whether a particular guru is favourably disposed to dakwah movements in any of their variants, ABIM, Darul Arqam or Tabligh, or more immersed in the syncretic or Sufi Islam of the Malay kampung, whether he sees Islam as an adjunct to

Malayness or as transcending it, whether of reformist or conservative bent (Kaum Muda or Kaum Tua), whether PAS or UMNO, royalist or "independent," his élite status and class position still stand. Religion, like other ideologies, can "interfere" with full class expression, as Poulantzas points out (ibid.:88-89), and even obscure it completely. This is equally true of dakwah and of Islam in its more traditional forms. More frequently, religious rhetoric seizes on social alignments which ignore or cut across objective class interests entirely, as observed in the aliran of Indonesia. In the face of the dakwah competition from outside, many rural ulama take pains to identify themselves with their kampung congregations against the intruder, and castigate the newcomer's attempts to convert villagers to the practice of inappropriate Arab customs as the whims and fancies of an alien group "coming in big cars from town." By such assertions, the ulama deflect attention away from objective class differences between themselves and their flock (even though some ulama also have big cars). By playing up the equality of the moral community they direct the strains of a basic social inequality into religious channels.

THE DAKWAH REVIVAL AND SOCIAL JUSTICE

As yet, the leadership of the new school of dakwah, based largely on younger urban intellectuals, can hardly be said to have attained the degree of religious legitimacy or level of social standing as the rural ulama nor to have become a religious élite in any sense. It is thus particularly difficult for these young professionals, whose training has more often been obtained in western or secular institutions than in centres of Islamic culture, to garner credibility when discoursing on an "Islamic banking system," the merits of zakat and sedekah, the levelling mechanisms made possible by an Islamic treasury (bait-ul-mal), and the justice of the elusive Islamic state. Neither in matters of theology or social theory have the dakwah proponents managed to improve much upon the well-worn platform of PAS, whose constituency is also older and better established. In this respect, ABIM, Darul Arqam, Tabligh, and Aliran are at an equal disadvantage.

Of all the four movements, Aliran, the least "typical" in the religious spectrum, is most clearly and actively devoted to issues of social justice and reform, along lines resembling class interests rather than ethnic boundaries. The self-declared goals of Aliran are to fight corruption, injustice, unbridled racism, and other ills of Malaysian society. In this capacity they have become the champions of a variety of causes relating to labour conditions and union rights, including problems of freedom of organization, wages, working conditions, women's status as workers, and divisions created by management tactics. Aliran has also taken on the cause of numerous other victims of injustice, such as that of an entire fishing village whose livelihood was almost wiped out by pollution from a powerful industrial complex, and cases of consumer exploitation by unprincipled commercial interests. In some of these enterprises it co-operates with the local Consumers' Association, itself regarded as something of a radical force. Aliran tends to concentrate particularly on cases which span ethnic lines. Yet while the spirit of its operations clearly favours the interests of class rather than "race," the language of class conflict is not prominent in its rhetoric. Unity is sought, not in the bonds of class, but through other kinds of universalistic ties, such as those of "equality," "compassion," "justice," and "harmony." On the ground, Aliran agitates for what are unmistakably the "gut" issues of the exploited and oppressed, but ideologically (or possibly politically), it divorces itself from the inevitable association, and like some of the PAS religious leaders, uses a different vocabulary, much of it religious.

Of the other dakwah movements, ABIM, whose one-time president was a close friend and confidant of the president of Aliran, is probably most oriented towards broader social problems and causes. The roots of ABIM's wider interests can be traced back to the days of its emergence from the PKPIM, when the issues of the era related to the Vietnam War, to mistreatment of minorities in South Thailand, and to students' rights in general. As an independent body, its first major social commitment, which almost precipitated ABIM's downfall, was in the Baling demonstration of 1974. Ideologically, it is more difficult to determine how far ABIM followers were involved in that capacity or as members of a wider constituency of youth and students. It must also be asked to what extent Baling was seen as an example of an exploited peasantry qua peasantry or as a show of solidarity with fellow Malay peasants.

The question of motives and ideology underlying Baling also concerned the Malaysian government at the time. Almost predictably, it saw communist and even Chinese complicity and even found "evidence" through the Chinese Language Society at the University of Malaya. Just as predictably on the other side, many student spokesmen blamed the situation of the avarice of western capitalism and imperialism. In each case, the villains of the piece were some sort of ethnic category. What this ritual interchange tended to obscure (although not totally) was the growing cleavage between rich and powerful Malays, on the one hand, and poor peasant Malays on the other, a case of a class in itself on the brink of becoming a class for itself. Some university students, schooled in western social science, undoubtedly recognized this for what it was. Yet while the government was unable to avoid considerable criticism for its own policies and mishandling of the problem, the ground was not completely ripe for a full-blown class confrontation in a population still largely unaccustomed to the concept. But the possible consequences of an eventual public realization of the situation, and its effects on Malay unity (and the UMNO vote), contributed to the government's heavy-handed retaliation and attempts to discredit the demonstration.

At this time, ABIM spokesmen made a number of statements of their own, which can be distilled into the basic message that Baling represented a violation of the principles of Islam, of the equality of man, and of a just distribution of wealth. They also made a plea for less corruption in high places. Even the religious language could not disguise the inequalities within Malay society. This was the first time too, when the current prime minister, Tun Abdul Razak, tried to co-opt Anwar Ibrahim into UMNO and to harness his strength to the party's wagon. Anwar's refusal (and subsequent endurance of detention under the Internal Security Act) is probably testimony to the intensity of his religious and ideological convictions at the time. Certainly, it was well known that the enthusiasm and prominence of ABIM followers in both the Baling affair and in several other, less dramatic or publicized incidents[2] in which students played a part were out of all proportion to their actual numbers. Subsequently, in 1982, Anwar surprised the Malaysian (and much of the Islamic) world by finally lending his power and prestige to the UMNO[3] of a later prime minister and one of his colleagues from college days, Datuk Sri Mahathir. This move, following years of adulation as a pillar of integrity and dedication to an independent religious cause, came as a shock and to many as a personal blow. Anwar's turning political in a formal sense surprised no one, for like many of the rural ulama and guru who feel their impotence in a changing world, there were obvious limitations to what he could achieve through an emasculated ABIM alone. The surprise consisted of his choice of party, which was expected to be PAS. Extrapolating from 1982 to 1974 makes it all the more difficult to evaluate the true ideological position of Baling whether by Anwar as an individual or by ABIM as an organization. There is no doubt that from 1974 onwards, both were officially considered to be politically dangerous and that ABIM was a "marked" organization. Attempts were made to curtail ABIM's activities through "legal" means, including restrictions on its rights to present public lectures and issue publications and by keeping them firmly under the jurisdiction of the umbrella consortium of Malaysian Youth Associations (MBM).

Given that all the action and justification for it by ABIM was in the name of religion, all official attempts to discredit it had to be in the appropriate language of "heretical," "unorthodox," "deviant," and "wrong." For whatever the terms of the verbal debate, it could barely disguise the covert class implications of ABIM's and other student activities of the early 1970's. The existence of a body of "dissident" and "ungrateful" youth, many of them scions of established UMNO and middle-class urban families (like

Anwar) and most of them recipients of Bumi scholarships, turning against their patron was totally out of keeping with the Malay feudal protector tradition. The phenomenon of students' "biting the hand that feeds them" recurred dramatically in late 1979, when twenty-four Malay student associations in the United Kingdom, among them many with strong dakwah leanings, issued a joint statement condemning Malaysian government racial and educational policies, particularly as embodied in the NEP, and hinting strongly of corruption in high places. It was a pungently worded document, and it was eminently clear that the protest was being made first of all in the name of Islamic values and justice, noting with regret the government's habit of belittling dakwah with unkind epithets. It also defended a more universalistic approach to Islam, in which, for example, the category of saudara baru would be eliminated and converts encouraged to integrate with the Malays. The statement then proceeded to attack the racial aspects of the NEP, with its Bumi privileges and Malay nationalism, as unjust and indefensible. It also voiced a frank recognition of the government's strategies of scapegoating even within the Malay community by transferring the responsibility for some of its own failed policies to the inadequacies of the Malays themselves. In no uncertain terms, the statement accused the NEP of simultaneously exacerbating ethnic tensions, expanding the gap between rich and poor Malays, and propagating an undue emphasis on materialism, from which the ruling élites themselves benefitted most of all. It concluded with a plea for the implementation of an "Islamic social system," where there would be no room for inequality, injustice or unbridled nationalism (*Watan* 21/9/79).

If such statements reveal a sensitivity to class issues and inequalities, they do not seem to use its language. In this case religious ideology apparently interferes with a full-bodied class expression, as Poulantzas noted (1973), and may even preclude its emergence altogether. The public rhetoric remains religious, and this is why government spokesmen and detractors have to resort to considerable casuistry in their responses. It is not possible to attack Islam in whose name the demands and accusations are made. What has to be raised is the spectre of a sinister conspiracy or of a manipulator (*dalang*) behind the scenes, dictating the action and making use of (*memperalatkan*) religion to nefarious ends. Sometimes the dalang is the communists collectively, and dakwah supporters have been painted as "communists in white hats." Sometimes it is the collective non-Malays, as it was the Chinese Language Society in the Baling affair. Otherwise, the challenge must be directed to the particular brand or interpretation of Islam by the opposition, which can then be dismissed as deviant. By this stroke, it is scratched from the map of legitimate opposition, and it also gives UMNO a monopoly over religious orthodoxy.

As the acrimony and restrictions of 1974-75 recede into the past, ABIM has lost some of its caution and has begun, for example, to make less timid statements in favour of land reform, which is in fact also an oblique tilt against the landowning aristocracy and royalty (*Risalah*, No. 2 1980:19). In 1980 ABIM also raised its voice in opposition to the tightening of the labour laws, which introduced stringent controls over strike action, empowered the registrar of trade unions and the minister of labour to declare strikes illegal, and curtailed the unions' rights to affiliate to unions overseas (*Asiaweek* 15/2/80:24-25). ABIM's (if no longer Anwar's) unconcealed sympathies for PAS in no way detract from its religious integrity, for this is consistent with Islamic social conscience and commitment. But in contemporary Malaysia, by throwing in their lot with an established party, members of ABIM inevitably lose some of their pristine virtue and religious virginity in the eyes of some critics and thereby become tainted. So far, however, ABIM (again without Anwar) has managed to steer a middle course by remaining uncommitted as an organization, yet allowing ex-members to run for PAS.

The evidence suggests then that ABIM has been able to display a public social conscience which has led it to diagnose many of the ills of Malaysian society as the result of class inequities, though using the protective language of religion and dakwah. On the other hand, ABIM supporters are not willing to be identified as "socialist" (which in Malaysia usually means the communism of the Chinese and of the Emergency), hence scrupulously avoid all references to "Islamic socialism." Like PAS, it favours the retention of free enterprise, open trade, private property, and wealth, as long as the latter is acquired in ways approved by Islam. Predictably, it favours banks based on profit-sharing (*mudarba*) rather than on interest, but is not as anti-materialist as is, say, Darul Arqam. In the vocabulary of the proponents of the Islamic state, the villains of the piece tend to be a fusion of the capitalist, imperialist, westerner, Chinese, non-Muslim/infidel, and sometimes even socialist, all in one breath. Class awareness may emerge as a discernible moral or analytical principle, but it can only be inferred from the context. The moral and ethical rationale, the historical and social charters, and the legitimacy all derive from the religious system.

In comparison with ABIM, Darul Arqam and Tabligh are generally less vocal and less intimately involved with social issues beyond their own immediate dakwah-related interests and the Malay/Muslim cause. As we saw in Chapter 4, Darul Arqam's economic theory and organization are attempts to implement its own idea of truly Islamic principles which makes no mention of class, either its presence or absence, desirability or not. Arqam's plan is designed for Malays and Muslims alone, and it is as much an antidote to non-Muslim and Chinese institutions as an articulation of the interests of a dispossessed class. Certainly, Darul Arqam's programmes do not encompass the non-Muslim dispossessed. Unlike ABIM, Arqam's followers are not known for any connection, verbal or active, with specific causes, grievances, or social problems. Their politics consists more of non-action or withdrawal, of refusal to co-operate with the political centre. In their forays into rural society, Darul Arqam's principal concerns lie in expanding their own trading network and religious schools, with little discernible interest in the problems of the peasantry as a class. Arqam's economic projects are intended merely to secure their own viability and by extension that of the Muslim Malays rather than as an alternative or outlet for the landless or unemployed sectors of the population.

Even more extremely, the reputation of Tabligh in matters of social and political concern is one of the dissassociation. In the words of many of its followers, one of Tabligh's main virtues lies in its social neutrality, whether in matters affecting its own members or on behalf of other constituencies. In urban areas Tabligh was traditionally associated with an entrepreneurial class of traders and merchants (principally Indian), while its expansion to rural areas does not appear to have involved it in anything other than spiritual exercises. As an organization it is sufficiently low-key for some covert activists, for example, clandestine PAS supporters among certain ulama to take "refuge" under an organization which is seen as politically innocuous.

From the Darul Arqam and Tabligh record to date, there is little evidence of radicalization, nor that these revivalists are likely to play the classic role of the intellectual consciousness-raisers of the peasantry or proletarian from outside. In these cases lack of radicalization cannot be the result of a burgeoning social conscience and political restrictions alone, for as we have seen, ABIM has revealed underlying radical tendencies which may even become overtly politicized. However, it may still be asked how far ABIM, like PAS, is more concerned with its own political self-interest, treating social issues as a means to this end, rather than as an end in itself.

Muslim scholars have long emphasized that the Islamic economy is *sui generis*, being neither capitalist nor socialist, although with the better elements of each. But it is in the interpretation of such generalities by actual religious groups that the real economic and social attitudes surface. The most striking conclusion about Malaysia is the variability rather than the unanimity, ranging from religio-ethnic chauvinism to a more universalistic sense of social justice. Yet nowhere in Malaysia, not even in the growing religious consciousness recently being displayed by the PSRM, is Islam (whether in dakwah or other form) explicitly harnessed to the defence of class interests as a motivating ideology for social action.

At the other end of the scale, neither the interests nor ideology of PAS emerge on balance as particularly radical, as witness the indifference of the Kedah ulama PAS leaders on the question of land reform (see Chapter 2).

Neither do they have the image of champions of the peasant qua peasant in Kedah, except insofar as the peasants are supporters of the party. Following the Alor Setar rice-farmer uprising of January 1980, official investigators managed to pin the blame on an arm of the underground religious army, Sabilullah, whose acronym, P.A.S. (*Pasukan Angkasa Sabilullah*), was conveniently but confusingly, identified with that of the party. It was widely felt, however, that this was an accusation of political convenience by UMNO, and that party PAS submitted rather meekly. On this occasion, a demonstration was held by a group of padi-cultivators from the Kedah Muda rice cultivation scheme dissatisfied with a clumsily administered system of coupons which replaced part of the cash paid for the sale of padi by the government rice-marketing agency. A crowd of several hundred peasants marched on the state government headquarters in the state capital and hurled stones at its windows. This was the first major articulation of peasant grievances since Baling. Responsibility for the uprising was never established by open legal proceedings, and no group came forward spontaneously to take advantage of the case as "protectors" of the peasantry, least of all PAS or any of the dakwah groups. Ironically, therefore, this was one instance when UMNO almost involuntarily forced PAS into the reluctant role of champion of the peasant, even against their will. In UMNO's view, the circumstantial evidence of the similarity of the initials of PAS and P.A.S. and the overlapping membership of the two organizations, admitted in private "confessions," was sufficiently incriminating. Insofar as confessions were made by certain individuals, they claimed to be defenders of their "race, religion, land and rajah," hardly a class-like statement. As one PAS M.P. asked rhetorically but reasonably, "what is wrong with such sentiments as these?" As a consequence of UMNO's stand, a campaign of mild police harassment followed, especially of religious and dakwah figures. As one old and respected haji complained, "anyone in a green or white cap and robe" was open to police abuse for some months afterwards. In other words, the government, faced with a minor peasant revolt, refused to face the obvious and, after toying with the predictable "Chinese conspiracy" in the familiar ethnic mould, decided to find its scapegoat in the ranks of the religious. So the basic issues were side-stepped. Again in 1980, on the occasion of a parliamentary debate on the Internal Security Act (ISA), PAS rather surprisingly came out in support of the more radical and largely Chinese Democratic Action Party (DAP), although this too may be construed as a political tactic to attack UMNO and as a defence of some of its own (PAS) detainees.

On the other hand, there are also many parallels between UMNO and PAS attitudes, each of which promotes the Malay ethnic cause in its own way, and each supports its own élites, mostly preoccupied with their own political self-preservation. This much is (pace Kessler) probably also substantially true of PAS in Kelantan. Given the basic similarities of their interests and strategies and the fact they champion the same constituencies for the same reasons (and these have nothing to do with class), they preserve their separate identities through religion, or their respective interpretations of it. So it is the political game is played out in religious rhetoric, sometimes subtle, sometimes blunt, of kafir-mengafir, described in Chapter 2.

Possibly the only grounds where PAS is open to accusations of radical or revolutionary inclinations lies in its public endorsement of the Iranian régime of Khomeini, which, by implication, makes revolutionaries of PAS supporters and all that might mean for their potential role in Malaysia. However, one more radical PAS supporter, not a religious leader or dakwah sympathizer, did once privately confide to the writer that the party should pay more attention to the interests of "poor Muslims" at home, rather than making waves over Iran and Afghanistan.

As the examples cited above show, the disadvantaged and alienated peasantry and labourers in Malaysian society are not entirely without means to articulate their grievances. Their strategies and level of organization, however, are limited, and mobilizations tend to be ad hoc, sporadic, and localized. In the recent past, for example, there have been a number of "invasions" of unoccupied rural land by landless peasants, including the famous episodes under Selangor leader Hamid Tua in the 1960's. Others have occurred more recently in separate incidents in Perak, Selangor, and Kedah (*Mimbar Sosialis* Sept.-Oct. 1979; Nov.-Dec. 1979). Where large-scale mobilization is not possible, the peasant sometimes reacts through petty obstructionism, deliberate "misunderstanding" of a situation or non-compliance with the authorities, forms of passive resistance described by Scott (1978). In such cases, sacks of padi destined for payment of zakat to the state religious council simply get "lost" or else its quality is unusually under par. Indirect forms of protest may also be made through the circulation of anonymous "flying letters" (surat layang),[4] often left lying in mosques and other public places. One of these missives, found in several Kedah mosques in 1979, did manage to convey an Islamic version of a class-like sentiment by purporting to be from the "Ayatollah Malaysia," encouraging the peasants to overthrow their government and even recommending the assassination of Tunku Abdul Rahman, a member of the Kedah royal family. Flying letters, of course, require a certain level of literacy, and this, added to the fact that one or two have been mailed from Australia, suggests the helping hand of a force outside the peasantry itself, possibly some ABIM students; but this remains unproven.

Since the late nineteenth century and throughout the active colonial period, the history of Malay peasantry has been marked by the occasional eruption of small, localized religious cult movements which appear to have been, at least in part, expressions of other (non-religious) grievances and thwarted interests in the absence of any effective, alternate means of political articulation. Among these are the various incarnations of the Sabilullah, and a series of invulnerability cults, combining traditional Indic and Malay martial arts elements with an overlay of Islamic symbols somewhat in the style of Nasrul Haq. Such cults were central to the Perak War of 1875 and the Pahang rebellion of the 1890's (Stockwell 1979:156). It is also rumoured that the embryonic UMNO movement under Datuk Onn made use of certain cults to enhance its appeal in rural areas. There is no evidence, however, that any of the contemporary Sufi and other cult activities in present-day Kedah have any such political significance, despite official fears as to their political potential and their condemnation by the religious courts as heretical and forms of "magic" (syihir). The abrupt official volte face over Nasrul Haq in 1977 can probably be attributed to such fears over a potentially explosive combination of invulnerability cults and traditional Malay sentiments with a few eclectic dakwah and other Islamic elements by a volatile youth. The popularity of Nasrul Haq among both rural and urban Malay youth of lower social and income brackets, where landlessness and unemployment portend a bleak future, was not, of course, reassuring to the authorities. Further, it may not be without significance that the mystical cult in Sik (Auratismailiyyah), so severely condemned by the Kedah Syar'iah court in 1979-80 (see Chapter 2), arose in the Baling area, still one of the poorest in Kedah. This cult may have assuaged some dissatisfactions among the participants, their frequent trances and mystical adventures transporting them beyond everyday hardships and reality. However, it is doubtful if Auratismailiyyah or any contemporary tarikat in Kedah has any strong political or class orientation. The dramatic 1980 attack on the Batu Pahat police station too was the result of action by an invulnerability cult group recruited from a number of FELDA schemes in which there was a high rate of dissatisfaction owing to low incomes, slow growth rates, and incompatible combinations of settlers of different origins. The increasing incidence of dakwah behaviour on other FELDA schemes (of which about 10 per cent are said to be affected) is acknowledged by one FELDA director to be a response to unsatisfactory conditions. The usual response by the administration is a mixture of arrogance and paternalism, and the proffered solutions consist of "changing the workers' attitudes (*sikap*) or of inculcating a facsimile of a "father/son relationship." In any event, both cult and dakwah movements are invariably condemned, if necessary, followed by an antidote of "government dakwah." Once again, any hint of dissidence "from below" elicits the protector instinct with its combination of patronal, paternalistic and sometimes overbearing lordliness.

In summary, religious ideology by itself does not appear to propose any radical force for social change nor does it, either in its rural or urban revival form, seem to mesh closely with the objective class interests of the peasant or worker. As long as the ulama and PAS leaders are concerned for their own status and wealth and dakwah activitists have their eye on power for themselves, with little to contribute to the social or material life of the peasantry, then religious ideology is relatively autonomous as a social force, and cannot reflect economic or class realities (cf. Poulantzas 1973). The moral egalitarianism of Islam does not necessarily translate into social or economic equality for all its followers. Even the sultans may use Islam to buttress their personal powers, and, reciprocally, there still remains substantial loyalty to the idea of the royal protector. PAS ulama and UMNO leaders are equally élites in their own way, representing separate class fractions, defending their own power and legitimacy, and having their own followings among the peasantry. Meanwhile, the peasants themselves, divided between PAS and UMNO, have similar interests in relation to the mode of production and compete for the same goals—economic well-being, freedom from poverty and injustice, and so forth, and they even have a variety of strategies for articulating these. Each cohort, however, has its own, non-class, ideologies. The UMNO cohort could be characterized as the Bumiputera Malay, where the promotion of Malay interests would permit co-operation with non-Malays, and the UMNO brand of Islam tries to justify this. The PAS Malay on the other hand is more fundamentalistically Islamic and champion of a political state which would minimize co-operation with the unbeliever (kafir).

The events of Baling and Alor Setar, however, and the largely unknown quantity of the shadowy Sabilullah may portend a more conscious and active mobilization of the peasants as a class in Kedah in the future. Undoubtedly, religious institutions and ideology will continue to provide most of the language and motivation of action and source of legitimacy for the leaders. But eventually the two (religious and class interest) may increasingly come to converge in a common cause, rather than to cut across one another as at present. The Kelantan hypothesis notwithstanding, this stage has yet to be reached in rural Kedah.

It is probably instructive to note that none of the dakwah activists, nor anyone involved in the religious revival, has shown any sign of making common cause with the PSRM, whose socialist taint probably makes it an unacceptable partner in any alliance. The closest secular parallel to the relationship between PAS and ABIM (prior to Anwar's defection) is possibly that between PSRM and a small body of students at the National University (mostly Malays) who have formed a loose association along Aliran lines but without any religious ideology behind it. This group is more concerned with issues of class and socialism and publishes a monthly news journal which regularly exposes, in PSRM style, some of the inequalities and abuses in Malaysian society. Although none of this group would be so rash as to declare an anti-religious stand (some even claim sympathy for the more liberal forms of dakwah), religion is not a major underpinning of their views or authority.

We are left with the conclusion that, if the religious revival in Malaysia has any significant social content, its sympathies lie more closely with the peasantry and rural poor than with the urban worker. This suggests that, given the ethnicity of the bulk of Malaysia's peasantry, beneath the Islamic veneer is a strong streak of Malayness. It also suggests more than a hint of political self-interest, and here the potential (or actual) link with the opposition party places ABIM, at least, in a position of direct competition with UMNO, by vying for the loyalties of the same constituents. Where UMNO would have Islam unite the Malay community, by dakwah it is fragmented.

Yet dakwah revivalism still has a long way to go in the rural kampung. Not only is it regarded with caution by much of the rural population, it has yet to show positively what it can contribute to peasant well-being, and here communication appears to be a problem.

Finally, where objective class interests and threats to Malay political unity (the security of the UMNO élites), come dangerously close to the surface, the responsibility is swiftly deflected into other channels. In urban and national contexts, the scapegoat is usually "racial" or ethnic, while in rural areas the blame is laid at the door of religion. This alone may foster an illusion of greater religious involvement in social issues than is actually warranted. Certainly, the language of debate and incentives to mobilize in Malaysian society interfere with a full and uninhibited expression of class. Social ideology and objective interests remain somewhat independent of one another and autonomous. Were the two to combine, however, it would be a powerful alliance indeed. It is in anticipation of this eventuality that the different ideological strands and constituencies of Malaysian society must be constantly monitored and trained into the normative pattern and political format favoured by UMNO, in an effort to maintain the system in its familiar and controllable order.

9

The Wheels Still Turn:
and Grind Exceeding Small

Our four-century perspective of the evolution of Malay identity shows how Islam played a progressively larger role in defining that identity, contributing many essential elements to Malay culture. What is more, the sharing of the faith was probably the single most important source of political unity beyond the level of the original petty principalities or sultanates, and this too was motivated by Islamic symbols, literature, and culture. The bearers and mediators of this religious culture were the itinerant ulama, through their pivotal position as leaders of Sufi tarikat and cult movements, and as an emergent élite stratum at the kampung level. Culturally, socially, and eventually politically, the ulama network was extended by yet more far-flung links beyond the "Malay world" to the Middle Eastern heartland and to Arab culture at its source.

The Malay universe has gradually expanded from the local domain and personalized following of a paternalistic and particular ruler to membership in a community which transcends the boundaries of Nusantara or even of Southeast Asia. The recent dakwah revitalization, which self-consciously and actively draws on Middle Eastern connections and ideas, has served among other things, to place the Malays "on the map," both of Islam and the world. A recognition of their existence by outsiders and a gradual enhancement of their status in the Muslim world are by-products of this recent intense religious involvement, which in turn inspires even stronger religious commitment.

The steady rise of Islam as an integral element of one kind of Malay identity, however, has never managed totally to eclipse the other, continuing strand of pre-Islamic, pristine Malayness (Melayu). This has its present-day expression in the residual, so-called "feudal" mentality and absolute loyalty syndrome, with its political consummation in the UMNO party, and its native son, the Bumi Malay. While these two strands, Islam and Malayness, have become intertwined, they have never perfectly fused, creating a permanent tension that lies at the heart of both past and current developments in Malaysian politics and society. Part of the tension consists in the opposing pulls of ethnic particularism and religious universalism which lie at the root of the problem of Malay identity. The idea of masuk Islam being equated with masuk Melayu has appealed in principle to both Malays and non-Malays for its implicit promise of assimilation through religion. But the elegant simplicity of this equation was ever vulnerable to other factors, such as the demographic pressures of massive alien immigration, ethnic division of labour, and, lately, of party politics.

While the equation is an indirect affirmation of the universalism of Islam, in that it makes room for Muslims of different ethnic origins, it has in Malaysia taken on a peculiarly particularistic twist by creating different categories of Muslim, each with its separate status. In the resulting hierarchy, the Malay Muslims are the ones who set the tone of Islam in the peninsula, while Indian Muslims and converts (saudara baru) are accorded a distinctly second class status. In fact, Malayness now has a double boundary: passing through the gate of Islam does not necessarily open the second door to the Malay community (bangsa).

The particularism of Malay Islam also shows up in the way in which the faith has been appropriated as the principal symbol and core of Malay identity. This has assumed even greater importance as the other cultural boundaries of language and custom have gradually evaporated. In its new, revitalistic role under dakwah, Islam is seen as the last bastion of ethnic exclusiveness and political mobilization. Whatever universalism remains tends to "leap over the heads" of local, non-Malay Muslims, linking Malays with fellow-Muslims overseas rather than at home. This reinforces the isolation of the non-Malay Muslim in Malaysia and is compounded by the "bornagain" emphasis of dakwah.

In one sense religion has served as the unifier of a people emerging into nationhood, as the handmaiden of a transformation into a politically self-conscious and mobilized constituency. Now the need to project a strong image and distinctive character is more pressing than ever, but it is threatened by the growing cleavage between the Muslim/dakwah Malay and the Bumi Malay, with their conflicting ideas of leadership and charters of legitimacy. It is just this conflict which compromises the burgeoning national consciousness and troubles an incumbent political party. The goal of Malay unity, on which its status depends, suddenly becomes elusive, when the apparently firm foundation of traditional Malay leadership is challenged by an alternate, but equally formidable authority, that of Islam. Forced to pick up the Islamic gauntlet, the game must be played to Islamic rules, for its principles cannot be questioned. Ways and means must be found to unseat the challenger without impugning the values on which his claims are founded. Hence the tactics of kafir-mengafir, consigning the opposition (dakwah or PAS ulama) to the status of unbeliever or at best the doubtful realms of deviants and heretics. In solving one, religion has created another crisis of identity for the Malay community.

In its first incarnation, as an identity resource, the dakwah revitalization was, and continues to be in large measure, a closing of the ranks against the non-Malay. Aside from its internal political implications, dakwah participation for the average follower (always allowing for differing levels of sophistication of interpretation between grass-roots and leaders) is a nativistic re-affirmation of Malayness in a new form. It has provided a rich new repertoire of rituals, such as style of dress, certain Arab customs, conspicuous withdrawal from inter-ethnic dining and other acitivities, so that non-Malays are intimidated and fear to approach. Thus the communities draw further apart. The parallel revival of religious consciousness in the Chinese and Indian communities too, whether as a response to similar social conditions or ethnic backlash, also entrenches the retreat into ethnic exclusiveness on all sides.

Despite the revivalists' lack of a formal political organization or platform, their engagement in much theological debate over such topics as the Islamic state, Islamic justice, and the qualities of political leadership, are sufficient to inject a political element into the dakwah movement. Futher debates over an Islamic economy also create political ripples by questioning the official plans for modernization and development and the NEP. Thus even before ABIM members made moves in the direction of PAS, the more farreaching implications of Islamic social theories were recognized with some apprehension by the incumbent powers-that-be, which led to their treatment of all dakwah groups somewhat in the manner of an opposition party. Darul Arqam's conspicuous dissociation from government plans and agencies and its cultivation of its own autonomous, Islamic economic system likewise threatened official development programmes. And ABIM's declared moral support for the Iranian revolution has awakened other kinds of political fear. Jemaat Tabligh alone poses little apparent political threat, as it quietly goes about its task of spreading its message and incorporating its "marginal" Indian Muslim followers into communion with the Malays.

Fears about dakwah's revolutionary potential relate partly to its origins, the phoenix from the ashes of the student movements of the 1960's and of the militant Malay Language Society, and to its involvement with the 1969 riots. Moreover, the principal dakwah leaders and actors are also the survivors of that heady, pre-Universities Act era or else their faithful disciples. In short, the association of dakwah with youth, students, and the urban-educated intellectuals brings together in a volatile combination a number of constituencies traditionally identified with radicalism, rebellion and social change the world over.

A glance at the contemporary situation in other Muslim countries shows the predominance of these elements in both religious revitalization and also in some of the political movements. In Egypt, a constant irritant and thorn in the side of the incumbent régimes for over a generation has been the youthful (Al-Azhar) university-connected Muslim Brotherhood, Al-Ikhwan. In Egypt too, as in Malaysia, there is more than one revival organization. To the venerable Al-Ikhwan has been added another fundamentalist, Pakistani-influenced group, the Jama'at Islami, also with a strong following in the universities and schools. Like the Malaysian government too, before his death, President Sadat had tried to create his own religious antidote in the form of his League of Islamic and Arab Peoples. Meanwhile, the branches of the Al-Ikhwan in Syria and in the Sudan have gone even further politically than in Egypt and openly engage in militant politics in their quest for temporal as well as spiritual power.

In Iran, some of the most enthusiastic supporters, if not the leaders of the 1979 revolution were likewise the educated youth, many with extensive western contacts and experience, although alienated from its materialism and secularism. Unlike Malaysia, however, in Iran the intellectual guidance and leadership was firmly in the hands of the traditional ulama and rohani-yat, who in Shi'ite Islam wield substantially greater power through their acknowledged right to reinterpret the scriptures and to issue fatwa of their own, in a permanent process of *ijtihada*. The Iranian revival then represents more than the mere removal of the régime of the Shah and the influence of the west, but the latest return to a fundamentalist religious tradition of which there have been many throughout the country's history. Within the broad parameters of the revival, each ayatollah and mullah has his own style and personal following, in keeping with the individual isnad tradition of Muslim scholarship. Besides Khomeini, the ulama at the holy city of Q'um, especially the Grand Ayatollah Shariat-madari, are deeply involved in the kind of mission that recalls lapsed Muslims to the obligations of their faith. What in Malaysia is known as dakwah is referred to in Iran as tabligh (not to be confused with the Indian-based Jema'at Tabligh, associated with the dakwah movement in Malaysia).

In Pakistan too, fundamentalism Al-Maudoodi style has captured the hearts and minds of the young, and it is from this source that has sprung much of the organization and most of the publications which fuel the revival movement around the world. Following its master guru, Maulana Al-Maudoodi himself, and in general tune with political and economic developments in the third world, Pakistani youth is anti-western and beginning to re-examine its lifestyle. As in Malaysia, insecurity over future economic and employment prospects and over the Zia military régime has led to a politici-zation of some wings of the religious movement under the party banner of the Jama'at Islami which seeks to follow the "way of the Prophet" (Nizami-i-Mustafa). And somewhat reminiscent of Malaysia too, Islam in Pakistan has become the new source of inspiration and hope for students and intellec-tuals following the disillusionments of the events of the Bhutto years. With the growth in urbanization and its associated industrialization and literacy, Islam as a solution to the resulting social and personal dislocation, has stirred urban workers, labour unions, and even women to a new militancy. As edu-cation and literacy creep into the countryside, so does some of the influence of Jama'at Islami, which as in rural Malaysia, has to compete with Zia's Islam, mediated in this case through more traditional ulama and even local "saints" (*pir*).

What is simply labelled the "Islamic revival," or dakwah in Malaysia, represents the confluence of several different streams and styles of faith and behaviour, fundamentalist, ascetic, mystical, nativistic, millennial, political, and personal. It cannot be characterized by any single feature, but varies with the condition of each country and region. Each is in some measure unique, and the Islamic resurgence fulfils its special needs. Thus Malaysia is distinc-tive for its unusually deep ethnic divisions, which are finding new expression in religious terms. In Iran it served the needs of a revolutionary movement hostile to a particular secular régime. In other respects, however, all of these countries are undergoing similar crises and challenges which may also underlie some of the appeal of religious revitalization. They all share the experience of recent, rapid and sometimes uncontrolled urbanization and industrialization, pervasive western influence, and the spread of literacy with the burgeoning of a critical, educated class without precedent in traditional society. The combination of these processes generates the kind of situation which Islam is well qualified to satisfy. In its "great tradition" form, it is a religion deeply committed to social problems and causes by political involve-ment and as a more personal system of ethics. Indeed, as a system of values, a total "way of life" (al-Din), it can provide the missing meaning and uncer-tain identity for the timid urban migrant, rural-born university student, or neophyte civil servant, where few secular models or precedents exist. Its impact is particularly potent where these developments are combined with a growing mistrust of western values and models, to which Islam is able to contribute a coherent, viable alternative. For the intellectuals, especially the educated youth, access to the steady stream of new religious literature, different from that traditionally available from rural ulama coupled with a sense of their own role as future teachers and leaders, has led to the religious explosion now so deeply felt in the schools and campuses of the Muslim world. Apart from the doubts in many minds as to the value of the western contribution to knowledge, and especially as to its ethical and social implications, there is the more elemental question of loss of identity in the homogenizing process of western scientism, technology, and overall style of life which follow. Identities are often expressed in terms of basic binary oppositions. In many cases, the antithesis to the Muslim world is the Christian west. In other contexts, it takes the form of the Jews/Israelis, socialists/communists, or in Malaysia, the "non-Malay." This is why the spirit of religion and nationalism appear to be so close and why the symbols of one so readily translate into the language of the other. Thus ethnic particularisms easily replace the more universalistic aspects of Islam, and religion itself partakes of ethnic-like sentiments.

As the young Muslims of the world refind and rekindle their faith, one of the casualties of their personal relationships arises in the form of an exaggerated generation gap. The contrast between the ardent, sometimes self-conscious zeal of the youth, intensified by the critical scrutiny of their peers, often bewilders, irritates, and even angers their parents and elders, many of whom have long comfortably settled into middle-class, urban, and westernized lifestyles. Even pious rural parents have evolved their own patterns of religious observance, which are adjusted to social requirements of another kind, as in the adat of the Malay kampung. Urban and rural parents alike are often startled by the vehemence and seeming arrogance of the assault on their own religious practices (or lack of them) made by their juniors and agonize over the latter's marriage chances, careers, and futures. The contrast should not be overdrawn, for some of these same parents also respect the religious commitment of their offspring and are awed by their rising academic and professional statuses. But the web that binds this contemporary wave of young Muslim revivalists is very much a horizontal one, spanning countries and political boundaries more than generations.

Meanwhile, back in the village, both in Malaysia and elsewhere, such international exposure and experience is largely limited to the travelled ulama, who combine this with their local cultural traditions. Thus a lively and more irrepressible form of Malayness, still with its feudal, martial, magical, and mystical overtones, survives parallel to the more fundamentalist version of the faith which now frowns on such activities. Both constituencies are concerned with cultural survival in their own way, and both see their identity at least partly in religious terms.

Islam in Malaysia, as elsewhere, can also serve as a vehicle for sensitizing and mobilizing people against oppression and injustice, even within their own religious community. In Iran it overthrew the Shah, and in parts of the

Mahgrib (North Africa), it has become radicalized to the extent of entering into "unholy" alliances with socialism. While a comparable level of consciousness and mobilization has yet to be reached in Malaysia, the potential is always there. Traditional rural discontent has found a voice, first through the sporadic cult movements of colonial times, and more recently through the religious party, PAS. In the past decade, however, such events as Baling and Alor Setar are not so clearly in line with this ulama-managed tradition, although if ABIM and other urban dakwah activitists become more involved in such issues, a radical social reform movement could conceivably emerge, with all the political consequences which that would entail. For Malaysia, with its aversion to any hint of class and class conflict, this alone would be revolutionary enough, even with a substitution of religion for an overt class ideology. Whether these possibilities will eventually become reality will depend, among other things, on whether ABIM (without Anwar) can penetrate more effectively into the villages, how far they will be confined to the PAS mould and mode of acting in the rural areas, and to what extent entry into more open politics is met with government resistance and penalties. Much will also depend on the resolution by dakwah leaders of the nature of the Islamic state and, more important, on the legitimation of this leadership in the eyes of the rural population. While some religious fundamentalists seem prepared to take up the cudgels of class interest, if under another name, so some of the socialist leaders of the PSRM remain open to the harnessing of religion to their cause. None of these leaders evince the antipathy to religion that is often expected of socialists. To the contrary, there are signs that these men are affected by the society-wide religious climate, and are rediscovering a faith for themselves and not merely as adjunct to their political interests.

The signs are that Islam will increasingly become the principal language of Malaysian politics, beyond the mere symbol of Malay ethnic identity. Whether from choice or not, UMNO now regularly seeks legitimacy in religious terms and engages in "holier than thou" campaigns against both PAS and dakwah supporters. It has intensified its aid to religious institutions and causes, and launched its own dakwah programmes, if only to co-opt the unco-opted before they go over to the other side. Engagement in kafir-mengafir as a form of political discourse reaches both the depths of banality and the heights of refinement in party campaigns and even in the daily life of some kampungs. Since assuming the premiership from Datuk Hussein Onn, Dr. Mahathir has made great publicity and political gain from his trips to the Middle East, his promise to open a branch of an Islamic bank, his turning away from ties with the west, and his plans for a grand new Islamic University (the latter on ABIM's agenda for over a decade). Government leaders can no longer rely so securely on the precedents of feudal Malay tradition alone for their authority, and this is particularly true for Mahathir, who is not an aristocrat. For their part, urban dakwah leaders try to turn their newly claimed religious authority to more established roles and institutions, such as guru, and by their fundamentalist reversion to the past to inject a note of tradition into their authority.

Viewing it in a longitudinal perspective, the present-day variety of religious politics may be seen as the culmination of—or possibly just another stage in—the ambivalent relationship between the secular ruler and the religious establishment. Today in Malaysia, there are ongoing conflicts between government and party, the sultans (as Heads of Religion in their states) and state religious councils, the independent rural ulama, and the various forms of urban dakwah movement. The question of ultimate authority between these four elements has yet to be resolved and, as such, feeds and adds colour to most aspects of Malaysian politics.

As a polity, Malaysia also differs from many other Muslim countries in its large non-Muslim "minority," whose fate in the Islamic state is by no means resolved. One solution, as promulgated by PERKIM, is to promote their conversion to Islam, although the experience of the Chinese mu'alaf or saudara baru is not an encouraging example. The particularistic social image of Islam as a Malay religion still persists. The independent dakwah people, on the other hand, show little interest in introducing non-Malays into the fold, preferring to concentrate on Malay spiritual renewal. Twice-born Muslims are favoured over those who enter for the first time. This approach is most characteristic of Darul Arqam. Although the public ideals of ABIM are more universalistic, in practice they have little impact on the average follower. At an ideological mid-point, Tabligh seems to be fairly effective in providing, through dakwah, one mechanism whereby Indian Muslims at least can acquire Malay status. Otherwise, Malay and Bumi ranks appear to be closing ever more firmly in the political sphere, and even some non-Tabligh Indian Muslims, who had been accustomed to "oscillating" back and forth between Malay and Indian status, are encountering a new rigidity. Thus PERKIM's solution seems increasingly remote, and ethnic divisions continue to be reflected in religious rationales.

The recent religious revivals in the Chinese and Indian communities, whether charismatic Christianity, canonical Buddhism, millenarian movements or Sai Baba, may well represent a similar preoccupation with ethnic boundary maintenance or else a backlash in response to Malay dakwah. On deeper reflection, however, these revivals are probably also symptomatic in part of some of the same basic ills and insecurities afflicting Malay youth, and may fulfil similar needs. But as long as religious movements are identified strongly with particular ethnic communities, the prognosis for the erosion of ethnic boundaries, or for greater unity in any kind of state, Islamic or other, is not encouraging.

Given the low probability that ethnic integration or national unity in Malaysia will be achieved by Islam alone, what are the possible alternatives for the country's future?

In some plural societies, such as Israel and even the United States, it has been suggested that a form of civil religion could perform this task of integration (cf. Aronoff 1981). In such a situation, religious symbols of a very high level of generality, such as those of "belief in God," human dignity, justice, compassion, and brotherly love, could provide a common and indisputable set of values which no community could deny. This is one proposition put forward in a multi-ethnic seminar on religion, "One God, Many Paths," sponsored by Aliran in 1980. Such an approach would neither preclude nor explicitly favour the use of Islamic symbols, ideas and values, just as Israel draws heavily on Judaism and the United States on Christianity. But these would be in a suitably generalized form and "diluted" of some the more specific and onerous obligations on those not prepared to undertake them. It would in theory allow Muslims and non-Muslims alike to share common sentiments and experiences. This would be particularly important in the choice and effectiveness of myths, symbols, and rituals of the state to achieve the loyalty and commitment of all its citizens. Already in Malaysia some national events and occasions are inspired, but not limited, by Islamic observances, for example, the ceremonies of Independence Day and the Installation of the King. Indeed, this is the kind of Islam that had been developing prior to the rise of dakwah, one eminently suited to UMNO goals and needs. It was an era too when even specifically Muslim holidays, such as Hari Raya Puasa, were sufficiently "secularized" to incorporate more non-Muslim friends. Even non-Muslims had begun to model their own religious holidays on the Malay-Muslim "open-house" pattern. Meanwhile, the fact that many national, non-religious events were accompanied by Muslim symbols, did not unduly impinge on or threaten the citizens of other faiths. The reading of Islamic prayers and the carrying of religious banners in a National Day parade had become so routine a part of the ceremonial, as to be totally acceptable to all.

The recent revival, however, has caused whatever implicit and fragile unity might have been evolving in the form of elements of a civil religion to evaporate, in the face of the religious and ethnic polarization now resurfacing. Even the religiously neutral "ethics" classes, compulsory for non-Muslim school children, are now being transformed into instruction on basic Islam. In its place, we are now more likely to see moves in the direction of the Islamic state, acceptable only to Muslims, and probably only to certain

Muslim constituencies at that. For as long as it remains in control, UMNO will unquestionably attempt to compromise in this sphere, even while paying greater lip service to Islam as the all-embracing religion of Malaysia.

As Malaysia enters the 1980's, the conflict now shaping up is between two types of authority, both with strong tendencies towards absolutism and a rigid rule of law and demanding uncompromising loyalty: Islam and the latter-day "protector" variety of Malay leadership. Both are also fundamentalist in the sense that they draw on tradition as an inspiration for action and a source of legitimacy. Finally, both are eminently legalistic and adhere tenaciously to a code of law which requires total obedience and submission to the ruler or to God. The immediate future of the country will depend much on which of these two traditions is able to set the tone of society and stamp its seal most deeply on the institutions and peoples of the country as a whole.

Glossary of Special Terms
and Abbreviations

ABIM   Angkatan Belia Islam Malaysia, or Malaysian Muslim Youth League, one of the most prominent of the recent revival or "dakwah" religious movements.

Adat   Traditional Malay custom, usually referring to pre- or non-Islamic forms.

Al-Din   "Religion," in the sense of its provision for the entire range of needs of this world and of the next; religion as a "way of life."

Alim (Pl. ulama, q.v.)   Religious scholar, in all parts of the Muslim world, often independent of schools, formal authority, etc.

Al-Ikhwan   A Muslim Brotherhood, particularly political organizations with fundamentalist / revivalist religious tendencies, for example, in Egypt and Syria.

Aliran   Literally, a "stream" or "current," used especially in Indonesia to refer to interest groups and coalitions cutting across obvious class lines. Also the name adopted by a specific religious / political reform movement in contemporary Malaysia.

Baitul-mal   The treasury, or a committee entrusted with the state's funds in an Islamic polity.

Bangsa   Descent or "ethnic" group, race, social community.

Barisan Nasional   National Front, the formal consociational alliance of political parties which hold a collective majority in Parliament and rule Malaysia.

Bersanding   A central event in many Malay rites of passage, in which the individual(s) undergoing the rite are publicly presented on a decorated platform, for example, the bridal couple during a wedding.

Bilal   One who makes the call to prayer in the mosque.

Bomoh   Traditional Malay medical practitioner or curer.

Bumiputera   Literally, "prince" or "son of the soil," now applied to Malays born in the peninsula, as the basis of their entitlement to certain privileges. By extension, also refers to other indigenes, for example, orang asli.

Dakwah   A generic term for any missionary activity which recalls lapsed Muslims to the faith or makes new converts. In Malaysia, used in a rather restricted sense to refer to specific, urban-based national revival movements.

Dalang   Originally the manipulator of the puppets at traditional puppet shows (wayang kulit), now used for any (political) wheeler-dealer or background organizer.

DAP   Democratic Action Party, an avowedly non-communal and somewhat radical opposition party, popularly associated with the Chinese.

Darul Arqam   Literally, "House of Arqam," one of the three principal revival or dakwah organizations in Malaysia, distinctive for its attempts at economic self-sufficiency.

Fatwa   An official Islamic doctrinal ruling by a religious council, regarded as binding in its domain.

Guru   Any kind of teacher, religious or secular (derived from the Sanskrit).

Halal   Permissible by the standards of Islam, especially of food.

Haram   Forbidden by Islam; unclean of foods.

Ijtihad   The tradition, in Islamic scholarship, of constantly reinterpreting the faith according to the needs of contemporary society.

Imam   A mosque official, who normally leads the Friday prayer.

Isnad   The "chain" of religious authority between scholar and pupil linking regions and generations.

Jema'at Tabligh   One of the three major religious revival or dakwah organizations in Malaysia, of Indian origin.

Jihad   A holy war or crusade to defend Islam against non-believers. By analogy, any kind of religious sacrifice or striving.

Kampung   Malay settlement or village, rural or urban.

Kathi   An appointee of the Muslim Religious Court (Syari'ah), usually concerned with registration of births, marriages, conversions and deaths, etc.

Kaum Muda   Literally the "Young Faction," referring to a progressive Malayan Islamic revival movement in the 1920's and 1930's.

Kaum Tua   Literally the "Old Faction," or the conservative opposition to the religiously progressive Kaum Muda (q.v.) in early twentieth century Malayan Islam.

Khatib   One who reads the sermon at the Friday prayer.

Lebai   Religious teacher, usually of lesser status and reputation than other ulama or ustaz.

Madrasah   Type of religious school, modelled on Arab prototypes, in which some "secular" subjects may be taught along with the religious.

MBM   Majlis Belia Malaysia, or consortium of most of the Malaysian Youth Clubs at the national level.

Mu'alaf   A new convert to Islam. In Malaysia tends to be used derogatorily.

Muballigh   A Muslim missionary.

NEP   The New Economic Policy, or series of policies first put forward in the Second Malaysia Plan (1971–75), to eradicate poverty and improve the economic status of the Malays.

PAS   Partai Islam Se-Malaysia, the predominantly Malay Islamic opposition party.

Pawang   Traditional Malay curer, of pre-Islamic origins.

Penghulu   Traditional Malay title, originally applied to lesser "chiefs," but now the lowest appointment in the bureaucratic hierarchy of the state, usually at the level of the mukim (parish) unit.

PERKIM   Pertubahan Kebajikan Islam or Muslim Welfare League, a Muslim missionary association.

Pondok   A type of (usually rural) religious school, in which the pupils resided in small huts around the house of their teacher.

PSRM   Partai Sosialis Rak'yat Malaysia, or non-communal people's socialist party.

Riba   Interest derived from money-lending or usury, forbidden in Islam.

Rohaniyat   The religious leadership (ulama) in Iran.

Salasilah (silsilah)   Arabic term for genealogy. Frequently used for "intellectual" line of descent of scholars, particularly of religious teachers.

Saudara Baru   Literally, "new associate," used for new converts to Islam in Malaysia, especially the Chinese.

Shi'ah   Branch of Islam, parallel to the Sunni, but separate from it, with several distinctive beliefs, practices, and styles of leadership, most prominent in Iran.

Silat   Generic term for the entire spectrum of traditional Malay martial arts, of which there are numerous branches, for example silat gayong, silat lincah etc.

Sunni   Numerically largest branch of Islam to which the Malays and most Indian Muslims belong.

Surat Tauliah   Letters of accreditation, from Sultan or Religious Council, authorizing religious teachers and other functionaries to carry out their tasks.

Syari'ah   Muslim religious court, most commonly those dealing with civil and personal law, relating to marriage, family, inheritance, etc.

Syura   A religious committee.

Ulama (sing. Alim)   Religious scholar and/or teacher in all parts of the Muslim world.

UMNO   United Malays National Organization, or senior political party in the Barisan Nasional.

Usrah   Small, face-to-face group meeting for religious purposes and discussions, etc.

Ustaz   Religious teacher or instructor in Islam, usually attached to a formal school.

Notes

NOTES TO THE INTRODUCTION

1. The Federation of Malaya was originally created out of nine historically independent sultanates and three Crown Colonies or Straits Settlements, Penang, Malacca, and Singapore, the last of which joined the federation as the western section of what was to be renamed Malaysia. Each sultan was permitted to retain royal status and privilege, including the right to participate in the rotating kingship of Malaysia, by which each ruler undertakes a five-year turn as Head of State (*Yang di Pertuan Agong*), although not all have chosen to do so in practice.
2. The term "western orientalist" has come into recent currency as a popular, derogatory way of referring to western scholars who rather arrogantly set themselves up as experts on Islam and who, in so doing, misrepresent the faith or try to squeeze it into Christian-centric categories.
3. A useful lead in this direction has been provided by Mendelssohn (1975), in his analysis of the Buddhist sangha in Burma, in which he takes account of both the ideological and political (factional) aspects of internal religious divisions.

NOTES TO CHAPTER 1

1. The dates of some of these annals are by no means as established or as accepted as was once thought. Originally, there were two principal versions of the *Sejarah Melayu*, the first of which, the "Raffles version" (JMBRAS XVI (3) 1938), was assumed to have been composed before 1536, and the second, the "Shellabear version" (recently republished in full by Oxford University Press, Kuala Lumpur, 1967), is believed to be of seventeenth-century provenance. Johns (1975), however, suggests that some of these apparent dating anomalies may be reconciled by regarding the *Sejarah Melayu* as an ever-evolving and cumulative set of manuscripts, with constant accretions and changes in successive periods.
2. The word adat itself is in fact of Arabic origin, and it is somewhat curious that a term which was presumably introduced with Islam could (so swiftly) acquire this exclusivist association with a local royal line, only later to be transformed back into an approximation of its original meaning, as "custom," "daily life," etc.
3. Hang Tuah, one of the best-known heroes of Malay history, was one of a cast of characters in the *Sejarah Melayu*, an aristocrat and subject of Sultan Mahmud of Malacca in the seventeenth century. He is celebrated in Malay literature for his unswerving (and uncritical) support for his master in all the latter's enterprises, in the course of which Hang Tuah was required to perpetrate deeds (including murder) unacceptable to Islam.
4. The *Tuhfat al-Nafis* was composed in Riau in the late 1860's, and although still preoccupied with providing a legitimate charter of descent for the Rajah, it also deals with a different kind of identity: the relationship between the Melayu and the Bugis, as determined by place of origin. The *Hikayat Abdullah* was the creation of a scholar-commentator of mixed Arab and Indian descent, who lived in the colonial world of nineteenth-century Malacca and Singapore and whose sensitivities to identities by origin, language, and culture were influenced by consciousness of his own mixed descent and the British colonial atmosphere.

5. The renowned Muslim exegesist, philosopher, and social commentator Al Ghazali even claimed that an unjust but strong ruler is better than no ruler at all in the interests of social stability. A totally different point of view comes from the Egyptian social thinker, Muhd. Qutb, who, in his "Islam, the Misunderstood Religion," states that a "word of justice, uttered before an unjust ruler is the greatest jihad (holy crusade)" (1964:291).

6. Curiously, the term for "religion" itself, as used by modern Malay Muslims is the Sanskrit word agama, as is the word for prayer, *sembahyang*. Certain other terms, such as that for "mankind" seem to use Arabic (*mahkluk*) and Sanskrit (*manusia*) forms interchangeably. Most of the vocabulary pertaining to royal power and courtly ceremonial is, not surprisingly, of Sanskrit origin, thus underlining the Indic base of Malay temporal rulership. However, in most cases, after the introduction of Islam, the Malay rulers changed their titles from the Indic *rajah* to the Arabic *sultan*.

7. Jawi is a term derived from Jawa (Java) and commonly used in the Middle East to refer to many items of Malay (and sometimes, by extension, to other Southeast Asian) origin. Its usual frame of reference is to language and custom and occasionally to the people. In Malaysia itself, Jawi refers to the Arabic script (modified) for the writing of Malay, mostly in religious texts.

8. Among his many preoccupations concerning the interests, achievements, and potential of the Malays for progress, Abdullah paid particular attention to the role of language. He made the point that language is crucial to the development and maintenance of a people's identity as well as a means of communication and mobilization.

9. The close association between Islam and the Malay language is further illustrated by the fact that in the eighteenth century, Malay and Jawi were used as the medium of royal genealogies (salasilah) at Muslim courts in such far-flung places as Sulu, Mangindanao, and Maranao, in what is now the southern Philippines (Cesar Majul 1971: 51).

10. Of the nine Malay states affected, five, Kedah, Johor, Kelantan, Trengganu, and Perlis, were officially known as the Unfederated States, while the rest, Pahang, Perak, Negri Sembilan, and Selangor, were designated Federated States. In the latter the sultan's powers were more severely curtailed and largely abrogated to a British "resident." In the Unfederated States, relatively more powers were left in the hands of native rulers, who were expected only to consult their British "advisers," established in each of their states (cf. Emerson 1937; Ratnam 1965; Means 1970).

11. On the other hand, it has been claimed by Al-Attas that colonial intervention actually reinforced the rulers' feudal power, so that the "feudal mentality" was in effect perpetuated and validated by western imperialism (1978:173).

12. This is not meant to imply that such movements were necessarily un-Islamic, but that they drew more heavily from secular political ideologies in their quest for identity.

13. The original Straits Settlements, Penang, Malacca, and Singapore, were administered by the British directly from London as Crown Colonies, and their residents were regarded as British subjects. Many of the immigrant traders, such as the Arabs and Indians referred to, found in the Straits Settlements greater freedom than in the Malay states, which was one reason for their opposition to the authority of the sultans.

14. It should be noted that, years later, other "immigrant" Malaysians have refused to swear an oath of allegiance to the sultan of their state of residence, for example, in 1978 when several Chinese state political leaders refused to pay homage to the Sultan of Perak as members of the State Assembly.

15. Meaning "son of the soil," the term Bumiputera has been in intermittent use since at least the 1930's (cf. Roff 1972). Its range of meaning has varied somewhat over the years and according to the issues at stake, and its legal status is still uncertain. It is generally understood to refer to anyone of Malay or other aboriginal descent, including the tribal peoples of the Malay peninsula (orang asli) and the natives of Sabah and Sarawak in East Malaysia. To date, non-Muslims (in the above categories) have been admitted to Bumiputera status, although no serious issue has yet put this question fully to the test. So far, its greatest significance has been in determining eligibility for New Economic Policy (NEP) benefits. See Siddique and Suryadinata (1981) for a fuller historical account of the use of this term.

16. Etymologically, the term Kling, commonly used for Indian Muslims in Malaysia, probably refers to the putative origin of many of that population from the Kalinga area of South India. The meaning of Jawi Peranakan is literally "one born of Jawi parents," i.e., people of Malay parentage, but with the implication also of an input of other, non-Malay lineages, hence not a "pure Malay" (Nagata 1974a; 1979). Most Jawi Peranakan were in fact descendants of unions between Malay women and immigrant Indian, Arab, and other (Muslim) males, many of them traders, and some religious scholars. Saudara baru ("new associates") are recent converts to Islam, principally Chinese, who are rarely acknowledged as Malays, but are relegated to a separate and marginal status (see Chapter 7).

17. Nusantara is an even more diffuse concept of a vague cultural and linguistic domain, extending beyond the Malay and Indonesian archipelagoes to a broader area of "Malay-speaking peoples" which would even include parts of Madagascar. Clearly this generous coverage eliminates any question of Islam as an essential component of Malay culture or identity at this level. Once again, in the late 1970's, some conferences in Malaysian universities on themes pertaining to "Malay culture" have adopted this all-inclusive interpretation of the "Malay world."

18. For a fuller account of the cultural and political ideology and strategies of the KMM, see Roff (1967); Rustum Sani (1976); Funston (1976); and Stockwell (1979). In Malaya, members of the KMM tended to be English-educated intellectuals from such institutions as the Sultan Idris (Teacher) Training College, while many of their Indonesian counterparts were active in the Committee for the Preparation for Indonesian Independence.

19. This, of course, had implications for immigrant non-Malays, whose lack of political allegiance (as well as lack of Islam) placed them completely outside the pale. This was most dramatically illustrated in 1946, with Malay rejection of the British Malayan Union proposal, whereby immigrants would have been accorded equal status as citizens along with "native" Malays by the principle of *ius soli* (cf. Ratnam 1965; Stockwell 1979).

20. Once the religious casuistry got going, its refinements led to such questions as to whether the Sanskrit term baginda (majesty), used for modern Malay sultans, is appropriate for reference to the Prophet Mohammed (as is customary in Malaysia), for its confusion of Malay feudal values with religious authority.

21. Under the present constitution the Malaysian state is a secular one with Islam as the "official" religion and permitting freedom of worship to all other faiths as long as they do not interfere with Islam.

NOTES TO CHAPTER 2

1. In the Shi'ite (non-Sunni) tradition of Islam, dominant in Iran, the concept of ijtihad is built into the very structure of the faith. In this tradition, every teacher and scholar (*mullah/ ayatollah*) is free (and expected) to establish his own interpretation and following, sometimes in competition with other ulama. Thus they are sometimes also known as mujtahid, or of ijtihad. This is in keeping with the messianic anticipation of the coming of the twelfth (hidden) imam, for whom every religious leader is preparing in his own way. Iranian ulama are thus more authoritarian and absolutist.

2. Salasilah is the Arabic for "genealogy," both of the family variety and, by extension, of an intellectual kind.

3. It should be emphasized that this refers to the question of leadership in a generic sense, rather than to specific rulers of dynasties, such as the various caliphates of the early Islamic era in the Middle East.

4. It is partly for this reason that proposed variants for the ideal "Islamic state" have ranged from (Islamic) socialist (cf. Fazhur Rahman 1974) to General Zia's military rule in Pakistan. It is worth noting that, when the Muslim League Al-Jinnah in colonial India initially launched the idea of the Pakistani state, many ulama, among them Maulana Al-Maudoodi, were opposed to the idea on grounds of the alleged vested property and commercial interests of the League's leaders.

5. In Kedah alone there is no true mufti as such. The role and functions of the mufti in that state were fulfilled in the early part of the twentieth century by a Syeikh al-Islam, who was later replaced (in 1935) by a fatwa committee. Subsequently, a special fatwa committee of the religious council, formed in 1948, assumed these functions.

6. The sizeable Muslim population, mostly of Malay ethnic origin, in the southern four provinces of Thailand has long been pressing for greater autonomy in religious affairs and even for union with Malaysia. This has resulted in a series of guerilla activities along the Malaysian border. At least four organizations are said to exist on the Thai side of the border, and the Communist Party is also alleged to be aiding the cause. On the Malaysian side (Kedah shares a common frontier with Thailand), some PAS members are also involved. Both the Malaysian and Thai governments are co-operating to provide military opposition to the insurgents.

7. UMNO is the party of the incumbent federal government, and senior partner of a grand consociational coalition (once called the Alliance, now the National Front) of several parties. Many of these represent ethnic interests (e.g., Malaysian Chinese Association—MCA, and the Malaysian Indian Congress—MIC). Others are in theory multi-ethnic, but in practice tend to be associated with one ethnic group, as is the Democratic Action Party with the Chinese. PAS, as described in Chapter 1, is the religious-based Malay opposition party, although for a few years (from 1972 to 1977), it was temporarily a member of the Front, until the uneasy alliance proved untenable to all concerned.

8. The term Sufi is said to be derived etymologically from *sūf*, meaning "undyed wool," possibly referring to the ascetic clothing habits of the original followers. The Sufi tradition generally emphasizes personal and mystical religious experiences, and so cultivates trance, dance and other mood-influencing methods as a direct path to God. Organizationally, Sufism has been carried across continents by brotherhoods (tarikat), each with its own charismatic-like leaders and unique local variants. Sufism is an offshoot of the Sunni branch of Islam, although often considered deviant by other Sunni followers.

9. One particular case concerned the question as to why commercial beer, with 5 per cent alcoholic content, should be forbidden (haram), while an indigenous drink made from rice (*air tapai*), whose alcoholic content may be twice that of the beer, is tolerated. The verdict, by one ingenious alim, was that the high level of sugar in the latter makes it permissible. Moreover, it is a "native" (asli) drink and not one of the invidious, imported concoctions of the west (*Berita Harian* 1/6/76).

10. The family of the groom is usually expected to contribute a substantial sum to the cost of the (non-Islamic) part of the ceremonials, including a feast and entertainment for many guests, and to provide an impressive display of gifts to the family of the bride (*hantaran*).

11. It is probably significant in this regard that there are remarkably few religious schools or established religious traditions in fishing areas, where subsistence levels and economic stability are generally lower and less predictable than in the wet ricelands.

12. Malaya never had a Syari'ah Act like that of India (1937), by which all "custom" was explicitly subordinated to religious law (cf. Moshe Yegar 1976:145).

13. Safar is the month of the Prophet's death and is always considered one of the least auspicious times of year, when, for example, weddings are rarely performed. The bathing (*mandi*), either on coastal beaches or in rivers, has often become one glorious picnic and day of recreation (although rationalized as "purification"), involving a mingling of the sexes in a manner unacceptable to orthodox Islam.

14. The persistence and success of the Matahari communities, despite their heretical stigma and frequent persecution by religious authorities and social ostracism by other Muslims, may be attributed in part to an effective leadership. The Matahari leaders were obviously able to fulfil the needs of their followers and also placed the communities on a solid economic footing through their entrepreneurial skills, notably the operation of printing presses. Members claim that they have profitably substituted funds which would otherwise have been "wasted" on religious obligations and expenses (e.g., the pilgrimage) on business investments instead.

15. FELDA or the Federal Land Development Authority of Malaysia is a federally sponsored body which, since 1957, has been responsible for the opening up and development of new land (over a million acres to date) and new cash crops (e.g., oil palms), on which large cohorts of landless Malays have been resettled. Despite the apparent bonanza to the settler, in terms of access to prepared land and fairly reliable financial returns, socially, and in terms of personal satisfaction, some settlements have been less than successful, with the result that settlers may be vulnerable to the appeals of new leaders and ideologies.

16. Strictly, in Islam, as in mediaeval Christian scholarship, there is no clear distinction between "sacred" and "secular" education or the premises from which such knowledge is derived, (as, for example, between "science" and "religion"). Thus for Muslims, even (modern) science can be the product of inspirational knowledge (wahyu).

17. The mosque officials normally include an imam (who leads the prayer), a bilal (who makes the call to prayer), a khatib (reader of the scriptures), and a siak (who is responsible for the physical upkeep of the building).

18. Government schools for all their subsidies still entail greater expense per pupil in the cost of the uniforms and for the greater number and variety of text books and other equipment required for its more expanded curriculum, which students are expected to supply for themselves.

19. This does not mean that their religious education is entirely neglected, for most offspring of ulama or teachers receive religious instruction at home or in the father's school, at least part-time, at hours which do not conflict with the government school. In contrast to the previous generation, most children and grandchildren of ulama today attend a government school, particularly in view of the attraction of the national language policy and of special education and occupational quotas for Malays.

20. These promotional examinations are: the LCE or Lower Certificate of Education (*Sijil Rendah Pelajaran*), taken following Form III; the MCE or Middle Certificate of Education (*Sijil Pelajaran Malaysia*), taken after Form V; and the HSC or Higher School Certificate (*Sijil Pelajaran Tinggi*), taken in Form VI in preparation for university entrance.

21. In Kedah, sekolah agama raky'at and other co-operating schools receive $20 per pupil per year from the religious council and between $30 to $40 per pupil annually from the Ministry of Education. To make up any deficit, pupils may be charged a nominal additional fee by the school, usually in the range of $15 to $20 per month.

22. This kind of dual system has long been institutionalized in the state of Johor, in what is generally acknowledged to be a successful combination. Since the school "day" in the national curriculum is, in fact, only half a day, either morning or afternoon, the people's school arrangements do not compromise the Ministry requirements.

23. A survey by Ahmad Kamar of the educational background of thirty-four Kedah PAS leaders shows that four had pondok schooling only; eleven were graduates of madrasah; one had attended Al-Azhar university in Cairo, and one a university in India; eight had only primary Malay education, while six more had reached lower secondary Malay school; finally, only three had received English-medium education (unpub. ms. 1979).

24. Some non-political ulama ignore party differences and make attempts to recreate or extend marriage alliances with the "new" religious élites by marrying into the families of government imams.

25. In practice, most Malay villagers, even zealous PAS followers, tend to have high aspirations for material goods, in emulation of their city cousins.

NOTES TO CHAPTER 3

1. A series of educational reports, starting with the Fenn-Wu Report in 1951 and continuing with those brought down by Razak in 1956, Talib in 1960, and Barnes in 1968, resulted in the gradual standardization of a national education curriculum. By 1980, the only official use of vernacular languages in schools (Chinese and Tamil) is at the primary level. In secondary

schools, English and Chinese are only found in private, "national-type" schools. Since 1970, Malay has been phased in as the universal language of instruction, from Grade One to university, a process to be completed by 1983, save in certain highly specialized technical and professional subjects where sufficient Malay texts do not yet exist. All promotional examinations (see Chapter 2, n.20) are now in Malay. The Ministry of Education has embarked upon an ambitious programme of school construction all over the peninsula, both to make education more available to the rural child and to increase the Malay enrolment in secondary and tertiary institutions, as a channel for the occupational opportunities constantly being opened up. Since 1969 when only one university existed in Malaysia (the University of Malaya), four more have been created, the National University, the Science University, the Agricultural University, and the Technical University), which must be fed from the growing stream of Malay-medium high-school graduates. Language policy has been, since 1970, an officially "sensitive" issue and cannot be challenged publicly. It is well known that the Chinese community has long been thwarted in its bid to establish its own Chinese-medium (Merdeka) university, which now seems unlikely to ever be approved. So far, it has had to be satisfied with a college of lesser status, Tunku Abdul Rahman College.

2. For details of the elections and other events leading up to the riots but from different perspectives, see: Gagliano, *Communal Violence in Malaysia: The Political Aftermath* (1970), John Slimming's *Malaysia: Death of a Democracy* (1969), and *May 13th: Before and After* by Malaysia's first prime minister, Tunku Abdul Rahman (1969).

3. Outspoken criticism by some severely disaffected non-Malays of late has led to a slight amendment to the balance since 1978. As a result, the National University now has 16.5 per cent non-Malay students. In the 1978 intake of new students into all five universities (aggregated), out of a total of 4,400 recruits, 2,881 were Malay, 2,110 were Chinese and 309 Indian, i.e., about 50 per cent non-Malays, which approximates to their proportions in the national population (*Far Eastern Economic Review* 20/10/78:13.)

4. In 1977 there were reported to be over 40,600 Malay students overseas, including 16,100 in the United Kingdom, 5,000 in Australia, and 3,200 in the United States (*Utusan Malaysia* 22/12/79).

5. The precipitation of the Baling affair was a series of convergent disasters, including a decline in world commodity prices for the principal cash crop of rubber, a rapid increase in inflation, and a perceived neglect of the peasant condition by government programmes and policies. The result was so serious a deterioration of rural living conditions there were rumours that peasants in Baling, Kedah, were dying of starvation and that eating poisonous tubers to stave off hunger had resulted in two deaths. An angry cohort of peasants themselves marched independently to the local district office to draw attention to their situation. This quickly caught the attention of many urban-dwellers, particularly students, who staged a number of massive rallies in Kuala Lumpur and Penang, culminating in the "Starvation Parade" (*Perarakan Kelaparan*) on 30 November 1974, in which the number of participants was variously estimated to have been 13,000 and 30,000 (*Far Eastern Economic Review* 13/12/74; 10/1/75). These events were followed by a severe official crackdown and jailing of several student leaders.

6. Since 1975, a series of further minor amendments to the Universities Act has gradually accumulated, now controlling visits and lectures on campuses by any "political figure" and denying recognition to "political societies," which in effect means any association which makes public statements or publications on government policy. In either case, the term "political" can be interpreted as broadly as the authorities desire.

7. At present, only one Malaysian university, the National University (Universiti Kebangsaan) has a full-fledged Faculty of Islamic Studies, while at the University of Malaya it is possible to major in Islamic Studies. At the other three universities, individual courses only are offered in religious studies. At MARA Institute of Technology, certain religious courses are compulsory. Other colleges specialize in religious education, e.g., the successor to the old Islamic College, now called the Maktab Perguruan Islam, and Nilam Puri in Kota Bharu, Kelantan, which was recently annexed as a branch of the University of Malaya. Graduates of the National University's Faculty of Islamic Studies provide the bulk of new religious teachers, both in the public schools and in various dakwah capacities.

8. One measure of the political interest of youth is the high correlation between Malay Youth Club membership (including UMNO Youth) and the Malay dominance of the national political scene. Of a total youth club membership in Malaysia of 1,077,064 in 1977, 73 per cent were Malay (*Berita Minggu* 24/6/79). For many reasons, it is less profitable and regarded as more "chauvinistic" for the youth of other ethnic groups or political parties to be politically active.

9. Datuk Harun was accused, among other things, of misappropriating funds from the Bank Negara for his own personal interests, but there was always some question as to whether his growing power among the Youth was partly responsible for his downfall.

10. Note that the English term "bonus" is used to distinguish the return from the prohibited "interest" or usury (riba; *faedah*). The "bonus" is justified on the grounds that it results from a natural expansion of the principal capital through legitimate economic growth.

11. These requirements have effectively eliminated the role and services of one traditional institution in the ports of Malaysia (especially Penang), namely, that of the *Syeikh Haji*, originally a combination broker / travel agent, who arranged accommodation and contacts in the Holy land for his clients.

12. Nasrul Haq itself claimed to be a branch of the already established and accepted school of silat lincah.

13. The minister was assailed for his attempt, in his capacity as minister of culture, to support the resurrection of the dubious mandi safar ceremony (see Chapter 2) in Malacca and was accused of being unable to distinguish between Islam and adat once again (*Dakwah*, Feb. 1978: 28-50).

14. There are stories of mosques in Pahang facing the wrong way (i.e., not in the direction of the *khiblat* in Mecca) and of misinterpretations of Syari'ah law in some cases of marriage eligibility.

15. In the original Second Malaysia Plan, the target of Malay equity / capital ownership and employment quotas was to be at least 30 per cent by 1990, but at a Bumiputera Economic Congress in 1980, ten years before the arrival of the deadline date, calls were sounded by delegates to raise the target to 50 per cent or more.

16. Successful consociational politics depends upon an (often uneasy) coalition between the leaders of different ethnic (or other interest) groups, who maintain their fragile unity and precarious dominance by rallying their own grass-roots to support them and the status quo by appeals to ethnic loyalty. Any horizontal linkages, e.g., along class lines, which could erase some of the ethnic conflicts, threaten both the leadership and their alliance. See Lijphart (1977) for a comprehensive analysis of consociationalism, and Enloe (1977), on the ethnic calculations and strategies in the Malaysian situation.

17. The phenomenon of mass hysteria is regularly reported in the Malaysian media in a number of authoritarian situations and institutions, particularly in boarding schools, hostels, and factories. It is characterized physically by forms of spontaneous and uncontrolled shivering, laughing, crying, or vomiting and claims of possession or assaults by ghosts and spirits (*penunggu*; *hantu*). Sometimes this is accompanied by partial undressing and behaviours normally inhibited or proscribed. Although hysteria often begins with just one individual, it is highly "contagious" and rapidly convulses an entire group (for example, a class or factory floor), and as even the most cynical or detached of observers has discovered, it can usually only be stopped by the intervention of a traditional Malay curer (bomoh) or exorcist, who normally sacrifices a goat or introduces a charm (*tangkal*) to appease the offending spirit. Foreign factory managers have learned too that the only sure and immediate "cure" is by these traditional methods. As for the deeper causes, of repression and need for expressive outlets, these remain untreated. Mass hysteria has been acknowledged by Malaysian social psychologists as a form of "covert individual conflict," a substitute for personal confrontation (Lee and Ackerman 1981).

18. This group, which held the Grand Mosque for several days, was initially characterized in the international media as an example of an undisciplined, irresponsible, and extremist youth group or sect, disowned by every other branch of Islam. Subsequent investigations, however, revealed that the group in fact probably represents a tribal-based opposition movement

to the Wahhabi Saudi monarchy, with supporters from sympathetic radical elements from neighbouring Muslim countries including Egypt, Lebanon, Syria, and Iran.

20. The term "dakwah" is not used in the Middle East in the same specialized and restricted sense it has acquired in Malaysia, but only in its original and generic sense of "mission," implicitly understood to be the duty of every Muslim.

21. This period, following World War II, was one of constant armed struggle between the Malaysian government and jungle-based guerilla remnants of the wartime Chinese People's Army, dedicated at first to combatting the occupying Japanese, later transferring their allegiance to international communism and a renewed focus on China.

NOTES TO CHAPTER 4

1. It was reported that when one of the daughters of past-Prime Minister Tun Hussein Onn returned from England as "dakwah," she was swiftly and unceremoniously transported to a secret location for "de-programming" sessions under a chosen religious scholar, who managed to persuade her to manifest her religious convictions in a less public, or at least visible, form.

2. Despite Peacock's claims (1978b) that his Kedah sample displayed reformist tendencies, his conclusions are based entirely on questionnaires administered by "remote control," without benefit of personal observation or even a visit. My own feeling is that what the Kedah findings really reveal is a deep religious commitment and knowledge, not surprising in an area with so extensive an ulama/pondok tradition, but less of an interest in reform per se. The Kaum Muda of the earlier part of this century was also short-lived there, and little evidence of its influence now remains.

3. The Malay College, modelled on the English "public" school, was founded in 1904 by the British to groom sons of the Malay nobility for the civil service. Subsequently, the College was opened up (by scholarship) to Malays of humbler background, but it retained both its Malay character and its high academic and social reputation.

4. The Faculty of Islamic Studies was founded, along with the university itself, in 1970, and initially only had "squatters' rights" in the Islamic College in Petaling Jaya. In 1974, it graduated 32 B.A.'s and in 1979 over 800. Now it also has a postgraduate programme, granting M.A.'s and Ph.D.'s.

5. In view of ABIM's precarious status as a registered association owing to its alleged political interests, restrictions have been placed on some of its publications. At first, *Risalah* was restricted to subscribers only (that is, it could not be sold on open newstands), but since 1981, its licence (KDN) has been withdrawn completely.

6. The pass rate, as of 1980, has been approximately 75 per cent (namely, 30 out of 40 candidates) at the level of the Middle School Certificate, and 31 out of 44 in the Higher School Certificate.

7. Fees are graded according to level of study, with a maximum of M\$32 per month for Form VI, and are further adjusted according to the means of the student's family.

8. The fashion sections of some women's magazines now reflect in content, if not so much in spirit, dakwah trends in dress, by featuring designer-co-ordinated "dakwah ensembles," in which the emphasis is on colour and type of cloth, rather than cut. They inform their readers that they can be "groovy and dakwah too"!

9. It is significant that, before ABIM became so obviously powerful a political force (and before Baling), more friendly attempts were made to channel its influence in the direction of government interests. It is rumoured that in 1974, then Prime Minister Tun Abdul Razak proposed to Anwar that he run for office on the UMNO ticket and follow in his father's footsteps, but that Anwar did not take up the offer (*Utusan Malaysia* 4/9/78). It is thus the more surprising that he should finally accept a similar offer, by Prime Minister Mahathir in 1982 and that he should then run for elections on the UMNO ticket in his father's old constituency of Bukit Mertajam.

10. This hostel was almost completely destroyed by fire in May of 1980, the result, it is said, of the unsupervised cooking efforts of pupils preparing their own meals.
11. Both Syamelin and the Darul Arqam system have ancient precedents in Islamic history. One of the major features of the traditional Muslim city (cf. Lapidus 1969) was invariably a strong economic underpinning in the form of trade guilds and networks, independent of non-Muslim merchants whose principles of operation were deemed incompatible with their own religious values.
12. It is often pointed out that, since the mosque is a public place for all Muslims, no imam has the right to deny entry or the convening of a religious meeting to any of the faithful, technically permission for use of the building is not required. What Tabligh missionaries are seeking, however, is the stamp of legitimacy and respect as well as useful local contacts. Nowadays, they are expected to obtain a letter of permission (surat tauliah) to lecture from a state religious council, which is rarely refused.
13. Strictly, in Arabic, khalwat merely means "isolation" or "seclusion" and was even used to refer to the Prophet Mohammed's retreats for meditation. In modern Malay, khalwat has come to be associated principally with illicit sexual relationships, including fornication and adultery. Most state religious councils have recently introduced (and enforced) strict new penalties for those caught *in flagrante delicto*. Penalties range from one to two months imprisonment or a fine of from M$200-300 for the first offence, with increases for all subsequent offences. Some zealous individuals have devised a new pastime of searching out "khalwat couples" in dormitories, hostels, cars, and corners of public buildings, sometimes with embarrassing results.
14. The lone survivor of the Kerling incident was eventually tried for "destruction of property." Subsequently, the involuntary Hindu killers were also put on trial and finally given prison sentences of two and one half to four years each, which observers feel represents a concession by the courts to the strength of dakwah sentiment in the country (*Asiaweek* 18/1/80:14).

NOTES TO CHAPTER 5

1. It is not my intention here to discourse at length on the extensive literature on ideology. Suffice it to say that for present purposes, I use as a working definition of "ideology," "a pattern of beliefs and concepts (factual and normative), which purport to explain complex social phenomena, with a view to directing and simplifying the social and political choices facing individuals and groups" (Johnson 1968:76). Ideology is thus a conscious set of symbols with conative functions, and includes myths, ethics and intellectual ideas, all constantly reforming into new patterns.
2. All males, in all collateral lines, of the first ascending generation are called by some variant of "father" (*pak*), and females by a "mother" term (*mak*). In the second ascending generation, by the same principle, all males are tok (grandfather) and females *nenek* (grandmother). Those of the same generation are called by a sibling term, and those of the first descending generation by a form of anak (child). All of these forms, in the same generation as ego and above, can be further graded by relative age and order of birth within the same generation set, thus pak *long* and pak *su*, as oldest and youngest males respectively in father's generation set, in any collateral line (or "uncle").
3. The Boria, peculiar to the city of Penang, is a form of musical drama and repartee, interspersed with short skits, songs, dances, and slapstick comedy, dating from colonial days in the late nineteenth and early twentieth centuries. It is said to have originated in the Jawi Peranakan (Indo-Malay) culture where it often became a vehicle for political satire, especially of the colonial authorities. It was in view of this last attribute that it was supposedly abolished in the 1930's, but it was later resurrected as a popular form of "traditional" entertainment, performed on public holidays and now in annual competitions.
4. Surat layang (literally, "flying letters") are a traditional device by which attacks on authority were sometimes made by peasants (or those acting on their behalf) to articulate grievances

without direct identification of source. The letters were usually left lying in a public place, for example, a mosque.

5. See Nagata (1968; 1974) for a detailed analysis of the interaction of ideology and factional politics contributing to religious sectarianism in an Amish-Mennonite community. Although ideological and theological rationales were invariably invoked, most cases of division in Mennonite communities, including the formation of totally new sub-sects, can be traced to conflict over authority, political ambition, and personal disputes in the original parent group.

NOTES TO CHAPTER 6

1. Most of the ''born'' Chinese Muslims are descended from a small but significant minority of Muslims whose faith was probably acquired from Central Asian traders to the west and from maritime Arab merchants who are reported to have established colonies in Canton as early as the fifteenth century. The Muslims distinguished themselves as a separate people, the Hui, different from the Han Chinese and living in separate communities. In both China and Malaysia, the most common Chinese Muslim surnames are Ma and Beh, and the dwindling representatives of these families are still to be found in the urban areas of Penang, Kuala Lumpur, and Singapore. Until the recent past, most of these families seem to have been in the process of resinification through intermarriage with other Chinese, under pressure of the surrounding Chinese community, and lack of adequate social support groups of other Muslims.

2. Normally, for the first six months following the registration of a conversion to Islam, the convert is eligible for up to M$30 per month for the purpose of buying religious books and financing instruction in the new faith.

3. These same Middle Eastern sources are also constantly providing contributions to all manner of religious projects in Malaysia, both to the dakwah organizations and for such items as religious libraries, schools, and colleges and now for the conversion of ''tribal'' peoples.

4. Merdeka University was first proposed by the MCA in the early 1970's, when it became clear that, under the quota system, university places for even qualified Chinese would be increasingly difficult to find and as costs of overseas education escalated. It should be clear that the Chinese never asked for an alteration of the education policy itself, only for approval of the request to establish a university in which the medium of instruction would be Chinese, without neglecting the national language. The finances were to be the sole responsibility of the Chinese community. Merdeka University has been a perennial electoral issue since 1970.

5. Until the 1970's, one of the deepest lines of internal differentiation within the Chinese community was between the English- and vernacular-educated. The former moved in a separate social and occupational world, were often professionals or connected with the MCA or civil service, while the latter formed the core of a more traditional Chinese community with its intricate family and business networks and other associations.

6. In 1980, the first year in which Chinese-educated primary schoolchildren entered the compulsory Malay-medium secondary schools (via a remove class), the parents of pupils in one community petitioned the State Department of Education to have their children transferred from an ''old'' Malay-medium school to one which had originally been Chinese-medium, under the threat of a total class boycott. They were successful in their bid, probably because the incident occurred in predominantly Chinese Penang, where many of the educational officers are also Chinese.

7. The spelling, or mode of transcription of Arabic loanwords in Malay and Indonesian can have devastating effects on their meaning. For example, the Arabic word transcribed as *da'wah* in Malay (Roman script) means to ''accuse,'' but it can easily be confused with dakwah with quite a different meaning!

8. Few Chinese or Indian students major in the fine arts; given the premium on university places for non-Malays and the problems of subsequent employment, they cannot afford to

major in subjects with so few prospects for the future. For Malay fine arts graduates there is potential employment in the media, especially national radio and television.

9. By another twist of religious argument, a woman's voice can be considered as part of her modesty (aurat) and an extension of her charms, which should be hidden from men.

NOTES TO CHAPTER 7

1. It should be pointed out that the situation is made even more complex by variations in different states. Today, in Kedah and Perlis, a "Malay" is a person of the "Malayan race of Arab descent," but may also include Muslim Siamese, thus giving priority to the religious factor. In other Malay states, for example, Kelantan and Trengganu, a Malay is one "belonging to any Malayan *race*" (italics mine), but explicitly excluding Arabs, Indonesians, and other Muslims. Here bangsa takes precedence over religion.

2. Perfect consistency in all of his pronouncements over time does not emerge. For on one occasion, Anwar is reported to have declared that, if every Muslim in Malaysia were to convert one non-Muslim, many of Malaysia's problems would be solved. This suggests something of a volte face on Anwar's part or else that his private convictions differ from most of his rank and file. On other occasions, however, Anwar went on record as opposing even the pro forma attendance of Malay Muslims at non-Muslim religious ceremonies, even by officials and politicians. His most recent "contradiction" came with his lightning switch to UMNO, now seen as less corrupt and more religious and an effective vehicle for religious and racial harmony.

3. In 1970, the percentage of Malays in the total Malaysian population was 53 per cent with the inclusion of the tribal peoples, which really therefore refers to Bumiputera. Without the benefit of the tribal component, however, the proportion of Malays alone comprised only 46.8 per cent of the total (Chander, 1972:24).

4. Of course, it is impossible, without longitudinal studies of individuals over time, to know whether the move to Islam represents the truly "final" solution or just another of the stages in an ongoing quest.

5. The so-called New Villages were artificially created settlements of Chinese rural dwellers during the Emergency between the years 1948 and 1960. They were established with the aim of aggregating a potentially disloyal population to control their movements and limit their possible collaboration with the guerillas. Thus all the residents were quite literally behind barbed wire.

6. Unfortunately, most of this information is qualitative and based on conversations with officials of both PERKIM and the religious councils, who admit that their statistics are not always sufficiently systematic or detailed clearly to differentiate converts for reasons of marriage from others.

7. Technically, all that is required of a convert is a verbal statement, before two Muslim witnesses, of the basic credo (khalimat syahadah) of Islam, "there is no God but God, and Mohammed is His Prophet," without any further testimony.

8. Of the two principal varieties of Buddhism, the Mahayana, with its greater emphasis on ritualism and on the intercession through "saint-like" Boddhisattva or spirit mediums, is the dominant form in East Asia, while the Theravada or Hinayana branch is largely confined to Sri Lanka and Southeast Asia. The latter adheres more closely to the Pali scriptures and to an emphasis on individual religious merit through good works and personal morality, without the use of religious intermediaries. Among the Chinese, Mahayana Buddhism has become fused with other Chinese religious (for example, Tao) traits and with ancestor worship. On occasion, however, there have been episodic revivals of interest in Theravada Buddhism in Singapore (Topley 1967), usually in times of crisis and among intellectuals of a philosophical bent.

9. The term taukeh is used widely in Southeast Asia to mean a rich Chinese businessman or "tycoon."

NOTES TO CHAPTER 8

1. The Muslim Brotherhood (Al-Ikhwan al-Muslimin) was founded in 1928 by Hassan al-Banna, a renowned Muslim theologian and social activist. It now has powerful branches in most Middle Eastern countries, including Syria, Saudi Arabia, Iraq, Lebanon, and Sudan. The original aim of the Brotherhood was partly anti-colonial in Egypt's fight against foreign occupation and, by extension, a force of resistance against Christian evangelism and all infidels (including Egypt's own Copts). It is basically a fundamentalist, anti-communist movement, advocate of a full Islamic state, and it gathers many of its recruits from schools and universities.

2. Prior to the clampdown of the Universities Act in mid-1975, students were essentially continuing the tradition of the 1960's, coming out in support of a variety of social causes. Among these were the defence of Malay land-squatters in Johor, joining forces with Thai students in opposition to the Bangkok military régime, protesting American support for Israel in the 1973 war, and demanding an upgrading of the MARA Institute of Technology to the level of a university.

3. The announcement of Anwar's dramatic switch, from president of ABIM to candidate for an UMNO seat just prior to the general election of April 1982, took the entire country (and many outsiders) by surprise. Even more astonishing was the claim by Anwar that he had actually been a secret member of UMNO since his schooldays, through the thoughtful annual renewal of his registration by his parents, long pillars of the party. Anwar's justification was that he would better be able to "achieve his goals" through UMNO than through ABIM, although whether because he had come to the conclusion that ABIM is a lost cause or because he is basically eager for more personal power is not clear. However, on his election he was awarded a deputy minister post in the Prime Minister's Office. Certainly his personal connection to Dr. Mahathir played an important part, thus reinforcing the view (Chapter 5), of the significance of interpersonal ties and of the strength of the connections of the shadow network behind the "front" that exerts so much pressure on commitment to particular causes.

4. It may be recalled that this tactic was also adopted by some university students protesting against an unpopular and "un-Islamic" lecturer of religious history.

Bibliography

Abdul Jalil Ali. "Nasrul Haq: Persoalan Sebenarnya Apa?" *Dewan Masyarakat* 16(5) 15 May: 3-4. 1978.

Abdul Manaf Bin Sa'ad. "Persatuan Ulama Kedah 1365-1376 H (1946-1957M)." In: *Islam Di Malaysia*. Kuala Lumpur: Malaysian Historical Society: 148-158. n.d.

Abdullah Al-Qari bin Haji Salleh. "To' Kenali: His Life and Influence." In: William Roff ed., *Kelantan: Religion, Society Politics in a Malay State*. Kuala Lumpur: Oxford University Press: 87-100. 1974.

Abdullah Taib. "The Place of Islamic Religious Education in Malay Society, with Special Reference to Kelantan." *Akademika*, Journal of Humanities and Social Sciences, Universiti Kebangsaan Malaysia. 2:29-46. 1973.

———. "Malay Students on an American Campus: A Study of Social Interaction, Ethnicity and Islamic Ideology." University of Kentucky, Ph.D. Diss. (unpub.). 1978.

Ackerman, S.E. & Raymond L.M. Lee. "Communication and Cognitive Pluralism in a Spirit Possession Event in Malaysia." *American Ethnologist* 8(4):789-99. 1981.

Ahmad Kamar. "The Formation of Saberkas." In: Asmah Haji Omar ed., *Darulaman: Essays on Linguistic, Cultural and Socio-Economic Aspects of the Malaysian State of Kedah*. Kuala Lumpur: University of Malaya Press: 179-84. 1979.

Alatas, Syed Hussein. "Feudalism in Malaysian Society: A Study in Historical Continuity." *Civilisations* 18(4):1-15. 1968.

———. *Kita Dengan Islam: Tumbuh Tiada Berbuah*. Singapore: Pustaka Nasional 1979.

———. "Islam dan Kebudayaan Melayu." *Analisa (Journal Persekutuan Bahasa Melayu)*, University of Singapore: 1-9. (1970-71).

Al-Attas, Syed Muhd. Naguib. *The Mysticism of Hamzah Fansuri*. Kuala Lumpur: University of Malaya Press. 1970.

———. *Sufism among the Malays in Malaysia*. Singapore: Malaysian Sociological Research Institute. 1963.

Al-Attas, Syed Muhd. Naguib. *Some Aspects of Sufism as Understood & Practised among the Malays*. Singapore: Malaysian Sociology Research Institute. 1963.

———. *Preliminary Statement on a General Theory of the Islamization of the Malay-Indonesian Archipelago*. Kuala Lumpur. 1969.

Aliran. *One God, Many Paths*. Penang. 1980.

Andaya, L.Y. *The Kingdom of Johor, 1641-1728*. Kuala Lumpur: Oxford University Press. 1975.

Andelson, Jonathan C. "Routinization of Behavior in a Charismatic Leader." *American Ethnologist* 7(4):716-33. 1980.

Apter, David E. "Political Religion in the New Nations." In: Clifford Geertz, ed., *Old Societies and New States*. New York: The Free Press: 57-104. 1963.

Aronoff, Myron J. "Civil Religion in Israel" *Rain* 44 (June). 1981.

Baharuddin Bin Ahmad. "Pengaruh Islam Dalam Perbentukan Keperibadian Bangsa Serta Semangat Kebangsaan Melayu." B.A. Academic Exercise in Malay Language, Literature and Culture (unpub.). Universiti Kebangsaan Malaysia. 1977.

Bailey, Fred. *Strategems and Spoils*. Toronto: Copp Clark. 1971.

Bellah, Robert and William, and G. McLaughlin eds. *Religion in America*. Boston: Houghton Mifflin. 1968.

Boissevain, J. and J. Clyde Mitchell. *Network Analysis: Studies in Human Interaction*. The Hague: Mouton. 1973.

Bronson, Bennet. "Exchange at the Upstream and Downstream Ends: Notes toward a Functional Model of a Coastal State in Southeast Asia." In: Karl Hutterer ed., *Economic Exchange & Social Interaction in Southeast Asia: Perspectives from Prehistory, History and Ethnography*. Ann Arbor, Michigan. Papers on South and Southeast Asia, 13:39-52. 1977.

Cesar Majul. *Muslims in the Philippines*. Quezon City: University of the Philippines Press. (2nd ed) 1973.

Chander, Ramesh, ed. *Population Census of Malaysia, 1970 General Report: Vols 1 & 2*. Kuala Lumpur: Department of Statistics. 1975 & 1977.

Chandra Muzaffar. *Protector? An Analysis of the Concept and Practices of Loyalty In Leader-led Relationships within Malay Society*. Penang: Aliran. 1979.

Chandrasekaran Pillay. "Protection of the Malay Community: A study of UMNO's Position and Opposition Attitudes." M. Social Science Thesis, Universiti Sains Malaysia. 1974.

Dahlan, H.M., ed. *The Nascent Malaysian Society: Developments, Trends and Problems* Kuala Lumpur: Universiti Kebangsaan Malaysia, Jabatan Antropologi dan Sosiologi. 1976.

Department of Statistics. *1970 Population and Housing Census of Malaysia: Community Groups*. Kuala Lumpur: Government Printer. 1972.

――――. *Social Statistics Bulletin, Peninsular Malaysia, 1976*. Kuala Lumpur: Department of Statistics. 1978.

Drewes, G.W.J. "Review of Malay Sufism by A.H. Johns." *Bijdragen Tot-de-Taal en Lande-en-Vokenkunde*. 115(3):280-304. 1959.

Education office, Penang. *Laporan Tahunan*. Jabatan Pelajaran Pulau Pinang. 1978.

Eickelman, Dale F. "The Art of Memory: Islamic Education and Its Social Reproduction." *CSSH* 20(4):485-516. October 1978.

Emerson, Rupert. *Malaysia: A Study in Direct and Indirect Rule*. New York: Macmillan. 1937.

Enloe, Cynthia. *Ethnic Soldiers: State Security in a Divided Society*. Harmondsworth: Penguin. 1980.
————. "Internal Colonialism, Federalism and Alternate State Strategies." *Publius* 7(4):145-60. 1977.
Epstein, A.L. "The Network and Urban Social Organization." In: J. Clyde Mitchell ed., *Social Network in Urban Situations*. Manchester University Press: 77-116. 1969.
Fatimi, S.O. *Islam Comes to Malaysia*. Singapore. 1963.
Fazhur Rahman. "The Sources and Meaning of Islamic Socialism." In: Donald E. Smith ed., *Religion and Political Modernization*. New Haven: Yale University Press: 243-58. 1974.
Federspiel, Howard M. "Islam and Nationalism." *Indonesia* 24:39-85. 1977.
Fortes, Meyer and E.E. Evans-Pritchard. *African Political Systems*. London: Oxford University Press. 1940.
Funston, N.J. "The Origins of Parti Islam Se Malaysia." *Journal of Southeast Asian Studies*. 7(1):58-73. March 1976.
Gagliano, Felix. *Communal Violence in Malaysia 1969: The Political Aftermath*. Athens, Ohio: University Center for International Studies. 1969.
Gallagher, Charles F. *Contemporary Islam: A Frontier of Communalism: Aspects of Islam in Malaysia*. American Universities Field Staff S.E. Asia Series 14, 10 (Malaysia). 1966.
Geertz, Clifford. *Old Societies and New States*. New York: The Free Press, 1963.
————. *Islam Observed: Religious Development in Morocco & Indonesia*. New Haven: Yale University Press. 1968.
————. *The Social History of an Indonesian Town*. Cambridge: MIT Press. 1965.
————. *Negara: The Theatre State in Nineteenth Century Bali*. Princeton: Princeton University Press. 1980.
Gibb, H.A.R. *Mohammedanism: An Historical Survey*. New York: Oxford University Press, Galaxy Books. 1962.
Gilsenan, M. *Saint and Sufi in Modern Egypt: An Essay in the Sociology of Religion*. Oxford: Clanendon Press. 1973.
Goitein, Solomon. *A Mediterranean Society: the Jewish Communities of the Arab World as Portrayed in the Documents of the Cairo Geniza*. Berkeley: University of California Press. 1967.
Green, Arnold H. *The Tunisian Ulama 1873-1915: Social Structure and Response to Ideological Currents*. Leiden: Brill. 1978.
Gullick, John. *Indigenous Political Systems of Western Malaya*. London: Athlone Press. London School of Economics Monographs on Social Anthropology, 17. 1958.
Haji Mohd. Sanusi Bin Haji Mahmood. *Kamus Istilah Islamiah Sanusi*. Kota Bharu. n.d.
Harun Haji Salleh. "Angkatan Belia Islam Malaysia: Satu Kajian." B.A. Hons. Thesis (unpub.). University of Malaya, Dept. of Anthropology and Sociology. 1976.
Hill, A.H. annotated & ed. *The Hikayat Abdullah*. Kuala Lumpur: Oxford University Press (original ed. 1849). 1970.

Jajuli, H.M. "Undang Islam: Pelaksanaanya Bagaimana?" *Dewan Masyarakat* 16(7) 15 July: 12-15. 1978.

Inglis, Christine. "Chinese Education in Southeast Asia." Australian National University: Development Studies Center Monograph 10. Ch. 7: 108-36. 1977.

Ismail Kassim. *Problems of Elite Cohesion: A Perspective from a Minority Community.* Singapore University Press. 1974.

Israeli, Raphael. "Muslims in China: The Incompatibility between Islam and the Chinese Order." *T'oung Pao* 63(4-5):296-323. 1977.

Jackson, Karl D. *Traditional Authority, Islam and Rebellion: A Study of Indonesian Political Behaviour.* Berkeley, University of California Press. 1980.

Johns, A.H. "Aspects of Sufi Thought in India & Indonesia in the First Half of the Seventeenth Century." *JMBRAS* 28, Pt. 1, 169. 1955.

———. "Islam in Southeast Asia: Reflections and New Directions." *Indonesia* 19:33-56. 1975.

Kamaruddin Jaafar. "Beberapa Pendekatan Terhadap Masalah Masyarakat Majmuk." *Risalah* (Jan.): 24-28. 1980.

Kapferer, Bruce. "Social Network & Conjugal Role in Urban Zambia: Towards a Reformulation of the Bott Hypothesis." In: J. Boissevain & J.C. Mitchell eds., *Network Analysis.* Mouton: 83-110. 1973.

Kassim Ahmad. *Hikayat Hang Tuah.* Kuala Lumpur. 1964.

Kemper, Steven. "Reform and Segmentation in Monastic Fraternities in Low Country Sri Lanka." *Journal of Asian Studies* 40(1):27-41 (Nov.). 1980.

Kershaw, R. "Of Race, Class & Clientship in Malaysia." Journal of *Commonwealth and Comparative Politics* 14(3) (Nov.). 1976.

Kessler, Clive S. *Islam and Politics in a Malay State: Kelantan 1938-1969.* Ithaca: University of Cornell Press. 1978.

Khoo, Kay Kim *The Western Malay States 1850-1873: The Effects of Commercial Development on Malay Politics.* Kuala Lumpur: Oxford University Press. 1972.

Lapidus, Ira M., ed. *Middle Eastern Cities: A Symposium on Ancient, Islamic & Contemporary Middle Eastern Urbanism.* Berkeley: University of California Press. 1969.

Lim, Kah Cheng. "Class & Ethnic consciousness among Women Factory Workers in Penang." M. Social Science Thesis. Universiti Sains Malaysia. 1979.

Lim, Linda Y.C. *Women Workers in Multinational Corporations: The Case of the Electronics Industry in Malaysia and Singapore.* Ann Arbor: Michigan Occasional Papers No. 9, Fall. 1978.

Lim, T.G., David Gibbons & Shukur Ahmad. "Universiti Sains Malaysia-Mada Land Tenure Study: Final Report." Centre for Policy Research, Universiti Sains Malaysia. 1980.

Lijphart, Arend. *Democracy in Plural Societies: A Comparative Exploration.* New Haven & London: Yale University Press. 1977.

Lyon, Margo. "The Dakwah Movement in Malaysia." *Review of Indonesian & Malayan Affairs* 13(20):34-45 (Dec.). 1979.

Ma'arof Salleh. "Aspects of Dakwah in Singapore." *Sedar, (Journal of Islamic Students Society)*. Singapore: 19-25. 1979.

Malaysian Historical Society. *Islam Di Malaysia*. Kuala Lumpur: Malaysian Historical Society. n.d.

Malaysian Historical Society (Persatuan Sejarah Malaysia). *Tamadun Islam di Malaysia*. Kuala Lumpur. 1980.

Manderson, Lenore. *Women, Politics and Change: The Kaum Ibu UMNO, Malaysia, 1945-1972*. Kuala Lumpur: Oxford University Press. 1980.

Mansur Othman. "Hakmilik Tanah Padi dan Politik Di Kedah." Universiti Sains Malaysia. M. Social Science thesis (unpub.). 1978.

Matheson, Virginia. "Concepts of Malay Ethos in Indigenous Malay Writings." *Journal of Southeast Asian Studies* 10(2):351-71 (Sept.). 1979.

Maudoodi, Abdul Ala al Ash'ari, ed. *Purdah and the Status of Women in Islam* (trans. by editor). Lahore: Islamic Publications (original published in 1939). 1972.

McIntyre, Angus. "The 'Greater Indonesian' idea of Nationalism in Malaysia and Indonesia." *Modern Asian Studies* 7(1). 1973.

Means, Gordon. "Public Policy Toward Religion in Malaysia." *Pacific Affairs*, 51(3): 384-405. 1978.

Means, Gordon. *Malaysian Politics*. New York: New York University Press. 1970.

Mehden, Fred von der. "Religion and Politics in Malaya." *Asian Survey* 3:609-15. 1963.

Mendelssohn, Michael. *Sangha and State in Burma: A Study of Monastic Sectarianism and Leadership*. Ithaca: Cornell University Press. 1975.

Metcalf, Barbara. "The Madrasah at Deoband: A Model for Religious Education in Modern India." *Modern Asian Studies* 12(1):111-34. 1978.

Milne, R.S. *Politics in Ethnically Bipolar States: Guyana, Malaysia, Fiji*. Vancouver: University of British Columbia Press. 1981.

Milne, R.S. & Diane K. Mauzy. *Politics & Government in Malaysia* (2nd rev. ed.). Singapore & Vancouver: Times Books International and University of British Columbia Press. 1980.

Milner, A.C. *Kerajaan: Malay Political Culture on the Eve of Colonial Rule*. Tuscon: The University of Arizona Press for the Association of Asian Studies. 1982.

Ministry of Culture Youth & Sports. *Asas Kebudayaan Kebangsaan* Kuala Lumpur: MAS Printer. 1973.

Ministry of Education. *Laporan Jawatankuasa Kabinet Mengkaji Pelaksanaan Dasar Pelajaran*. Kuala Lumpur: Ministry of Education. 1979.

Mohd. Jani Naim. "Sekolah Agama Rakyat Di Sabak Bernam Hingga 1945." In: *Islam Di Malaysia*. Kuala Lumpur: Malaysian Historical Society: 52-61 n.d.

Mohd. Nor bin Ngah. "Some Writing of the Traditional Malay Muslim Scholars found in Malaysia." In: *Tamadun Islam di Malaysia*. Kuala Lumpur: Malaysian Historical Society: 9-12. 1980.

Mohd. Razha Rashid. "Industrialization and Proliferation of Cultural Division of

Labour: A Case of Ethnic Urbanism in a Malaysian Town." In: Gordon Means, ed., *The Past in Southeast Asia's Present*. Selected Proceedings of the Canadian Council for S.E. Asian Studies Annual Conference 1977. McMaster University: 199-206. 1978.

Mohd. Taib Osman. "Islamisation of the Malays: A Transformation of Culture." In: *Tamadun Islam di Malaysia*. Kuala Lumpur: Malaysian Historical Society: 1-8. 1980.

Mokhtar Mohamad. "Sistem Pondok dengan Pendidikan Islam Zaman Pembangunan." B.A. Hons. Thesis (unpub.), Universiti Kebangsaan Malaysia. 1965-75.

Muhammad Salleh B. Wan Musa. "Theological Debates: Wan Musa b. Haji Abdul Samad and His Family" In: William Roff ed., *Kelantan: Religion, Society and Politics in a Malay State*. Kuala Lumpur: Oxford University Press; 153-69. 1974.

Muhammad Uthman El-Muhammady. "Peranan Islam dalam Pembentukan Kebudayaan Melayu." In: *Islam dan Kebudayaan Melayu*. Kuala Lumpur. Ministry of Youth, Culture & Sports: 62-87. 1977.

Mulder, Niels. *Mysticism and Everyday Life in Contemporary Java: Cultural Persistence and Change*. Singapore University Press. 1978.

Nagata, Judith. "Coalition and Segmentation in a Mennonite Community" *Anthropologica* N.S. 14(1):43-60 . 1972.

———. "In Defense of Ethnic Boundaries: The Changing Myths and Charters of Malay Identity." In: Charles F. Keyes ed., *Ethnic Change*. Seattle: University of Washington Press: 87-116. 1981.

———. *Malaysian Mosaic: Perspectives from a Poly-Ethnic Society*. Vancouver: University of British Columbia Press. 1979.

———. "Perceptions of Social Inequality in Malaysia" in J. Nagata ed., *Pluralism in Malaysia: Myth or Reality*. Leiden: Brill: 113-136. 1975.

———. "Tale of Two Cities: The Role of Non-Urban Factors in Community Life in Two Malaysian Towns." *Urban Anthropology* 3(1):1-27 (Spring). 1974.

———. "The Chinese Muslims in Malaysia: New Malays or New Associates? A Problem in Ethnicity." In: Gordon Means, ed., *The Past in Southeast Asia's Present*. Selected Proceedings of the Canadian Council for Southeast Asian Studies, Annual Conference 1977, MacMaster University: 102-27. 1977.

———. "What is a Malay? Situational Selection of Ethnic Identity in a Plural Society." *American Ethnologist* 1(2):331-50. 1974.

Ness, Gayl D. *Bureaucracy and Rural Development in Malaysia*. Berkeley: University of California Press. 1967.

Nik Abdul Aziz Haji Nik Hassan. "Islam, Kepimpinan dan Nilai-Nalai Hidup Dalam Masyarakat Melayu Tradisional." In: *Tamadun Islam di Malaysia*. Kuala Lumpur: Malaysian Historical Society: 87-93. 1980.

———. "Islam Dan Masyarakat Kota Bharu Di Antara Tahun 1900-1933." In: *Islam Di Malaysia*. Kuala Lumpur: Malaysian Historical Society: 18-33. n.d.

Noer, Deliar. *The Modernist Muslim Movement in Indonesia 1900-1942*. Kuala Lumpur: Oxford University Press. 1973.

Noor Azam. "Kearah Penyempurnaan Undang-Undang Islam." *Dewan Masyarakat* 16(7) (15 July): 7-8. 1978.

Obeyesekere, G. "Sinhalese-Buddhist Identity in Ceylon." In: George de Vos & Lola Romanucci-Ross, eds. *Ethnic Identity: Cultural Continuities and change* Palo Alto: Mayfield Publishing Co.: 231-58. 1975.

Othman Bin Bakar. "Haji Saleh Masri: Pengasas Al-Masriyyah, Bukit Mertajam." In: *Islam Di Malaysia*. Kuala Lumpur: Malaysian Historical Society: 62-74. n.d.

Othman Ishak. "Some Aspects of the Administration of Islam in Kedah." In: Asmah Haji Omar, ed., *Darulaman: Essays on Linguistic, Cultural and Socio-Economic Aspects of the Malaysian State of Kedah*. Kuala Lumpur: 185-92. 1979.

Othman Ismail. "Pimpinan Politik PAS Dalam Masyarakat Tani Kawasan Tunjang, Kedah: Satu Tinjauan Dari Aspek Organisasi; Faktor Mobiliti Dan Manifestasi Pimpinan Politik." University of Malaya. B.A. Hons. Thesis (Anthropology and Sociology). 1974.

Othman, Mohd. Aris. "Ethnic Identity in a Malay Community in Malaysia." Ph.D. Diss. University of Illinois (Urbana). 1978.

Paine, Robert, ed. *Politically Speaking: Cross-Cultural Studies of Rhetoric*. St. Johns; Memorial University of Newfoundland. Social and Economic Papers No. 10. 1981.

Parliamentary Debates, Dewan Rakyat. Official Report: Second Session of the Second Parliament of Malaysia. Vol. II, Session 1965-66 (13 Nov). Kuala Lumpur. 1965.

Peacock, James. *Muslim Puritans: Reformist Psychology in Southeast Asian Islam*. Berkeley and Los Angeles: University of California Press. 1978.

———. *Purifying the Faith: The Muhammadijah Movement in Indonesian Islam*. Menlo Park: Benjamin Cummings Publishing Co. 1978.

Poulantzas, Nicholas. *Political Power and Social Classes*. London: Humanities Press. 1973.

Ratnam, K.J. *Communalism and the Political Process in Malaya*. Kuala Lumpur: University of Malaya Press. 1965.

Reid, Anthony and Lance Castles, eds. *Pre-Colonial State Systems in Southeast Asia*. Monographs of the Malaysian Branch of the Royal Asiatic Society, No. 6. Kuala Lumpur. 1975.

Richter, William. "The Political Dynamics of Religious Resurgence in Pakistan." *Asian Survey*. 19(6):547-57. (June) 1979.

Roff, William. *The Origins of Malay Nationalism*. Kuala Lumpur: University of Malaya Press. 1967.

———. *Kelantan: Religion, Society and Politics in a Malay State*. Kuala Lumpur: Oxford University Press. 1974.

Rozlan bin Kuntum. A General Survey of Muslim Religious Schools in Malaya. B.A. Hons. Thesis (unpub.), University of Malaya. Department of Malay Studies. 1957.

Rustam A. Sani. "Malaya Raya as a Malay Nation of Intent." In: H.M. Dahlan ed., *The Nascent Malaysian Society*. Siri Monograf Jabatan Sosiologi dan Antropologi, Universiti Kebangsaan Malaysia. 1976.

Sahlins, M. "Rich Man, Poor Man, Big Man, Chief: Political Types in Melanesia and Polynesia." *Comparative Studies in Society and History* 5:285-303. 1963.

Saman bin Shariff. "Madrasah al-Haji Taib, Kampung Parit Jamil, Muar." In: *Islam di Malaysia*. Kuala Lumpur: Malaysian Historical Society: 86-97. n.d.

Siow, Molly. "Conflict, Consensus and Political Change: A Case Study of Interethnic Divisions in West Malaysia." Unpub. Ph.D. dissertation, New School for Social Research. 1979.

Shils, Edward. "Primordial, Personal, Sacred and Civil Ties." *British Journal of Sociology* (June): 130-47. 1961.

Said, Edward. *Orientalism*. Random House: Vintage Books. 1979.

Scott, James C. "Some Notes on Post-Peasant Society." *Peasant Studies*. 7(3): 147-54. 1978.

Seminar Kebudayaan. *Islam dan Kebudayaan Melayu*. Kuala Lumpur: Persatuan Mahasiswa (July) Universiti Kebangsaan Malaysia. 1976.

Siddique, Sharon & Leo Suryadinata. "Bumiputra and Pribumi: Economic Nationalism (Indigenism) in Malaysia and Indonesia." Singapore: Institute of Southeast Asian Studies Working Paper m.s. n.d.

Slimming, John. *Malaysia: Death of a Democracy*. London: John Murray. 1969.

Smith, Donald E. *Religion and Political Modernization*. New Haven: Yale University Press. 1974.

Spencer, Martin E. "What is Charisma?" *British Journal of Sociology* 24:341-54. 1973.

Stockwell, A.J. *British Policy and Malay Politics During the Malayan Union Experiment 1942-1948*. Kuala Lumpur: Malaysian Branch of the Royal Asiatic Society Monograph No. 8. 1979.

Syed Hussein Ali. *Malay Peasant Society and Leadership*. Kuala Lumpur: Oxford University Press. 1975.

Talal Asad. "Politics and Religion in Islamic Reform: A Critique of Kedourie's Afghani & Abduh." Review of Mid-Eastern Studies 2:13-22. 1976.

Tambiah, S. *World Conqueror and World Renouncer: A Study of Buddhism and Polity in Thailand against a Historical Background*. Cambridge University Press. 1976.

Tan, Chee Bang. "Baba and Nonya: A Study of the Ethnic Identity of the Chinese Peranakan in Malacca." Unpub. Ph.D. Diss. Cornell University. 1979.

Taufik Abdullah. "Adat and Islam: An Examination of Conflict in Minangkabau." *Indonesia* 2:1-24. 1966.

Topley, M. "The Emergence and Social Function of Chinese Religious Associations in Singapore." In: Lloyd Fallers ed., *Immigrants and Associations*. The Hague: Mouton: 49-82. 1967.

Trimingham, S. *The Sufi Orders in Islam*. New York & London: Oxford University Press. 1971.

Troeltsch, Ernst. *The Social Teaching of the Christian Churches* (Trans. O. Wyon) New York: Macmillan. 1931.

Tunku Abdul Rahman Putra Al-Haj. *Looking Back*. Kuala Lumpur: Pustaka Antara. 1977.

————. *May 13th: Before and After*. Kuala Lumpur. 1969.

Turner, Victor. *The Ritual Process: Structure and Anti-Structure*. Chicago: Aldine Press. 1969.

Wan Halim Bin Othman. "Ethnogenesis: A Case-Study of the Malays of Peninsular Malaysia." Unpub. Ph.D. Diss. University of Bristol. 1979.

Wawancara. Noor Azam dgn Datuk Sheikh Abdul Majid, Yang di Pertua Majlis Agama Islam Kedah Undang Syari'ah di Kedah." *Dewan Masyarakat* 16(7) (July): 30-31. 1978.

Weber, Max. *The Sociology of Religion* (Trans. Ephraim Fischoff). Boston: Beacon Press. 1968.

Wertheim, W.F. "From Aliran Towards Class Struggle in the Countryside of Java." *Pacific Viewpoint* 10(2):1-17. 1959.

Wilson, Bryan. "An Analysis of Sect Development." *American Sociological Review* 24(1):3-15. 1959.

————. *Sects and Society*. London: Heinemann. 1961.

Winzeler, Robert. "The Social Organization of Islam in Kelantan." In: William Roff ed., *Kelantan: Religion, Society and Politics in a Malay State*. Kuala Lumpur: Oxford University Press: 259-71. 1974.

Wolff, Kurt. *The Sociology of Georg Simmel* (trans., ed. & Introd. by K. Wolff). Macmillan Free Press: Toronto. 1964.

Yahaya Ismail. *Masaalah Melayu Pulau Pinang*. Kuala Lumpur: Dinamika Kreatif. 1978.

Yegar, Moshe. "Islam & Islamic Institutions in British Malaya, 1874-1941: Policies and Implementation." Ph.D. Diss. Hebrew University of Jerusalem: Israel. 1977.

Zainun Ahmad. "Pimpinan PAS Kelantan: Satu Kajian Tentang Latarbelakang Sosialnya." Universiti Kebangsaan Malaysia B.A. Hons. Thesis (Anth. & Soc.). 1977.

Appendix 1

Genealogies

Genealogy No. 1

1. Farmer, born in N. Sumatra, emigrated to Negeri Sembilan, Malaya
2. Daughter of farmer in N. Sumatra
3. Born in Negeri Sembilan, farmer
4. Married Negeri Sembilan farmer
5. Wealthy haji and businessman in Province Wellesley, become patron, adoptive father and later, father-in-law, of founder of madrasah
6. Sent away to study religion, both in Malaya and in Mecca, later adopted by (5) and married his daughter. Founder of famous madrasah in Province Wellesley
7. Wife of (6) and daughter of patron
8. Star pupil and adopted son (later, son-in-law) of madrasah founder
9. Well-known Arab Sheikh, for many years Mufti of Trengganu
10. Well-known Arab Sheikh, born in Saudi Arabia, now Saudi ambassador to London where he lives with his wife
11. Star pupil of madrasah, adopted by Arab Sheikh, married into the madrasah family, and sent by him to study in Mecca and Al-Azhar, Cairo. Now chief administrator of the madrasah
12. Well-known Arab Sheikh, now oil minister of Saudi Arabia, where he is a citizen and lives
13. Owns and runs a bus company and bookstore, source of some of the madrasah's funds
14. Head religious instructor at the madrasah
15. Current headmaster of the academic section of the madrasah, allied with the ABIM branch
16. Assistant in father's bookstore
17. Student at Al-Azhar University, Cairo
18. Student of religion in Al-Azhar
19. Once a teacher in the girls' section of the madrasah

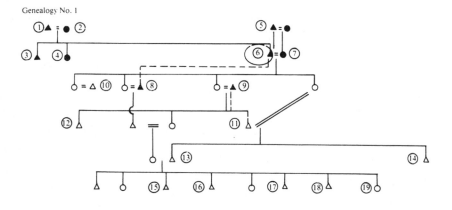

Genealogy No. 1

Gen. No. 1

Genealogy No. 2

1. Well-known imam of Kedah mosque
2. Famous pondok religious teacher, Kedah
3. Village headman
4. Religious teacher
5. Imam of mosque
6. Village headman
7. Informal village religious leader
8. Current administrator of pondok religious school
9. Daughter of wealthy farmer
10. Founder of two well-known pondok religious schools, in Kelantan and Kedah, now in hands of wife's brother (12)
11. Still resides in school, and assists with teaching of girls
12. Currently head of pondok religious school, taken over from sister's deceased husband (10)
13. Religious teacher in Perlis
14. Religious teacher
15. One of teachers at pondok religious school of uncles (8, 10 & 12)
16. Religious court kathi
17. Science teacher
18. Religious teacher
19. Religious teacher in the army
20. Secondary school teacher
21. University student (secular)

Genealogy No. 2

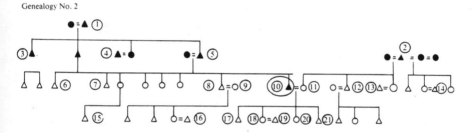

Gen. No. 2

Genealogy No. 3

1. Born in N. Sumatra, descended from long line of rajahs
2. Well-known alim, in N. Sumatra
3. Daughter of N. Sumatran district chief
4. Famous district chief in N. Sumatra
5. District chief in N. Sumatra
6. Religious teacher in N. Sumatra
7. Religious scholar in Mecca and Medina
8. Religious teacher in N. Sumatra
9. Founder of famous religious pondok school in Kedah
10. Founder of well-known madrasah in N. Sumatra, later moved to Kedah
11. Founder of distinguished madrasah in Kedah
12. Founder of religious pondok school in Kedah
13. Imam of mosque
14. Religious teacher in Kedah
15. Kedah religious teacher and PAS candidate
16. Religious teacher, graduate of Al-Azhar University
17. Police chief
18. Kedah religious teacher
19. Secondary school teacher
20. Student at Oxford University
21. Nurse
22. Teacher of technology
23. Official in Kedah State Religious Council

Genealogy No. 3

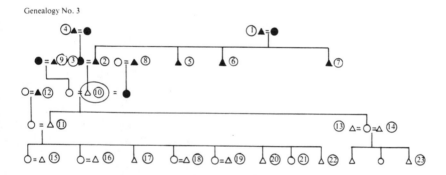

Gen. No. 3

Appendix 2

Education and Occupations of Children and Grandchildren of Twelve Religious Ulama in Kedah

Religious Leader	Generation*	Predominantly Religious Schooling			Predominantly Secular Schooling		
		Children	Sons-in-law	Grand-children	Children	Sons-in-law	Grand-children
1	I	3/3	3/3	7/14	0/7	0/3	7/7
2	I	12/19	2/3	3/9	7/19	1/3	6/9
3	I	15/21	2/2	2/9	6/21	0/2	7/19
4	I	6/6	1/2	11/18	0/6	1/2	7/18
5	I	9/9	3/3	2/11	0/9	0/3	9/11
6	I	8/8	2/3	–	0/8	1/3	–
7	II	2/8	–	1/1	6/8	1/1	–
8	II	5/9	3/4	–	4/9	1/4	–
9	II	5/6	2/2	–	1/6	0/2	–
10	II	0/10	0/2	–	10/10	2/2	–
11	II	8/8	2/3	–	0/8	1/3	–
12	II	0/8	0/3	–	8/8	3/3	–

Family data on education and occupations of children and grandchildren of 12 religious scholars ployment.

N.B. Where total number of children in "schooling" exceeds total in "occupations," some are school, some are still of pre-school age.

  * "Generation I" refers to religious leaders born before 1920, and "Generation II" to those

							Wives	
Religious Occupation			Secular Occupation				Originated from religious families	Members of elite families
Children	Sons-in-law	Grand-children	Children	Sons-in-law	Grand-children	No		
1/2	3/3	3/14	1/2	0/3	11/14	2	1	1
6/8	2/3	–	2/8	1/3	–	4	2	2
6/21	1/2	2/2	15/21	1/2	0/2	4	2	1
1/3	1/2	4/7	2/3	1/2	3/7	1	1	–
5/9	0/2	0/2	4/9	2/2	2/2	3	3	–
5/6	1/3	–	1/6	2/3	–	1	–	–
3/5	1/1	–	2/5	1/1	–	1	1	–
6/7	3/4	–	1/7	1/4	–	1	1	–
5/6	2/2	–	1/6	0/2	–	2	1	1
0/9	0/2	–	9/9	2/2	–	2	2	–
5/6	1/3	–	1/6	2/3	–	1	–	–
0/3	0/3	–	3/3	3/3	–	1	–	1

and teachers, showing a general trend over time towards more secular education and em-

not (yet) employed. Where total number of children or grandchildren exceeds number in

born after that year.

Index